Row House
to
White House

Lawrence M. O'Rourke

Reston, Va.   Aug, 2013

To order additional copies of this book, contact:
Xlibris Corporation
1-888-795-4274
www.Xlibris.com
Orders@Xlibris.com
103277

CONTENTS

DEDICATION

To my wife, Trish, my children, Chris, Katie, Jenny, and Tim, and my grandchildren who provided hopes and dreams as I completed this book, and to my parents, Lawrence and Margaret, for the strong roots they provided, which enabled me to grow.

ACKNOWLEDGEMENTS

Since this is the story of a reporter revealing for the first time conversations and experiences I had with well-known figures in the White House, Congress, major political campaigns, and leading newspaper offices, I am totally responsible for the contents. Much of the material revealed here for the first time was drawn from hundreds of notebooks I filled in 40 years as a Washington newsman.

I am in debt to many who helped me put this story together. Arthur Omohundro, John Maher and Michael B. Sisak III provided valuable editing and fact checking along with caution and encouragement. Richard A. Ryan gave wise counsel. Frank Aukofer and Peter Osnos contributed advice on publication. Historian James H. Hershman, Jr., endorsed the idea that history deserves the truth, even when it may make the powerful uncomfortable. David Whitney and Milton Jaques offered friendship and reassurance through hard times.

Above all, Patricia Coe O'Rourke patiently drew on her quarter century of experience as an editor and 44 years of marriage to get me through many rewrites and difficult places. Without her love and prodding, this story would be buried in musty piles of paper.

CHAPTER 1

Start of a Journey

M Y JOURNEY FROM a row house in West Philadelphia to the pressroom of the White House and the corridors of power in Congress and national politics was launched at a moment of national mourning following the assassination of President John F. Kennedy.

In a sense, my career as national political correspondent in Washington was an accident—built on a tragedy. I shall never forget a conversation I later had with Robert F. Kennedy during his campaign for the Senate from New York. "You can't plan your life," Bobby Kennedy said. "You look for opportunities. You make opportunities when you can. And when you find them, you take them."

This book is my story of taking advantage of opportunities, many flowing from good luck, told through my perspective, perhaps unbalanced in my favor, but as truthful as I can make it, of a professional life in the golden age of American print journalism. I am grateful for the chance to have participated, as an observer and as a player, in many of the events of my time. And so I begin.

In November 1963, I was the *Philadelphia Bulletin's* reporter on the public schools beat. The *Bulletin* had the largest circulation of any U.S. afternoon broadsheet newspaper. Philadelphia public schools were de facto racially segregated. White people of Philadelphia largely looked upon public schools as places to provide African-American kids the least costly education possible. The effort to end segregation and improve those predominantly African-American schools was a fantastic story to cover, and I loved the job.

I spent the morning of Friday, November 22 in a public school classroom in North Philadelphia where a young woman teacher tried to teach seven-year-olds how to read. I rode in a taxicab from the school toward the Board of Education headquarters building on Benjamin Franklin Parkway. I planned to interview an assistant school superintendent about reading challenges for the thousands of children failing in a failing system.

"Did you hear?" the cabdriver said as we went south on Broad Street.

"Hear what?" I said.

"Somebody shot Kennedy."

"Where?"

"Texas? Just heard it on the news."

"What's Kennedy's condition?"

"Don't know."

Skeptic as I was by personality and job description, I didn't know if the cabby's story was real or a hoax.

At the Board of Education building, the hallways were empty. I raced to the office of David Horowitz, an assistant superintendent whom I knew to have a television set. It was there that I heard Walter Cronkite tearfully announce that John F. Kennedy had been assassinated in Dallas, Texas.

I cancelled my interview with the reading expert and rushed by cab to the *Bulletin* building at 30th and Market Streets. The fourth floor newsroom was hectic, but functioning with discipline. Bayard Brunt took dictation from Dallas from Robert Roth, the *Bulletin's* Washington Bureau chief and White House correspondent.

Fred McCord took dictation from Washington from Anthony Day, the *Bulletin's* congressional correspondent. Sam Boyle, the city editor, worked with John McCullough, the *Bulletin's* superb political writer and a veteran of Washington reporting, to get a plane to Texas.

Boyle told Adrian Lee, a solid political reporter, to get ready to go to Texas or Washington. Boyle dashed among the desks where I sat with other beat reporters, telling us to call this person or that person, to get reaction statements. Boyle sent me to the *Bulletin* morgue—or library—for clippings to put together a story on Kennedy's visits to Philadelphia.

*   *   *

Only a few weeks earlier Boyle assigned me to Philadelphia's Convention Hall when Kennedy visited to make a speech raising money for local Democrats and to impose unity on a fractured local Democratic Party. My job was to work with Roth to identify local Democratic politicians and to interview them for a sidebar story. It was my first meeting with Roth, a legendary figure at the *Bulletin* and a highly respected political journalist. My first impression was that Roth carried the world on his shoulders. I found him to be a short, somber man in his 60s with dark clipped hair with a trace of gray; dark rimmed glasses and an intensity and indefatigability. He was fabled in the *Bulletin* newsroom for his ability to dictate stories on the run. He made numerous trips around the world with presidents. An ability to dictate stories was essential for a *Bulletin* reporter. We were an afternoon newspaper, and we prided ourselves on getting up-to-the-minute news into the paper. I was slowly learning the technique as the *Bulletin's* education writer because so many events—news conferences, school board meetings, state Legislature sessions—were held in the afternoon, as our final deadline approached. There was no time to sit down and write a story. We would do that after the last deadline, putting a fresh angle on what we called overnights.

On the night of the Kennedy visit to Convention Hall, Roth took me around the press filing center and introduced me to Merriman Smith of United Press International, Bill Lawrence of *The New York Times*, Bill Kent of *The Chicago Sun-Times*, and others whose names I recognized and whose reputations I envied. These national reporters asked me questions. I was flattered that they wanted me to sort out the players in the city's Democratic power structure. Roth took me to the head table where Kennedy was seated, but just as Roth was about to introduce me, Kennedy began to talk with Bill Green, chairman of the Democratic City Committee, so I never had the opportunity to meet John F. Kennedy. But I did meet Pierre Salinger, Kennedy's press secretary, and others whose names now blur. It was a heady evening for a 25-year-old reporter. It was also exciting just to talk with Roth, a legend I never expected to spend much time with. Roth, after all, was at the top of the profession while I was a young education beat reporter.

*   *   *

On the November afternoon as I researched a story on JFK's visits to Philadelphia, I could visualize Roth at work in Texas. I envied McCullough, Lee and other reporters ordered by Boyle to work the assassination story. To my disappointment, Boyle ignored me for a major role in covering the story from Dallas. He had far more experienced reporters available than me. The final edition of the *Bulletin* that afternoon was dominated by stories by Roth and Day of the Washington

Bureau. As I worked on the story about JFK visits to Philadelphia, I delayed writing my story about reading in the public schools, seeing little space for it in the weekend papers. I grabbed copies of the *Bulletin's* final edition as a keepsake and went home to West Philadelphia. I talked with my parents about the assassination and the new president, Lyndon B. Johnson. That evening, I watched on television as Air Force One, carrying Kennedy's coffined body, Jackie Kennedy and LBJ, landed at Andrews Air Force Base outside Washington.

As details of Kennedy's funeral were announced, I decided to go to Washington on Sunday to see the cortege pass on Pennsylvania Avenue and to walk by the body of Kennedy lying in state in the Capitol Rotunda. I had been to Washington three times—once to Dwight Eisenhower's inauguration as president, one time on a high school graduation trip, and a third time briefly when my plane stopped at Washington National Airport on a flight from San Juan, Puerto Rico, for home leave from the Army. I had a strong memory of the Capitol and Washington Monument lit at night.

When I broached my idea of going to Washington, my mother was immediately positive as was my 15-year-old brother Johnny. My father declined. He said he had to work on Monday and needed his rest on Sunday. "You go by yourselves if you want to. I'll be all right," he said. My mother expanded the idea by inviting her younger sister, Mary Higgins, who enjoyed travel and spontaneous invitations.

At six on Sunday morning, when it was still dark, we set off in my blue-green station wagon. Our route included Interstate Highway 95. Only a few days before, JFK traveled to the border on I-95 between Delaware and Maryland to dedicate a portion of the interstate. To this day, I note the spot as I drive by.

We arrived in Washington a few blocks north of the Capitol before 10 a.m. and found a parking place on the street. My mother, in the family tradition, had packed ham and cheese sandwiches. We ate them before setting out on foot for Pennsylvania Avenue at the foot of 14th Street. Little did I know that across Pennsylvania Avenue and up the slight hill of 14th Street was the National Press Building. Nor did I know that on the 12th floor was the *Bulletin* bureau office. I wasn't there on behalf of the *Bulletin*. I was there to experience a moment in history.

We were standing on the south side of Pennsylvania Avenue when a man listening to a portable radio announced that someone had just shot Lee Harvey Oswald in Dallas. My first thought was that it was somebody's sick idea of a joke. But the guy turned up the radio. It wasn't a joke at all. We were stunned. We stood in silence as the Kennedy procession passed us. It was an awful moment for me to see the horse-drawn caisson bearing the flag-draped coffin, to see the rider-less horse with the boot turned backward, to see the Kennedy family walk down the middle of the street, surrounded by Secret Service agents. We stood reverentially, as if in church, as the press buses and police motorcycles moved in the procession.

As the crowd dissolved, we found a nearby restaurant for a quick lunch and headed to the Capitol to join the line to walk through the Rotunda past the casket. We naively thought that it would be a short line and we would be off on our return to Philadelphia shortly. But as we climbed Capitol Hill and came to the east side of the Capitol, we found the end of the line to the left of the Supreme Court Building, heading away from the Capitol. We didn't know how far it stretched before it turned around. Though we were lightly dressed, it was still tolerably warm for a late November afternoon. Though my mother was 51 and Mary was in her 40s, neither ever indicated any desire other than to fulfill our goal of passing the catafalque.

I neglected to bring a portable radio, but others in line had. They explained the frequent 20-minute stops in the line. Announcers reported that a Kennedy family member or U.S. politician or foreign leader arrived and security officers closed the Rotunda to ordinary visitors. As the sun sank beyond the Capitol, we got very cold. We needed more food. We needed a bathroom. Fortunately, gracious people along the line that stretched several blocks to Lincoln Park and back along East Capitol Street invited those waiting to use their homes. Corner grocery stores had red-letter days as hungry people ducked out of line to buy anything.

After eight hours in line, we got to the Capitol about midnight. We climbed the white marble steps, entering the building with instructions from military and police to keep moving and take no pictures. I walked past the raised closed casket draped in a U.S. flag. It was my first visit inside the Capitol. I went as slowly as I could, but spent probably no more than a minute in the Rotunda. Then it was out the west side, and down the hill where, we knew from the radio, Jackie Kennedy had walked a few hours earlier.

We returned to Philadelphia. At 9 on Monday morning, I called Boyle and asked if he had anything for me. He said no. There was really no need for a junior reporter in the office. I told Boyle I would take the day off. See you tomorrow, he said. On television, I watched the funeral procession from the Capitol, the Requiem Mass at St. Matthew's Cathedral and the burial in Arlington National Cemetery.

* * *

I was barely at my desk in the *Bulletin* newsroom the next morning when Boyle came up, "Dickinson wants to see you," he said.

I was taken aback and didn't consider it to be good news that Dickinson wanted to see me. Dickinson was William B. Dickinson, the patrician, white-haired, fastidious man of few words who was the managing editor of the *Bulletin*, the real power in the newsroom. He made the rules and enforced them.

So here I am, the week after the Kennedy assassination, walking with Boyle to Dickinson's office, wondering what is the current mess I'm in. Was I about to be fired because I hadn't shown up for work Monday, the day of the funeral? Had I been wrong in not filing my story on the reading teacher in the North Philadelphia school? I felt that the eyes of the newsroom were on me as I sat down in front of Dickinson.

"I've been thinking," Dickinson began, "that this new Johnson administration is going to make quite a bit of news. So I've decided to expand the Washington bureau. It should also be good experience for reporters to get a year in Washington and return to Philadelphia. Are you interested in going down to Washington for a year?"

Though stunned, I answered immediately. "Yes, sir, I am." Dickinson didn't smile or pause. "You'll be working with Bob Roth and Tony Day," Dickinson said. "You'll need to find yourself a place to live for a year. Think you can be settled and get to work by the first of the year?" "I think so," I said. "I can start on that right away."

"OK," said Dickinson, standing up. He shook my hand, and that was it. The meeting lasted no more than three minutes. Boyle took me to his office. "If you have to move any furniture, do it as cheap as you can," Boyle said. "The *Bulletin* doesn't pay for first-class moves. And keep in mind that you're the first to be put into this one-year program. If you don't come back, you'll mess it up and we won't do it again. And remember that your future is here in Philadelphia. You've been on a fast track to an important job in this newsroom. I can't tell you where you're headed because I don't know how you'll do in Washington or any other job at this newspaper. But don't forget the big opportunity at this newspaper is here in Philadelphia."

My parents did not seem delighted when I told them the news that evening over dinner. My father recalled that as a young man the Gulf Oil Co. offered him a job in Washington as sales representative for Virginia and other Southern states. His mother didn't like the idea because she thought he would not be able to take care of himself. At her insistence, he took a room at a boarding house in Roslyn across the Potomac and rode the trolley car back and forth to the office downtown. "I didn't like it," he said. "I was all by myself. I didn't know anybody. I missed my mother." He stayed six weeks, quit Gulf, and returned to Philadelphia. My mother was not about to impose her will on me, but she was of mixed mind and emotion. She saw my move to Washington as a great chance to do interesting things, but she wondered if I could really manage living away from home.

In fact, my mother couldn't have imagined how eager I was to move out of the family home. One of the main reasons I joined the Army in 1960 was to get out of the family home. I viewed it as a wonderful place, where my every need was anticipated, but at 25, I also felt uncomfortable living in my parents' home and depending upon them. I also felt hemmed in. I was aware that they knew the hours I was keeping, and the friends I was seeing. I felt I couldn't go off on a trip to New York or the seashore without asking them if they wanted to go along. Living at home had its benefits, but they were outweighed by my desire to be independent. To an extent, the *Bulletin's* rule that I would have to return to Philadelphia in a year was a consolation to my parents who believed that I would be driving back regularly on visits and spending holidays with them.

When word of my move to Washington spread, my colleagues at the *Bulletin* were envious and congratulatory. Many predicted that I would not return. George Staab, an ultraconservative curmudgeon, was blunt, "You'll get taken over by all those liberals in Washington and drink so much Scotch Mist you'll never be normal again." I hadn't the faintest idea what Scotch Mist was and I hadn't yet developed a clear political philosophy.

*   *   *

On the first Sunday night in December 1963, I boarded the Pennsylvania Railroad train at 30th and Market Streets and went down to Washington. I bought, at the *Bulletin's* expense, a first-class ticket.

It was only a few dollars more than regular coach, but I felt entitled to special treatment. I booked a room at the Washington Hotel at 15th Street and Pennsylvania Avenue, a block from the National Press Building. I showed up bright and early the next morning at the *Bulletin* bureau. Grace Andrews, the office manager, led me to my office. It had a window into the interior courtyard. I could tell the weather and look onto journalists in other offices. In Philadelphia all I had was a desk in the newsroom. Only executives had offices. Now I had an office with a wall to hang pictures, a telephone where I could talk in private, and an Underwood typewriter to pound out stories. My stories—called copy—would be taken two blocks up 14th Street to Western Union for "punching" on the wire to Philadelphia. I knew that if stories broke during the day, I would dictate them to Philadelphia.

Roth welcomed me formally and said my assignment was to cover the Philadelphia area delegation in Congress and whatever other local area stories might break in Washington. That had been Tony Day's responsibility. Tony would now write about the Supreme Court, the White House and national security issues as the country seemed to drift toward an expanded war in Vietnam. Roth would continue as main White House correspondent and he would write his column three times a week. Roth didn't waste a lot of words on small talk. It turned out he was a painfully shy man who rarely criticized or commended. I don't remember a single occasion when he read one of my stories and said it was good or bad. Usually, he never read my stories at all. I wrote them and gave them to Grace Andrews for delivery to Western Union or walked them up myself. It was on the way to the bus stop.

Roth said that since I'd be working mainly on Capitol Hill—The Hill—Tony would introduce me around. Tony and I were friends from our days on the *Bulletin's* nightside. My first chore in Washington was to find a place to live that I could afford and that was convenient to the office. I needed an address so that I could apply for congressional and White House credentials. Roth and Day pointed out that I'd probably never use the White House pass, but it would be good to have.

Roth took me to lunch at the National Press Club, where I would become a member in due course. It was a club for white men only. It was another few years before a black was admitted, and only after that, did the club admit women. Women assigned to cover speeches in the club ballroom were required to sit in the balcony. The bar at the press club was crowded when Bob and I arrived. I took note of the

LAWRENCE M. O'ROURKE

celebrated naked Phryne painting on her back over the bar. The all-male club cherished the painting by Brazilian artist Antonio Parreiras. After the admission of women as members, the painting was removed. Under Phryne's gaze, Roth took me the length of the bar, introducing me to people whose names I recognized promptly. I was awed to be in such august company.

Roth and I sat at a table set with a big basket of bread and rolls and a plate of pickles and green tomatoes. "The Club has excellent hamburgers," Roth said. I ordered one and a glass of milk. At the end of the meal I paid my share of the bill, 60 cents for the burger, 25 cents for the milk, and I left 15 cents, and from what I could figure out, that was the right thing to do. For me, a $1 lunch was high living.

It was time to look for a roof over my head. I figured what I could spend. I was paid $360 a month. I got a raise only a few months back and now I knew from Dickinson and Boyle that there would be no more money for working in Washington. I figured that after I paid taxes and expenses for food, drink, clothing, gasoline and tolls for trips back to Philadelphia, I better watch my dollars. So I figured I could pay about $75 a month for rent. Tony suggested that since I was only going to be in the capital for a year, I should get a place within walking distance of the office. Besides, I'd be working late a lot, and transportation wasn't good after darkness set in. Tony said to try 16th Street. I found vacancy signs on apartment buildings there, but when I inquired, I learned they were $200 a month and up. I made calls to places on bus lines in Virginia and Maryland, and didn't find much cheaper. Finally, looking in the paper, I found an ad for a two-bedroom apartment with a street parking space near Catholic University in Northeast Washington for $77 a month. It seemed like a steal. I took a cab, liked the place, and rented it on the spot for a year. The Fort Totten Apartments at 4900 Fort Totten Drive had the additional benefit of being racially mixed. I discovered it had one big disadvantage. It was not on a direct bus line to downtown. So I had to ride two or three buses.

Then with Tony leading the way, I visited the Senate offices of Democrat Joe Clark and Republican Hugh Scott and the House member offices. All six House members from Philadelphia were Democrats. Tony took me to the press table in the Senate dining room. I followed his suggestion and ordered coffee and cinnamon toast. When the waiter came by, Tony said, "Larry, I want you to meet the special waiter for this table, King."

I reached out my hand to shake his hand. King hesitated, but I refused to lower my hand. Finally he offered his hand for a limp, quick handshake. "Glad to meet you, Mr. King," I said. Keeping his eyes lowered, he said, "Please call me King." He must have been well into his 70s, a shuffling black man with white hair who never looked you in the eye, and said, "yassuh" with abject humility. A few reporters would gently tease King. I later discovered that he would roll his eyes and shake his head and laugh, but never offer a rejoinder. I drank a lot of coffee and ate a lot of cinnamon toast served by King. After a while as soon as he saw me in the morning, he brought my ritualistic order without asking. We all tipped him generously by 1964 standards, a quarter for serving a cup of coffee and toast. The rumor when he died was that he was immensely rich.

On that first morning tour, Tony Day introduced me to two friends who were certainly among my heroes as Washington reporters, Anthony Lewis of *The New York Times* and Joseph R.L. Sterne of *The Baltimore Sun*. Lewis worked mainly at the Supreme Court. He was the country's best Supreme Court reporter, as his Pulitzer Prize attested. Sterne worked the Hill, and I often worked it with him. He was energetic, loaded with contacts, and perhaps above all, enthusiastic. Joe Sterne taught me just how important it was to develop sources on the Hill and to ask questions right away because these busy people, senators and House members and senior staff members, were not likely to give reporters much of a second chance.

*   *   *

After my introductory visit to Washington, I screwed up the courage to ask Dickinson for more money. I figured that $90 a week wouldn't be enough, even with a $77 per month apartment and 65-cent hamburgers at the press club. "I had a great week, got a lot of good advice from Bob Roth and Tony Day, and found an apartment," I told him. "But I do have a problem. I need a little more money." He looked at me for a few seconds and said he could not raise my salary, but had an idea. Every Friday night, he said, treat yourself to a $15 dinner at the press club. Put $15 on your expense account for dinner every Friday, even if you are not able to eat the $15 dinner that week. Thus I learned of the Washington bureau expense account.

As I spent my final days in Philadelphia, introducing Gene Herman as my successor on the education beat to my contacts, buying furniture,

LAWRENCE M. O'ROURKE

and saying see-you-in-a-year to my colleagues, I felt pretty good about myself, perhaps smug. Here I was 25 years old, not far from being a copy boy, the first of my extended family to have graduated from college, the grandson of Irish immigrants, heading for the big-time of American journalism, the Washington beat, as a member of the bureau of one of the country's proudest and most respected newspapers.

In feeling good about myself, I also felt confident that I could be a good reporter in Washington. For being a good reporter is what I wanted to be. I frankly had no great dreams—at least at that point—of globetrotting or punditry. I knew I could be a good reporter. I had already won prizes for my reporting. Politicians didn't awe me. I was already used to talking with them directly and aggressively to get the story I needed. I figured that as pretentious and celebrated as Washington reporters might be, they were still people with notebooks and typewriters who asked questions, got frustrated trying to run down stories, worked long hours, and in the end were judged the same way as any other reporter—by quality, accuracy, access, and speed.

But I also knew that Washington reporters got their plum assignments for a reason. They had worked hard at their home papers and proved themselves worthy, as had I. I was ready for my next step on my journey as a reporter.

CHAPTER 2

At The Ironing Board

WHEN I WAS a young reporter, the goal of a good newspaper story was to tell readers what the story was about in the first paragraph, and to get to the point in a hurry before the busy reader shifted attention elsewhere on the page or tossed the paper aside. Charlie Johnson at the *Bulletin* was among copy editors who schooled me: "Don't bury the lead." He warned against "getting cute with the story." That may no longer be the style, but I think that as readers are pressed for time, newspapers overuse the anecdotal lead. Another pet peeve is the sports story that doesn't tell the score until several paragraphs down. For most stories, I like the traditional who, what, when, where, how and why style.

*   *   *

While I opened this memoir with my arrival in Washington, where I built my career, my story begins long before that fateful November day that Kennedy died. It begins in a row house, 2112 South Cecil Street, in Southwest Philadelphia, where I was brought after my birth on March 12, 1938 in nearby St. Vincent's Hospital. I entered the world with help of Dr. John O'Connell, who 26 years before in 1912 attended the birth of my mother, Margaret Mary Cecilia Higgins, in the Higgins family home at 2208 Lombard Street in center-city Philadelphia.

Our block of Cecil Street was wide enough for one car, but we didn't need much more space. During World War II and immediately thereafter, few people on our block owned cars. Those who did parked them half on the sidewalk, half in the street. The police came through rarely. We had weekly visits from horse-drawn trash and ash collection wagons. They made it through slowly, as did the man delivering bread or milk in the early morning, the truck dropping off the odd piece of furniture or the ton of coal that was dumped by chute into the basement, or the truck that dropped off kegs of beer at McGarvey's, the saloon at one end of the block. We didn't need a wider street. It was wide enough for kick ball when we used imaginary lines from front steps or car fenders as goals, or for hose ball when we made a fire hydrant or lamp post the base.

There was little danger you could get run over if you played on Cecil Street. Cars didn't go fast enough to hurt anybody. Mothers pushing baby carriages chatted across the street without raising their voices. One of the best things about our street was that light traffic preserved the macadam and made Cecil Street great for roller-skating.

The 2100 block of Cecil Street ran from Woodland Avenue to Greenway Avenue. We called our houses row houses because they were all connected. They were wood and 15 feet wide. Families could hear each other through the thin walls. Since a set of front steps served two houses, you eased to the side to let the neighbors go up and down. The closeness and ambiance encouraged good neighborliness, except when neighbors didn't like one another. Fights between neighbors made life tough.

We had narrow front porches ideal for summers without air-conditioning. You couldn't say anything on your front porch and keep it secret long. But there weren't many secrets to keep. We went to the same church, Most Blessed Sacrament at 56th and Chester. The kids went to school there before going on to West Catholic High School. Rare was the kid on Cecil Street in the local public school or John Bartram High School. We shopped at the Acme on Chester Avenue and bought meat at the Tilles Market across from the rectory. Mr. Tilles, of course, was rationed by the war. My mother often said with gratitude that when she told Mr. Tilles she had company coming, he gave her an extra quarter pound of beef, even though she didn't have the right ration button. Mr. Tilles provided meat to priests in the rectory.

Most people on Cecil Street went to the same doctors and dentists. Most of us were Irish-Catholic, with a sprinkling of people with German names, and a few Italians. In my childhood, when the United States was at war with Germany, Italy and Japan, we kids used our fingers to shoot the Nazis and "Japs." Of course, we had no Japanese living on our street, or Latinos. The German-Americans on Cecil Street were the first to fly the U.S. flag on holidays and to comply with blackout rules.

We didn't have Jews or African-Americans on our block of Cecil Street, though Jewish people were said to live around the corner. The idea of blacks living in Southwest Philadelphia never entered my consciousness, so of course we had no overt racial prejudice. To my Irish-Catholic ethnic group, "Eye-talians" were the rivals.

During the war, many fathers were in uniform. A few mothers worked in the military industry. There was an airplane parts factory two blocks down 58th Street. But most women were at home, many young moms tending kids and dreading notices from the government about spouses. Several houses had flags with gold stars in their windows, signifying death in battle. As a child, I never thought we were in hard times. This was how life was. Air raid drills and standing in line with my mother with ration coupons to purchase eggs, sugar, butter and soap were normal. If a mother needed an extra cup of sugar or stick of butter to make a birthday cake for her child, she could "borrow" it from neighbors. After all, all the kids would likely be invited to the birthday party.

*   *   *

My father, Lawrence M. O'Rourke, was not away in the military. I don't remember this story, but my parents told it often. My father came home one day in the early war years and announced that he was not going away like other husbands and fathers because he was not "physically fit." He was 36 when on Jan. 20, 1937 he married my mother who was 24. He was 41 when Japan attacked Pearl Harbor.

At the war's outbreak my father was a bookkeeper at the Bellevue-Stratford Hotel in downtown Philadelphia. Two years into the war, the Penn Salt Co., a chemical firm in Cornwells Heights, a suburb northeast of Philadelphia, hired him. He spent about 90 minutes each way in trains, and arrived home from work five nights a week about six o'clock. He had the four-star edition of the *Bulletin*. He bought it at the railroad station in downtown Philadelphia. He insisted on the four-star, which I later learned, went to press about 5 in the afternoon. It was not much different than the three-star that went to press an hour earlier. But my father insisted that if he were spending three cents on the newspaper he would get the best. During the war, the *Bulletin* published Monday through Saturday, but my father said the Saturday paper was not worth buying for three cents because it was such a thin paper. It was not until the late 1940s that the *Bulletin* started a Sunday edition. My father complained it was too expensive at 15 or 20 cents on the sidewalk outside church. My father refused to buy the morning

Inquirer. He explained that he would not be able to read it during the day at work and why not wait for a paper he could read at home. He said he trusted the *Bulletin.* He said the *Inquirer* ran certain stories because "all they want to do is sell papers." It was never that way with the *Bulletin,* my father said.

He read the *Bulletin* from cover to cover. He started on the train and continued in the tiny living room at 2112 until my mother put dinner on the table. After dinner, he went back to the living room and read more of the *Bulletin.* My mother washed the dishes and did other chores. He occasionally read to my mother or to me important news from the *Bulletin,* but my father was a man of few spoken words.

I got the sense from my father that the *Bulletin* was the ultimate authority, the source of all that was worth knowing. The *Bulletin's* slogan was "In Philadelphia, nearly everybody reads The *Bulletin.*" I grew up thinking that the *Bulletin* was as vital to life as the weekly *Catholic Standard and Times, the* diocesan newspaper my father got at church and consumed with equal fervor. My parents did not subscribe to magazines or buy books. My mother played the radio in the kitchen and my father had a floor-model radio in the living room. He used it mainly to listen to broadcasts of games played by the Philadelphia Athletics, the American League team managed by Connie Mack. My father never listened to the Phillies games. Asked why, he replied, "I am an American League man." He hated the Yankees. During the war, broadcasts of road games by the A's were not real play-by-plays from the site of the game, but rather embellished accounts by announcers in studios in downtown Philaelphia reading from a wired report. My father knew that, but he loved hearing baseball pitch by pitch.

When my father left for work in the early morning, he left behind on the dining room table the thoroughly read *Bulletin* from the previous afternoon. My mother, who made my father's breakfast, then had her turn at the *Bulletin.* She got her three-cents worth in between cleaning the house, preparing meals and minding me and the children of neighbor women in jobs left vacant by men at war. After I entered first grade at Most Blessed Sacrament at age five in September 1943, my mother took in even more children. She supplemented the family income and provided me, an only child until I was ten, with after-school playmates. Somehow my mother found time to read the *Bulletin*—everyday, a habit she continued into her 90s. My parents wanted more children. My mother miscarried once during the war years. I remember how sad the moment was, though I, of course, didn't know why until many years later when my mother confided. She would have been much happier with many more children, and so would I. Then on May 1, 1948, my brother Johnny was born. We were 10 years apart. Much to my regret we were more members of a different generation than siblings.

*   *   *

Unlike my father, my mother was a woman of many words. As my father spent evenings with the *Bulletin,* and my mother went about household chores, she was rarely silent. I vividly remember sitting on the bottom step of the stairs at the end of a long hallway. My mother always had what she called curtain stretchers leaning against the long wall. It was a dreadful device. Hundreds of nails emerged from narrow strips of wood in a rectangle adjusted for the size of the curtain she was stretching. She always seemed to be stretching curtains, either our lace curtains or those of neighbors. They paid a small fee. My mother had the knack of stretching the curtains on the nails without pricking her fingers. She was very fast putting the curtains on the nails. As I grew up amid the stretched curtains, I was often detailed to the task. I never acquired her skills and rarely escaped without puncturing a finger and producing a drop of blood. My mother brushed off my complaints as malingering, and she was probably right. "Offer it up," she said about bleeding fingers and virtually every misfortune that came my way. My mother was constantly "offering things up" to God.

When my mother wasn't hanging curtains, she ironed in the long hallway. In that pre-permanent press era, days, my mother painstakingly ironed my father's shirts. Sometimes she took in ironing for other families. Later on, when I was an altar boy, she spent hours washing and ironing the white surplices I wore. My mother let me iron handkerchiefs. We had many handkerchiefs; perhaps someone always had a cold. My father never stretched curtains, ironed or did housework. He liked to say, "I don't even know how to boil water." One job I hated was putting wet clothes through the drying wringer in the basement. I was terrified of catching my arm in the wringer and never satisfied by my mother's reassurance there was an automatic release whenever something as big as a child's hand entered the rollers.

As far back as I can remember, all the time my mother stretched curtains or ironed or set the table or cooked, she talked to me. She had stories she told over and over. Many were family stories, often involving her parents and grandparents, brothers and sisters, cousins and childhood friends. She talked a lot about what she read in the *Bulletin*. I learned from her about places where U.S. soldiers, sailors and Marines were fighting Germans and Japanese.

Several months before my time to enter first grade, my mother acquired first-grade reading books from her Aunt Ann, known as Sister Agnes Regina, a member of the St. Joseph's order. Aunt Ann was a gentle, cheerful woman who taught primary grades. My mother set out to have me reading from the red covered books before school began for me. She succeeded. On my first day of first grade, I was well beyond Dick and Jane and their dog Spot, the main characters in the first reader.

*   *   *

My ability to read early created unforeseen problems for me in the first grade at MBS. We had 108 children in that class under a nun who could not have been more than 25 years old. The poor nun must have been terrified to look at us; two to a desk in what we were told was the largest elementary school in the nation, if not the world. I look back in wonder and admiration for that young woman. She was always addressed as "Ster"—our version of Sister. It still rings, "Yes, Ster" or "No, Ster" and nothing else was to be said other than recited lessons.

In her black habit that revealed only a bit of her face and her hands, and with her knobby clicker that served as both a signaling device and a potential blackjack, under the watch of Christ on the Cross, and with statues of the Blessed Virgin and the Lord's angels and saints gazing at us throughout the room, we first graders were terrified. I was slightly less terrified owing to frequent contacts with Aunt Ann and with Aunt Mary, known as Sister Stella Margaret, another of my mother's aunts. Aunt Mary taught eighth grade at St. Columba's near Shibe Park. I also had Aunt Helen, or Sister John Laurentia, a Franciscan, my father's sister who taught middle grades in various Catholic schools, I was used to nuns. Often on family visits I played school in my aunts' classrooms.

Teaching was largely by rote, starting with the Baltimore Catechism—Who made us? God made us. Why did God make us? God made us to know, love, and serve him in this world and the next. The rote continued into reading, all 108 present expected to read aloud the words about Dick and Jane running and jumping, with their little dog Spot by their side. We learned arithmetic by rote, reciting the two times table, the three times table, over and over for hours. For me, it was a bore. My mother made sure I memorized the times tables as well as the Baltimore Catechism. I won several catechism contests and was expected by family members and the nuns to become a priest—a conclusion largely based on my ability to recite the catechism.

As amusing as this may seem seven decades later, it was not all that much fun at the time. I was restless in school, and the nuns sent frequent notes home to my parents telling them that I did not pay attention or recite in rote as I was told. I got 90s in spelling and arithmetic, but I got many C grades, the worst, in behavior. It was a mark of shame. My father was irritated at his uncooperative son. How many times did he ask me, "Do you know how to spell obedience?" and I would have to spell it. My mother tried to keep me busy at home by encouraging me to fill my time and use my energy reading. That, of course, only made the boredom issue worse, particularly in a culture where conformity was highly prized and individuality was viewed as rebellion. We all looked alike from a distance in our school uniforms and were expected to act alike and to think alike, to stay in line, actually and metaphorically.

The reading material most available in our home was the *Bulletin* and I began early on to read it—starting with the funny pages, but also more grown-up stuff. I don't know how much I understood or absorbed, but, prodded and aided by my mother, I could read the words—often saying them to my mother at her ironing board.

In school and on Cecil Street, I had another strike against me. I was usually the youngest in my class. In sports—a great elementary school measuring rod—my age and physical development put me at distinct physical disadvantage. Since I started first grade at age five, earlier than most of my classmates who were six, I was too young and inexperienced to play the games of childhood with schoolmates. At football and basketball and tag and some game I remember as "buck-buck" with kids jumping on one another's backs, I was a loser. When it came to choosing sides, I was usually picked last or not at all, left to await the next game and another round of rejection. They probably didn't have the word at the time, but I was a nerd. I defended myself with a vocabulary and sharp tongue that only worsened matters, especially when I said something back to the nun. That was soundly condemned as "back talk." It often produced a note to home, a parental visit to school, and chastisement by my stern, mortified father.

LAWRENCE M. O'ROURKE

*　　*　　*

My social life got decidedly better in fifth grade, in 1948, when my brother Johnny was born. We had outgrown the house at 2212 South Cecil Street, and my father made no secret of his annoyance at lack of privacy. My mother told me in later years that she and my father were offered the house at 2112 for $900 in the war years, but could not afford it. Instead, they paid $25 a month rent.

By 1948, my father had saved a little money. James Neville of St. Charles Savings and Loan Society, the de facto family banker, recommended a new house at 742 South Cecil Street as a good buy at $4,500. It was a stretch for my fiscally prudent father in 1948. The new block of Cecil Street seemed a little more upscale. It was wide enough for two cars, not that we had one, but it was considered higher-class. Porches were enclosed and walls were thicker, thus providing more privacy. Our house adjoined that of Mrs. Shalet, a middle-aged Jewish widow, who, as my father put it, "kept to herself." I thought Mrs. Shalet one of the nicest people I knew. She always had a smile for me and constantly told my mother and me that if we ever needed anything, all we had to do was knock on the wall or tap the glass that separated our enclosed porches. She volunteered to watch my baby brother in his coach and now and then asked me to run to the store for something she had forgotten, which normally got me a nickel or dime. On occasions when I was locked out of the house when my mother was not at home, Mrs. Shalet invited me into her home for a glass of milk and a safe place to wait.

I was happy to move from 2112 to 742. I hoped to escape my reputation in the old school as smart aleck and troublemaker. The new school was Transfiguration at 56th Street and Cedar Avenue. I adapted quickly, hoping to keep a lower profile and get along.

My elementary school friends were usually those I sat near in the classroom and met on the walks between home and school. I soon met John Hone, whose parents were immigrants from Ireland. His father, like my grandfather O'Rourke who died before I was born, and my father during his youth, worked for the Pennsylvania Railroad. I met Jim Feerick, whose immigrant Irish father owned a saloon on Grays Ferry Avenue, and Larry McAlee with distinguished Irish roots, as well as Jack Friel, Jim Breslin and Billy Roche. Billy's father was the undertaker across from the church. There was Danny Devine, also from a large Irish family, and Jim McCoy, a quiet and serious youngster who seemed ill at ease with rowdier classmates. I often encountered Tommie Hardie, an outgoing youngster on our trips with schoolbags on our shoulders.

Hone became a successful businessman. Feerick and McAlee became lawyers in Philadelphia. Friel had a successful career at the Centers for Disease Control in Atlanta. Devine and McCoy went into St. Charles Seminary and were ordained as Roman Catholic priests. Hardie wrote engagingly in our high school alumni newspaper about our lives as schoolboys and the old neighborhood. Breslin tinkered with cars and died young of a heart ailment.

After the war, fathers were home and eager to do things with their kids. Families had money to spend and went out more to dinners and movies. After May 1, 1948, the day my brother Johnny was born in Philadelphia's Misericordia Hospital, my mother was busy with the baby and I had new freedom. I was finally allowed to venture beyond Cecil Street. There were football scrimmages in Cobbs Creek Park, and three-on-three basketball games in the Roche back yard next to the mortuary. I became an altar boy and was quickly tapped to be a magister, a job that had me sit in my black cassock and starched white surplice on a little chair on the floor of the main altar. I had a tiny metal clicker called a cricket. I would click and then stand, kneel or sit as appropriate during the Mass or other religious celebration. The young altar boys—called popes in their white cassocks—and the congregation behind me dutifully observed me and followed my lead. In our community, that was big power, and I loved the attention. The Transfiguration pastor, Father Joseph Cavanuagh, assigned Norman "Okie" O'Connor and me to be his altar boys at the monthly First Saturday celebration. Okie was the acolyte and I was the censer bearer. I lit the charcoal and held the censer steady while Father Cavanaugh spooned on incense. I swung the device as we processed up and down aisles. Joe Cavanaugh often gave us 50 cents each, a bonanza. When Cavanaugh became an old man and moved into a retirement villa, he wrote and asked me to visit. I wrote back and we exchanged a few letters, but I never visited. I am sorry about that now, but it taught me—if too late—that it is wise to seize the moment. As an adult I had little patience with procrastination.

*   *   *

Given more freedom, I found the library branch at 58th Street and Baltimore Avenue and realized I was no longer confined to the children's area. I began an aggressive reading program, often spending hours with novels I could not bring home because if my parents caught me reading them, there would be a price to pay, minimally a lecture about what kind of stuff I was reading, possibly even a prohibition on my free run of the library. I kept my growing interest in adult ideas to myself. I hid books I wanted to read in a little used line of books.

I learned about sex from Okie O'Connor while we stood in line waiting for a movie in the Transfiguration auditorium. I was shocked and disbelieving. But Okie insisted he had the facts of life right.

*   *   *

My fraternal grandmother, Bridget O'Rourke, born in Carramanagh, County Galway, Ireland, influenced my life. She came to the United States as a serving girl at 17. She raised her three children with frugality. She decided during the war to spend a little and rent a place on Long Beach Island, New Jersey, 60 miles east of Philadelphia. My parents and my father's brother John were expected to abide by her wishes, that is to say, to do what she ordered, which meant weeks at the shore every summer for me. We stayed in Ship Bottom, in a cottage called Tammany Hall by the owner, Mary McNulty. I stood with my mother the night of V-J Day as people poured from their homes to celebrate the victory over Japan and the end of World War II.

Up 22nd Street toward the beach there was a drug store that sold newspapers. My mother permitted me to walk there on summer evenings and buy the *Bulletin*. It wasn't the four-star that my father prized—that was confined to center-city Philadelphia—but it was the *Bulletin*. Buying and reading the *Bulletin* became even more imbedded as a ritual. I supplemented the *Bulletin* every week with Collier's magazine. I was hooked on Collier's as a child, mainly stories by John O'Hara.

I grabbed Collier's or a book after breakfast every morning and headed to the beach. I lay on my stomach with the sun beating down on my bare back and legs. It's no wonder that starting around age 50, I had to visit the dermatologist every few months and undergo surgery for skin cancer.

Three years after the war, my grandmother bought a cottage on stilts at 207 West 8th Street in Surf City, the next community to Ship Bottom. Starting with the summer of 1948 after my brother's birth, my mother, brother, and I were driven to Surf City the weekend after school closed to spend summer at the shore. My father came by bus on Friday nights and went back on Sunday. My grandmother came for two weeks, during which my mother and brother were sent home, but I stayed. Not eager to hang around the house with admonitions by my grandmother to drink raw eggs, as my uncle and father did, or to help with perpetual weeding, I continued all-day visits to the beach, armed with books, Collier's and the *Bulletin*. I kept the books and Collier's hidden from my grandmother, who never read in my presence except from a small prayer book. I had the feeling she would not approve of my ritual.

One of those summers, in 1950 when I was 12, a boy at the shore whose father was the town policeman, let me ride his two-wheeler bicycle. I had never done such a thing. Without my mother knowing, I took to the bike. When we returned to Cecil Street for the new school term, I wanted a bicycle. After many warnings about the danger, my parents said I could have a bicycle if I bought it myself. That requirement may have appeared formidable, but it was the key to my career in the newspaper business.

*   *   *

The *Bulletin* relied on young boys after school and on Saturday afternoon and Sunday morning to deliver the newspaper at the front doors of customers. A garage around the corner from us was the *Bulletin's* distribution center for our neighborhood. At the garage, I met Ralph Burton, a white-haired man who was the local circulation manager. I watched as the *Bulletin* truck from the center-city printing plant delivered bundles of newspapers. Under Burton's watch, a boy called the branch captain cut the wire on the bundles and counted out the papers for the carrier boys. The boys filled canvas bags with *Bulletins* and headed to their routes. It looked like fun and there was money in it.

Burton said he had an open route with 60 customers. He said there were houses where people didn't take the *Bulletin*, so there was a good chance to expand the route. I could make eight dollars a week to start and more if I got additional customers. I took the deal. I rushed home from school. I took my wagon on days when the newspaper was heavy, especially on days when the *Bulletin* was full of food ads.

I learned to fold the newspaper to toss it as close to the top step as my arm and aim allowed. On Thursdays every week, I started the process we called "collect." That meant going door-to-door, asking thirty cents for the week. With the proceeds I paid Burton on Friday what I owned the *Bulletin* for the week's papers. I pocketed the profit. Customers on Ellsworth Street were good at paying. Some tipped me 10 or 15 cents. You can bet they got their paper on the top step. I opened an account in a bank at 58th and Baltimore across from the library. By the winter I had $60 to buy my beautiful blue and cream Schwinn bicycle. It was my first business equipment investment. I could deliver papers much faster from a bike than from a wagon.

I liked delivering the *Bulletin* and turned up reliably every day. I was still at it in the fall of 1951 when I entered St. Thomas More High School. It became tougher to be a *Bulletin* boy at that point because I had to ride a bus and trolley car between school and home. The Philadelphia Transportation Co. schedule did not always fit my needs. Thus on many an afternoon my mother became the *Bulletin's* delivery boy. When I didn't get home from school on time to be at Burton's garage, my mother substituted. I usually caught up to her as she trudged to Ellsworth Street, but there were times when I didn't, and so my mother delivered the entire route. She let me keep the money and never complained. She took special delight when customers called her the *Bulletin* boy.

In the fall of 1952, Burton held a meeting of delivery boys to announce a *Bulletin* contest. If we got ten new customers in the next few weeks, we would win a trip to Washington on January 20, 1953, to attend the Inauguration of the next president of the United States. That would be Republican Dwight D. Eisenhower or Democrat Adlai E. Stevenson. I had read plenty in the *Bulletin* about the campaign. I knew more than the average *Bulletin* boy about the election. I spent a few hours that fall passing out literature for Stevenson. Stevenson's national campaign manager, James Finnegan, lived a block from my grandmother O'Rourke on Springfield Avenue. Finnegan and my father were boyhood friends. We were a family of Democrats. I asked my father if I could meet Finnegan. My father walked me down the street one evening to talk with Finnegan. After I expressed my support for Stevenson, Finnegan, who acted as if he had nothing more important to do than enlist a 14-year-old in the campaign, inquired if I would like to deliver Stevenson brochures around the neighborhood and at trolley car and train stops. I was delighted to spend many hours promoting Stevenson's candidacy.

When the votes were counted on that November Tuesday and Eisenhower was elected, I was disappointed, but my interest in partisan politics and enthusiasm for the *Bulletin*-sponsored trip to Washington for Inauguration Day was undiminished. I had never been farther south than Chester, a few miles below Philadelphia. I had never taken a train ride by myself. The idea of attending a presidential inauguration was beyond my dreams.

But first there was the matter of getting ten new customers for the *Bulletin*. I went door to door with a simple message: Take a *Bulletin* subscription and send me to Washington to see Eisenhower become president. Whether it was my persistence, my salesmanship or the notion of a neighborhood kid at Ike's swearing-in, I never knew. But I rang up ten new customers. Burton put me on the list.

*　　*　　*

Early on the morning of Jan. 20, 1953, a date that was also my parents' 16th wedding anniversary, my mother took me to the Baltimore and Ohio Railroad Station by the Schuylkill River at Walnut Street. Showing my congratulatory notice from the *Bulletin*, I was given a red, white and blue knit hat and a train ticket. More than 50 years later, I still have the hat. I went proudly with the other winners to Washington's Union Station and the U.S. Capitol grounds. We were in the peanut gallery, but that made little difference to me. We were there. After the ceremony, we got box lunches and were led down Pennsylvania Avenue to bleachers on the sidewalk in front of a large government building. I watched Dwight and Mamie Eisenhower and Richard and Pat Nixon pass, flanked by Secret Service agents. I saw large trucks bearing reporters and photographers. The Eisenhowers and Nixons were followed by bands and floats. I snapped pictures with a Brownie camera. The site on Pennsylvania Avenue was later cleared for the Newseum, a museum of the news business. After the parade, we walked to the Uline Arena, adjacent to the railroad tracks above Union Station and were fed a meal. The Uline Arena building is still there. Whenever I ride by it on an Amtrak train or the Metro, I remember the 1953 Eisenhower Inauguration and the *Bulletin*.

As I left Washington after attending the great quadrennial moment in America—the inauguration of a president and the promise of renewal—I told myself: I'll be back.

CHAPTER 3

The Boys of Tommy More

ONCE PRESIDENT EISENHOWER'S inauguration was behind me, I decided to quit as a *Bulletin* carrier. I had stayed primarily to win the trip to Washington.

I thought I was too old to be a paperboy. After all, I was all of 14, a sophomore in high school, and certain in my mind that I knew just about everything that was worth knowing. It was a long while before I discovered that the older I got, the less I knew. But with sophomoric confidence that I could accomplish whatever I set out to do—a mental outlook that remained with me through life—I embarked on a series of time-consuming school extracurricular activities. I enjoyed them a lot more than rushing home every afternoon to pick up a bundle of *Bulletins* in Burton's garage.

I was no less confident in my imagination than everybody else in our neighborhood that I was born to be a gifted athlete. But realism conquered imagination. Though I had a decent outside jump shot, being short and slow and young, I could not make the St. Thomas More High School varsity basketball team. I was on the freshman team, but rarely got into games. But I was crazy for the sport, as were most of my friends. I signed on as manager of the basketball team. The legendary coach, Joseph "Tubby" Walker, appointed me team scorekeeper with responsibility at home games for posting the right score on the electric board in the decrepit school gym, keeping tab of timeouts and starting and stopping the clock as signaled by the referees. Tommy More had a distinguished basketball record. Only a year before I got there, the team had won a post-season championship at Glens Falls, New York. John "Misty" Fannon went on to play at Notre Dame. Al Giuliani became a fine player at St. Joseph's. My classmates included Nick DeCurcio, Danny Devine, Butch Jenkins, Tom Hardie and others I played against in Roche's back yard. I knew I couldn't compete with them.

I joined the school band and attempted to master the tenor saxophone under the tutorship of a very patient band instructor, Adolph Sorian. I approached the sax the way I approached my studies. I was a quick study, but never, except for English and history and a few courses I favored, put in the time and attention that would turn me into a scholar, nor a musician. But I learned enough on the saxophone to fake it.

I signed on to the student newspaper and competed on the cross-country team, embarking innocently enough on two of the activities that marked my life—newspapers and distance running. The newspaper came out every month or two and I was assigned minor articles to write. Our cross-country training was around the park across from the school at 47th Street and Wyalusing Avenue. I ran in basketball shoes.

Looking for a job to replace the *Bulletin*, I launched into the food distribution industry. Classmate Harry Johnson led me to an after-school job as a shopping cart collector and gasoline station attendant at the Penn Fruit Market on Market Street. I don't recall anybody asking me how old I was. Perhaps they were grateful they had someone willing to work in the cold and dark. I kept at it for a couple of months for two evenings a week and on weekends until I was told I would have to join the union. I didn't object to joining the union until I learned that the initiation fee was the equivalent of about a month's part-time work and the dues would eat up a fourth of my minimum wage. I gave up that job.

Meantime I stepped into a more interesting grocery job at the American Stores Co. outlet at 58th and Christian Streets, around the corner from our home. American Stores was fondly regarded in the neighborhood since Irish immigrants founded it in 1891. A classmate, Bruce Long, a stock boy at the local store, told me about an opening. I was hired to stock shelves and carry bags of groceries home for people who could not do so. After a few months, Bill, the manager, tapped me to work behind the counter. At that store, inefficient as it was, but a friendly place to shop, customers asked for items—typically, four cans of Campbell's tomato soup, a two-pound bag of sugar, a box of oatmeal, a quart of milk. Those items were shelved behind the counter. The customers picked up their own bread and potatoes and placed them on the counter, but they couldn't go behind it.

My job was standing next to one of the countermen—each of them named Bill. When a customer asked for an item, I pulled it from the shelf and put it on the counter. Bill wrote the price in pencil on the shopping bag. When the customer was done ordering, Bill added the

LAWRENCE M. O'ROURKE

prices he had written and announced the cost of the order. Both Bills were whizzes at addition and never checked their numbers. We suspected that our customers did when they got home; if they discovered the tiniest mistake they would have come back with written proof. I never heard a single complaint. If the customer didn't have enough money, Bill and the customer usually removed items until the bill met the customer's ability to pay. That was often a sad moment. I packed purchased items into a brown paper bag and returned deleted items to the shelves. Bill took the money and put it in the hand-cranked register.

I quickly learned more than I should have about my neighbors—what they ate was a starter, but what they couldn't afford was an insight. It was painful watching a mother turn back a can of stewed tomatoes or a handful of apples because the family could not afford them. Now and then a mother would say she had a little extra money at home and would come by later if only she could have the items. The Bills were gracious and trusting, until the point when a customer had run up such a debt that it was evident it would not be paid. The Bills didn't keep a written tab. The storekeeper and customers trusted each other, and I don't recall any disputes.

With no supermarket within easy walking distance of our neighborhood, the store was busy. After a few weeks as a counter gofer, Bill the manager asked me if I could add as fast as the other Bill. No, I said, he's really fast. Let's try anyway, Bill the manager said to me. You wait on the customers just as the other Bill does. So I, at age 14, was assigned space at the counter. I did what the Bills did, including writing the numbers in pencil and adding them. I had access to the cash register. I was paid 50 cents an hour, but sometimes at the end of a good, busy day, Bill the manager asked me if I wanted to take home sugar or oranges or cookies or some such luxury item, and I was delighted to do so. He sometimes slipped me an extra quarter tip. Bill the manager gave me the keys to the store to work on Sundays. Alone in the store, I restocked shelves from the back room. I didn't have to restock meats, but the butcher said I could eat lunchmeat if I would take out the trash and sweep the floor. On busy business days the butcher called me from the grocery counter and had me grind hamburger meat. A "pound ground" was a popular order in our neighborhood. My mother was pleased at my expanding opportunities in the grocery business. She reminded me that her uncle John McGonigle owned and operated the grocery store near St. Patrick's Church in center city and he made a good living. My father was delighted to hear from neighbors that I was a whiz at arithmetic.

High school wasn't a lot of fun. A year or two younger than my classmates, doomed to modest athletic skills, with braces on my teeth, unkempt hair, and protective parents who wanted me home for dinner every night with no going out after dark, I was not part of the in-crowd. As for studies, I did enough to get by. Blessed with a great memory, I picked up required material quite quickly. I can look back and see the genetic roots for my memory. My mother was skilled at telling stories in amazing detail, remembering names, dates and places with stunning ability. She also loved to write letters.

In all my life, I never encountered anyone with my father's ability with numbers. I remember my father playing cards around our dining room table with his friends from his old South Philadelphia neighborhood or the San Domingo Council of the Knights of Columbus. On rare occasions they'd have a shot of whiskey, but they were usually confined to tea served by my mother. My father always was funny and outgoing while playing cards, traits he rarely displayed with the family. Mostly they played poker or pinochle, hand after hand for three to four hours with most talk about the cards or baseball or politics. From a corner chair, I watched and listened as they bet quarters, dimes and nickels, building pots once in a while that amounted to as much as three or four dollars. At the end of the night, usually 11 o'clock on Friday, the men would go home and my father would run through the hands he had played, telling me how he had made his decisions to bet or fold. He usually came out even or with a few quarters profit. Reviewing hours of poker and pinochle transactions, he talked in detail about who had what cards, the order they were played, and calculations that had been made. I never developed a gift for poker or other card games that required bluffing. I lacked the "poker-face" that my father said was mandatory. But I marveled at his skill at card games and his astonishing memory, not to mention his capacity at mathematics and love of numbers—gifts that were to give me an edge as a student and as a young journalist.

My father could be voluble about statistics, especially numbers from his chemical plant job. Often on weekends, he worked on those numbers at our dining room table. He could also recite batting averages of American League players, games between the Yankees and the A's won and lost, and election results. He and I did not talk about much other than baseball, politics and my dodging my duties around the house. My father was not a man given to personal conversation or idle chatter. He readily answered factual questions, but bristled when asked "why?"

*   *   *

The fact that I was in St. Thomas More High School was a bit of a fluke. Our parish, Transfiguration, sent its eighth grade graduates to West Catholic High School, run by the Christian Brothers at 49th and Chestnut Streets, a long walk of home. I spent the summer of 1951 expecting to enroll at West Catholic in September and become a "Burr." My father arrived at Surf City one August Friday with a letter to me that I expected was my instruction for arriving at West Catholic. I opened it on the beach and discovered that I was bound for St. Thomas More. West Catholic was overcrowded.

I was shocked and heartbroken. I knew St. Thomas More as a small school, too far from home to walk, not much of an athletic power, never having beaten West Catholic in decades of football competition. My parents said it might not be so bad, but I didn't believe them.

A few weeks later, summer at the beach over, I dutifully arrived at Tommy More to discover dozens of Transfiguration classmates who made clear they were as miserable as I was. Unlike West Catholic, Tommy More had no adjoining football field. It had a bandbox gym, a cafeteria with long tables and rollout seats. In my four years in high school, I never saw anyone sit on one of those seats at lunchtime. We put one foot on the seat and ate standing up, usually the lunch in the brown paper bag that our mothers packed. The school sold hot dogs, milk and soft drinks, but I didn't have the money or inclination to buy. At first blush, everything at Tommy More seemed institutional—narrow hallways, dim lights, aging bathrooms, rows of desks fixed to the floor, an auditorium with a small stage and an ill-working sound system.

Most teachers were diocesan priests whose Roman collars suggested unchallengeable authority to the adolescent lot of us. We heard stories from older boys in the neighborhood that some of the Christian Brothers at West Catholic were young and fun to be around. They could even be seen after school playing basketball in shorts and undershirts. On arrival at Tommy More, we had little prospect that the priests we would face would ever shed their collars, much less expose their legs.

My mood wasn't helped when the first thing I learned only a few hours into my first day at Tommy More was the omnipresence of Rule 9. "As soon as the bell has rung for the beginning of the class period, students are to be in their seats and in silence." I learned that the rule was rather strictly enforced and liberally applied. It didn't take much errant behavior to run afoul of Rule 9. Punishments were usually collective. Rare was the time when an individual student would be singled out as a malefactor. I suppose that the idea was to have classmates put peer pressure on those who were not in their seats and in silence, but the effect was to bring us together as victims. Violations were punished with a command to write the rule 50 times that night, or perhaps 100 times over a weekend, in ink on loose-leaf paper. It was the first thing collected at the beginning of class the following day. I can't recall any student ever showing up without the required Rule 9 penalty completed. Writing Rule 9 put a crimp into free time. As for me, it was always an infuriating exercise in wasting time, with resentment building with each line. Many a time I performed my Rule 9 obligation first and skipped studying.

We were grouped in classes by expectations. I was placed in the premier class, known as D-1. One of our classes was Latin, a subject that I later realized was perfectly appropriate for kids likely to enroll in college liberal arts studies. But the pedagogy was menacing. The upperclassmen who briefed us through the grapevine on what to expect were unanimous in their fear, if not loathing, of the teacher. He was a big man who wore a cassock that accentuated his rotund mid-section. It was frequently marked with chalk dust. As a student, I found the man terrifying.

He introduced us to conjugation and declension, by rote, and I have no trouble recalling endless group recitations of such Latin verb forms as amo, amas, and amat. But I didn't love Latin and I hated the class—conditions that were probably shared universally in the classroom and undoubtedly anticipated by the experienced teacher. It's not that I didn't learn Latin. I did. The teacher's take-no-prisoners style was to enter the classroom and remove from a holder on the wall, near the Crucifix, a U.S. flag on a thin stick perhaps two feet long. With us sitting in silence and dread, he went to the rear of the room and either began the group recitation or asked an individual student to recite. Such a request brought added terror to the student because he knew that the teacher had rolled up the flag and moved within striking distance of the student. The student either got it right or faced a sound whack on the back of the neck with the flagstick. Old Glory did not soften the blow. The style of teaching encouraged preparation and attention and I had no doubt then, nor now, that fear was a powerful stimulant to learn or conform. But while I rarely got hit with the stick, I lived in constant fear of it, harboring within myself a deep dislike of that teacher and a resentment of bullies, even if they were priests.

Never in my high schools years did I experience or have any sense of sexual abuse or sexual misconduct by any priest. I thought about that after revelations decades later that priests had sexually abused children. We were certainly vulnerable.

Though that teacher was an aberration, he is near the top of bad memories from high school. But to be fair, virtually all priests I encountered during four years at St. Thomas More were outstanding teachers and kind and gracious human beings. They were by and large distant and authoritarian, but they constantly conveyed concern. I never doubted that the priests cared deeply that I learned. It did not take me long to develop a loyalty to the school I had not wanted to attend. Before the football season ended—with another Tommy More loss on the football field to West Catholic—I was beginning to realize the advantage of attending a small school with a dedicated teaching staff. The fact that we had fewer than one thousand students—less than half the enrollment at West Catholic—meant expanded opportunity to get involved in extracurricular activities, and so I was soon busy from the band to basketball to the newspaper, while still working on weekends at the grocery. It was boot camp for multi-tasking.

*   *   *

Much to my gratitude later in life, Tommy More teachers believed in large doses of daily homework. I had a lot of writing to do for English classes, history to memorize and analyze, math problems to work out, along with general science, Latin and, of course, religion. The religion was dogmatic Roman Catholicism, but several priests, to their credit, encouraged challenges, even if only to knock them down sufficiently for their young charges. One excellent religion teacher was Father Gerald McDevitt, later a bishop, and despite that, a man without pretension.

One religion teacher, Father John Nugent, was also on the pastoral staff at my church. On several occasions I served as his altar boy. One Saturday afternoon I came to the church for my confession of sins, and who should be on the other side of the confessional screen but the familiar Nugent. I recited my list of sins, was given my penance of prayers and recited my Act of Contrition while receiving absolution. That done, Nugent said, "Larry, it's cold here. Please run over to the rectory and get me a sweater." I did that before offering my penance. I realized I didn't have many secrets from the priest.

The St. Thomas More science courses were terrific, even if chemistry turned out to be my worst course in high school. Looking back, that was largely my fault. While there was a consistency and logic to chemistry, I never fully grasped it because I stumbled miserably at learning basic elements. It was one course I could not fake. On the other hand, I did well in biology, taught to us by the young Father Louis DeSimone, who later became a bishop and always struck me as the kind of priest who knew the most important part of his job was to prepare us to be decent men in our families and in our world. My English teachers, Fathers James Simon and David Thompson, were superb. Simon introduced me to the joy of poetry and an appreciation of drama. Thompson put great emphasis on clear simple writing. He worked hard at correcting papers because I have some that he gave back to me with notations for improvements. From him, I began to grasp the importance of re-writing. He also bears some of the credit for my approach to journalism. Write the story fast and don't worry about style. Then come back and fix it.

One summer during my high school years, I dashed off in a few hours at the beach a piece of fiction. It was published in the literary magazine. It was my first byline and I welcomed the notoriety it got me, mostly from my mother and family members to whom she circulated it with pride. I liked seeing my name and writing in print, a foretaste of things to come.

In my junior year, I enrolled in a mechanical drawing course. It was taught by Gerald McCauley, a layman born in Ireland who kept up a line of patter as he went from drawing board to drawing board to see how his young charges were getting along with their straight edges. I remember that our final assignment was to draw our dream house. I know that mine included a large basketball court, but a very small kitchen and bathroom. Years later, after I had public attention through my newspaper columns in the *Bulletin*, Gerry McCauley wrote me a couple of letters about high school days. I was too much into my own life to send more than perfunctory replies. I now regret that I missed an opportunity to strike up a friendship and to learn a bit about his and my Irish roots.

LAWRENCE M. O'ROURKE

My most pleasant memory of high school was as a performer. I played the saxophone in the high school marching band and in a dance band, the Stardusters, organized by an enthusiastic young priest, Father James Mortimer. During football season, the marching band practiced several mornings a week before class on the grounds of St. John's Orphanage, a few hundred yards from our high school building. They were good mornings for me because I got a ride to the practice with Jim Feerick, a Cedar Avenue neighbor who played the clarinet. Jim's father, owner of a bar on Grays Ferry Avenue, had a big Chrysler that was more comfortable than the bus. He had an Irish brogue and was a good-natured fellow who asked lots of questions.

Father Jim Mortimer, only nine years older than me and fresh out of the seminary, loved music and musical theater. He recruited two of his classmates from St. Joseph's Prep to produce an annual variety show called the Varsity Follies. It included a chorus line of dancers, the majority of them athletes with limited potential for starring on "American Bandstand"—the hit TV afternoon show of my generation. Varsity Follies athletes dressed in full skirts in our version of female Parisian garb to dance the can-can. It always brought down the house. It was regarded in our neighborhood as quite risqué.

I had no recognized skill and certainly no experience at dancing and my singing voice was always judged insufficient for a solo. But I could bellow out lines, and I was called on to act. In one show, Tom Hardie and I were cast to go before the curtain while they changed the set on the stage behind us. Hardie and I went through a long forgotten dialogue that brought laughter, applause and admiration for knowing all those lines.

* * *

It was not until my senior year in high school that I thought about going to college. Looking back, I think I gave my future no serious thought at all until St. Thomas More sponsored visits by college recruiters. The guidance office made one point emphatically: we were expected to attend a Catholic college, preferably a local one, and to attempt to do otherwise, would delay them sending our transcripts.

As was custom, I took an examination in junior year to see what occupation I might be suited for. The results said I should be an electrician. That delighted my mother. Her father, Edward F. Higgins, did the family's electrical work, such as installing and repairing outlets and doorbells, and fixing appliances. He was famous for his Christmas platform that included not only a tree loaded with lights, but sets of electric trains and houses with lights. My mother surmised that electrical work came to me naturally. I learned electrical repair skills from my grandfather, as well as my mother who shut off the power and worked on malfunctioning outlets. She also enjoyed painting and wallpapering. In her 80s, she still climbed ladders with long sheets of wallpaper.

In helping to shape careers, the school sent us on field trips to Philadelphia factories. While I wasn't keen on manual labor, I convinced myself that I could work in inventory control or be a long-distance truck driver.

*   *   *

One reason I didn't give much thought to attending college was that there was little college in my family history. On my mother's side, there was a great-uncle who attended college. Nobody seemed to know how he managed to go to college or even what college he attended. What they said about him is that he lived in Baltimore and they had lost contact with him. There was no one on my father's side who attended college. My father, as instructed by his immigrant Irish mother, quit high school at 16 after his sophomore year and went to work.

Such was the background when in my senior year at St. Thomas More High School, I brought up the subject of attending college. My quest to attend college created tension in the family. My father opposed the idea and said he talked it over with his mother and she saw no need for it. "Get a job and if you really want to go to college, you can attend night school," my father said. "I can't afford to send you to college," he said. "Do you think I'm made of money?" I had no idea of family finances, but had no answer to his argument. Still I saw friends preparing for college. My high school teachers pushed me to enroll in college.

With my father in opposition, my mother immediately seized on the idea and never stopped talking it up. This contributed to friction between my parents. I moved cautiously.

Under Tommy More's rigid rules, I effectively had three college to pick from: St. Joseph's, the Jesuit college on City Line Avenue in Philadelphia; LaSalle, the Christian Brothers college in north Philadelphia, and

Villanova, the Augustinian college in a western suburb. I thought about two other schools, the University of Pennsylvania just a few miles from our West Philadelphia home and Fordham University in New York City. I had often been to Penn's campus to basketball games and museums, but I knew that as a non-Catholic school I had virtually no chance of getting there. I had never seen Fordham, but found the idea of going away to New York exotic.

The discussion waged for months. My father suggested that I get a job at the Post Office or as a shipping clerk. I could decide down the road on night school. Yielding a bit, my father said he would find money to help pay night school tuition at St. Joe's or LaSalle if I studied accounting. I believe that no matter how skilled he was with numbers (he was called a cost accountant by his company), he envied those with college degrees in accounting that did the same job and were paid more.

In my teenage years, my father and I were often, perhaps even usually, at odds. I was no good with my hands or, frankly, performing household chores as taking out ashes and trash, cutting the lawn, or picking up my clutter. He reminded me frequently that I spent too much time reading books for my own good and lacked common sense. My proposal to study English Literature at Villanova only seemed to accentuate our differences.

Meanwhile, my mother kept pushing me to do what I wanted to do, often further alienating my father. Furthermore, she made it clear that my father should pay my tuition. She didn't have any money. Nor, it appeared, did my father have much. Two decades later, I learned that he was paid very little by his company, but had bought U.S. savings bonds in $1,000 increments once or twice a year to get through retirement. He spoke about the Great Depression, savings lost, families thrown into poverty and onto charity. He was determined to avoid such misfortune. My later review as his executor of his detailed financial records showed his reluctance to spend money on himself, even late in life when he no longer had reason to fret about money.

Scrambling to work something out with my father, I offered a compromise. Since I had no interest in accounting or business, I would study to be a teacher. I tried to convince him that there were always teaching jobs, even in the worst of economic times.

In late spring, as the deadline for college applications arrived and my high school asked where I wanted my transcript sent, my father announced he would pay a large part of my first year tuition at whatever local Catholic college I picked. I read catalogues, and submitted applications to St. Joseph's, LaSalle and Villanova, got accepted at all three, and picked Villanova. I had never been there. I had been to the LaSalle and St. Joe campuses for high school sports events, but I thought it would be neater to attend college on the Main Line. My reasoning was no more sophisticated than that.

As a condition of paying my tuition, my father said I had to work to buy books and pay fees, and he suggested I take a summer job at the chemical plant where he worked in Cornwells Heights. Before daylight on St. Joseph's Day, March 19, a school holiday, I traveled with my father via the railroad to Cornwells Heights. He turned me over to one of the foreman and at the end of the day I was told I could have a summer job cleaning and painting steel cylinders used for shipping chlorine.

With that in mind, I finished at St. Thomas More and began to dream of Villanova. On the 10th of June 1955, I was handed my high school diploma in the auditorium of St. Thomas More, the school I had not wanted to attend, but had come to cherish.

I had been thinking about cleaning and painting chemical carboys and daily early-morning trips with my father. I looked for alternatives. My father was irritated, and he said he would give me a week to find another job, but that if I didn't have it, I would have to choose between the carboys and Villanova.

I set out on a frantic job search. With my modest list of accomplishments, I went to every potential employer I could think of. Every day ended in disappointment. Finally it was Friday, June 17, and I was desperate. That morning, I went to the main post office at 30th and Market Streets and submitted a job application. But all summer openings were filled. I left the post office building and looked across Market Street to the majestic exterior of the Pennsylvania Railroad Station. I glanced to the left, across a plaza, and saw the four-story stone *Bulletin* Building. An electronic sign streamed the day's news.

It was worth a crack, I thought to myself. I entered the *Bulletin* Building and was directed to the personnel office on the second floor. A clerk took my résumé', had me fill out an application form, and said all job applicants were required to take a written test. I took the test, and was thanked for coming by. I rode the number 34 trolley car to home, visions of carboys and Villanova competing in my head.

CHAPTER 4

Bear Meat

I T WAS A Friday before Vatican II, and I dutifully observed the Catholic Church's rule to abstain from meat on Friday under penalty of mortal sin. As my mother prepared her favorite Friday lunch of grilled cheese sandwiches, I recounted my frustrating morning of job hunting and my unease about working the summer cleaning and painting carboys. The phone rang. It was the *Bulletin's* personnel office. Are you still interested in a job with us? Yes. Can you come back to our office? On my way.

Within minutes, I was back on the 34 trolley. The personnel manager noted my work experience, including my years as a *Bulletin* carrier and my time behind the grocery counter. She led me down a corridor into a large room where several dozen middle-aged women wearing headphones talked and typed. Behind them was a man whose desk was stacked with piles of paper. The personnel chief introduced him as Mr. Gibbons.

Mr. Gibbons (I didn't call him Frank until years later) said the women were taking classified advertising, such as death notices, help wanted, rooms for rent and articles for sale. My job would be to keep the women supplied with the *Bulletin's* four-by-five inch classified ad forms, to collect completed forms, to detach one copy and file it alphabetically under the customer's name. I was to make sure that there were no forms in the file indicating that the customer was a deadbeat. I would separate another copy for delivery to a second file elsewhere in the building, and I would put remaining copies on Mr. Gibbon's desk. He would review them and I would periodically, and alertly, pick up a pile of approved forms and take them to the composing room on the third floor.

I would work with a lovely young girl named Monica. Her job was to mail a copy to the customer and when the bill was paid pull the forms from the file I built.

"Can you do all this?" Gibbons said with gravity and sincerity.

It looked a bit daunting, but Mr. Gibbons added immediately he was sure I could do it, especially since I was a graduate of St. Thomas More High School. He said he would, of course, not hire me if I were only going to be working at the *Bulletin* until the fall when I might start college. Happily for me, he never asked my plans, and I didn't volunteer information. So to get the job, I didn't lie. I evaded.

I saw Monica across the room. I had never worked with a girl, and had rarely talked with one my age. We had no girls at Tommy More. Our elementary school was segregated by gender. I went to my high school prom with a neighbor girl, Marnita Benedetto, daughter of Nicholas Benedetto, an accordion player, and her very religious mother, Mary. Our mothers arranged the prom date as they walked home from daily Mass. I saw working side by side with Monica over the *Bulletin's* classified advertising files as a rich new experience.

Gibbons said I'd work from 8.30 in the morning until 5 in the afternoon with an hour for lunch. To his questions, I assured him I was punctual, in good health, and not likely to call in sick. Well then, the pay, he said, is $26.50 a week. I would also get a free copy of the *Bulletin* to take home Monday through Friday.

*   *   *

My father was disappointed. He said I would have been paid $50 a week on the carboy line, with the possibility of overtime. Looking back, I also suspect—and hope—that he was disappointed that we would not share three hours together on the journeys between home and Cornwells Heights. Those journeys might have been a breakthrough in our relationship. We might have shattered the awful pattern of stern father-obedient (or disobedient) son we had constructed. Certainly he would have enjoyed introducing his college-bound son to Penn Salt workers. But it was not to be. It was many years before we were able to carry on warm conversations.

My summer at the *Bulletin* was glorious and eventful. Monica was charming and funny and, much to my surprise, she acted as if I were the same. The work was not as demanding as Mr. Gibbons warned, and so Monica and I talked a lot. I learned that Monica had the job because her older sister, Betty, worked in the *Bulletin's* payroll department. Monica and I never saw one another outside the office. We didn't even have lunch together. I spoke to her only once after that summer when, years later, she phoned me from her job as secretary to the *Bulletin's* publisher. She said there was talk of the *Bulletin's* sale, she had reviewed records and discovered I had retirement money on deposit. She suggested I withdraw it to avoid loss. I took her advice.

*　　*　　*

While Monica was at lunch with her sister, I developed a lunchtime pattern. I brought to work in a brown paper bag a lunch prepared by my mother. Under an arrangement with my parents, I saved my full take-home pay, and my mother gave me trolley fare and 17 cents a day to buy chocolate milk at a canteen run by the *Bulletin* for pressmen, paper handlers and truck drivers. The canteen was in an attached building that housed the presses and shipping departments. It had a balcony that overlooked the presses. The buildings were new and the presses were state of the art. The *Bulletin* was rightfully proud of them and it conducted guided tours. I toted my lunch to the canteen, bought chocolate milk, and took a seat in the balcony.

I watched a conveyer belt deliver curved metal plates that pressmen put on the presses. Plate after plate came down the line. Activity speeded up at edition time. On a signal from the foreman, the presses rolled, amazingly fast to my eyes, and folded newspapers emerged onto another conveyor belt that carried them onto the floor above. Most pressmen wore blue shirts and trousers, the better to deal with the mist of ink and occasional spills. They wore square hats fashioned of newsprint. Foremen wore white shirts and no hats. On a rare day, men in suits (I suspected they were executives) grabbed the first newspapers off the conveyor belts and looked at the front pages. Once or twice that summer the presses stopped abruptly, metal plates were quickly replaced, and the presses rolled again.

I explored the next floor up and watched men remove stacks of papers from the conveyer belt, wrap them with wire and deposit them on yet another conveyer belt to a loading dock where the bundles were stacked in trucks. I knew that one of those trucks was headed to Burton's garage and to other distribution sites where hundreds of boys, and perhaps a few mothers, waited to begin delivery rounds.

Gradually that summer I worked my way at lunch hours through the room where the plates for the presses were made, through the composing room where dozens of men pounded away at linotype machines, others assembled type in metal frames, and others made impressions from the metal frames onto thick fiber sheets that were rushed to the press room for conversion to the metal plates.

It was a stunningly busy, yet controlled and flowing, operation. I was captivated.

I told Mr. Gibbons of my lunchtime activity and he did not object. He warned me to stay out of the way and not get him into trouble. He suggested that I visit the newsroom—the heart of the paper. He told me that if I went to the newsroom at a quiet time, I could ask the sports department for a discount pass for Connie Mack Stadium. The sports department people were gracious and gave me yellow passes. With a pass and 50 cents I bought general admission tickets to see the Phillies. In this way, I learned about one perk of the newspaper business—free or cheap tickets. I always liked perks.

I often visited the newsroom. No one chased me away. Everybody in the newsroom seemed to be constantly busy, though I didn't know what they were doing. Phones rang. Machines clacked. People with headsets talked on the phone and typed. Others, several in eyeshades, edited stories and wrote headlines. Boys my age dashed from desk to desk. A boy responded promptly whenever one of the people shouted, "boy." The tempo was upbeat, and there were moments when it burst into overdrive. It was the most exciting place I had been.

True to Mr. Gibbons' promise, a pile of newspapers was in the corner every afternoon at 5 o'clock quitting time. Another perk. I grabbed a copy for the trolley ride home.

August arrived. The first day for Villanova neared. I got my first look at the Villanova campus one weekend day that summer when I made a practice run on the Philadelphia and Western high-speed trolley line (we called it a train) from the 69th Street terminal to the Villanova campus. I walked around in awe at the size of the campus.

It was finally time to tell Mr. Gibbons I was going to end my career as a classified advertising clerk. He didn't seem at all surprised. He startled me by asking if I intended to work while in college. If so, he had an idea. Would I like to work in the *Bulletin's* newsroom? I was stunned and instantly accepted. Well then, he said, go to the fourth floor and ask for Barney Devine.

* * *

LAWRENCE M. O'ROURKE

E.J. (Barney) Devine was what we in those days called, for lack of a better word, a character. He was certainly different from anyone I knew. He was a retired Philadelphia cop hired by the *Bulletin* as chief of copy boys. I was to be a copy boy and Barney immediately made clear that he didn't think much of me and thought it unlikely that a fancy college boy such as myself could do the job. He showed me around as if he were the commissioner of police giving a suspect a preview of what would come unless I did everything to his liking. He said I had been hired to work eight hours on Saturday and 12 hours on Sunday from 11 a.m. to 11 p.m., as a copy boy. In addition, I could work holidays and even nights if my school schedule allowed.

Quickly calculating, I saw advantages of at least a 20-hour a week job, possibly more, enough to pay many school expenses and to reassure my father that I was doing my share. The deal was even more attractive when Barney said I'd be paid a full $1 an hour, more than I made as a classified advertising clerk. Barney asked if I could start work the next morning—just days before the start of classes at Villanova. I said yes.

"Do you know how to make books?" he said. I admitted my ignorance. He dispatched me to the back of the room. I met Ernie. Ernie was the son of a prominent and wealthy Main Line family. I caught the famous last name and was impressed that I would be associated with him as a copy boy making books. Ernie showed me the ropes.

I learned to pick up a piece of off-white 8 by 10 inch paper called copy paper and fold it at the mid-line. I then inserted sheet by sheet alternatively, double-sided carbon paper and thin white paper called flimsies. I created a *Bulletin* book with the original on top and six interior sheets, and a copy paper bottom sheet. These books went to reporters and rewritemen writing stories, or, creating "copy." Copy boys stood by to take the typed-on books from the writer's hand. The copy boy rushed the top or "hard" copy to the copy editor's desk, and distributed flimsies to the news editor, the city editor, the picture editor, and the library. One flimsy was "spiked" or punctured on a sharp metal upright on the writer's desk. The writer spiked his notes. At the end of the shift, copy boys cleared the spikes into envelopes that were filed indefinitely in case of error or lawsuit.

My first job in the *Bulletin* newsroom was to make hundreds of books a day. Ernie was an interesting lad. He had limited ability to carry on a conversation, but he knew call letters of hundreds of radio stations and frequencies around the country. He challenged me. I was to name a city and he would provide the radio information. So we began, side by side, making books, with me trying to outwit him with little known communities. Ernie snapped back his answers. Ernie provided a radio list for me to check his accuracy. He was invariably correct. At first this was a pleasant diversion while making books, but Ernie didn't take it lightly. When I told Ernie I couldn't think of more communities, he said to start over. And so every time I came across Ernie we resumed this dialogue.

Before leaving Ernie, I note the most visible effect of working for hours with carbon paper. My fingers were black and I literally became an ink-stained wretch. No amount of washing with either the gritty soap in the *Bulletin's* washroom or at home removed the ink. I seemed to leave a stain on everything I touched. Ernie and his family had no apparent concern about this occupational hazard. Ernie came to work every day in a clean white shirt. He rubbed his hands on the shirt so that by the end of the day it was well inked. Ernie seemed to like making books because as I moved along in the copyboy ranks, he remained forever a bookmaker.

After weeks making books, the *Bulletin* hired another copyboy. Barney Devine promoted me to the ranks that ran copy from the writers. Each writer had a style for summoning a copyboy. On the front row, Fred McCord uttered a soft "copy." Adolph Katz and Jerry Dietz snapped "copy boy." Bayard Brunt snarled "boy" spaced multi-syllabically and you better be there in an instant or he would snarl it again quite loudly.

In the back rows of specialty reporters, Frank Hanlon, the obituary writer with an undertaker's demeanor, looked until he spotted a copy boy and silently waved the copy for attention. George Staab, the hard-bitten labor writer, shouted, "Hey, you kid." Writer Jim Perry favored a gentle "copy boy" while Peter Binzen seemed abashed as if asking for personal service.

I learned voices and intonations so that even if my back were turned while serving one writer, I would know whom to deal with next. Sometimes I was called to "the desk," the horseshoe where editors sat. I took calls and ran errands for Charlie Johnson and his colleagues on the copy desk, assistant city editors Len Murphy, Sam Boyle and Phil Schaeffer, and city editor Stanley Thompson. Johnson was famed for editing with a pen. Others used pencil to allow for mistakes. Johnson said he never made mistakes.

Thompson, known as the "Colonel," was not expected to have to ask for a copy boy. Barney Frank sternly warned me that I was to constantly keep my eye on Mr. Thompson. If I ever even suspected that he needed anything, I was to stand a few feet from him and wait for his soft-spoken command in a Southern accent. I became familiar with the hierarchy of the newsroom and the personalities. Boyle wanted a new cup of coffee every 20 minutes. He had a stack of cups, sometimes 20 inches high at the end of his shift. You didn't want to approach Dietz from the left or you might step into something he left on the floor when he missed the spittoon. Schaeffer always looked relaxed and he thanked you for errands, Murphy asked how you were doing except near deadline when you better keep out of his way. I'm sure his angry voice could be heard outside the building. The copy editors used scissors and glue to "paste up" inserts, and you better never let Johnson's gluepot run dry. Buck Sawyer mumbled constantly as he snipped and edited. Once I cleaned the hardened glue from a glass gluepot with a razor blade and I let it slip. The doctor in a nearby hospital emergency room put in four stitches on my left thumb. I got no sympathy from Barney Devine or anyone else.

The mood in the newsroom shifted. When a big story broke near deadline, editors and reporters shouted to each other, with editors sometimes demanding one paragraph at a time from the writer. That ate up a lot of books. After a deadline passed, I sensed from the kidding taunts and low-keyed insults when they were quite happy with their work. If Bayard Brunt got to grill a politician over the phone for a big story, the entire room hushed so that people could hear the penetrating interrogation for which he was famous.

Seventeen years old and participating in this scene, even as a "boy" making books, running copy, fetching coffee or filling a gluepot—it was starting to grab me.

*   *   *

In our Cecil Street backyard we had a tiny plot of earth. I grew tomatoes and peppers that summer between high school and college. I harvested a few tomatoes to complement my mother's grilled cheese sandwiches (my father, who suffered for years with a terrible digestive system, did not eat tomatoes). Two days before the reporting date for Villanova I ate some peppers. Shortly thereafter, I had terrible stomach pains and began vomiting. My mother said initially it was nerves over Villanova. She told my maternal grandmother, Catherine Higgins, who advised drinking large amounts of Coca-Cola. We didn't normally keep

Coke in the house and I rarely drank it. But I downed several bottles on the eve of my first day at Villanova. I headed to the campus famished from not having eaten in two days and jumpy with caffeine. I have avoided hot peppers ever since, and rarely drink Coke, but peppers and Coke remind me of Villanova.

On my first day as a collegian, I stepped off the P&W car at the Villanova station and was greeted by young men in white hats and blue jackets screaming at me, "What do we eat?' Dumbfounded, I was prompted to say, "Bear meat." A few feet on, the white hats demanded again, "What do we eat?" and I knew enough to say, "Bear meat." A few feet more and other white hats insisted that I roll up my trouser legs three times. And once across Lancaster Avenue and on the campus, I was handed a beanie and told not to remove it, perhaps ever again. In beanie and rolled-up trousers as I approached the field house for registration, I several more times shouted, "Bear meat."

So this is college, I thought.

It turned out that Villanova's football team was to play the Baylor Bears in Municipal Stadium in South Philadelphia, in a game dubbed the "Grocery Bowl" because the athletic department arranged for supermarkets to distribute discount tickets. The young men in white hats were members of an orientation committee carrying on a Villanova tradition designed to generate school spirit, shock away our apprehension, and guide us across the campus. We had a couple of days of intense orientation in which we frequently addressed the theme of Bear meat. It turned out we were required to wear beanies with trousers rolled for the first few weeks of class. A leader of the 1955 reception committee was J. Patrick Nicholson, later a Republican politician in Toledo.

Thrust into classes with strangers, I reached out for new friends, often during informal gatherings between classes in the Pie Shoppe, a wooden frame structure built as a barracks during World War II when Villanova trained U.S. Navy officers. The Pie Shoppe's long wooden tables were used by "dayhops" eating lunch. The tables facilitated chess matches. One Tommy More classmate, Daniel, spent a lot of time at chess. He was a whiz. A very earnest fellow who exuded hard work and scholarship, Dan was at the top of our high school class. Unfortunately, Dan flunked out of Villanova after one semester. Whether there was a connection between Dan's chess-playing and early departure, I never knew. For some classmates college offered too many choices. On the other hand, we had older veterans in our class who worked very hard and seemed to put a higher value on their opportunity than many who had gotten it easily. The experience fed my admiration of veterans and my skepticism of kids with obvious wealth.

We dayhops were commuters. It was clear that to many "residents" who lived in on-campus dormitories, we dayhops were second-class. The elite, including football and basketball players, runners, hurdlers, and high jumpers, lived on campus, as did student council members, editors of the student newspaper and yearbook, and the orientation committee guys who authoritatively made us roll up our trousers and wear beanies.

In 1955, Villanova was a male campus. We were told there was one female undergraduate, and she was admitted because her father was a professor. We were told that Villanova might establish a nursing program that would attract women, but it had no plans to admit women in other undergraduate programs.

Villanova was growing and it welcomed far more students than it could house in dorms. Under construction was a student union center called Dougherty Hall across from the Pie Shoppe. We tracked through a lot of mud. And I had a do a lot of tracking because I often had class at one end of the campus and the next class at the opposite end, a distance that took a lot longer than the ten minutes allotted between classes. No one would dare leave class early or arrive late. Professors were stern about attendance. We wore shirts and ties, jackets and dark trousers. One disadvantage as a dayhop was we had to carry all our books for the entire day of classes. It was quite an armful. Residents switched morning books and afternoon books during lunch hour.

* * *

My Uncle John O'Rourke asked about what was happening at Villanova. A quiet and gentle man in his 40s, he lived with his mother apart from his few months in a Christian Brothers novitiate. He dutifully gave his mother his paycheck from the Signode Steel Strapping Co. where he was a salesman, and received an allowance from his mother that permitted no frivolity. He made me an offer. He would give me his car—a black 1947 Chevrolet with under 40,000 miles. I liked the car. I often rode in it between Philadelphia and Long Beach Island. It was a tight fit when Uncle John drove, my father sat in the right front seat, and I crowded into the back seat with my mother, my brother, and my grandmother, not to mention food, bed linens, tools and whatever items we could not fit in the trunk. It was a quiet ride. My grandmother insisted we do nothing that might "distract the driver."

We stopped halfway on the 60-mile two-hour journey for my grandmother to serve two raw eggs each in a glass to my uncle and father. She said they needed "energy for the journey." I resisted the raw eggs, despite her advice that they were good for me. On every trip, except on Friday, I got a wax-paper wrapped boiled ham sandwich with butter and a touch of mustard on whole-wheat bread. There was a canister of hot coffee for the men. My mother didn't eat or drink before or during the journey. The entire event was a ritual that replays in my mind more than a half century later as I write these words.

We had a ritual every time we came to the tollbooth of the Benjamin Franklin Bridge that crossed the Delaware River between Philadelphia and Camden, New Jersey. At one time the toll was 20 cents. As we came to the booth, Uncle John asked for money. My father said he had it, but my grandmother insisted she would pay. She was profusely thanked. Grandmother rooted in her black bag for a quarter, handed it to my father, who held it for John until we came to the toll collector. John took the quarter, paid the toll, got back a nickel, handed it to my father, who handed it to my grandmother who put it into her handbag. The choreography was splendid. It never varied.

*   *   *

On the morning of Thursday, December 8, 1955, the feast of the Immaculate Conception, a religious holy day and school holiday, Edward F. Higgins walked from his home at 6326 Kingsessing Avenue to our home at 742 South Cecil Street with his hammer, screwdriver and drill. He had telephone wire, electric tape, wire cutters, and screws.

The man I called Granddad went to work on the plywood platform I set up on horses on our enclosed front porch. He admired the Lionel trains I had purchased a few days before. For many years, one of my delights at Christmas time was visiting my grandparents' home at 2208 Lombard Street in center city. In the large living room, my grandfather had a Christmas display that dazzled me. It was the full width of the room. On a platform a foot off the ground, a train ran around and around. In the center was the large Canadian Balsam tree, decorated with strings of lights and balls. There was a two-story dollhouse with tiny furniture. The platform was decorated with tiny figures. My cousins and I would take turns at the Lionel transformer, speeding up the train to the point when it seemed ready to spin off the track and slowing it down just in time to avoid that calamity. We were consistently successful.

With money earned at the *Bulletin,* I purchased a Lionel set, a Plasticville collection of church, school, firehouse, farm and houses, with figures, including livestock. My grandfather was there to show me how to set it up. We worked together for hours, talking about school as he taught me how to fasten track, drill holes, and attach wire. When we got the train running, I thought it a truly historic moment. It was. I have tried every Christmas since to set up the trains, and I still have on my platform the Lionel freight train set and some pieces belonging to my grandfather. He told me he was making for me a control board that would have three plugs: one for tree lights, one for train transformers and one for lights in the buildings on the platform. When my grandfather left, I promised to come soon to his front porch where he was setting up his Christmas trains.

*   *   *

Four days later, on December 12, 1955, I drove to Villanova in the 1947 Chevy. When I got home that afternoon, my mother wasn't there, a very unusual occurrence. My mother was always there, flowing with questions about what I learned that day, what the professors said, what work I had to do at home, and what would I like to eat. My seven-year-old brother was nowhere to be seen. His schoolbooks could usually be spotted near the dining-room table while he was off with friends.

The phone rang in the kitchen. It was my mother, grief-stricken. My grandfather had walked to the corner store and was returning with a purchase. My grandmother watched from the doorway as he chatted with the next-door neighbor sweeping her sidewalk. He turned toward his front steps and collapsed. An ambulance took my grandfather to Misericordia Hospital. My mother rushed to the emergency room. Edward F. Higgins was dead of a cerebral hemorrhage. My mother identified him.

*   *   *

My grandfather was buried on December 16. Joseph Gilligan, my biology professor, excused me from class. He said I could catch up with the lecture and do lab work later. It was a fiercely cold day as we stood over the grave in Holy Sepulchre Cemetery. We passed the Villanova campus on the ride back to Kingsessing Avenue. My grandmother sat with her sisters Mary and Ann—the nuns. They asked about Villanova, reminding me that college was a precious opportunity. My grandfather's unfinished train platform was on the front porch. I found in the basement the control board he made for me. I took it home. It was the last time I ever saw his trains. An aunt who took over my grandfather's affairs said the trains were useless and trashed them.

*   *   *

My grandfather's death was the first death I experienced. It devastated my mother. Her long memory for detail now became a burden. Through the rest of her life, she couldn't let go of the memory of her father or the memory of dark moments that occurred in our family, as in most families. She made it all too true that Irish never forget and never forgive. My family experience attests to that. My parents dealt with the dark moments of their lives in different ways. My mother never stopped talking about them. My father never said anything about them. She was irritated by his long silences. Her irritation and volubility only aggravated his silences. The situation nourished a sense of guilt as every slight, every mistake, took on a weight far greater than justified.

*   *   *

Villanova and expanding opportunities at the *Bulletin* shielded me somewhat from silence and guilt at home. I continued my high school pattern of plunging into courses that interested me and doing the minimum to survive courses that didn't. I did very well at biology, igniting a notion that I might become a medical doctor. But the more I worked at the *Bulletin*, the more I became intrigued by the newspaper business. *Bulletin* sports editor Jack Wilson and scholastic sports writer Jack Ryan asked if I had an interest in covering high school sports along the Main Line. They gave me a press card that identified me as a *Bulletin* reporter. Many afternoons I drove from campus in my '47 Chevy to games, walked the sidelines of football fields or sat at press tables at basketball games. I interviewed players and coaches and phoned my reports to Ryan. I was paid $3 a game. The cost-benefit ratio wasn't the key to prosperity, but it sure was fun.

In the spring of my freshman year, I decided that if I could be a reporter for the *Bulletin*, maybe I could be a reporter for the *Villanovan*, the undergraduate weekly. The editors were delighted to get a volunteer. After a few weeks, they had me interview professors about world and national events within their expertise, as well as cover student activities. My work got the attention of Eugene Ruane, the university's director of public information and moderator of the *Villanovan*. He liked newspapers and was a frustrated reporter. Although we were later to have our battles over the amount of editorial freedom for *Villanovan* editors, we were to become lifelong friends. One of his sons, Michael, became a superb reporter for the *Washington Post*.

*　*　*

My work at the *Villanovan* and involvement in an incident in Dougherty Hall once got me into such trouble that I feared I might be expelled from Villanova and even prosecuted. The dining room for athletes was 25 feet from the *Villanovan* office. I often walked past it and through the open doors and glass windows saw football and basketball players and other campus stars. Not only did they get from their special kitchen meals in content and quantity different from other undergraduates, but also they had available to them at all times an endless supply of ice cream. Through the glass I saw large containers of ice cream in many flavors. One evening I worked late on the *Villanovan* and walked down the hallway. I saw the door open to the athletes' dining room and the ice cream. So I stepped in and filled a bowl. I happily continued my story for the student paper with the assistance of ice cream. But I had been spotted. The next day, I was summoned to the office of the campus police chief and confronted with the accusation that I had stolen ice cream. What could I do but confess and acknowledge the error of my ways. The chief said he would report my misconduct to the university president, who would decide the appropriate sanction. Word got around. The police chief and Gene Ruane shared the same suite of offices. Ruane questioned me about my miscreant behavior. Gene didn't seem to have the same disapproving attitude as the police chief. In any event, I never heard from the university president. But I didn't heist any more of the athletes' ice cream.

In the summer between my freshmen and sophomore years at Villanova, I was promoted by the *Bulletin* into the job of slot copy boy. It was the top-of-the line for copy boys. I sat inside the editors' horseshoe, just behind the news editor, and within a few feet of the telegraph editor, the city editor, the copy editor, and the picture editor. And I was within easy hearing range of the managing editor and the executive editor when they took their seats on the outside of the slot. My job was to take the edited copy from the news editor, who in theory had read everything processed by the city and telegraph desks, as well as the copy editor. I put the copy on a conveyor belt that carried it down one flight through a hole in the wall to the composing room. As soon as the type was sent, it was printed as a proof, and the proof was sent up the conveyer belt. I had to read every proof quickly to determine the right editor to give the final sign off. I could hear every exchange among the editors as they decided what stories and pictures to put in the paper and how to play them. When a big story broke, the executive editor or managing editor came to the desk to mark up the dummy, a drawing on a pink sheet on how the top brass wanted the front page to look. The makeup editor, Carl Cressman, usually attended the making of significant dummies. Editors sometimes clashed over how to play stories, but once the top editor made a decision, it was final. My job as slot copy boy was to stand beside the news editor. When the dummy was complete, I rushed it down the stairs and started the process of putting page one together.

Between editions, the editors sometimes talked with me about their work and inquired into my studies. Work was enormously exciting. I couldn't wait to take my post in the slot every day. It was with great satisfaction each afternoon that I carried the four-star dummy to the composing room. Step by step, I fell in love with the newspaper business.

One night when I was at home studying when the phone rang. A giant grain elevator across Market Street from the *Bulletin* had exploded, damaging the *Bulletin* buildings, as well as overhead tracks of the Pennsylvania Railroad. Could I come in to work the slot? I was there within a half-hour. The newsroom was as chaotic as I had ever seen it. Windows were broken. Cabinets were upended. The blast had bounced heavy equipment. Building engineers feared damage to the presses could not be fixed in time for the next day's editions. The explosion caused multi-alarm fires. The police cordoned off the neighborhood. My *Bulletin* pass as high school sports reporter got me through. When I entered the slot as the copy boy, the news editor told me they needed reporters more than copy boys. He said go report. I grabbed copy paper and hit the street, observing and interviewing. After hours of this, I came back and unloaded my notes to a rewriteman. The next day, my reporting was in the newspaper.

*   *   *

In the spring of my sophomore year at Villanova, I was required to declare my major in the College of Liberal Arts and Sciences. I said that I would major in English literature and minor in political science. In reality, I majored for the remaining two years at Villanova in the *Villanovan.*

I was named managing editor of the newspaper, an unusual procedure since that position usually went to a junior to be served during senior year. I was to be managing editor during my junior year and presumptively editor during my senior year.

My boss as editor was Robert Mulcahy III, a superb campus politician and a decent admirable young man. Bob and I were a wonderful combination. He guided the editorials, encouraged and soothed the staff, negotiated with the administration, and dealt with student complaints while I ran the newspaper—alienating reporter and editors as I pushed an all-volunteer staff for better stories and pictures. The *Villanovan* became the core of my life at Villanova. I tolerated classroom work, but it was the student newspaper that took my time and dominated my interest. The *Villanovan* week started on Wednesday when we gathered copy and prepared it for the printer. The *Villanovan* office on the second floor of Dougherty Hall had the feel of a newsroom—reporters arriving with notes for stories, and editors at typewriters turning those notes into readable copy. Eventually all of the copy came to me for a final reading and my dummying of pages. I assigned headlines to section editors. Villanova did not have a journalism department. We were mostly English, history and business majors with one or two science majors, and one or two nursing majors. An engineering student showed up now and then with a story from his school or his club, but engineers had the reputation of being grinds, too busy for campus activities.

Because I had genuine newspaper experience, as a copy boy with time in the *Bulletin's* slot watching the paper put together, I had a modest understanding of the mechanics of putting together a weekly paper 12 to 20 pages. Since I was hooked on getting enough copy to fill the paper before I quit and discharged the staff, I often worked through the night, sometimes grabbing a couple of hours sleep on a cot made available to me by the university for that one night. On Thursday morning, between classes, I delivered the copy to the printer, Long Publishing, in downtown Philadelphia. I soon discovered that Gene Ruane, the university public relations man, would visit Long's to read copy and make sure there was nothing too controversial. He would sometimes change copy. I tried on Thursday evenings to return to Long's, after Ruane left, to change it back the way I wanted it. Ruane and I never discussed this system—though he must have been aware that I was reversing him—but it gave him the right to say he had "fixed" something the administration might not have liked.

I next showed up at Long's, with associate editor Joe Kinney, features editor Bill Jones, and others on occasion, to read the entire paper and make any needed changes before it went to press. In those pre-computer days, the stories were glued onto cardboard sheets. So changing anything meant working carefully with razor blades to cut out offending words or paragraphs or stories and replacing them, sometimes letter by letter or word by word from previous paste-ups. It was a stunningly time-consuming process—especially after dinner. Villanova gave Mulcahy a budget to buy dinner for the staff. It was enough to pay for thick sandwiches, usually corned beef with coleslaw and Russian dressing in my case, and a bottle of beer.

This process—which we called paste-up, lasted until arrival of daylight the following morning when, after another sleepless night, we'd go back to campus for classes. I imagine we looked like quite a sight to our professors. Somehow I managed to stay awake, even through early morning classes. Long's printed the paper on Tuesday afternoon and delivered it to campus for free distribution by Wednesday morning. At that point, the cycle would begin anew.

Mulcahy might have to spend the day explaining to administrators and students why we played up this story or didn't use this story. Bob was good at it. I was not. Mulcahy used his talent brilliantly. As a Democratic politician, he was chief of staff to New Jersey Gov. Brendan Byrne and mentioned as a gubernatorial candidate himself before he became head of the New Jersey Sports and Exposition Authority, developing the Meadowlands. He was the state's first commissioner of the Department of Corrections and served 10 years at Rutgers University as director of athletics. Joe Kinney earned his doctorate in English and became a Villanova professor and dean, teaching among other courses Shakespeare. Bill Jones became a *Bulletin* reporter, spokesman for the Philadelphia Board of Education and spokesman for a Pennsylvania power corporation.

*　*　*

I often worked at the *Bulletin* on Friday nights, sometimes a double shift from 4 in the afternoon until 8 on Saturday morning. I might grab a couple of hours sleep on a cot in the editorial department from 2 to 4 in the morning.

City editor Stanley Thompson—"The Colonel" to the staff, Mr. Thompson to me—usually arrived at 7.30 on Saturday morning for a busy day. He had to deal with Saturday matters before turning to the first deadline of the Sunday paper in mid-afternoon.

I had not said 100 words to Mr. Thompson until one Saturday morning in late spring when I saw him at his desk in his private office, the door open as I passed. I knocked, was admitted by his grunt, and said to him, "Mr. Thompson, I was wondering if you might have a reporter's job open this summer that I could apply for."

"I don't think so," he said. "But I'll keep you in mind if I do." I knew there would be several reporters' jobs open that summer because it was the *Bulletin* style to give bright young men, sometimes the sons of advertisers and friends, the opportunity to work a summer as a reporter before they went on to other things.

After my first approach to Thompson, I made a ritualistic Saturday morning visit to his office with a single sentence or two to remind him of my interest. He would usually dismiss me with a noncommittal "all right." Then one Saturday morning, Thompson, barely looking at me, said, "We'll try it." Had I heard correctly? "Talk to Schaeffer," he said. I did, and so I was hired for the summer of 1957, between my sophomore and junior years at Villanova, as a reporter on the summer nightside of the *Philadelphia Bulletin* for $50 a week, $5 for night differential and $5 for driving my own car to work. What more could a boy ask?

*　*　*

With the value of hindsight, it's clear that my career was set. I spent my final two years at Villanova working at least 25 hours a week on the *Villanovan*, with one year as managing editor and one year as editor. I much preferred the managing editor's job. I enjoyed the process of gathering information and producing a newspaper more than I did responding to critics. I learned that the better course of valor for me was to remain loyal to my staff. On the *Villanovan*, I was assisted by a wonderful group of young men, including Jack Curtin who became a journalist, Tom Goldschmidt who became a teacher, and Bill Christie who became a lawyer. I was busy with other activities, including the student council and the literary magazine. I was selected to National Who's Who Among Students in American Colleges and Universities. I passed my exams and got my class work in on time, often with the help of my father, who heroically typed the thoughts I scribbled during quiet moments on *Bulletin* assignment. My mother spent several afternoons in the public library on research for papers I was writing. There's absolutely no doubt but that my parents deserved a large measure of my college diploma.

At the *Bulletin*, I did my share of obituaries and three-paragraph stories on accidents and crimes phoned in by field reporters. My favorite assignment was the midnight to 8 a.m. shift in Room 619 of City Hall where I monitored the police and fire radio, and responded to emergencies throughout the city. I had a lot of adventures. Once I stood in a burning theater in West Philadelphia interviewing the fire chief. A few minutes after we stepped out, the ceiling collapsed. I went to the homes of murder and car crash victims and compiled histories of the dead. I got booted out of political meetings and rallies of the local corrupt Teamsters' union. It was not work for the fainthearted.

While I was sorry to leave the *Villanovan*, graduation from Villanova was pretty much a non-event. Unlike my fellow grads who had to scramble for jobs, I went to work the day after graduation at the *Bulletin* and pretty much continued what I had been doing, except now instead of part-time work of 20 hours a week I did full-time work of more than 50 hours a week. The *Bulletin* did not pay overtime. It was a mark of honor that none of us wanted to leave the story until it was ready for the paper.

CHAPTER 5

Sergeant O'Rourke

BEFORE SUNRISE ON Thursday, June 30, 1960, I climbed out of bed in the back second-floor room at 5663 Springfield Avenue. I dressed in old clothes and came down to a full breakfast my mother had set. She said you don't know when you'll get your next meal or what it will be. It looked as if she had been awake all night, which is likely. My father was there. I was struck by how much he talked over eggs and scrapple. He cautioned me to keep out of trouble, mind my own business, and do what I was told—themes echoing our conversations of my younger years. It was wise, kindly offered. I did not dissent. Though stepping into the unknown, I was mellow.

I was 22 years old, a rising newspaperman at the *Bulletin.* I was happy in my work and my editors were satisfied. So why, on this beautiful day, was I entering the United States Army for two years? Some relatives, including Aunt Helen, warned me that I was too soft for the tough life of a soldier and that I talked too much for my own good. The taciturn and secretive O'Rourkes were consistent in that they opposed what they regarded as too much talk. Friends said bluntly that I was crazy, a fashionable word, though not used clinically. My parents were the most perplexed. I had not explained to their satisfaction why I was leaving my comfortable and easy life. My mother seemed to suggest that I was abandoning her forever.

I didn't know what lay ahead. Where would the Army ship me? In my mind, shaped by stories and movies, horrors of basic training were recognized, even mythologized. Would I survive? How would I do meeting new people, especially those outside my comfortable arc of Catholics, Irish, Northerners, and Philadelphians?

On the enclosed porch, I said goodbye to my parents and my brother Johnny, just turned 12 and summoned from bed for the occasion. I promised to let them know as soon as possible where I was and when we might meet again. It sounded as if I were a convicted felon headed for prison. The night before, I emptied my wallet of all but driver's license, a few dollars, and a slip of paper with phone numbers. I was leaving my identity behind as I stepped into a new one of unknown definition. I yielded my keys. The morning promised a warm and clear day. I looked affectionately at my black humpbacked 1947 Chevrolet with the Philadelphia Police Department sticker on the rear window, parked out front.

I was beyond the point of asking myself why I was doing this, and was not given much to second-guessing. I may be slow in making decisions, but once made, I don't agonize over choices. If facts change, if there's a new hypothetical, then I acknowledge that I am on the wrong course, and adjust. I use mistakes as experiences for future decisions, not as punishment for flawed choices. I made a calculated decision to enter the Army. I did it carefully after extensively reviewing my status in life. It was not spur of the moment. I had not been attracted by the artful ads of recruiters or stirred by martial music, the lure of a uniform or patriotism. I was a bit scared, but I had no regrets. Nor, from the vantage point of a half-century, have I ever regretted. Serving in the Army for two years turned out to be one of the best experiences of my life.

I volunteered for the Army. Volunteered means I told them to draft me, to come get me. They did. I signed on for two years, stopping short of enlistment for a three-year hitch, a prelude to a military career. Of that I wanted no part. I considered the National Guard and Army Reserves, each available for a short basic training followed by monthly weekend encampments and two weeks every summer, probably at Indiantown Gap in Pennsylvania. I wrote stories on the Guard and Reserve and was familiar with their benefits and duties. After thinking about it, I went in May to the Selective Service System office near Independence Hall and told them to draft me for two years. Two weeks later I went on a 10-day trip to Canada with my mother, brother, and Aunt Mary Higgins. We were in Boston, returning to Philadelphia, when I called my father. He said a letter arrived from Selective Service. At my request he opened it and read: Report 30 June.

Many people were shocked when I told them I was entering the Army. Among them were *Bulletin* editors. I worked the nightside five days a week starting at 6 until 2 or later in the morning. Fellow nightsiders and I stayed until the work was done, work that meant rewriting stories until they satisfied the editor. I didn't complain about the hours or the

LAWRENCE M. O'ROURKE

mandated rewrites. I was learning and that's what I wanted. The night editors, among them Bill Lohan, Henry Yocum and John Gerfin, were good editors. I felt they pushed me with my best interest in mind. They wanted a quality newspaper and I felt we delivered it to the *Bulletin's* hundreds of thousands of readers. I had a good share of bylines and an intriguing list of assignments, many dealing with government and politics—increasingly my favorite topics.

My decision to enter the Army surprised also my professors at Villanova where I was in graduate studies in Theater. Few of them had served in the military. I was heading to a master's degree, enjoying research and writing. In fantasy, I thought of being a newspaper critic or even a playwright. Mostly, I liked school and its demands on the mind. Not only did my professors want me to complete the course work, but they also advised me that as a graduate student I could be deferred from military service. There was a notion that educated men of my background served in the Army as officers, not as Army riflemen. Villanova had a Navy officers training program. I had no interest in being an officer and spending three years or more in uniform.

Working at the *Bulletin* often resembled a monastic commitment, leaving little room for a social life. With a pretax *Bulletin* salary of $50 a week, take home about $43, auto expenses, and personal care bills to pay, graduate school costs, and ambition to put aside a few dollars a week for travel, I was dependent on the largesse of my parents who provided free room and board.

Moreover, I had a *Bulletin* schedule that consumed more than 50 hours a week at night, not counting afternoons spent covering high school sports for $3 a game and not counting hours in the Palestra on my college basketball column for the *Catholic Standard and Times*. There was little time for conventional dating. As a young unattached reporter, I was always assigned by the *Bulletin* to work on weekends—Friday, Saturday and Sunday nights.

*　*　*

Not everybody my age was being drafted, and I had a reasonable chance of avoiding a summons into uniform. It would have been a reasonable gamble, but not for me. As a young reporter with the possibility of military service hanging over my head, the *Bulletin* would never promote me to a beat such as politics, labor, education or science where it could take years to build up expertise and contacts that enriched stories. I was cannon fodder for the nightside. At 22, I saw indefinite employment as a general assignment reporter in the dark hours, chasing politicians, cops and car accidents, rewriting stories by beat reporters, and, of course, writing obits. I didn't fault *Bulletin* editors for this.

I had no plans to change my draft and life status by getting married and thereby shielding myself from a draft notice. I had a lot of living to do, a long list of places I wanted to see, before I settled down. The *Bulletin* didn't promote marriage. One person, much less two, could barely scrap by on the $75 a week it paid young married reporters.

There were at least two other factors in my decision to volunteer for the Army. Like many young reporters, I convinced myself that I was smarter, quicker, wiser, not to say more honest, than politicians I covered. And there was envy. I admired Philadelphia's two dynamic Democrats, U.S. Sen. Joseph S. Clark and Mayor Richardson Dilworth, men I often talked to. I became friendly with a young Democratic prosecutor who later switched parties to become the longtime Republican Sen. Arlen Specter. (He switched back to the Democrats in 2009, but lost in 2010). The *Bulletin* often sent me to cover political stories. When I considered my future, I thought about practicing law and engaging in politics. I reasoned that a career in politics required a tour of military service. I heard political candidates tout their experiences in uniform and denigrate their opponents as draft dodgers.

But the overriding reason for volunteering for the Army was a wish to shake up my life. I was restless for experiences that I read about. I lived a safe, predictable, orderly life, centered in Philadelphia and the Atlantic coast of New Jersey, with side trips to New York. There must be something more exciting, I told myself. As much as I enjoyed the comforts of home, a pass to the Palestra, and challenges on the job, I don't want to do this for the rest of my life.

*   *   *

The Route 13 trolley ride that June 30 morning took me through 30th Street Station, the stop for the Pennsylvania Railroad and the *Bulletin* Building. I wondered what the big story would be that day and whether any nightside colleagues made it on the front page in the first edition, soon to hit the streets. If I hadn't taken off from work last night to get ready for the Army, would I have a byline today?

From the City Hall station, I walked about a half mile to the induction center at 401 N. Broad. I had my letter ordering me to report by seven in the morning. It warned of dire consequences for being late. I got there early, of course, and there were a few of us, hardly looking at each other, perhaps to avoid emotion. The sergeant told me to sit down and wait. More than an hour later, after others had straggled in, we were told, if as we needed to be reminded, why we were there. Thus in the first hour I learned an Army maxim—hurry up and wait.

The first jolt came with the order: take your clothes off and get in line. The doctor, if that is what he was, made as perfunctory an exam as a glance would allow. My father suggested that I might not be "physically fit" and would be sent home. He recalled how he was exempt from the military at the outbreak of World War II because he was not "physically fit." He was also 40 with a baby when the Japanese struck Pearl Harbor. The doctor said I was physically fit.

There were papers to fill out and hours to kill in silence until just after three that afternoon when I was sworn into the United States Army. Stand straight, raise your right hand, repeat after me the oath, and take one step forward. It was done.

I wasn't elated. I was hungry. There hadn't been a lunch break though we had enough time for a five-course meal. I was grateful to my mother for stuffing me at breakfast. I wished I had accepted the sandwich she offered. The sergeant announced that we were to be taken on a bus across the river to the reception center at Fort Dix, N.J. He said we were to sit and not speak until we got to Dix. He suggested ominously that trouble awaited us at the other end. For no discernible reason, he announced that I would be in charge of the bus and that the others were to do everything I told them to do. Fortunately on the ride over the Delaware and along the roads of New Jersey, I had nothing to tell my fellow riders. But I immediately sensed deference, if not hostility. Young men rankle at authority, and I felt it. But rank, I knew, has its privileges, no matter how fleeting or trivial. The entire front seat behind the driver was reserved for me. The sergeant handed me envelopes with papers that I was to hold until relieved.

My authority and duty ended abruptly when we pulled into Dix. Someone took the papers and yelled at the ragtag lot of us to get off the bus and into formation, whatever that meant. We were pushed into lines, encouraged, one might say, by sustained profanity. Army representatives told me for the first time, though hardly the last, that I was "lower than whale shit."

In my lowly status, I marched to the mess hall where the first meal of my military career could have been something from a cavity of the whale, accompanied by a stale roll and a mysterious liquid. Fortunately there was catsup to add zest. Was it what the Army called a hamburger? Don't question too closely. Shouted at, I ate quickly in silence and reassembled for another march to an ancient wooden barracks where I was assigned to a lower berth in a row of bunks. Shortly thereafter, lights went out. I had a sleepless night as I imagined the nightside and home. You're in the Army now.

Whistles, shouts and clanging of sticks on steel beds roused us early the next morning. After breakfast we marched to a barber who within seconds had me shorn of all but a stubble of hair. Some fellow recruits were teary eyed as they emerged from the barbershop. My attitude was: so what? I didn't have much hair to lose since I had kept my hair short and bristled. We marched to a warehouse where we were told again to strip and line up.

I got a duffle bag and began a journey down a long counter. They guessed our sizes. We were told how to dress ourselves, from skivvies to fatigues. The fatigue outfit included a soft hat that simultaneously reminded me of the beanie I wore my first weeks at Villanova and the cap worn by prisoners in World War II movies. The low point came at the boot station when I was handed one pair of black boots and one pair of brown. "You have to make these black," the clerk said, gesturing to the brown. I was to spend scores of hours kneading black polish with my bare hand into the brown leather. The black polish didn't stick well, especially when the boots got wet. I shined the brown boots to a phony black and never wore them. That violated orders to rotate boots daily. It was my first breach of military orders. But it saved hours. I never caught the dreaded foot rot we were warned would befall us if we wore the same boots every day.

After dropping off our duffle bags in the barracks, we marched to our first work detail. We entered a village of barracks, all unoccupied. We were told that the barracks on one side of the street contained steel beds and mattresses for both rows of barracks. The barracks with the furniture were to be painted and so our detail was to move the furniture across the street to the facing barracks. And hurry up, they said, because the work must be done before we could eat our next meal. The thought of missing another meal of the same sort as last night was not inspirational, but the shouted threats of our superiors, replete with reminders of our linkage to whales, got us hopping. It was July 1 and hot as we in new fatigue uniforms and caps, breaking in new boots, lugged furniture across the street. It went on for hours.

That night, I had a few minutes before lights out to begin taking notes on my Army experiences. As a journalist, I took notes on just about everything. I saved my Army notes until I wrote tales of my adventures in letters sent home. Reading the letters years later, I found them jovial, full of the absurdity of my daily existence, a bit cynical, and never self-pitying or morose.

The next morning, the Saturday of Independence Day weekend, the Army had to find something to do with us. We marched to the same set of barracks where the day before we demonstrated our skills at furniture transfer. Perhaps it was a different set of superiors or perhaps they had forgotten. But we were again told that the Army intended to paint a row of barracks and we had to clear them of furniture before the craftsmen arrived. Thus we reversed the flow of the furniture. We had to work quickly, our superiors said, because we wouldn't eat until we finished. A certain mindless repetition took over my life. I hesitate to call this set of events ridiculous, for what else was the Army going to do with a bunch of young men on July 4 weekend than keep our hands busy and our minds confused if not void. I learned that in the Army, as in life, there is a distinction between keeping busy and appearing to keep busy. So I didn't wear myself out toting furniture, but worked at a measured pace. The threat to deny us food was also empty, I realized. Though we did not complete our moving task by mealtime, we were nonetheless fed. One final note on this furniture moving: a few days later, chance would have it that we marched past the barracks on our way to meet the chaplain and our first lecture on the Uniform Code of Military Justice. I saw another group of young men in newly acquired fatigues and soft caps moving furniture across the street. The Army was unimaginative at busy work.

On July 4 we were permitted to celebrate by having visitors. In the afternoon, my parents and Johnny arrived to find me in uniform. I apologized for yielding a strong odor. Though this was my fifth day in the Army, I had not showered, shaved or cleaned my teeth since I left Springfield Avenue. We had not been issued towels or soap and we had not gotten razors and toothbrushes. My parents must have been stricken by my appearance, but I found the entire event hilarious, as I explained the furniture transfer and living arrangements. I was boosted by the picnic lunch my mother prudently packed. On the next morning, we marched to the PX to buy the luxuries of towels and personal care. There was no provision for providing these items to people without money. I got my first shower and shave of the Army that night.

The next day was for packing duffle bags for our first flight as soldiers. Some recruits had gone wild in the PX and bought cameras and radios. Those in charge of our packing made a startling announcement. We could only take with us on the plane to Fort Benning items issued by the Army. Anything else—civilian clothing, razors, soap, shaving cream, aftershave lotion, not to mention cameras and radios—had to be left behind. So I had the sympathetic experience of watching fellow recruits who had gone overboard at the PX hand their material to sergeants readying us for our journey. I avoided that trap, since I purchased only bare necessities at the PX. However, I wondered how our instructors in the art of packing were able to use or dispose so much equipment, especially if it happened with each wave of recruits. Was it, I thought, a scam that produced a steady stream of military booty?

*   *   *

The next day we hoisted duffle bags and went by bus to McGuire Air Force Base. I was glad to be done with Fort Dix and furniture moving. We flew to Columbus, Georgia, landing after dark to a scene of generated chaos that I vividly recall a half-century later. On a steamy summer night, I walked from the plane to the shouts of our basic-training reception committee. "Whale shit" was among milder epithets. A seven-letter adjective seemed to be applied to every noun, most of which concerned our anatomy. I don't mean to be prudish, but the obscenities and vulgarities quickly lost value as incentive. Many greeters wildly waved ammunition belts, some close enough to my head to prompt instant compliance with their orders to get on the bus with my duffle bag. I didn't want to be hit and I was not hit. I was, I readily acknowledge, quite frightened by that experience. Of course, that's what they intended and I'll not challenge their effectiveness. In the Army at least, they break you down and then they build you up. There was a resemblance to Villanova's hazing. Perhaps they do it in the seminary as well. The night was only beginning. On arrival at Fort Benning and our barracks, we were

LAWRENCE M. O'ROURKE

assigned bunks, and instructed on how to put items in footlockers and wall closets. Practicing the rolling of socks and underwear at two in the morning was a brutal experience, especially when it involved dumping the items repeatedly onto bunks and repeating the process until all of us seemed to get it right. There was no room for variance. When we were awakened before dawn the next morning, drill sergeants put us through rudimentary close-order drills, with such commands as attention, parade rest, about-face, and left face and right face. The drilling lasted until night mercifully arrived. On Sunday morning, I took advantage of a chance to attend Mass, if only to get away from drilling. The march to church let me look out of the corner of my eye at Sand Hill, our new neighborhood. I saw a movie theater, but was told it was off-limits to recruits. We marched to the PX to buy personal items. This time, my fellow recruits skipped the cameras and radios.

*   *   *

We were told we were to be trained as riflemen for assignment in Korea with the 2nd Infantry Division. At Fort Benning, we would have a week of orientation, drilling, and testing. We would have eight weeks of basic combat training, learning how to use rifles and bayonets, throw hand grenades, march long distances, bivouac, survive gas attack, crawl an infiltration course, and respond instantly to commands. After that, we were told, we could begin to think of ourselves as soldiers in the U.S. Army.

If we completed basic training successfully, we would get a furlough. Then we would ship to Alabama for advanced weapons training. Then off to Korea we would head for the rest of our hitch—20 months on the 38th Parallel facing a ruthless and relentless enemy.

To prepare, our sergeants told us, we would have long and demanding days with heavy emphasis on physical conditioning. (You had to complete several pull-ups to enter the mess hall and you were not permitted to walk outside the barracks. You either marched or you ran.) We were told that North Koreans and Chinese attacked late at night, so often we were to be called out at night for maneuvers, to prepare us for waking and falling asleep on cue.

There were fundamentals to learn. All officers were to be saluted and addressed at least once in every sentence as sir. No sergeants were to be saluted, but responses to them were always to be yes, sergeant, or no, sergeant. Sergeants had names, but not for us. Our platoon sergeant was Jose Albino and he was from Puerto Rico. But to us he was platoon sergeant, no more or less, and the same extended to all sergeants, whether in the mess hall or laundry or anywhere else. If they had stripes, you did what they told you to do and did it right away. Whenever you passed an officer or were addressed by a sergeant, you stood at attention with hands at your side, unless you were told at ease, which turned out to be rare. It was authoritarian and intimidating, while simultaneously irritating to a young political reporter with a streak of independence and skepticism toward authority. I suspended and suppressed rebelliousness.

One of our first chores at Sand Hill, our home in a patch of Fort Benning, was to learn the military chain of command, starting with squad leader and running through platoon sergeant and company commander through the Benning post headquarters and beyond to the Pentagon and the White House. We were given lists with titles, ranks and names and were told we would be tested and punished if we failed to memorize and recite them accurately.

Sure enough, on Friday of orientation week, we were called into formation on a drill field. As we stood stiffly at attention, eyes straight ahead, officers went down the line asking each of us to recite the chain of command. I listened as they came toward me. Not a recruit near me got it right. Some got as far as the battalion commander, but none got beyond the confines of Benning. The Pentagon and White House seemed far from Sand Hill.

It was my turn. Looking straight ahead, making no eye contact as ordered, I went up the list, reaching the Pentagon and the name of the Secretary of Defense. All we had to do, we were told, was to give the last name. But I, with perhaps more bravado and ego than common sense, was on a roll. "Sir, the Secretary of Defense is Thomas Sovereign Gates, Jr., Sir." Gates was a business executive in Philadelphia before entering the Eisenhower cabinet. I talked with him in May before a function in a downtown hotel. I wrote a story about his speech.

Before I could get to President Dwight David Eisenhower, the officer told me to repeat the secretary of defense's name. I did. "How do you know his full name?" the officer inquired.

"Sir, I interviewed him a few weeks ago and wrote a story about him in my newspaper, Sir," I replied. There was a pause and the officer moved on, without ascertaining if I knew the commander-in-chief's name. (As it happened, I had been introduced to Eisenhower only a few weeks

LAWRENCE M. O'ROURKE

before when he attended a function in Philadelphia and I covered it for The *Bulletin*. But Ike never came up on the hot afternoon at Benning.)

When the officers left and we recruits were dismissed, Sergeant Albino summoned me and asked for details of my meeting with Secretary Gates. He seemed skeptical at first, but maybe my sincerity and fright convinced him that I was not making the tale up. He asked about my job and education. He asked if I could type. "Yes, Sergeant," I said. He dismissed me. But the sequence of events that started with recitation of Gates' name turned out to be a fortuitous moment that likely altered my military experience. The critical Gates moment lay ahead.

*   *   *

Army combat training began early the following Monday morning, and it was hard. I usually collapsed exhausted into bed at the end of a day, often to have sleep interrupted by orders in the night as part of the preparation for facing the dreaded North Koreans and Chinese. If the Army has a rule for a number of hours of sleep for trainees, it was more honored in the breach than in the observance. Acclimating myself, I did what I was told, and with as much genuine enthusiasm as I could muster in my weariness. Basically I set aside judgment and followed orders.

I had continued at the end of the day to write notes about my experiences. Often I wrote in the latrine where there was light all night. I scribbled on sheets of paper I stored inside the dress green uniform jacket in my wall closet. I have no idea if the Army would have been receptive to the idea of a recruit recording details of training. On weekends when it was time to write home, I used my notes to refresh memory.

*   *   *

I weighed too much when I entered the Army and I had few developed muscles or physical skills displayed by many fellow recruits. The one thing I could do well was run. Perhaps it was a legacy of my high school cross-country training or laps around the track at Villanova. Perhaps it was an O'Rourke gene producing at the right time. Maybe it was an inheritance from my father who was a great walker. He walked miles every day at a brisk pace. He walked between the Cornwells Heights railroad station and the Penn Salt Co. factory where he worked. He walked between our home and his mother's home at least once a day, every day. My father walked as a determined man on a mission. I often joined him on those walks. It was hard keeping up.

However, in the year between graduation from Villanova and entry into the Army, I did little to keep in shape beyond a rare round of golf and an occasional basketball game with *Bulletin* co-workers. Now and then I'd swim at Villanova. There wasn't much time for exercise and I didn't value it as highly as I did later in life. I liked to run and when the Army said, run, I ran, and well.

I ran through the bayonet course, poking the bayonet at the end of my rifle into cotton dummies, waiting for the command "hit it" to dive for cover in a prone position until the command "move forward" meant get up and resume attack. What sticks out in memory were the sergeants or lieutenants at attack posts asking, "What is the purpose of the bayonet?" I answered, "Sir, (or Sergeant), the purpose of the bayonet is to kill." I shouted with a straight face.

I ran through woods and across fields with my rifle held high and a heavy pack on my back responding to commands to hit the ground or move forward. As tough as those events were in the summer of '60 at Fort Benning, they were exhilarating. I could feel myself becoming stronger and confident that I had strength and durability—enough for the 2nd Infantry Division in Korea.

What I remember most was training to fire the M-1 rifle, Sergeants reminded us it was our best friend. We learned to take it apart, clean it, and reassemble it while blindfolded. I and other trainees spent hours sitting on the floor of our barracks cleaning and practicing with our rifles.

We learned about the M-I shoulder, the jolt when we fired the weapon. On several nights we slept with our rifles. They were unloaded, but they reminded us of our intimacy and dependency.

Finally it was time to march to the rifle range and to fire the rifle in various positions—standing, sitting, kneeling, squatting, and lying prone. Squatting was my nemesis. I could hold that positions for only a few seconds.

The commands on the firing range are indelible. As I got the order to "lock and load" live ammunition into the rifle, nine rounds of 30-caliber bullets, I looked hundreds of feet across the field at a red flag and the target. "Ready on the right. Ready on the left. Ready on the firing line. The flag is waving. The flag is up. The flag is down. Commence firing."

Peering through the sight at the target, I squeezed the trigger. There was a sense of awe and power every time I sent a bullet across the field. How relieved I was when word came that I hit the target. We knew that unless we fired our rifles with accuracy we would be recycled in basic training—caught in another eight weeks of drilling and boot polishing and rifle training. We would remain the droppings of whales on the ocean floor. Fortunately, I passed rifle tests and got a marksman badge that indicated competence, if not proficiency. I wore it proudly.

Other episodes of basic training stand out. On the infiltration course we crawled with heavy backpacks and rifles ready to fire under barbed wire and around obstacles. Explosions shook the ground and bullets shot overhead. This was most terrifying at night when explosions lit the sky. Red tracer bullets a few feet over our bodies made clear it would not be wise to lift a head or shoulders or rump off the coarse sand. Some trainees wrapped elbows and knees in sanitary napkins for protection against the sand, but I tolerated the loss of skin without a wrap.

Toward the end of the basic training we made long marches bearing heavy loads that included half a tent, food for a couple of days, and our rifles, bayonets, and other combat gear. We were prodded by sergeants and periodically ordered to "hit it" wherever we could instantly find shelter against the prospective enemy. It was not a game. At the end of exhausting all-day treks we dug foxholes and established guard posts. Through nights we rotated sentries and responded to whistles and other signals that alerted us to mock attacks by North Koreans and Chinese. Morning meant packing up and moving on, always keeping rifles clean. We were subjected to frequent inspections to make sure we were ready to engage in firefights that might develop. It wasn't war, but for those days it sure felt like it. I remember eating canned rations and I recall four sheets of toilet paper allotted each day. I gave the issued cigarettes to fellow recruits.

One of my fond memories of Fort Benning was returning at the end of a long march to the barracks. We cleaned up and stored equipment. I showered for the first time in days and collapsed into bed anticipating that the alarm would soon sound and I'd be back in gear to be ready for attack. But the next thing I was aware of was sunlight streaming through the windows. I hadn't slept through a sunrise in more than two months, but on this glorious morning the Army let us sleep in. Years later, I remember my gratitude. The Army, it appeared, wasn't so bad after all. Perhaps that's an example of the Stockholm syndrome.

The greatest terror during basic training was the gas chamber. I spent hours practicing with the gas mask. I learned how to take it out of its case, how to blow into it to clear it of any gas, how to make sure it was tight around my face to prevent gas from leaking in. Sergeants built the tension, warning that if we failed to use the masks correctly in the chamber we'd suffer damaged eyes and would be sick. We would do it over until we got it right.

With dread I marched to the gas chamber and stood in line waiting my turn. It was frightening as a few fellow recruits were pulled from the chamber. They lay hollering on the ground about their burning eyes. Some retched.

Finally, in I went. I stood with my mask in its case on my hip as my skin began to burn. We were forbidden to shut our eyes tight. The sergeant talked through his mask. He ordered us to don our masks. I did it as I had drilled, focused on nothing beyond survival. I succeeded and stood there until the sergeant appeared in front of me. "Take it off," he said. This was a surprise. Dutifully, I did, my eyes starting to burn. After what seemed to be a long time, he said, "Put it on." With hands shaking, I did my drill again. I did not clear the mask entirely and left a little gas inside. But through blurred vision, I was able to peer through the glass as the instructor moved on. Seconds later, I was ordered to march from the chamber into the sunlight of an August day in Georgia. My eyes cleared and my spirit stirred with relief and pride. Bring on those North Koreans and Chinese. I'm ready.

Our evenings at Sand Hill often included an hour of close-order drill. Left turns and right turns and about-faces and to-the-rear marches and forward marches seemed to be as natural as eating. I learned, as the Army wanted, to follow orders, immediately, unhesitatingly, totally.

One evening as I reported for drill, Sergeant Albino remembered that I could type. He ordered me to the orderly room. I was handed handwritten documents that I was told to type. On other evenings, I typed schedules and reports. At one point, I typed the orders that were to move us to Korea. I remember typing my own orders. I was not pleased with assignment to Korea, but had little choice, so I didn't grieve. They were the days before computers and so each order had to be separately typed, using abbreviations ordained by the Army.

We were in our final week of basic training when one evening there was no call to type in the orderly room. I was drilling on Sand Hill. My uniform was soaked with sweat and I was covered by dust from boots to

LAWRENCE M. O'ROURKE

helmet, which we called our steel pots. A jeep arrived. A soldier in khaki uniform stepped out and approached our drill sergeant. He stopped the marching and called my name with an order to get into the jeep. I had not the faintest idea why. We came to what I could see was the Fort Benning headquarters. The soldier led me down a hallway to a colonel.

"Recruit O'Rourke, reporting as ordered, Sir," I said, with a salute while standing at attention.

"Sit down, son," he said, motioning to a chair beside his desk. The words burned into my memory. I knew that colonels, no more than drill sergeants, called recruits "son."

He asked a few questions about my civilian work and why I volunteered for the Army. I answered truthfully, wondering what was going on. He noted I had orders for Korea.

"We're forming a team of officers and enlisted who will travel around the southern United States, visiting schools and other places to recruit soldiers," the colonel said. "Enlisted men may be called upon to speak to some groups. Are you interested in joining this team?"

"Sir, yes, Sir," I said, pushing Korea further back in my mind. The colonel wasn't done.

"And the United States Government has an arrangement with the Commonwealth of Puerto Rico to teach English to Spanish-speaking young men who are eligible to serve in the U.S. military," the colonel said. "Are you interested in going to Puerto Rico as an English instructor?" he said. "Sir, yes, Sir," I replied. "Which do you prefer," he continued, "the recruiting team in the Southern states or the Puerto Rico teaching assignment?"

"Sir, Puerto Rico, sir," I said. "I figured that," he said. "I'll cut orders sending you to Puerto Rico. Dismissed."

"Sir, thank you, Sir," I said, with one of my more snappy salutes. I was driven back to Sand Hill, but suspect I could have flown.

The deed was done. When the orders were handed out in the final days of training, the one I had typed for myself sending me to Korea was gone and I was dispatched to Puerto Rico. I've often wondered why. I pulled no strings. I did not try to win favors as a trainee. What I suspect to this day is that by knowing the full name of Thomas Sovereign Gates, Jr., as secretary of defense, and identifying myself as a journalist in civilian life, I had somehow catapulted myself first into the orderly room as the relief typist and beyond that to Puerto Rico. After I got my orders, Sergeant Albino told me he was from Puerto Rico and was pleased I would be going there to teach English. Had he played a role in assigning me to Puerto Rico? I never asked, to my regret. I have often thought that I would enjoy having a beer and a talk with Albino.

*   *   *

At the graduation ceremony, we marched in pressed khaki uniforms and stood at attention through the national anthem and exhortatory speeches. I was taken by bus on a long ride to the Atlanta Airport and a civilian plane. As we flew into Washington National Airport, I looked at the Washington Monument and U.S. Capitol. The next stop was Philadelphia for a round of hellos and goodbyes with Puerto Rico beckoning.

I didn't know a thing about Puerto Rico. I drove with my parents to New York and visited the Puerto Rico tourist office. While walking on Fifth Avenue, I got a flier that John F. Kennedy would speak at a campaign rally in a nearby hotel. I was there when the Democratic presidential candidate came in. I don't recall a word he said, but I was impressed by the horde of reporters and photographers that came with him. That, for me, was the exciting part.

*   *   *

A few days later I was back in New York, at Fort Hamilton in Brooklyn, boarding the USS Geiger, a troop ship. The less said about the four-day trip to Puerto Rico the better. I slept, or at least lay in, a sling with my nose no more than six inches from the sling of the soldier above me. They called us to meals three times a day, but I largely existed on saltines. Many fellow travelers were sick the whole way as we rode through an October storm off the East Coast into the Caribbean. Near the end of the journey we were permitted on deck and I observed flying fish and felt the warm sun. Through my life, whenever anyone suggested a cruise, I thought of the Geiger to Puerto Rico, and said no thanks.

*   *   *

In a khaki uniform and with a duffle bag slung across my shoulder, I stepped off the Geiger in San Juan to a new culture—and a new life. I suddenly encountered the warmth, the colors, the swaying palms, the blaring Latino music pumping from the wildly-painted and always

LAWRENCE M. O'ROURKE

jampacked taxicabs. The old buildings and the open-air food stands with tantalizing smells, and the Spanish street signs and billboards and the loud sounds of upbeat music. It was vibrant.

I rode in a small bus from the ship dock a short distance to the San Juan outskirts and Fort Buchanan, instantly recognizable as a military facility by sentries at the gate, the U.S. flag, and precise directional signs and streets and sidewalks and painted white buildings. It had a golf course, movie theater, large PX, basketball and tennis courts, a swimming pool, chapels, and a school for children. It sure wasn't the 38th Parallel in Korea. I reported to Training Company C, U.S. Army Training Center Caribbean.

The bus turned into a cul-de-sac to the barracks that would be my home while I served as an English Language Instructor. I had never taught, but was confident I could. The barracks, under palm tress and ringed with flowers, were fit for the tropics with a screened door and windows. Inside, in various states of dishevelment, were young men like myself. They read, played the guitar and talked. It looked like a college dorm. Within minutes, it was as if I had lived there for years. The Army culture turns strangers into friends that must rely on one another.

There was a bunk for me, draped with bug netting. From my duffle bag, I pulled the woolen olive drab dress uniform I would wear again only once, on a furlough in the States. In a locker I hung the green fatigues I wore through basic training. I didn't realize it then, but I was to wear them only once or twice more. The next day, I was issued my new uniform as an English Language Instructor—khaki shorts, khaki short-sleeve shirts and high khaki socks with black dress shoes. My well-broken-in combat boots, both the original brown and the original black, found a home in the closet and but for two occasions stayed there for the duration. The crowning touch of my new uniform was a khaki pith helmet. Adorned thus, I felt like a British Army officer downing gin and tonic at Raffles in Singapore.

The instructors were between cycles. A week earlier they finished a course for several hundred young Puerto Rican boys. The Puerto Ricans were now being tested to see if they were ready for the journey they hoped would lead to entry into the U.S. military. The instructors waited for a new shipment of Puerto Rican boys. In the interim the instructors had little to do. So they read, talked and played bridge for fun, not money, went to movies, spent evenings at the noncommissioned officers club with 15-cent beers and talked some more. It was for me the college life I had never experienced. I had turned my clock backward and instantly liked it.

The company commander was a Captain Jose M. Gil Lamadrid, a Puerto Rican. He was to leave the post a few months later. In the time I was under his command we rarely met except on paydays. The Army required enlisted men to report to the commander who sat behind a desk with money and a revolver. The captain counted out my pay to the penny. I picked it up, thanked him, saluted, and we were gone from each other's company for another month.

The morning after my arrival I met First Sergeant Angel M. LaFantaine, a Puerto Rican who was friendly, approachable and ready to make the point that if the English instructors didn't bother him, he wouldn't bother them. The chief English instructor at my arrival was John E. Willey, whose obvious goal was to complete his tour of duty in a few weeks with minimum fuss. I was introduced to the incoming chief instructor, or team leader, Thomas F. Somerville, a tall and earnest young man who soon was to let me know he liked to sing and direct choral groups. I was soon a member of the Company C glee club that sang in the San Juan area at Christmas time under Somerville's direction. Strange as it may sound so many years later, I learned that Tom was a Protestant with a wealth of Christmas carols that I had never sung and had never heard in the Catholic churches where I celebrated the Christmas season. One Somerville favorite stood out, "We Three Kings of Orient Are." Somerville led us in "Star of Wonder, Star of Light, Star of Royal Beauty Bright." Ever since, every time I sing that carol, I think of Tom Somerville and Puerto Rico. He had us sing "Allegria" in Spanish, my first use of Spanish words in music.

Somerville told me that I would teach English Group 10. The students were classified according to tests and interviews. By these measurements, my students were among the poorest. I thought it a bit odd that the experienced teachers got the best students and the greenest, meaning me, got the worst. But who could challenge the Army.

Somerville handed me an Army manual of how to teach English to native Spanish speakers. It was based on the Army Method developed at the military language school in Monterey, California. None of the teachers had been to Monterey or put much stock in the Army manual. They explained that each class was different. Each teacher had his own style that defied regimentation. The Monterey manual had to be followed in theory, but with a wink.

I was struck by the dedication and intensity of the teachers. Virtually all were in the Army against their will, counting days until they were "too short to care" and homeward-bound. Several seemed drawn into uniform by reasons that had brought me to this place—escape, adventure and ticket-punching. Many were teachers in civilian life; that's what they would be after two Army years. They were career teachers. There wasn't a career soldier in the bunch.

I was one of five new teachers in Company C. We were all ranked as recruits, meaning we had fewer than four months in the service. But we were immediately ordered to put on corporal's stripes—needed, it was explained, because we were authorized to command troops and the corporal's stripes were the sign we had to be obeyed.

One newcomer was Arthur T. Omohundro of Chicago. Art attended the University of Chicago. He earned undergraduate and master's degrees in English and enrolled in a doctoral program. He completed course work and was writing a thesis at Northwestern University on the aesthetics of English writing when the draft notice came. Arthur was an outstanding distance runner. After the Army, he had a distinguished career as an English teacher in New Trier High School in Evanston, Illinois, one of the nation's premier public secondary schools.

Another new teacher was Joseph M. Edwards of California. Merritt Edwards was a graduate of the University of California at Berkeley and an English teacher in San Rosa. A Mormon, he was a gentle and patient man who was frustrated by his students' lack of progress. With a missionary zeal, he was determined to teach them English. He returned to Santa Rosa—with Myrna, his Puerto Rican bride—after two years in the Army and resumed high school teaching.

Robert Bruce Waters was a graduate of Western Kentucky University and an English teacher in civilian life. Appropriate to his native state, he was an intense college basketball fan. With nary a cynical comment, he cared deeply for his students. After the Army, he became a magazine executive in Fort Lauderdale, Florida, and looked back on his Army years as some of his finest. In the Army, he got the nickname "Muddy."

David J. Rife was a graduate of the University of Florida and an English teacher all his life. He spent decades as professor of English and department chairman at a university in Pennsylvania, where students frequently voted him their favorite faculty member. Of his experiences in Puerto Rico, he wrote: "Here in isolated peacefulness, surrounded by mountains and the ocean, we lived together and taught. We were thrown back upon one another and upon the one thing common to us all—our literary interests. We read and wrote and discussed."

Within a few days of my arrival, two teachers who were memorable characters joined us in Company C. William G. Tolliver was a poet who told all who asked and didn't ask that he came from the "small coal-mining community" of Christopher in Southern Illinois. He was a graduate of Southern Illinois University and, before entering the Army, taught English and speech at Cave-in-Rock High School. Unkempt in both military uniform and civilian clothes, he constantly wore a camera around his neck and snapped pictures whether the subject was willing or not. He complained about how the Army was cramping his private life. But in later years, when his poetry and prose were published and after he served as a high school teacher, union organizer, policeman, and firearms instructor in Emporia, Kansas, he proudly proclaimed that he had served in the Army and said that it was one of the best events of his life.

Another arrival, who became one of my closest friends, was Gary Greenup of Seattle, a graduate of the University of Washington. Greenup and I discovered that on Saturday nights we could cadge free rum drinks at San Juan Airport and acquire Cuban cigars for a few pennies. We spent many a Saturday night on the top deck at the airport, drinking and puffing while the sun set over the Caribbean. We solved most of the world's problems. (I never smoked after leaving Puerto Rico.) Returning to Seattle in the summer of 1962 with the announced goal of "looking over the World's Fair and being a bum for a while," Greenup earned advanced degrees in literature and history and spent most of his life as a writer before dying in his early 60s.

The list could go on. What's amazing is that the Army found dozens of teachers (and in my case a journalist, albeit an English major and Theater graduate student) and brought us together in Puerto Rico, turned us loose on young Puerto Ricans, and got dedicated, unslacking effort. Left largely free to teach, we created a learning atmosphere that I never encountered elsewhere.

These short-time soldiers, some of whom were initially unhappy and bitter about being drafted into the Army and having their lives and careers disrupted, threw themselves into their work, making it more a labor of love than a duty to be performed. They could have faked it, but I cannot recall a single one of my fellow teachers during those two years doing less than his best—and that was consistently good, if not

LAWRENCE M. O'ROURKE

excellent. If awards were given to English language instructors for "going beyond the call of duty," I can name dozens who qualify for the prize.

That experience was critical to my thinking about creation of an all-volunteer Army, a goal of antiwar activists who thought it would reduce the threat of war. I never agreed. As a journalist, I wrote and spoke in favor of a draft to national service—either in the military or as a civilian such as a teacher or tutor in an inner-city school or as a worker to improve the environment or to assist in the care of the elderly and ill.

I doubt that an all-volunteer Army could bring together the team of English instructors who labored as hard and diligently as we did. If the Army were challenged to teach in the barrios of East Los Angeles, or the streets of Kabul or Baghdad or Gaza, peace and justice would be better served than through the use of arms. I can see today's version of Greenup and Edwards and Tolliver and Waters and Rife in those classrooms.

*   *   *

I was anxious and awkward when I faced my first class in November 1960. I was responsible at least five hours a day for 20 young Puerto Ricans in green fatigue uniforms. I was as alien to their culture as they were to mine. Neither of us knew what to expect, but I had a sense that they suspected my lack of experience and skill. Looking back, I don't blame them.

The Monterey manual told us to start by teaching trainees to recite, "I am a man." Because we were to use only English in the classroom, we were not supposed to tell them it was a translation of "Yo soy un hombre." Rather they were to recite the sentence in unison dozens of times and then I would take them to "He is a man." It would continue indefinitely with no translation. I understood rote recitation—the way I was taught catechism, spelling and arithmetic in elementary school. But I at least knew the language and what I was saying.

So from the outset, I broke the rules and told them in Spanish what I was about to have them repeat in English. The manual called for constant group recitation, with no provision for individual speaking. That struck me as ludicrous. How could I know if a student was saying words that I wanted him to say? I mixed group recitation and rapid-fire individual recitation.

I made the classroom work exhausting for students and teacher. After eight weeks with Group 10, I was frustrated that I did not succeed as well as I hoped. There were many reasons why. After we English teachers worked the students over Monday through Saturday, they went back to their Spanish-speaking sergeants who spoke to them only in Spanish. The students, of course, spoke to one another in Spanish. If I ran into a student in the mess hall or on a work detail and said something, he invariably responded in Spanish.

But I learned valuable lessons during that first cycle—mostly concerning discipline.

After a few weeks with me and the work of the classroom, students became restive. I often saw them look out the window and speak to each other when I tried to get them to recite. I surmised I had lost their attention and they had lost their fear of me. So one day I had an idea. I told them that they did not work hard enough and were lazy. After dinner at night, they generally hung about their barracks talking to each other in Spanish and listening to Spanish-language music on the radio. I told them in the fifth week that after dinner that night they were to report to the classroom where I had a plan to make them pay more attention to English.

This being the Army, they followed my order. We went for a run. As we ran I called out English sentences and had them repeat. They seemed to do a better job while running than in the classroom. I told them it was time they learned to sing in English. I had nothing fancy in mind, just some simple lines in cadence. And that worked too. To my pleasant surprise, the trainees sounded good. We did this for an hour before I sent them back to their regular evening activities. I was pretty worn out myself.

To my shock, many told me the next day that they enjoyed the run, the extra English lesson, and the singing. So I incorporated it into my teaching technique. Once a week for that cycle and all the others I taught in Puerto Rico, we had regular runs and sing-alongs.

I was especially proud of another use of my military authority—a tool I did not use. I had authority to deny passes to trainees to go home on weekends. Many instructors routinely withheld passes. I thought as a practical matter that denial would make trainees resentful and surly, surely not feelings that would enhance learning. I missed my family and friends and was certain that the trainees were in the same fix. I resolved that whatever breach of discipline might occur, I would never deny a weekend pass to a trainee. There were times when I was sorely tempted to break that promise. But then I began to see benefit to my leniency.

LAWRENCE M. O'ROURKE

I became known as the English teacher who did not revoke weekend passes, and that seemed to win over the trainees. Once that happened, I rarely had discipline problems.

I used unorthodox techniques in the classroom that I know were not in the Monterey manual. I kept a wide white board at the back of my classroom, and if I were having trouble that day with a trainee I'd order him to sit on the board on the floor for a few minutes. The board was a threat that I rarely had to use because trainees didn't want to be disciplined or embarrassed.

I made trainees stand when it was their turn to recite individually. I sought individual recitation by pointing at trainees and not calling their names. A few times early in every cycle I would point at a trainee when he would be looking out the window or have his mind detached from the classroom. There would be an awkward silence until the trainee discovered me pointing at him. Trainees didn't like that experience either, so I was quickly able to establish a pattern that trainees focused on me during the entire class.

We teachers were masters of our own classrooms. The team leader had responsibility. But he invariably let teachers do it their way. We had a civilian consultant, Edward Audas, who visited the classroom once in a while. He assured me that while some of my methods were unorthodox, I was doing just fine. He didn't pay any more attention to the Monterey manual than we did.

When I arrived in Fort Buchanan in the fall of 1960, the practice was for trainees to be tested at the end of the eight-week cycle to see if they had sufficient proficiency in English to certify them as reliable candidates to serve in a branch military service. Many failed and were sent home—usually to their disappointment and ours as their instructors.

Change was needed and change did come, and I will explain how. But before that, I digress to tell more about my life in Puerto Rico.

*   *   *

First, I shall confess the first time I got drunk. Terribly drunk. What are the words we have used over the years? Plastered, four sheets to the wind, wasted? I qualify for them all. I was coming to my first Christmas away from home and I was melancholy. I'm not looking for an excuse, but rather to put my conduct into perspective.

The chaplains announced they would host holiday parties. Attendance was not compulsory, but it would have been bad form to stay away. The first event was the Protestant chaplain's Christmas party, held on a Sunday in mid-December in a hall near the church that served all denominations. It was a very nice Christmas party, just what I, though inexperienced in Protestant ways, expected. The hall was seasonally decorated. Christmas music played on the record machine. The chaplain was gracious, chatting with us as he urged us to eat the cookies and drink the punch. There was a lot of gentle laughter. Some officers and noncommissioned officers and their spouses attended and the talk was informal, gracious. We talked about where we came from and a lot about the weather back home. We sang carols. The minister-chaplain spoke briefly to the group, nice, gentle remarks, cheering us up, stressing service to our country and reminding us we were about to celebrate a birth that marked the beginning of the great act of service that Christmas brings. I was glad I attended.

The Catholic chaplain announced he would have a Christmas party for the English teachers the following Friday night. I anticipated a repetition of the fine Protestant event and decided to arrive early, have a few cookies and cup of punch, exchange pleasantries, and then duck out, perhaps to a movie or a book. I arrived early and there was the priest-chaplain in informal clerical garb. After we went through the motions of figuring out where we came from and what the weather was like there, he suggested I have a bite to eat and perhaps a drink. Indeed the spread on the table was a young man's delight. But it was the bar—the open bar—that caught my attention. I confess that one rum drink followed another as the room filled and the laugher intensified. By the end of the evening, it was a case of who's counting. I had far more rum than sobriety would tolerate. Memory plays tricks, but I've thought about that evening often enough to recall being led with a few of the other lads across the field and into our barracks.

I awoke with a brutal headache and got a lesson from an English instructor who was an old hand at rum imbibing. He said that excessive consumption, no matter how free or whatever the season, was not for the squeamish. I learned my limits and never indulged so enthusiastically and fully again. That chaplain sure knew how to throw a party.

*   *   *

It was in Puerto Rico in the fall of 1960 that I cast my first vote for president. I voted for John F. Kennedy by absentee ballot. I had somewhat mixed emotions. I listened over Armed Forces Radio to the first debate between JFK and Richard Nixon, and I decided that Nixon won. I was impressed by his message, his logic, and certainly his eight years of experience as vice president. On the radio, Kennedy seemed to stumble a few times.

As I read news report of the debate the next day in *The San Juan Star* and listened to broadcast news reports, and read stories at the Fort Buchanan library in *The Miami Herald*, and *Time* and *Newsweek* magazines, I had a different view of the debate. Beyond recognizing the power of the press to influence public opinion in political campaigns, I became aware as never before of the importance of this new medium of television in U.S. politics.

There's no doubt that my vote for Kennedy was influenced by the fact that he, like me, was Irish Catholic. As an undergraduate at Villanova, I wrote a research paper on the 1928 election between Herbert Hoover and Al Smith. Since most of my research was done in the *Bulletin* library, I had an advantage in access to original material. However, the professor told me critically that I wrote too much like a journalist and not like an English major. That really didn't bother me very much. On the core point, I concluded that Smith lost because he was a Catholic. My father, who said that Al Smith made him a Democrat, reinforced that position.

Religion was in the forefront of politics in Puerto Rico when I arrived on the island that fall. The Catholic bishop of Ponce, the Most Rev. James E. McManus, wrote a letter instructing Catholics to vote for the Statehood Republican Party because the Popular Democratic Party (PDP) supported artificial contraception. He said that a vote for the PDP would be a sin.

The Kennedy campaign understood that the McManus statement could reinforce to voters on the Mainland claims by Protestant leaders that the Vatican would influence a Catholic president. Kennedy tried to reduce this fear in a Houston speech to Protestant clergy. Now the Catholicism issue erupted two weeks before Election Day. Cardinal Francis Spellman of New York and Archbishop James Davis of San Juan entered the fray, saying that a vote for Kennedy would not be a sin. McManus retorted that it would be sin without penalty, whatever that meant. Puerto Rican Gov. Luis Munoz Marin, who supported Kennedy, said McManus was for Nixon.

The imbroglio took center stage in the barracks of Company C. As a Roman Catholic and a political journalist, I came under fire from many English teachers, most of whom supported Kennedy. I tried a nuanced defense of the bishop's right to speak out on a matter of faith and morals—which birth control was for the official Church and many Catholics—and the importance in our society of separating church and state. I said that suggesting that Kennedy in the White House would take orders from the Pope in Rome was ludicrous. However, I was not as confident of that point as I sounded.

On election night, we gathered in the barracks to listen to broadcast reports. With Puerto Rico an hour ahead of the Eastern United States and with classes the next morning, I went to bed not knowing the outcome. I learned the next morning I was about to see changes in my chain of command. Tom Gates and Dwight Eisenhower left on Jan. 20. They were replaced by Robert S. McNamara as secretary of defense and JFK. I knew my chain of command, though I was no longer quizzed on it.

*   *   *

JFK's election meant more to me than I anticipated. Soviet leader Nikita Khrushchev tested the U.S. president by building a wall across Berlin. The Berlin wall ignited the Berlin crisis and edged the United States and the Soviet Union, the world's nuclear superpowers, closer to war. In response, Kennedy ordered a buildup of the U.S. military.

I was summoned to the training center command at the Caribbean Headquarters in El Castillo del Morro at the jutting tip of San Juan. Before explaining why, let me backtrack and say that it was my second trip to El Morro. In December 1960, I was taken to the military hospital in El Morro after getting a flu shot. The Army doctor said my high temperature, irregular heartbeat and neuralgia indicated I had rheumatic fever. He brushed aside the notion that the flu shot had made me ill. He ordered a battery of heart tests. I was wheeled on a gurney into a room, stripped naked, and told to lie still and flat as the technician attached a number of connectors to my body. He started to hook up wires when another technician dashed in and said that a senior officer had apparently suffered a heart attack and was on the way. My wires were disconnected and I was wheeled outside the testing room into a rotunda with various balconies. It was the main passageway for the military office complex. The technicians neglected to give me a sheet. So there I lay, in

LAWRENCE M. O'ROURKE

my birthday suit, for what seemed like an eternity while they worked on the officer. Eventually I was tested and the initial diagnosis was dropped. The military doctor told me that henceforth I should tell my doctors that I had a possible penicillin allergy. I was sent back to the classroom.

On the visit to El Morro prompted by the Berlin crisis, I was ushered into a meeting room where military people were assembled. Also there was Audas, the civilian adviser to the English language program. He explained that Kennedy's order to expand the military meant that more Puerto Ricans were to come into our care to learn English. It seemed that there was a backlog of Puerto Rican boys trying to get into U.S., military uniform.

Audas said we would take as many as 1,200 trainees at a time. There was not enough housing and classroom space for them at Fort Buchanan, so the military intended to open another facility on the island. Audas told me that I was to become the chief English Language Instructor at this new facility. No longer would I teach Puerto Rican kids; now I had full charge of their instruction and their teachers. I was promoted to sergeant, technically acting sergeant, but I was ordered to put three stripes on my sleeves and act like a sergeant.

The new campus was to be a Puerto Rican National Guard camp in Salinas, on the southern or Caribbean side of the island. The Pentagon wanted the facility opened and English classes started within days. To me that sounded impossible, but that was the order.

I flew with a team of officers the next day to Salinas. We inspected the sprawling camp and found villages of barracks. We decided that a ten-minute march up a mountain would be ideal for classrooms. Audas and I set out to start a school within two weeks. We rushed back to Buchanan and San Juan to find desks, blackboards, and office supplies to be trucked to Salinas.

In Salinas, I worked with engineers to convert barracks into classrooms. They made four classrooms, two on the first floor, two on the second, in each former barracks. For our first class of 1,200 students, we needed 48 classrooms. That would put 25 in each class, hardly ideal since the best learning of English took place when there were 15 to 20 students per class.

Since there was no fixed roof housing yet available at Salinas, we pioneers at the new school, from the colonels in charge to the likes of me, were each given a tent. But what a tent! Mine, like the others, was on a concrete block about 15-by-20 feet. It was enough space to shelter my bed, a desk with an electric outlet, a chair, and a steel closet. From one end I looked down onto the classrooms. From the other I could see the Caribbean Sea. Engineers built a shower and somehow supplied it with plenty of hot water.

With the construction of classrooms underway, my task was to pick the instructors for the expanded program. That was a challenge since many of my fellow teachers made it known they did not want to go to Salinas, but were quite content to remain in their barracks at Fort Buchanan, where they had virtually no supervision, a movie theater, PX and NCO club with beer at 15 cents a bottle, rum drinks at 30 cents, except on Mondays when prices were lower. I suddenly had a lot of people reminding me of how soon they would get out of the Army and how inefficient it would be to ship them elsewhere. I reminded them that the Pentagon had delayed their release because of the Berlin crisis. In picking the instructors I wanted at Salinas, I tried to exclude the married ones, but otherwise gave no favors to personal friends.

The Army command brought in officers and noncoms who had not served in Fort Buchanan and thus had no sensitivity to the burdens of teaching English as a foreign language or what had come to be the unique status of the instructors. Most incoming regular Army people seemed set on doing things by the book while the teachers under me did the minimum of military duty while they poured their energy into teaching. So it became my task to mediate between the two groups. And that on occasion meant that I had to pull rank and go Army. I remember one day that a group of instructors arrived and were told their new home would be a barracks that wasn't yet clean. Perhaps they expected someone else to clean it for the next thing I knew I was called in by a senior sergeant who had been shipped in from Panama and told that the Army would not tolerate soldiers tossing their duffle bags onto unmade beds in an unkempt barracks while they wandered about the facility in their civvies. The sergeant said that if I couldn't get things straightened out, he would. I got the point.

I gathered the instructors together. They grumbled so much that I called them to attention, told them to get into fatigues, to clean their barracks to my satisfaction, to make the toilets and shower room as spotless as they remembered it from basic training, to make their beds and stow their gear according to Army regulations, and to line up in military formation at a certain hour when I would conduct an inspection. Since I didn't do any of this gently, they got the point that Sergeant O'Rourke could be a hard-ass.

They did as they were told, no doubt uttering some remarks about O'Rourke in my absence. But they passed my inspection and got the regular Army people off my back.

Since the regular Army people knew nothing about English language instruction, I had an empty blackboard on which to write the rules. Fortunately, a young lieutenant, a recent West Point graduate named Paul Chalmers, was given day-to-day responsibility of the English language school. Chalmers and I were quite frank with each other. Initially, he wanted it done the Army way and that meant obeying customary rules and regulations. I wanted the trainees to learn English and that meant giving the instructors the flexibility to bend the rules. To my delight and relief, after extensive argument and negotiations, Chalmers agreed. He said that the mountaintop classrooms would belong to the English program and he would rarely be there and would give me ample warning when he or any other regular Army person, such as the commanding officer, might decide to visit. We hooked up a hand-cranked field telephone between my office on the mountaintop and his office in the valley below.

I prevailed on the regular Army people to understand that hours to be kept by the teachers included time in the classroom and time for preparing lessons. The teachers could not be routinely called on for other military-style tasks such as weapons training and drilling.

On most afternoons teachers donned civilian garb and headed for a watering hole in Salinas named Maya's. Though I was not one of them any longer, I occasionally joined for beer, fried plantains, rice and beans, and conversation. Out of that conversation came two actions quite extraordinary for the U.S. Army—creation of a literary magazine and establishment of a newspaper for the training center. Each was unofficial, written, edited and published by the teachers, largely intended only for the teachers, but with government printing and supplies.

I got the credit among English instructors for starting the literary magazine and newspaper. When I took the ideas to Chalmers, he cautioned that the Army might not be the place for such publications. I said they would be good for the Army because they would keep instructors engaged in what they do best—reading and writing English. Chalmers came around. I had a tougher time convincing sergeants who thought we were all a bunch of lazy, arrogant misfits.

The deal I struck with Chalmers and the regular Army was that the publications would be identified as unofficial, that they would not make negative comments or even slightly critical comments about the Army, anybody in our chain of command or Puerto Rico. They said they'd watch carefully and if we broke the agreement, my head would be on the block.

We set to work. On December 17, 1961, the first issue of *En Transito* rolled off the presses, actually the orderly room mimeograph machine. Edited by Dave Rife and Gary Greenup, it was read word for word by me before printing.

In their introduction, Rife and Greenup declared, "*En Transito* is a unique publication, as unique as the United States Army process in Puerto Rico which created the circumstances from which the idea of the magazine evolved."

The issue contained four poems translated from Greek by Joe Shaw of Brown University, poetry by Bill Tolliver, a short story called "The Firing Squad" by Gary Greenup, and a variety of other entries, including an essay by me claiming that James Michener and John O'Hara are the most important U.S. novelists because they wrote for ordinary people.

*   *   *

That was my Army. I have never forgotten my experiences in Puerto Rico, the friends I made there, and the lessons learned. I matured as a person in the U.S. Army, and I stand proud whenever I hear the Army's song played. I might have been enriched through service on the frontline with the 2nd Infantry Division in Korea or some other service. But that was not to be. I was lucky that my orders did not read Vietnam. Chances are high that, if I had entered the Army a few years later, I would have slogged through the jungle. They were the brave soldiers. They were the heroes. I served as an English teacher.

I'll end this chapter with the story in the *Training Center Journal* that appeared as I left Puerto Rico in May 1962 and returned to civilian life.

> Lawrence M. O'Rourke's first teaching cycle was a group ten in Co. "C." His next cycle was group three and for three cycles thereafter he taught group three. In his own words: "I found that the caliber of students I got in the upper middle groups responded best to my method of teaching."

LAWRENCE M. O'ROURKE

There was truth in what he said, for group three's motto during O'Rourke's teaching days was "Everyone knows in Company C. The best English group is number three."

Larry's teaching philosophy is "keep the student off-balance. Never let him know what to expect from you next."

One visit to an O'Rourke-conducted classroom and you got the feeling that here was English instruction as it should be.

In October 1961, O'Rourke assumed the team leadership of Co. "G" in Salinas. Thus began, by his own admission, and by the observations of those close to him, "his finest hour."

Co. "G" trainees respected Sergeant O'Rourke. He was a disciplinarian who could seemingly sense the correct manner of handling a problem. Night classes were a favorite punitive measure of Sgt. O'Rourke. English instructors who helped him conduct these classes were heard to say on more than one occasion, "Somehow, in spite of the fact that I'm missing NCO club time, I don't mind teaching at night for Larry."

Upon his return to Buchanan, O'Rourke became a member of the Testing and Retraining Committee, assuming the chairmanship in March.

Larry's reading habits are well-known in the training center. He doesn't read newspapers—he consumes them.

Perhaps this is the printer's ink in his veins.

Before he entered the Army he was a rewriteman and reporter for The *Philadelphia Bulletin*.

His love of the newspaper business manifested itself when he conceived the idea of and edited the *T.C. Journal*.

Philadelphia will claim its own soon. Larry will be discharged from the Army this week and will return to his job on the *Bulletin*.

CHAPTER 6

On the Road and On the Beat

O UT OF KHAKI, I looked forward to my newspaper attire: buttoned-down blue shirt and wrinkled suit, with scuffed shoes. But before returning to the *Bulletin*, I needed my Kerouac moment.

The day after taking off the Army uniform, I telephoned Earl Selby, the *Bulletin's* city editor. "Come in right away," Selby said. "We look forward to having you back." What I didn't tell Selby on the phone was that I wasn't coming back right away, that during my collegiate-like duty in Puerto Rico, I read Jack Kerouac's 1957 classic, "On The Road," and it spurred my wanderlust. I, a square if there ever was one, dreamt of being a temporary member of the Beat Generation.

I came to Selby's glassed office in the newsroom. Earl was a wonderful newspaperman, just what the *Bulletin* needed in drive, energy, commitment and example. An honors graduate who worked his way through Northwestern University as a short order cook and reporter, he came to the *Bulletin* in 1943 from *The Chicago Tribune*. He brought Ben Hecht's "Front Page" eccentricity and competitiveness to the more staid world of Philadelphia journalism and especially to the "gray lady of Filbert Street." Selby had a brilliant ability to sniff out a story and a flair for generating hot copy. Beyond hard work, endless energy and unlimited curiosity, his success was based on his skill in inspiring confidence—and fear—in sources through an "if you're not with me, you're against me" mentality that divided Selby's world into good guys (his sources and no-holds-barred, fully-committed reporters) against bad guys (the malevolent, those who didn't leak to him and reporters who relied on *Bulletin* tradition and style when gumption and edginess were needed.) Selby's approach wasn't pure, but it was mostly effective.

Earl was a difficult boss. While respected, he was not liked. With his burr haircut, eyeglasses perched on top of his head, herky-jerky style, rapid dashes around the newsroom, and air of superiority, Selby always struck me as a man with a dozen things competing in his mind simultaneously, with his issues far more vital than mine. As for small talk, Selby was at the bottom of the list. He didn't tolerate fools or bores.

In his office, Earl came, as usual, right to the point. He wanted me back right away, tomorrow if possible, next week certainly. "Earl, I don't want to disappoint you," I said. "I look forward to working again at the *Bulletin*. But I'm not coming back right away. I'm going to drive across the country, camp out, visit national parks, and go to the World's Fair in Seattle." That was my vision of beatnik. I would, of course, visit San Francisco.

"Oh, no," said Selby. "Either you are here June 1 or you don't have a job. Take it or leave it. If you want to be a newspaperman, if you want to work for this newspaper, you'll follow our rules. I have plans for you, but you have to follow my plans." That ended our conversation on a very confrontational tone. We understood each other.

I toured the newsroom, greeting old colleagues. First assistant city editor Sam Boyle and Len Murphy, an assigning editor, were there with the irascible but superb chief copy editor, Charlie Johnson. Along the rewrite bank were Fred McCord, Bayard Brunt, Jerry Dietz, and Adolph Katz. They greeted me warmly and asked when I'd start work. I fudged. "Trying to work that out," I said.

In my final months in the Army, I spent many hours plotting my trip across the country. Despite Selby's demand and my desire to work for the *Bulletin*, I wasn't going to revoke my commitment to myself. So a few days later, I called and said, "Earl, I'm moving ahead with my cross-country trip." His response was abrupt. "That's a mistake. Don't think you have a job at the *Bulletin*. Call when you get back." And he hung up. I figured that when I returned from Seattle, I'd have to look for a job—and it was not likely to be in the newspaper business, and certainly not with the *Bulletin*. Was I being stubborn or stupid? Like most decisions I made in life, once I made them, I didn't second-guess myself. Kerouac challenged me. I wouldn't let him down.

I bought a tent, sleeping bags, a stove, and a lantern. I had moved back in with my parents on Springfield Avenue. In the backyard I practiced setting up the tent. My mother planned campsite menus. On the first day of my brother's school vacation, I set off with my mother and brother to the West.

Our first overnight was a campsite in Western Pennsylvania. Then it was on to Chesterton, Indiana, for the Indiana Dunes where we camped next to a troop of Boy Scouts who partied all night. We went through Chicago, across Illinois and Iowa, and into South Dakota. Our first major sightseeing was Badlands National Park in Western South Dakota. What a delight that was, scanning a sky filled with stars, attending park ranger lectures, exploring canyons. The Badlands NP was the first Western national park I visited, and perhaps for that reason, it became my favorite. The visit opened for me a lifelong affection for the U.S. national park system. It is America's great treasure. People asked me what job in government I'd like if given a choice. Director of the National Park Service, I replied.

From the Badlands, we went through Wall, the South Dakota town known primarily for a hokey but fun drugstore emporium, Wall Drug. It offered free ice water. We toured the Black Hills and camped by Mount Rushmore.

We weren't seeing much in depth as we paused long enough at Devil's Tower to scramble over rocks and pose for photographs. My attitude was that this was a trip of a lifetime and I might never be on these roads again. I drove to the limits of toleration.

My mother kept a journal and wrote my father several postcards a day. She had one ready every time we passed a post office.

In a major concession to our schedule, we spent two days and nights in Yellowstone, experiencing "bear jams," road congestions caused by sightings of bears that came to eat human food, over objections by the Park Service. Human food is unhealthy for animals, and bear jams are dangerous for humans who get close to the bears. We weren't reckless, but bears climbed onto our car hood. We toured boiling mud pots, geysers such as Old Faithful, and hiked to the edge of the Yellowstone River and waterfall. As if we roomed there, we walked through the splendid Yellowstone Park Lodge, before retiring to our tent. I didn't envy those who stayed in fancy digs. Kerouac wasn't into fancy travel.

My mother was brilliant at striking up conversations with total strangers, so we met many interesting people. I had the Army experience, but the trip alerted my mother and brother to a culture different from West Philadelphia. We did not escape our roots entirely. One of my mother's primary concerns was getting to Mass on Sunday. Consulting guidebooks, phone books, newspapers, maps, and the locals, she made sure that we got to church on time, Beatnik or not.

Focused now on reaching the Space Needle that epitomized the Seattle World's Fair, we dashed through Montana (awestruck at the Anaconda smokestacks), Idaho and Washington State, before we found a campsite outside Seattle. Our goal in picking campsites wasn't convenience or amenities. It was cheapness. I didn't want to pay more than $1 a night, and that was tough with so many people coming to the fair. In Seattle I paid the outrageous sum of $3 a night. My mother scrupulously kept an expense tab. When I bought gasoline at 35 cents a gallon in the mountains, I thought it was larceny.

Nor were we big spenders on food. There were few fast-food chains, so we didn't find McDonald's. We stopped at grocery stores for bread, cheese and sliced meat for sandwiches made in the back seat as we moved on. For breakfast we had pancakes or cereal and coffee or tea on our campsite stove. We bought ice daily, marveling at differences in prices for 10-pound bags.

We sang, "This Land is Your Land, This Land is My Land." My mother listed state license plates she saw. She made notes on the news of the day reported on the car radio. She kept a list of songs played on the radio. My mother was a more detailed note taker than many reporters I traveled with in later years.

It was dry on our first day at the World's Fair, but it poured on the second. Packing a wet tent is grim. There was more rain as we drove south through Northern California's Redwood forests, stopping for pictures of ourselves with our station wagon in a passageway cut through a 2,200-year-old tree. Then it was on to San Francisco where we busted the budget by taking a motel on Lombard Street, offering my mother new opportunities to talk about life back at her growing-up home in Philadelphia at 2208 Lombard Street. One big treat was lunch on Fisherman's Wharf, at Alioto's Number 9, on a Sunday. We found a pay phone and called my father from the wharf, marveling at being able to talk to him 3,000 miles away. I took a walk through North Beach, but didn't spot Kerouac.

We drove down the coast, through Los Angeles and into Anaheim and the inevitable day in Disneyland. It was my first time on the Jungle Cruise and It's a Small World. I did not anticipate the number of times I would return to a Disney property, sometimes on assignment. Once I went to Disneyland with Richard Nixon's press secretary, Ron Ziegler, who before joining the White House staff was a tour guide on the Jungle Cruise. Ziegler did his spiel on headhunting pygmies and roaring hippopotamuses. I always thought Ziegler knew that steering through an imaginary jungle and representing Nixon required similar suspensions of belief. I never believed Ziegler lied deliberately for Nixon. He just didn't challenge anything he was told to say, just as he played the role as Disney's jungle guide.

Turning east, we looked at the Grand Canyon at night, camped on the South Rim, looked at the Grand Canyon in the morning, and hit the road. We could say we had seen the Grand Canyon.

We paused briefly at the Painted Desert, and drove through Tucumcari, New Mexico. The name fascinated my mother. Whenever she described the trip to friends, she said she had been to the World's Fair, Disneyland, and Tucumcari. From most people, that prompted a question, where is Tucumcari? Of course, that was my mother's intention. I picked up her technique and used it as a method to get conversations started.

Back in Philadelphia, I called Selby, not expecting a job at the *Bulletin*. "Come in tomorrow and we'll talk," he said. In his office, he seemed little interested in the trip, but shocked me by saying he had a job for me, and it was one I never expected. I was to be the *Bulletin's* assistant makeup editor for a few months. "Can you start tomorrow?' Selby said. "Yes," I replied. "OK," he said, "and here's your vacation pay." I was stunned to discover that the *Bulletin* welcomed me back with two weeks pay—money for doing nothing for the paper that had not guaranteed me a job before my western tour. To receive an unexpected gift is one of life's great pleasures. It binds you to the donor.

I was on the job early the next morning. Managing editor William B. Dickinson convened a morning meeting with the telegraph editor, city editor, picture editor, the feature editor, and the chief makeup editor, Carl Cressman, with me as the neophyte.

Bill Dickinson was pivotal in my newspaper career. A Kansas native, Dickinson was a combat correspondent in Europe and the South Pacific during World War II. He was the only journalist to land with Gen. Douglas MacArthur at Leyte and he was on board the USS Missouri when Japan surrendered in 1945. His circle of friends included Eric Sevareid and Walter Cronkite.

I was in awe and fear of Dickinson. My first contact with him was eight years earlier when I, as a 17-year-old copy boy, was assigned to the "slot," a chair in the middle of the large newsroom horseshoe that we called the desk. Dickinson had a chair on the outside of the horseshoe. Nobody other than Dickinson ever sat in Dickinson's chair. I was a few feet behind the news editor, whose back was to me and across from Dickinson's chair. The city editor was to my left, the telegraph editor to my right, the picture editor behind me, and an ever-rolling rubber conveyor belt just beside me. My job as "slot" copy boy was to be constantly on the lookout for copy edited by the city and wire desks and, if time allowed, vetted by the news editor and sometimes by Dickinson. These editors would hold up a page of copy they wanted put on the conveyer belt and sent to the composing room a floor below. Sometimes a proof of a story would come up the belt and I was to quickly look at it, decide who should get it, and walk it over and lay it in front of the right editor. It was a job that required constant attention. Nobody said, "Larry. Here's a sheet of copy. Please put it on the conveyor belt. Thank you."

If they waved the copy for longer than they wanted to wave it—and these editors had their own unchallengeable notions of how long that was—and I didn't take the copy, they yelled, "Boy." I got the message and dashed to them, embarrassed by my ineptitude.

It was in the "slot" that I first met Dickinson. He was the final decider, when he wanted to be, of everything that went into the newspaper, and where it went. If he took his chair at the desk, editors knew that he was to be given the chance to see all copy before it was sent to the compositor. As a rule, Dickinson read copy only on big stories, such as the Kennedy assassination, or the sinking of the Andrea Doria with Philadelphia's mayor aboard. On most days, Dickinson arrived at the desk in early morning to "dummy" the first edition, that is, to decide what stories got top billing and to lay out the front page on a piece of pink diagram paper. Then he came back about noon to dummy the home delivery edition, and he came back in late afternoon to dummy the final edition, the four-star, the pride of the *Bulletin*. The in-between editions were rarely re-dummied. But if a big story needed his command decisions, he would be called from his office to the desk. I had no idea what Dickinson did in his office other than to talk to staff members summoned there. He had glass windows. Everybody could see whom Dickinson was talking to. There was always guessing and rumors when Dickinson met somebody. Occasionally, "the Major," William L. McLean, Sr., the paper's owner and publisher, came to Dickinson's office. That triggered tidal waves of speculation.

Dickinson's word was final in the newsroom. One night I was assigned to attend a gathering of Hispanics who arrived in Philadelphia from Cuba. I was to do a story about their role in the Bay of Pigs invasion. I knew enough Spanish to interview them in their native language. One man told me that he was in a landing craft about to land on the beach when the order came to abort the landing. He told me that the Central Intelligence Agency trained him in Nicaragua, paid him, and dispatched him to overthrow Fidel Castro. While the CIA's role was widely understood, this was the first time, to my knowledge, that any survivor had shown up in Philadelphia and talked about it. I wrote the story big and the *Bulletin* put it on the top of the front page the next day.

A few days later, I was summoned to Dickinson's office. There were several men there. They looked at me with great seriousness. With them listening, Dickinson told me that the federal government challenged the accuracy of my story and wanted a retraction. Would I explain how I got the story? I did. Dickinson and the men questioned me. The visitors bore in. They insisted I should admit I was wrong when I wrote that the CIA had planned, paid for and directed the invasion. I said I couldn't do it because I had named and quoted my source and had attempted without success to get a response from the CIA and State Department. Dickinson told me I could leave and I did so, wondering what would happen next. I was relieved when nothing happened. The *Bulletin* did not run the requested retraction, and Boyle told me to forget about it.

*   *   *

Now I was slated to work closely with Dickinson. At his markup session, editors from the wire, city, sports, and business desks told Dickinson what news they had and suggested how it should be played in the paper, stressing the first three pages and the last page. Dickinson was very quick and decisive. He took a pencil and ruler and designed on a pink sheet of paper how he wanted the front page to look, producing a document called a dummy. He said what he wanted on pages two, three and the last pages. The editors put together a list of the headlines for subordinates to write. Dummy in hand, Cressman, as chief makeup editor, with me trailing, walked down a flight to the composing room where four large metal frames called chases sat on a metal table called a stone. Each of the four frames, or pages, under Cressman's charge had a compositor awaiting his orders.

I was responsible for a dozen or more pages partly filled with ads. Stories left over after Dickinson's dummy were given to me to fill empty spaces around the ads. The *Bulletin* had a practice of trying to touch every ad with a story. The *Bulletin* told advertisers that putting stories next to ads brought readers' eyes to the ads. I decided what stories went on what pages and what kind of headline they needed. As I decided, I used a phone on a pole to call the news editor upstairs. "Give me a 2-24 on crash," I would say, for example, for a two-column head at 24 picas for the story called, or slugged, crash. I might order a 4-head or a 5-head or a 7-head or a 9-head or a 12-head. It all went stunningly fast as pressure built to finish my pages—to "move them" along the multi-stepped process toward the line of modern presses in the adjacent building. As compositors placed the lines of lead where I directed, they left space for the headlines I ordered. I had as many as a dozen compositors waiting for my instructions. They belonged to the *Bulletin's* composing room union. I was management. I made the decisions. They carried them out. Most of them were wonderful men, on most days. But not every day. We usually got along just fine, especially since I knew what might happen if we didn't: they could "pie" type. This means they could drop it or scramble it in their hands—by accident, of course, since no compositor would admit to sabotaging the newspaper. Fixing "pied" type could take precious minutes at deadline.

My job was not only to keep the compositors hustling, but also to keep them happy. We talked about sports, my trip West, and my Army service, rarely of politics. Most compositors could talk about real military work since they had been in World War II. I frequently expressed admiration for their skill. I carefully avoided touching type, even when I could retrieve it from the typesetting machine. That was wise on my part. There was hardly a greater incentive for them to "pie" type than to have the makeup editor perform a task within the job description of the union guys. As I put my pages together, I made sure that the headlines rolling down the conveyor belt from upstairs and into type were attached to the right stories. I learned how to read type backward.

The challenge was to fill in completely the entire news "hole" around the ads, not a line of type less, not a line more. For me it meant trimming stories on the run, cutting out paragraphs when needed or adding words to sentences to make stories a line or two longer. It certainly wasn't the moment for fancy writing or editing.

Once in a while a big story broke between the time Dickinson drew the dummy and I locked up the pages. At such moments, Dickinson phoned Cressman and said he was sending down a story that he wanted substituted for another story, but he wanted the other story in the paper.

Cressman instructed a compositor to lift the first story and carry it down to me. Cressman yelled to me that I was getting a "must" story. I then decided what wasn't a "must" story, ordered it removed and replaced it with the "must" story. It forced me to throw out a story a reporter had written with loving care. When the paper hit the newsroom 45 minutes later, editors and reporters screamed at me for not running a story they considered far more important than the one I picked. They dared not scream at Dickinson. He authorized their paychecks.

Cressman and I worked together for the first edition, with a deadline of just before nine in the morning, and then again for a mid-morning edition and finally the main home delivery edition around one in the afternoon. Then Carl went home and I had the full makeup duty for the last three editions. On some days there was a lot of changing as Dickinson or the news editor ordered fresh stories onto page one and I found room for displaced stories back in the paper. Tension was often high, but I enjoyed it.

The most important afternoon edition was the four-star, so named because it had four red stars at the top right on page one. It could sell thousands of papers at newsstands in center city as workers poured out of offices after 5 p.m. and headed for the trolley car, subway, or Pennsylvania Railroad train. Most people rode on mass transit; few drove cars to work. The *Bulletin* regarded the four-star as a work of art, error-free, the reflection of fine minds on what people should spend commuting time and evenings reading. My father often came from work and said with pride, "I got a four-star tonight."

The timing of getting the four-star to the newsstands was critical. A few minutes delay could mean thousands of lost sales. A traffic jam on Market Street could be a major problem for the *Bulletin*. It lacked free run of the streets enjoyed by the morning *Inquirer* that shipped its papers by truck after midnight. For the four-star, an important job was to insert on page one a U.S. Treasury sum that the federal government announced at the end of the banking day. The Treasury sum that I was responsible for getting right and into the four-star was no trivial matter.

The final three digits in the Treasury number, as printed in the four-star, constituted the "number" for the day used by bookies to determine who among their customers had won. Bookmaking was a crime, of course, and here I was, a central, if unwitting, figure in the conspiracy. An editor in the financial news department got the Treasury number off the Associated Press wire. He sent it down to the composing

LAWRENCE M. O'ROURKE

room. The type came to me along with the original handwritten copy. It was my job to verify it before placing it into the paper. *Bulletin* editors impressed on me that while the *Bulletin's* number, even if incorrect, was accepted as the payoff number by the bookmaking industry, it would not be well for any of us to get it wrong. Someone in the bookie industry, and customers, would likely verify it, and, lo and behold, consider the consequences if we were incorrect. I was warned about a variety of scenarios. Might not a compositor have placed a bet with a bookie that day and adjusted the number to get himself a payoff? Indeed, might the makeup editor have stopped by his neighborhood bookie on the way to work? I didn't play the numbers, but I knew many bookies in West Philadelphia who did.

I put a lot of attention into getting the accurate number in the four-star.

*   *   *

From the newsroom, Selby occasionally squawked at me when I failed to include in the paper a story he favored.

Once he was relieved when I omitted a story he wanted. A rich and famous man died and his estate was revealed. Selby sent me a story for the four-star. He wanted it on page one. The news editor agreed and sent me instructions to put it at the bottom of the page under a two-column headline. The story was late getting from the newsroom to the typesetter, so it reached me with just minutes to spare before we had to move the pages to catch the commuters. Reading the story backward as the compositor slid it in the page one hole, I learned that the rich and famous decedent had willed his "historic grandfather's cock" to a family member. In the Philadelphia of 1962, that would have been a shocker. There was no time to reset the line of type. I ordered the story killed for the edition and substituted a story that had been previously deleted for space. When Selby saw what I had done, without waiting for an explanation, he charged into Dickinson's office, targeting my scalp. I was summoned—and fortunately for me, Dickinson said I had done right. The story would have gotten the *Bulletin* attention, but not the kind it valued. The story held until the next day when we detailed the decedent's estate with its historic grandfather's clock.

Selby and I had one very serious confrontation. One afternoon, I made a calculated decision that might have ended my job at the *Bulletin* if I guessed wrong. A few minutes before the four-star deadline, a correspondent in New Jersey called the city desk and said he heard from good sources that an airplane based at McGuire Air Force Base disappeared after takeoff. He said the plane had an atomic bomb on board.

Dickinson was not around, and it had been such a quiet afternoon that the news editor slipped out early, leaving Selby the top executive in the newsroom. Selby ordered me to hold the paper indefinitely until his reporters were able to assemble the story. I reminded him of my orders from Dickinson to move the pages on time. I realized the importance of the story. Also, I was aware of the possibility of thousands of missed customers and the return from newsstands of thousands of unsold newspapers. I also knew that if I kept the pages back, the *Bulletin* would have to pay overtime down the line. The compositors waited for my cue. The foreman pressed for my decision. I held on as long as I felt I could, and then ordered the pages moved—without the atomic bomb story.

In the newsroom, Selby went berserk. He had the entire staff working on the story. He stormed down the stairs and let me and everybody else know what he thought of me—not too much in a positive sense. I faced a sleepless night.

The imbroglio was big news at the paper. I had defied Selby. The next morning Dickinson called us into his office. The story had been a false alarm. There was no missing plane with an atomic bomb. Selby however said the issue was my defiance of him. He said that I wasn't paid to make that level of news judgment; he was. Dickinson made a futile attempt at mediation. He said I had to obey my newsroom superior, but that on this one I made the right decision. By my reckoning, it was a draw. Earl got over it quickly, as did I. But the notion someone had looked Selby in the eye and said no to him enhanced my reputation for toughness.

Within a year, Dickinson and Selby had a pitched battle. It ignited when Selby got into a struggle over placement of stories with one of Dickinson's top deputies, Mal Deans. It involved stories Selby wanted in the paper and how they were to be handled. The Selby-Deans row almost came to blows. I suspected that Dickinson welcomed the incident as a chance to dump Selby. Quit or be fired, Dickinson said. Selby quit. Before leaving the office, with class and dignity he went around the newsroom, shaking every hand, thanking all for giving their best to the *Bulletin*. However, few in the newsroom or Philadelphia politics seemed sorry to see Selby go. Earl and his wife Ann went to Europe for a spell, but could not stay away from the action. He went through a series of jobs, none as mighty as city editorship of the *Bulletin*. In 2000 he died at age 82, killed in a car crash in California. He was publisher of a computer magazine. He was driving to his home in Carmel from Las Vegas, where he had covered a story.

*   *   *

Earl was very much alive in the fall of 1962 when he called me into his office and said it was time for me to move from the makeup editor's job and return to reporting. I agreed. He complimented me on my work in the composing room and said it was an important step to my rapid advancement at the *Bulletin*. I was flattered.

But now, he said, he wanted me back on the nightside as a general assignment reporter and rewriteman. I readily accepted. I much preferred reporting and writing to the role of makeup editor. On the nightshift, I joined a superb crew. The *Bulletin* attracted talented young reporters, even if few remained long. Their departures were not surprising in view of their skills and the *Bulletin's* low wage scale. My salary was advanced to $65 a week.

On the nightside, the gifted Jack Morrison could take any story and make it sing. He was so good at turning stories into flowing prose that editors rarely let him out of the office, instead tossing at him the toughest stories to make readable. He did so with grace, accuracy, and gentleness. In daylight hours he wrote short stories. He would later join the *Philadelphia Daily News* where he frequently wrote long obits. They were works of art. Morrison's peeve was that he'd be in the middle of writing a tricky story when an editor told him to take an obituary. The editors wanted nightsiders to remember they were foot soldiers that could be sent into any battle.

Nightsider Anthony Day, a Harvard graduate and son of a Pulitzer Prize-winning editor at the *Baltimore Sun*, was not only a brilliant writer, but also a man of incredible depth and self-assurance. Tony famously won one of the pitched battles often waged at the decorous *Bulletin*. Until Tony fought it through, the *Bulletin* never used the word "rape." For years the *Bulletin* would not report on the crime. As time passed, it changed to say that a woman had been "assaulted." It was into the 1960s before the *Bulletin* acknowledged "sexual assault." Then one night Tony wrote that a woman had been "raped." He sent his story to the desk. An editor reminded Tony that no such word was permitted in the *Bulletin*. Tony was ready. He launched a strong argument on why the criminal act should get its rightful name. It was the next day, after a contentious conference of senior editors, that "rape" got into the *Bulletin*. There were complaints from readers, but Philadelphia and the *Bulletin* survived. The *Bulletin* never named a woman who was raped. I support that policy.

A few chairs from Tony Day on the nightside desk sat Lynn Ward, a graduate of Penn State University and resident of Malvern, a Philadelphia suburb. Lynn was a pioneer just by being there. The *Bulletin* was short on women reporters, except for the few who put together the Society pages, largely tidbits of gossip about the wealthy who lived on the Main Line or in Chestnut Hill. But Lynn proved that a woman could be a good reporter on every aspect of news. She was courageous as well, as she showed one night when she walked on a deserted path through Pennypack Park, site of several recent attacks on young women. Lynn was accompanied at a distance by a *Bulletin* photographer whose assignment, it appeared, was first to get the picture of Lynn being attacked, then to come to her rescue. To Lynn's disappointment as a reporter, but to the relief of her colleagues, she was not attacked. She wrote a fine story about the dark park. She regularly joined us on after-work forays to Chinatown where we discussed our stories, the *Bulletin*, and anything else that came to mind. Her wit and judgment were outstanding and soon Tony Day and Lynn married.

The nightside had a young reporter named Michael B. Sisak, 3rd, who brought enthusiasm and spirit to every assignment. He prodded editors for more and tougher stories, always wanting to learn. On New Year's Day in 1964, fire broke out in an abandoned warehouse called the Fretz Building in North Philadelphia. It was filled with paint and chemicals and quickly lit up the Philadelphia skyline. Mike was sent to the scene and walked closer to the blaze than safety and common sense would allow. Embers floated onto his winter jacket, and the soot and smoke darkened his face and hands while the heat burned them. He filled his notebook with impressions and wrote a lead that read like a memo to Selby: "A reporter walked though disaster last night." The *Bulletin* gave the story appropriate front-page play in big type, but, true to form, resisted his expense account entry to dry-clean his coat. Sisak later moved to *The New York Times* as a sports editor, but he wanted to be at the center of action. For years, he and his son, Michael, a reporter and photographer, worked the sidelines at Penn State football games.

I also covered the Fretz Building fire and chased down the owner. I persuaded him to talk. My interview with him on the contents of the building and the possible causes of the fire earned me a share of a Philadelphia Press Association award to the *Bulletin* staff.

The nightside had its share of eccentrics. Dick Cleveland kept snakes in his home and so it was appropriate that he left the *Bulletin* to do public relations for the Philadelphia Zoo. Tom Frayne lived in a Philadelphia house that once was the residence of Edgar Allen Poe. Frayne had an irrepressible wit and imagination. He favored wild shoes, including sandals in winter. He left to write on Fire Island. John Gordy was avuncular in his 20s, and I was seated next to him when he wrote a classic Gordy lead on a power failure: "The bright-as-day Vine Street underpass of the Schuylkill Expressway was dark-as-night this morning." Mary Ellen Gale had a penchant for precision, but she had bigger plans. She became a law professor in California and wrote eloquently of civil liberties. There was the fastidious Bob Brothers who one time went with us to a Chinatown restaurant and ordered a bologna sandwich. Dave Newhall, a Princeton graduate, was on the nightside, but he loved politics more than reporting. In 1976, Newhall managed the unsuccessful vice presidential campaign of Sen. Richard S. Schweiker, the Pennsylvania Republican tapped for that job by Ronald Reagan.

Of special memory from the *Bulletin* nightside was Myron "Mike" Waldman, who seemed to bleed every word from his typewriter. I couldn't sit close to him along the rewrite bank because he never stopped laughing or groaning as he struggled for the perfect way to tell the story. Once he felt he got it right, he showed it to other reporters. If I were less than wildly enthusiastic, Mike would interpret it as his personal failure. His face would reveal the agony of disappointment. Years later, Mike, then working in the Washington Bureau at *Newsday*, and I covered a story in Paris and we decided to visit the Folies Bergere. We filed our stories. Over dinner we talked about what we wrote. Over a splendid meal and a grand bottle of wine, Mike became agitated as he talked. I thought he had done a fine job and told him so. But, no, he said, he could have done it better, by changing word order, or putting in an additional fact or deleting a word here and there. He kept this up as we arrived at the Folies theater. Before the curtain went up, he called his office. He must have been thinking more about the story during the first act because he rushed after it to place another call to *Newsday*. This pattern continued throughout the evening. His colleagues said he never could let a story go without second-guessing. He was a wonderful interviewer and reporter. I was saddened when Mike, as a young man, died of cancer. I told the story of the Folies in the eulogy I delivered at his funeral.

Another unforgettable nightside character was Fred Hauptfuhrer, a tall gangly recent college graduate who was one of the most tenacious reporters I ever met. When Fred seized a story, there was no letting go. After he was assigned to write a story about the polluted Delaware River one night, he managed to find a new angle night after night, giving the river attention worthy of a Ph.D. thesis, but more copy than the editors wanted. Besides, when Fred was submerged in the story of the Delaware River, he wasn't available to write obituaries, crimes, fires, accidents and political events that were the main substance of nightside journalism. Fred later left the business, moved to London, and oversaw the restoration of the historic Asgill House overlooking the Thames. It was perfect for Fred and his love of detail.

One of Fred's techniques, or perhaps foibles, was asking "what?" after almost any words directed at him. It gave him time to ponder the answer. But it drove people mad. Leonard Murphy, then night city editor, sat fifteen feet from the line of reporters and often shouted out comments on stories or directions to head toward some event. Murphy was a busy man and he didn't long tolerate Hauptfuhrer's "what." I sat stunned one night when after a "what" from Hauptfuhrer, Murphy ripped into him, telling him that he better listen the first time or find another job. I was also there when Murphy confronted a politician who lied to him. "The next time I put your name in the *Bulletin* is when either you're arrested or dead," Murphy said.

My advice has always been don't lie, but especially don't lie to a reporter. This was verified when city editor Stanley Thompson told me to dig out information for the next edition on a fight that almost amounted to a riot on a boat that took passengers on a short cruise on the Delaware River between Philadelphia and Riverview Beach amusement park in South Jersey.

I called a man named Si, publicity agent for the cruise line. Si had many clients and he often brought stories to Thompson that served his client's interest. Si's bread and butter was getting stories in the *Bulletin*. Thompson often gave him a few inches and Si occasionally repaid with a genuine tip. To me, Si adamantly denied any trouble on the boat. I said the cops told me there was a big fight. Not true, said Si. "I've checked out that rumor and it isn't true. You got my word on that." I told Thompson and a minute later he was on the phone with Si. Again Si denied it vehemently. Meanwhile I heard from other cops who confirmed the fight. I wrote the story. Thompson had me listen to him call back Si. "Don't bother coming around any more with those stories you want us to put in the paper about your clients." Thompson said. "People who lie are not welcome in the *Bulletin's* newsroom." Si and his clients were *persona non grata* for months.

The practice on the Bulletin nightside was to work until all of us had our stories cleared by the copy editor and then head, often at 2 in the morning, to the South China Restaurant on Ninth Street where we talked over egg rolls, wonton soup and chicken fried rice for hours, sometimes to the first rays of sunlight. I thought of it as a graduate school seminar as I listened to Morrison, Day and others dissect their work of the evening.

I enjoyed visiting a public housing project in South Philadelphia for a page one story about children growing vegetables in a garden in a dumpsite. What fun it was when I interviewed Richard Rodgers and Oscar Hammerstein as they were honored by the Poor Richard Club. Of sadder memory are those times when I was sent to the home of a victim of an accident or crime to get the "house-end," the biography and photograph that illustrated the tragic loss of another life, often one as young as myself. On one such story, I was literally thrown off the front step and told I would suffer vague but distinctly unpleasant consequences if I returned. Once I interviewed a woman who had been in an accident on her way to work and learned she was a hooker.

Perhaps it is nostalgia, but I have found that those of us who boot camped our newspaper careers on the *Bulletin's* nightside cherish every memory. My nightside work ended early in 1963 when Selby again said it was time for a change.

* * *

My new assignment, he said, was to cover the Philadelphia public schools.

The Philadelphia public school system was de facto racially segregated. Thousands of children were victims of bias and indifference. Too many people didn't even think about public schools. The overwhelming majority of Catholic parents made significant financial sacrifices to send their children to outstanding parochial schools. They paid for this choice by contributions to the weekly collection basket and through other fundraising techniques Catholic schools employed to keep themselves afloat, such as Bingo, lotteries, carnivals, and candy sales. Beyond the working-class Catholics, wealthy families in other faiths sent their kids to the many excellent private schools in the area.

Later, I was pleased that my children attended quality public schools. The country's first domestic priority is education of its people. Access to quality public education for all is the keystone of a decent, caring society. Parents have the primary obligation for their children's education, and this might lead them to pick a religious based-school for their children. They often make financial sacrifices and they are to be respected. Later, I supported public education in many opinion columns I wrote in *The Philadelphia Bulletin*, as I argued for adequate spending at all levels of government to build a high-quality public school system.

When he called me into his office, Selby didn't ask my opinion on public and private schools. He wanted me to cover the public school system for the *Bulletin*. Peter Binzen was the *Bulletin's* education writer. He was a brilliant reporter. Peter built the education beat when he returned from a Nieman Fellowship at Harvard. Up until then, the *Bulletin* had relied heavily on news releases from the public school superintendent's office at 21st and Benjamin Franklin Parkway. A *Bulletin* reporter attended Board of Education meetings, but little happened there that was newsworthy. The board and superintendent met behind closed doors prior to the public meeting and smoothed out any differences they might have. Binzen set out to break that cozy deal. He developed sources inside the system and listened to critics outside it.

But now Binzen wanted to move beyond the public schools beat to stories about higher education and urban issues. With its wonderful range of outstanding universities and colleges, Philadelphia was a gold mine of creative thinking about problems facing the city and the world. Binzen had in mind a new beat about the economic health of the city and the region that focused not only on politics and public services, but also on the business community that generated jobs and revenue for those services. Binzen was a visionary for what newspapers can and should be. He later came to national prominence by authoring a book with Joseph R. Daughen, "The Wreck of the Penn Central."

On taking over Binzen's beat, my approach to covering the public school system began by asking officials to get me fully apprised of what they were doing and considering. I wanted to give my readers the whole

LAWRENCE M. O'ROURKE

story, not just what school officials wanted published after they had ironed out the wrinkles. I told them that being new to the beat I needed to ask many questions of school officials, including the superintendent Allen H. Wetter, his top assistants, and school board members. Wetter, his assistant said, was too busy to speak to the press.

As for complaints about racial discrimination, I was told that these were matters in the hands of the school system's lawyers and therefore not to be discussed by the superintendent and his staff. When I approached J. Harry LaBrum, the school board president and a prominent lawyer in Philadelphia, he graciously brushed me off, suggesting that the issues I raised were best dealt with beyond closed doors. Nobody, it seemed, was ready to swing open the door to me as the *Bulletin* reporter.

So I took a new approach. If the school board wouldn't talk, the plaintiffs would. And their response when I asked was, are you really going to put our position in the *Bulletin*? Their position had not previously received much ink. Black leaders were used to being patronized by the Philadelphia press as a whole. I made contact with black ministers on the frontline of battles to improve neighborhood schools. I made frequent visits to the headquarters of the Philadelphia Federation of Teachers (AFL-CIO), the main union representing Philadelphia's 11,000 teachers. I learned about problems inside schools from teachers and a few principals who would talk to me only after I promised I would not name them. Many were terrified of being fired if they said anything contrary to school board policy or were disclosed as sources for information the system wanted to keep secret. My practice was to gather information from whatever sources might be informed and helpful, and then carefully check it out with school authorities. The authorities understood that I was going to print what I had learned, if I regarded it as reliable, with or without the approval of the system's officialdom. "Here's what I have. What do you have to say about this?" I inquired.

Selby was enthusiastic about my approach and my stories. The *Bulletin* ran most of my stories on page one. The school system wasn't happy because I was reporting information about troubled schools that was quite unflattering to the system leaders. Those leaders complained to Selby, saying I was stirring up trouble. He told them bluntly that I was the reporter on the beat and they should deal with me. School officials went to the *Bulletin's* publisher. He said it was a newsroom matter and as far as he was concerned, the test was whether O'Rourke was accurate, not whether he was sympathetic to the school board. I was grateful and proud of the *Bulletin*.

The new mantra of the school board and the superintendent, after years of dealing with a docile press, was that I was unfairly presenting only the dark side of the story. I pointed out that I gave them a chance to respond, but they balked. I said I was always open to report stories they proposed. School executives wanted it told their way or no way.

David Horowitz, the assistant superintendent whose main job seemed to be building roadblocks to reporters, denied that the Philadelphia public schools were racially segregated. David and I talked several times a day. He said the school system went to extraordinary lengths to give special education to black children—they were usually called Negro children in that era. He said teachers of black youngsters got special training and the system made sure that there were sufficient books at the right level for the students. Those were changes recently initiated. Horowitz gave me numbers to support his contention that the system poured money and effort into remedial education in schools with the poorest families.

I'd like to visit one of those schools, I told Horowitz. But reporters aren't allowed to wander around schools, he said. I don't want to wander around, just sit quietly in the back of a classroom for a few days to see the class in operation, I said. But there's no teacher or principal that would allow a reporter in the classroom, David said. Suppose I find such a principal and a teacher, I countered. Working through the unions, I came up with several willing teachers, and we finally settled on a classroom I could visit.

Thus began my visit to a public school in North Philadelphia where the teacher, a young white woman, faced about 25 ten-and eleven-year-old black students. Test records showed that most of them were behind the city average in reading skills. The children behaved well as the teacher clearly poured her heart and soul into teaching them. While many youngsters stumbled over simple words, a few were advanced in reading. How difficult it must be, I thought, to deal with such diversity in achievement levels. I was honored when the teacher asked me to read stories to some children while she worked with slower learners. The students having trouble clearly tried and were obviously upset at their lack of progress. The teacher had a teddy bear in the classroom and when a child seemed to be about to crack, she gave the child the teddy bear to hold. It seemed to help a bit.

After a few days, I had an interesting story to tell. The teacher allowed a *Bulletin* photographer in the classroom. My story led with the teacher, her hard work, and her effort to teach reading. I included information from the school board about its special efforts to improve reading skills in the city's poorest neighborhoods. It was an accurate and interesting story. My story included the teddy bear angle and was illustrated by a picture of a child holding a teddy bear.

Officials in the Board of Education headquarters were furious with my story and the picture. They complained to Selby that I trivialized and distorted the story and the serious work of teaching children how to read by putting in the Teddy Bear reference and emphasizing that the school did not have enough books in the classroom for the children, that the children were not permitted to carry books home, and that they never read at home. Selby, complimenting me on the story, told the school officials that my story and the picture let our readers know the difficulty schools had in teaching children to read and the efforts being made to address the problem. I felt that the school superintendent and his aides could use a teddy bear to ease their discomfort, but the upshot was that the school system said I was not welcome to visit additional public schools.

Occasionally I managed to get away from the public schools to write about higher education. I interviewed the president of LaSalle College, Christian Brother Daniel Bernian, about new directions for his college. An innovator on many fronts, Bernian introduced lay vice presidents and created a faculty senate. Discussing the role of Catholic colleges and their teaching mission, I asked him about LaSalle's practice in teaching Catholic doctrine. I have never forgotten his reply. He said that LaSalle taught Catholic doctrine just as it taught any other curriculum entry—as an academic subject—where informed critical thinking was developed. "I figure that if at some point in the course, generally in the sophomore year, if a student doesn't ask himself why he is a Catholic, even having doubts about that choice, the course has failed," Bernian said. He added that this approach actually strengthened the religious faith of LaSalle's students, most of them Catholic. The story shocked many Catholics who said LaSalle was not doing its job properly in instilling Catholic values in it students, but Bernian told me later I had accurately reported his view.

I went to New York City to compare its efforts against Philadelphia's. I wrote that New York put in a much greater effort, particularly in the all-black schools. I concluded that the only solution in Philadelphia was to acknowledge that the public school system was racially segregated, as plaintiffs in a lawsuit claimed, and to adjust distribution of resources. Such adjustments would require extra money—a sore point with taxpayers. In view of the history and reluctance of current school system leaders to change, desegregation would require a new philosophy and leadership at the top.

I gave space in the *Bulletin* to a previously largely ignored group—advocates for racial integration and compensatory help to black youngsters. I interviewed these advocates, including Cecil B. Moore, president of the Philadelphia chapter of the National Association for the Advancement of Colored People. Moore was not accustomed to be taken seriously by the city's mainstream press, including the *Bulletin*. He occasionally led protest marches against the school board and was considered a rabble-rouser. It's true that Moore, like Al Sharpton several decades later, reached on occasion for outlandish things to say. His statements may have seemed to him as clever sound bites, but when printed, they backfired. I approached Moore not looking for soundbites, but for reasoned analysis of what he and his activists wanted. I found that when approached on that basis, Moore and the black ministers were happy to drop one-liners in favor of more substantive discussions.

Serving as the *Bulletin's* reporter on schools got me to interview two of the nation's great lawyers, William T. Coleman, Jr. and A. Leon Higginbotham, Jr. Coleman was the major author of the brief in the landmark 1954 Brown v. Board of Education school desegregation case. In later years, I interviewed him frequently in a different capacity—as Secretary of Transportation during the Ford Administration. Higginbotham, president of the Philadelphia chapter of the NAACP from 1960 to 1962, had a distinguished career, as the first African-American to serve as commissioner of a U.S. regulatory agency, as vice chairman of the Kerner Commission, and as a federal trial and appeals court judge. With Coleman and Higginbotham as counsel for the plaintiffs, the Philadelphia school board held a weak hand.

I gradually began to knock down the wall of silence about the low state of Philadelphia's public schools. Through leaks, I learned what was said behind closed doors of the boardroom and I put it in the paper. It didn't take long before the battle between the black community and the public school system became the hottest topic in Philadelphia politics.

LAWRENCE M. O'ROURKE

Readers wrote the *Bulletin* that I was overly sympathetic to black people. I heard wisecracks from reporters in the *Bulletin's* newsroom that I was the reporter on the black beat, not the school beat. Selby and Dickinson were enthusiastic about my stories.

It was on a fall afternoon that I received a phone call from a federal judge familiar with the lawsuit brought by black activists to declare the schools segregated and in need of remedy. The judge said he had been reading my stories and wanted to meet me, but only on an off-the-record basis. Not a word could be said to anyone, including my bosses, about our meeting, he said. I agreed. I went to his center-city home and we chatted agreeably. He insisted several times that our conversation was off the record and I acknowledged that. We turned to the subject of the litigation and he suggested that the court was reluctant to rule that the school system was racially segregated.

Rather than such a ruling that would plunge the court into the maelstrom of running the Philadelphia public schools and increase racial tension in the city, he said that the parties should negotiate a settlement. He said he felt that the civil rights organizations and ministers who were spearheading the lawsuit would settle for less than their demands, but that the Board of Education held out against concessions.

If only he could tell me what the deal would look like, he said. But of course, he said, he couldn't.

Now he said it was time to have a drink and view the sunset. He said we could go onto his balcony. I could join him or not. Oh, by the way, he said, the proposed settlement is in those papers on my table. He repeated that he could not show them to me. But he was going outside for 45 minutes or so. I could join him or let myself out. I decided to let myself out, but not before I rustled through the papers on his table and found the terms of the proposed settlement. I never wrote in my notebook quite so fast. I let myself out.

And there across the top of the front page of the *Bulletin* the next morning was my story about the deal that could be cut to end the racial confrontation over the Philadelphia public schools, if only the school board would bend a bit.

There was an open-to-the-press school board meeting that afternoon and my story was front and center. Reporters for other newspapers and television and radio scrambled to confirm my story. It may have been the most covered school board meeting to date in Philadelphia history. The board seemed unsure of what to do and refused to release either the proposed settlement or its own position. So I got another day with the story, adding details I omitted from the first story. The school board soon made its documents public.

I felt honored as a reporter when participants in this ruckus, including Horowitz, school board members Robert Williams and Elizabeth Greenfield, and NAACP attorney Isaiah Crippens told me that the *Bulletin's* publication of the proposed accord broke the dam and cleared the way to a new era in public education in Philadelphia. Soon after my story broke, the school board and NAACP declared an agreement to end overcrowding in several schools and to close part-time schools as first steps to end de facto segregation.

Crediting my stories doesn't belong to me as much as the *Bulletin* that gave me the beat and stuck by me through many battles. But I'm proud after a career in journalism that I can point to that set of stories that had a big impact on the city. It was proof of the power of the press to publish information vital to decisions affecting public policy. Reporting significant local matters should be the lifeblood of American newspapers.

The deal that I helped promote by no means brought an end to racial strife or the establishment of high quality in Philadelphia public schools. Former Philadelphia Mayor Richardson Dilworth replaced LaBrum as school board president. Mark Shedd succeeded Wetter as superintendent. Legal battles continued for decades, racial tension grew, de facto segregation prevailed and worsened, and the city's public schools steadily slipped.

*　　*　　*

But I wasn't around to chronicle the story of the Philadelphia public schools for readers of *The Philadelphia Bulletin*. I had a new beat with a new set of controversial choices, closed doors and secret dealings—in the nation's capital.

CHAPTER 7

A Boy on the Bus

I WAS 25 YEARS old when I arrived in Washington in January 1964 to cover government and politics for *The Philadelphia Bulletin*, the nation's largest broadsheet evening newspaper at the high-water mark of American print journalism. I wasn't half the age of the men I held as role models in American journalism. In 1964, there were few women in top-of-the-line jobs in the print press in Washington. Though I was a new kid on the block, I was confident I could compete with renowned journalists. However, I hid my confidence, or was it arrogance? I wanted them to teach me how to be a successful Washington correspondent. The best way for me was to watch and learn.

As an evening newspaper, *Bulletin* deadlines ranged from about 8.30 in the morning to 5 in the afternoon. The *Bulletin* wanted the latest news, lean and fast. In the Washington Bureau, I started on the local beat, covering Pennsylvania, New Jersey and Delaware delegations in Congress and news in Washington about those states. I expanded my assignment as quickly as I could from local to national and international.

My job meant a lot of breaking news that made it impractical to type stories and send them by telegraph. I dictated breaking news during the day from phone booths on Capitol Hill and in federal buildings to a rewriteman in Philadelphia. There was little margin for error since the *Bulletin* usually put my breaking stories into print and into the paper quicker than they could get them from the wire services. At day's end, I wrote overnight stories that included news and analysis. For those I had the luxury of a typewriter, time to reflect, and more space to explain the meaning of the facts I was reporting. When I knew something big would happen the next day, but lacked details, I wrote an overnight "holding story" with as much information as I could gather, creating space for the breaking news. My overnight stories often lasted in original form only one edition as events overtook them. Working for the *Bulletin* meant filing as many as six new stories or new leads a day. I was in the paper almost every day.

As I settled in at the *Bulletin's* office in Suite 1296 in the National Press Building in downtown Washington, I had no idea how exciting 1964 would be in learning about federal government and politics at the highest level, and becoming a close—sometimes an inside—observer of how the nation was managed. Lyndon Johnson was in the White House and there was excitement in Washington as he promised a progressive agenda of civil rights, urban renewal, an end to poverty, better education and health care, and more attention to natural beauty. On top of that, he promised to cut taxes and improve relations with the Soviet Union. Few asked how the nation could afford all this, or paid much attention to slowly worsening reports from the faraway country of Vietnam.

I plunged into stories experienced by few young reporters. I spent much of the year on the road, traveling the country with Johnson, Republican presidential nominee Barry Goldwater, Republican vice presidential nominee William E. Miller, Democratic vice presidential nominee Hubert H. Humphrey, and with Pennsylvania Gov. William Scranton who futilely tried to rip the GOP's White House nomination from Goldwater.

I covered historic events on Capitol Hill, including the debate that led to passage of the Civil Rights Act, arguably the most contentious and significant domestic measure in U.S. history. I covered congressional approval of a tax cut bill of just over $11 billion, a tidy sum in those days. Today we would scoff at such a sum.

Covering the Civil Rights Act debate was among the most memorable experiences of my Washington career. It got me regularly, sometimes daily, into the offices of a dozen key senators and allowed me to compete with great reporters. Nearly five decades later, I'm proud of my stories. They were accurate and fair, even as my enthusiasm for the civil rights movement jumps from the yellowed *Bulletin* clippings.

At the signing ceremony in the White House East Room on July 2, 1964, Johnson beckoned to leaders of Congress and reporters to stand near him as he signed the legislation. I was one of the invited reporters. Johnson used many pens and he handed them out, one to Humphrey, and one to Speaker of the House John W. McCormack of Massachusetts. And he gave me one. I have it framed on the wall in my office, with a photograph of me standing by McCormack and peering at the new law on LBJ's desk. Of my political memorabilia, none gives me more pride than that pen.

LAWRENCE M. O'ROURKE

*   *   *

Hours after the signing, I made my first trip as a White House correspondent to Austin, Texas, to cover Johnson on the ranch. I made 36 such journeys throughout LBJ's administration. I never tired of it.

White House correspondents covering presidents traveled in high style. We flew in a chartered jet, often a Pan American Airways 707. The White House employed a press travel staff that arranged flights and billing. I forwarded my bills to the *Bulletin's* main office. It paid promptly. The White House travel office tried to come out even—not to make a profit or sustain a loss for the government.

There was a pecking order aboard the charter. First-class seats usually went to newspaper, TV and radio correspondents. I enjoyed the luxury. Economy-class seats were given over to still photographers and TV crews and Secret Service agents. It was not discrimination but function that dictated seating. Correspondents needed space during flights to work on their portable typewriters (I, like most, carried an Olivetti before the electronic age when most of us began toting Radio Shacks that we called Trash 80s.) Photographers and film and sound crews hauled much more equipment, especially before the advent of minicams. Cameras and sound recording boxes and batteries were large, heavy and stowed on seats. Secret Service agents wanted to sit together and to get in and out of the plane fast.

On presidential trips, we watched Air Force One leave and then rushed onto our charter. We passed the presidential plane during the flight and landed earlier, in time to record the president's landing and greeting. This worked well on long flights when the press charter had many miles and time to pass Air Force One. It didn't work so well on flights of an hour or less. That often required Air Force One to circle to give the press time to set up. Presidents want to be photographed.

Service on the press charter was first-class. We were the pampered press. Cabin attendants had hot or cold towels, and food and drink ready so that the minute we sat down we could eat or write. The bar was open and some reporters drank too much. I skipped alcohol until the final flight of the day after my deadline. But on long flights, such as across an ocean or a continent, or the two-hour-50-minute flight from Andrews Air Force Base to Texas, I would usually have a drink. I preferred bourbon and water before I discovered Scotch and soda. I took every opportunity to have a Baileys Irish Cream on the rocks. Or maybe two over the Atlantic. On longer flights meals were multicourse, served on plates with real silverware. We had more cabin attendants (called stewards and stewardesses in those days) than did commercial flights.

One thrill of White House chartered travel five decades ago was the open cockpit door. From first-class, we could see the crew in action. We had an open invitation to ride in the cockpit. I did it many a time. I put on earphones and listened to the pilot-tower chatter. The pilots patiently explained where we were, how much fuel we consumed and still had to burn, and anything else we wanted to know. I remember seeing big cloud formations ahead and watching pilots maneuver around them. I left the cockpit when it was time to prepare for arrival and to let the pilots do their jobs in tranquility.

As much fun as charter flights were, it was great to ride aboard Air Force One, something I did numerous times. The back of Air Force One had seats for the press pool. The pool included two wire-service reporters, and a reporter each for newspapers, magazines, television and radio, as well as a photographer, cameraman and soundman. We were there primarily to report if the president came back and made news. As Air Force One pooler, I talked with LBJ, Nixon, Ford, Carter, Reagan, the first George Bush and Clinton. The president came into the press section with his press secretary and Secret Service agent. Sometimes we bantered. Sometimes the president made news. When I was the newspaper reporter on board, I wrote a pool report for reproduction aboard Air Force One and distribution to reporters on the ground the minute the Air Force One pool correspondent touched the tarmac. I had to get it right because what I said in the pool report quickly went around the world.

* * *

The most fun in 1964 was covering the vice presidential campaigns of Hubert Humphrey and Bill Miller during which I discovered that their public personas were mirror opposites of their private demeanors.

While I shared Humphrey's liberal politics and enjoyed watching him on the political stump, the closer I got to him, the less I liked him. I saw Humphrey's bad temper more than once. One time I was talking to a Humphrey aide when Humphrey stormed in. He tore into the aide for a transgression that I considered minor. In blue language that would have served the needs of a drill sergeant, Humphrey blistered the aide who

LAWRENCE M. O'ROURKE

stood at attention during the dressing down. From that aide and others, I learned how tough it was to work for Humphrey. Humphrey needed a two-hour rest period in the afternoon. He might nap or just use the time to collect his thoughts. It wasn't usually a problem in Washington. He slipped into his small office in the Capitol and locked the door. Aboard the campaign plane Humphrey curled up on a row of seats and the staff isolated him with blankets. They put together a schedule that provided a mid-afternoon break. A doctor was always along to monitor Humphrey's health and need for rest.

Despite the senator's short temper, Humphrey's aides wanted to work for him. He was their champion in great causes. I wondered if that's the way it is with great public figures. LBJ was manipulative. Kennedy, Nixon and Clinton worked scores of aides and volunteers on long hours with minimal compensation.

I heard this story about Humphrey from one of his aides. "One time I got a call from the White House that somebody, maybe it was the president, needed to speak to the senator right away," the aide told me. "I woke the senator up from his nap and he was an angry bear. He was ready to tear me apart. He frightened me, but he was calm enough by the time he made the call back to the White House. But I never want to do that again."

During a 45-minute conversation I had in 1964 with Humphrey on a helicopter ride from Washington to central New Jersey for a Humphrey campaign appearance, I asked him about his private life. While he was evasive about his temper, he acknowledged differences between his private personality and public identification. "I'm on a campaign of happiness," Humphrey said. "But I'm not naturally as upbeat as I appear in public." He acknowledged he was "full of steam and tension" much of the time.

For an experienced public speaker, he was insecure and undisciplined. I asked Humphrey about his upbeat public-speaking style. "It takes a real effort every time I make a speech," he said. "I get an inner strength from audiences. I need it." He frequently lost control of himself during speeches, seemingly unaware of how long he had gone on as if he was determined to talk until everyone in the room agreed with him. Aides signaled that it was time to wrap it up. He'd be late for the next appointment, a habitual problem during the campaign when he'd disrupt the daily schedule and keep crowds waiting for hours. But Humphrey ignored his aides' pleas. If Muriel Humphrey was by her husband on stage, the staff gestured to her to whisper to him or tug his jacket. After speeches, Humphrey was so excited he had to be pulled from platforms. But once out of public view, he sagged as if his energy had burned away.

As a self-proclaimed candidate of happiness and joy while in public view, Humphrey lived in fear during the campaign—fear that he would say or do something that would irritate Johnson. Humphrey was on a short leash. The LBJ team told Humphrey where to go and what to say. Spontaneity was not only discouraged, it was forbidden. Humphrey chaffed under the restrictions, but he even more feared getting chewed out by Johnson. The campaign built a protective wall around Humphrey.

I had two run-ins with Humphrey's staff that marked me as uncooperative and not to be favored.

The first came during a Humphrey visit to his childhood haunts in South Dakota. In Doland, in his old high school, he sat in the desk he said he used. An Associated Press photographer captured the moment—Humphrey with a broad smile, Muriel with her pocketbook and tiny hat standing by his side, and current school principal Irving Herther looking on. It was a happy scene, if marred by me, a few paces behind Humphrey with an unexpressive face writing in my notebook. The *Bulletin* and other papers ran the photo.

While my presence in the picture irritated the Humphrey staff, what I wrote ticked them off even more. I talked outside the classroom to Humphrey's brother, Ralph, a pharmacist, and a few of Humphrey's classmates. They told me that Hubert Horatio Humphrey's schoolboy nickname was "Pinky." It was too close to "Pinko" for the comfort of Humphrey strategists. In the context of the campaign and the era, the word "Pinko" had a bad connotation. After World War II when Red-baiting Sen. Joseph McCarthy of Wisconsin had his meteoric ride across the political sky, to be a "Pinko" was a catch phrase for sympathy to Communism.

Though he was a liberal who fought Communism in his rise to political prominence, Humphrey was nonetheless under attack in the campaign as too far to the left to be given the office a heartbeat away from the presidency. So when Humphrey's aides realized that I learned Humphrey's boyhood nickname and surmised—correctly—that I would include it in my profile of the vice presidential candidate, they tried to talk me out of using the nickname. Their reasons were many: it was a silly childhood name meaning nothing, certainly nothing political, and

I had gotten it from people who may have had memory lapses or didn't know I was a reporter, or perhaps I misunderstood, and what was the point of using such an inflammatory word.

The pressure backfired, as they should have realized. I darned well was determined to get "Pinky" into my story, and so I did. As it turned out, nothing came of it. Fear that Miller and other GOP advocates might start calling him Pinky never materialized. The pique of Humphrey aides slipped away, as it did after another incident during a Humphrey visit to the LBJ ranch.

I was on the lawn of LBJ's spread outside Johnson City, Texas, while the president and his vice presidential choice discussed campaign strategy inside the farmhouse. After the two men emerged to have pictures taken and to say a few words, Johnson invited Humphrey to join him for a walk. Humphrey was a few feet behind the president and I was next to Humphrey when he stepped into a pile of animal manure, no doubt deposited by LBJ's cattle. Humphrey looked at his brown-smeared shoes and quipped, "I'm standing on the Republican platform." Johnson heard and doubled over in laughter. I laughed while jotting Humphrey's words into my notebook.

I thought it was a funny line, certainly worth quoting in my story. But Humphrey's aides didn't agree. While I was writing my story, a couple of them asked me not to use the line, asserting among other things that it was off the record. I brushed off that nonsense. To me the only way a politician can put something off the record is to ask in advance and have my agreement. I habitually made it clear that I would consider anything said to me or in my hearing to be on the record unless otherwise agreed, and I made clear that when I consented, I did it grudgingly.

So I included the quote in my story and the *Bulletin* printed it. Bill Townshend, the wire editor, said there was no hesitation by editors in Philadelphia and that only a few readers complained. But what I had done was make it clear to Humphrey and his staff that I was a reporter doing my job fairly and objectively, not a Humphrey loyalist.

*   *   *

Traveling with Bill Miller was more fun than traveling with Humphrey, though I regarded many Miller ideas as absurd. I kept my views out of my news stories and reported the Miller campaign straight, which wasn't easy in view of Miller's cynicism.

Unlike Humphrey who looked inevitable as vice president, Miller had little to lose. Miller believed that most reporters liked Humphrey's politics and ridiculed his and Goldwater's viewpoints. Miller knew that most reporters in his plane or bus thought very little of him as a potential vice president. Miller's charm for reporters, however, rested in his evident conviction that he never thought he would be vice president or that the top of the GOP ticket, Sen. Barry Goldwater of Arizona, had a real shot at the White House.

Miller told me privately that he was stunned to be picked. After Goldwater won the nomination in the GOP convention in San Francisco, Miller recited to me, "Barry called me and said, 'Bill, it's going to be a long and lonely road. Do you want to join me?'" Miller accepted instantly, knowing that his job, as he put it, was "to give Johnson hell."

Miller had been chairman of the Republican National Committee and was a master at political hyperbole. He understood polling numbers better than almost anyone. He knew, he told me, that he and Goldwater were the "longest of long shots." Their strongest hope was for a Johnson mistake and a divide between Johnson and Kennedy liberals who disliked LBJ. Goldwater said he picked Miller because Miller "drove Johnson nuts." Miller did his best to goad LBJ into a mistake, but I saw no evidence that Miller was even a minor irritation to LBJ. In potential campaign problems, what Humphrey said and did was far more important to Johnson than anything said or done by Miller or Goldwater.

Miller liked risks and on one trip he put us all at risk. Flying out of Rapid City, South Dakota, Miller told the pilot to take us to Mount Rushmore. Miller joked that he wanted to see the spot for Goldwater. We flew over the Black Hills to the mountainside with busts of Washington, Jefferson, Lincoln, and Teddy Roosevelt carved in the granite. Miller came on the speaker system, "Let's take a closer look." The plane made two passes close to the mountain to give those on both sides a good view. It was as near as I ever wanted to be to Mount Rushmore. To me, it seemed there was very little space between the tip of the airplane wing and the presidential noses.

On the stump Miller delivered a message dictated to him by the conservative Goldwater camp that Miller, astute politician that he was, recognized as politically disastrous. As a congressman from northwestern New York, Miller, though more comfortable in the country club than with blue-collared workers, understood the need for government services for the unemployed, poor and elderly. Before one speech, he said off the record that I should be alert because he was about to deliver a message that would sink Goldwater and himself even lower in the polls, if that were possible.

Miller's new message came as Johnson and the Democrats talked up a plan to create a government health insurance plan for the elderly. (It became established in 1965 as Medicare.) On a campaign stop, Miller aggressively denounced the idea of Medicare as socialized medicine and an affront to the dignity of the elderly. Miller said that Goldwater needed to throw red meat rhetoric to hard-core GOP conservatives and had delegated the job to Miller. Miller pointed out, privately, then and on other occasions that LBJ and Humphrey were rolling to a landslide victory. Goldwater and Miller had to first solidify their base if they hoped for a reasonable showing at the polls in November. Despite their best efforts, they never got there.

On several occasions on the plane, Miller, playing bridge with reporters, wisecracked that he was about to scare away more voters with his next pitch. Miller made clear that all conversation over bridge was off the record.

Miller, like Humphrey, was a contradiction. Privately, Miller was funny, loose and charming. On the stump, he was a mean-spirited attack dog. In contrast, the in-private tart and reclusive Humphrey was a bundle of joy on the stump.

*   *   *

Beyond daily stories, I wrote a three-part series contrasting Humphrey and Miller. Reading those stories a half-century later, I see how I imposed rules on myself that protected each candidate. I wrote of the public men, not the private men. I scrupulously followed off-the-record rules. The *Bulletin's* style was to avoid personality and to attribute most everything I wrote. If I got to do it over again, I'd put much more emphasis on personality. The *Bulletin* gave my Humphrey-Miller stories big play on the front page.

The rules of campaign access would change rapidly after 1964. By the time I covered the presidential campaigns of Humphrey and Richard M. Nixon in 1968, there was virtually no private time with the candidates and few leaks from their staffs. By 1968 rarely would candidates come from the front of the plane to the press section. Nor would we be invited forward very often. By 1968, casual off-the-record access we enjoyed in 1964 may have disappeared forever.

*　　*　　*

Off-the-record conversations were valuable to me as a reporter because they gave me a glance at the personality and private thoughts of the candidate. I believe that in voting for president, we should put judgment at the top of the criteria list. We don't know what crucial decisions the occupant of the Oval Office might be called to make. I think voters are better served when reporters know candidates better. Now more than when I first hit the presidential campaign trails, campaigns are more the work of media manipulators. Politics and campaigns have become bitter, abetted by a press that thrives on controversy. There is less understanding of what candidates would do as officeholders.

I regard myself as lucky to have arrived in Washington in the golden age of American print journalism. Never before had so many print journalists had such access to politicians, channels to dispense their stories, and resources to cover the news. A combination of factors put Washington at the center of public interest and concern. John Kennedy's personality and political skills encouraged the presence of television in every living room. In turn, the power of TV and the exposure it offered politicians enhanced the ability of print—newspapers and magazines—to capitalize on burgeoning public interest in the personalities of Washington. Personality journalism was born and here to stay.

It wasn't entirely clear when I arrived in Washington that the politicians had opened their doors to television in the hope of manipulating it, as Kennedy did, for personal advantage, and that the print press had walked in right behind the cameras. But I knew that television made politicians larger than life.

The new emphasis on images worked against print journalists. Newspapers lost to the power of television to project into every home 24/7 without demanding much effort from viewers. I did not foresee in 1964 that television would steadily expand its influence and that politicians would increasingly see television with sound bites as far more important to their careers than journalists with pens asking questions.

Starting in 1964, I would be eyewitness to the decline of print journalism and the rise of the electronic media, though I did not anticipate the Internet, bloggers, tweeters, talk radio, 24-hour television, and technological breakthroughs that left us pencil scribes in the dust and changed American journalism forever.

*   *   *

As much as I enjoyed national political coverage, I was responsible to *Bulletin* readers in 1964 for Philadelphia area news in Washington.

My boss was Robert Roth, the *Bulletin's* Washington bureau chief. Roth was a respected Washington correspondent. At age 64, he had many years experience traveling with presidents around the globe, picking off top stories in the capital, and writing analysis and opinion columns. Politically, he was in the *Bulletin* mold—an advocate of honest progressive government, but subdued in style and argument. He advanced his views by raising questions, not by offering solutions. Bob wrote in the "on the one hand this, on the other hand that" vernacular that was gradually losing out to advocacy journalism. Roth, a man of sound judgment, was fading to flashier competitors.

Bob made clear to me—pleasantly because Roth was nothing but pleasant—that I was welcome in his bureau, but my success or failure would be my own. He did not intend to mentor or edit me. As it turned out, I had few conversations with Roth during 1964. He gave me full latitude to do my job the way I thought it needed to be done.

Roth introduced me to the office manager, Grace Andrews, a prim and proper lady who let me know that she would tolerate me graciously if I made no demands on her and let her attend to Roth's wishes. She opened Roth's mail, smoothed it and laid it neatly on his desk. Mine she left unopened on her desk until I gathered it and took it to my office. She liked to be addressed as Miss Andrews and always called Roth Mr. Roth. I made it clear that I was Larry, but she rarely used my name.

I began the local beat by attempting to meet the Philadelphia region's members of Congress. That was easy with the senators. Both Democratic Sen. Joseph S. Clark and Republican Hugh Scott were residents of Philadelphia who read the *Bulletin* as their hometown paper and wanted to be in it. But they also knew me from my days covering politics and education in Philadelphia. Clark was Philadelphia's mayor before he went to Washington. One of the New Jersey senators was Republican Clifford P. Case. Clark, Scott and Case invited me to contact them and their staffs to gather and interpret information. The other New Jersey senator, Harrison (Pete) Williams, a Democrat, was wary of my interest. He didn't want close coverage. No wonder. He resigned from the Senate in disgrace.

In my neophyte year of 1964, I sought help and sources to understand Washington. As a source, Case was the most generous. As a liberal Republican, he had access to both wings of his minority party, and because he was open to vote for Democratic initiatives, he could make the majority Democrats pay a price for his support. Case knew what was going on. He and his aides shared that information with me freely.

I had far less success in getting information from House members who represented Philadelphia districts. In fact, they wanted their names in the paper only when they had a federal benefit to announce and they intended to do that by sending me a piece of paper with the story written the way they wanted it to appear. Their aversion to newspaper coverage was neither surprise nor mystery. All were machine Democrats without a streak of independence. They took orders from the head of their delegation, the city Democratic chairman, and the House Democratic leader. They rode the train on most days round trip between Philadelphia and Washington. They regarded their seats in Congress as sinecures and they weren't about to jeopardize them.

Bill Barrett of South Philadelphia could usually be found at night in his South Philadelphia office as a Democratic city committeeman, seeing constituents and arranging favors. He preferred to be called "Mr. Chairman" because he was in line to head a subcommittee. He constantly adjusted his toupee.

Jimmy Byrne could be found in the evenings in his Philadelphia funeral parlor. Being an undertaker was a good post for a local politician. Sooner or later you would meet most families in the district. Byrne's nickname, naturally, was "Digger." If he ever had an independent thought, he hid it from public view. He rarely smiled.

Robert N.C. Nix was the delegation's black member, but he made clear that his task was not to speak publicly in Washington for his black constituents in Philadelphia, but to calm them with patronage and whatever he could work out for them with City Hall. Nix made it clear that the less I wrote about him in the *Bulletin,* the happier he would be. Since he never seemed to be doing anything in the Capitol, ignoring him was easy.

A new arrival in Washington in 1964 was Bill Green, son of Congressman William J. Green, for years the boss of the city's Democratic organization. When the senior Green died late in 1963, young Bill claimed the seat. He was easily elected in a special election and when he was sworn in as a House member, he was even younger than I. Bill had no intention of making waves. His motto was "keep your mouth shut." We later struck up a friendship through Georgetown Law Center where we were in the same class. Bill left school to run successfully as mayor of Philadelphia.

I worked most days out of the Senate and House press galleries. With security less tight in those days, reporters were allowed on the Senate floor 10 minutes before the start of the session. Under the deal, when the opening gavel was struck, I left the floor, even if the senator I was interviewing was in the middle of a thought or sentence. I enjoyed looking up from the well of the Senate to the galleries, knowing that for tourists I was part of the show in Washington. It was great fun to ask a question of Democratic Majority Leader Mike Mansfield of Montana and to try for an answer other than a "yep" or a "nope." In contrast, it was amusing to ask a question of the Senate Republican Minority Leader Everett McKinley Dirksen of Illinois. He could talk endlessly and say nothing—senators and press called it "oozing." During the session, when I wanted to speak to a senator, I sent in a note and asked to meet outside the door. Frequent contacts meant that senators got to know the "regulars" in the congressional press corps. They were more inclined to talk to a regular than an unknown reporter.

On the House aside of the Capitol, I could enter the members' cloakrooms and catch a member there or ask through a note that he or she come off the floor to meet me. Most members, aside from the Philadelphians, seemed delighted to have their name and words in the *Philadelphia Bulletin*. The prerequisite of becoming recognized as a good reporter in Washington was to work for a publication that had a solid reputation and a hefty measure of political clout. In 1964, the *Bulletin* scored in both categories. For a reporter such as myself, just being on the scene made a big difference. I got to be recognized and therefore achieved success if only because I showed up. Even then it was possible to report on Congress from the office, reading the mail and making phone calls. That became easier when C-Span covered the chambers live. I preferred firsthand reporting.

The Speaker of the House met with reporters before sessions in a room just off the floor. If the Speaker had a lot to say, he'd show up early and take questions. But if negotiations were still underway or there was a problem, he'd come just in time to list the business of the day. In all events, Bill "Fishbait" Miller, one of the many factotums employed by the House, stood by the speaker, brushing lint, real or imaginary, from the speaker's dark blue serge suit. "It's time, Mr. Speaker," the sergeant-at-arms would say. The speaker, following the mace, walked through the swinging door to the podium. I would dash up the steps to reach the press gallery before the first speech of the day.

My workday usually began shortly before 9 a.m. in the *Bulletin's* office in the National Press Building. I aimed to be out of there within a half hour for a five-minute cab ride to the Capitol. Only we never referred to the stately white domed building as the Capitol. It was "The Hill." I told the cabbie, "The House side" or "The Senate side." In those pre-terrorist days before barricades and magnetometers, I was driven under a portico. I carried a congressional press gallery card but after a few days on the Hill I rarely had to show it to the members, the staff or police officers. They recognized me.

I liked to grab a second cup of coffee, often with cinnamon toast, at a special long table reserved for the press in the Senate dining room. It was a good place to catch up on the latest news or gossip. Gossip was the raw meat of politics. It was useful to listen to reporters for the Associated Press or United Press international wire services since they were well clued in. The press galleries had wall fixtures loaded with statements by senators or representatives, ample copies of the *Congressional Record*, the latest committee reports, and witness statements delivered to committees. If I wished, I could fill a day and gather information needed for a story by reading from the bins. I often read for a couple of hours. A member of the press gallery staff in each chamber was tuned into what was important. From the chamber, he phoned to the gallery such messages as "Humphrey's up" or "Dirksen's back." That was my cue for dropping reading. I went through the swinging door and grabbed one of the round swivel seats in the gallery. I was allowed to bring in paper and to take notes, unlike tourists in the gallery who were forbidden to write or talk. Reporters could whisper to each other.

When a Senate heavyweight such as Richard Brevard Russell of Georgia, leader of the Southern Democratic coalition, or Dirksen or another powerbroker completed his say and yielded the floor to some backbencher, we vacated the gallery en masse. Senators often came to our gallery and occupied an overstuffed chair for a conversation with reporters. Because the chairs were so comfortable, some reporters routinely dozed in them. It was particularly amusing to watch Barnet Nover of *The Denver Post* place a newspaper over his face and fall asleep. His wife Naomi of the same paper would arrive, nudge him, and announce that she had a really great story. Naomi said all her stories were great. Barnet agreed. The gallery was full of such characters.

By 3 each afternoon I decided what I would write for the next day's *Bulletin*. I called Grace Andrews and dictated a budget line. I mentally wrote my lead as I took a cab to the press building. Although it sounds routine and predictable, there were surprises. One day I saw Malcolm X, known generally as a militant black Muslim leader with little regard for whites, in the Senate visitors' gallery. I asked to speak with him. He could hardly have been more gracious. In the hallway, we spoke at length about the civil rights bill then being negotiated behind closed doors. He had a strong command of its details and endorsed what appeared to be a compromise. Displaying keen sensitivity to congressional politics, he said that while he wanted a stronger bill, he knew it did not have the votes and he would settle on a weaker measure as a first step toward securing full rights for Negroes. I wrote the story exclusively and it got good play in the *Bulletin*.

It was not long after my arrival in Washington that I realized that covering the local beat was not as much fun as covering national stories. Within a month of my arrival on the Hill, Congress began work on a tax-cut package. Aides in the offices of Senators Clark, Scott, and Case who monitored local issues for their bosses helped me latch onto the tax-bill story. I called them every day and asked if there was anything local I needed to pay attention to. When they told me no, as they did on most days, I went after the tax story. To my pleasure, the *Bulletin* didn't care what I did, as long as I did not get beaten on a local story. My prime competitor, Jerry Cahill of the *Philadelphia Inquirer*, was a superb reporter, but his mandate was pretty much limited to the local beat. So I had a fuller field than Jerry to run on, even as I kept an eye on the local beat to make sure Jerry didn't beat me on a story. I cultivated sources inside the House Ways and Means Committee and the Senate Finance Committee. Though I knew next to nothing about the U.S. tax system or finance, I got leaks of the latest deals being cut on the bill. The *Bulletin* led the paper with many of my stories.

By the time hard talks on the civil rights bill got underway in March, I was almost completely off local stories. But I had a built-in excuse. Scott and Case were among the main Republican negotiators. Democratic leaders needed votes from liberal and moderate Republicans to break the Southern Democratic filibuster. I got good stories, often exclusive, into print with the assistance of Scott and Case, Russell and one of his Southern allies, Lister Hill of Alabama. I could not have been happier. They were going back and forth with conflicting ideas and demands and I was right in the middle of it.

*　*　*

I was fortunate in 1964 to be in the right time and place to cover a slice of the late-starting and soon-ending presidential campaign of the Republican governor of Pennsylvania, William W. Scranton. I knew Scranton and his staff members from *Bulletin* assignments in Harrisburg.

The Hamlet-like Scranton entered the race for the Republican presidential nomination after Gov. Nelson A. Rockefeller of New York dropped out. Rocky, symbol of the liberal wing of the Republican Party and despised by many Republican activists for his deviance from orthodox conservatism, reluctantly realized he could not stop Goldwater's march toward the nomination. Scranton, like Rockefeller, deplored his party's lurch to the right. He and fellow GOP moderates refused to accept the obvious—that the party was under the control of conservatives who blamed liberal or moderate Republicans for GOP losses, including Nixon's loss in 1960 to Kennedy. In persuading Scranton to challenge Goldwater, GOP leaders appealed more to his vanity than common sense. More a dilettante than a rough-and-tumble politician, Scranton was reluctant to be a sacrificial lamb for the Republican East and West Coast wings. Scranton never showed the zest for campaigning that Rockefeller displayed, but he was susceptible to appeals that he had to save the party as a matter of conscience.

When Scranton announced his candidacy, the *Bulletin's* John G. McCullough, a veteran political reporter and one of the finest human beings I ever met, was among the first reporters to sign on for the duration of the campaign. The *Bulletin*, as leading newspaper in Pennsylvania, had a special obligation to cover Scranton. When after weeks of exhausting coverage McCullough asked for a break, I got the call to replace him.

I rushed to Harrisburg to board the Scranton campaign plane. Within days I made a blunder that led me to fear that my career as a national political correspondent was over.

I flew on Scranton's plane into Detroit where he was to make a speech downtown. I rode in Scranton's motorcade to the speech site and after the speech back in the motorcade to the airport. I wanted to get a story on the speech into the next edition, so I ducked into a phone booth at the airport. Scranton's next stop was Lansing, the state capital, across the state from Detroit. Scranton was to meet Michigan's Republican Gov. George Romney and receive an endorsement. At the Detroit Airport, I was right up against a deadline and concentrated on getting a coherent story dictated.

That done, I stepped from the phone booth and realized that I was alone. I ran through the terminal to catch up. By the time I got to the gate, the Scranton plane was revving its engines at the end of the runway. Then it was up, up and away. And here was I, on a big political trip, on the ground.

My first instinct was panic. But I overcame it quickly. I rented a car—worrying that the *Bulletin* might not allow the expense—but too nervous to call the *Bulletin* for permission—and drove at breakneck speed the 90 miles to the Lansing Airport. I had minutes to spare as I checked in the rented car, found the gate for Scranton's plane, and boarded it just in time for the next leg—a flight to Chicago. I was mortified.

Hardly anybody had noticed my absence. Campaigns are circuses in motion and my experience was barely a sideshow—for everyone but me. The *Bulletin* paid for the car rental and my colleagues had a good laugh at my embarrassment. It was the only time I missed a plane, though I came close other times.

My coverage of Scranton included a trip to the Eisenhower farm outside Gettysburg, Pennsylvania. It was Scranton's last roll of the political dice—a bid to convince the former president to endorse him and oppose Goldwater. It didn't work. Eisenhower said he saw no reason to deny the nomination to the candidate who was the clear choice of the party. My story amounted to the obituary for the Scranton campaign.

*   *   *

In that wonderful summer of 1964, Bob Roth and Tony Day applied their considerable talent to covering the Goldwater phenomenon, leaving virtually all else on the Washington beat to me.

Two weeks after the post Civil Rights Act trip to Texas, I was back there again, this time getting an interview with LBJ on the ranch. Then there was a trip to Valley Forge, Pennsylvania, where LBJ spoke at the Boy Scout jamboree. There was a trip to New York for a Johnson speech to the American Bar Association. In the June to August period, I didn't spend two consecutive days in my Fort Totten apartment.

There was at least one story that I grossly mishandled. When I read it more than four decades later, I recognized how I failed to convey to readers the full meaning of what I was reporting. I was not alone, but I see now how I should have done better. It began on the morning of August 3. I was asked into the Oval Office. Johnson spoke, and I took notes. From that event I wrote via dictation to Philadelphia:

> "President Johnson has ordered U.S. naval and air forces increased in the Gulf of Tonkin off North Viet Nam and has instructed them to destroy any attacking force.
>
> "Mr. Johnson said today that he made the decision to beef up American strength in that Southeast Asia area following an attack yesterday morning on the U.S. destroyer Maddox by three North Vietnamese torpedo boats.
>
> "Mr. Johnson added with a somber tone: "These instructions were conveyed yesterday to the appropriate people and they "will be carried out." At the end of his seven-minute session with the reporters the President said he would stand by his statement and not answer any questions."

I led the paper that afternoon under the headline: U.S. Boosts Forces Off N. Viet Nam After Reds Attack Destroyer"

In the following days I wrote about the Gulf of Tonkin Resolution that Johnson was determined to move swiftly through the Democratic-controlled Congress. On August 6, in the Senate Foreign Relations Committee hearing room, I listened—and reported—as Secretary of State Dean Rusk urged prompt bipartisan approval. My story noted the dissent of Sen. Wayne Morse, a Democrat from Oregon, but said that committee chairman Sen. J. William Fulbright, a Democrat from Arkansas, proposed the resolution. The resolution passed Congress in a week. Little did I know at the moment that I had witnessed the expansion of the Vietnam War. I was clueless about the importance of the Gulf of Tonkin Resolution that served as LBJ's flimsy pretext for going to war. Nor did I convey to readers any sign whatsoever of what lay ahead. That was to come—the dying in Vietnam of friends and foe, dissent that ripped the nation, destruction of the potential for progress in battling poverty, disease and illiteracy that seemed so promising in the summer of 1964, loss of trust in government, and decay of confidence in the press.

*　　*　　*

In 1964, I was the youngest *Bulletin* reporter assigned to cover the Democratic National Convention in Atlantic City, 60 miles from Philadelphia and in the *Bulletin's* prime circulation area. Almost every Philadelphian of my generation was fond of Atlantic City—with its beach, Boardwalk, cheese steaks, bars that served minors, Steel Pier, and Miss America beauty pageant, even before it became a gamblers' delight. To me Atlantic City was wading into the gentle surf, dining with my parents in my father's favorite restaurant, Dock's on Atlantic Avenue. It meant chewing saltwater taffy, playing skeeball with dimes provided by Uncle Martin, my mother having fun with her children and conversations with Aunt Rose. It was the only place I heard my parents talk of their dreams for the future. They wanted to buy a house "at the shore"—Ventnor or Margate just outside Atlantic City so that they could ride the jitney into town and stroll on the Boardwalk for the sea air. And so it was that when the *Bulletin* told me I'd be in Atlantic City for the Democratic Convention, I thought life could hardly get any better.

I went to Atlantic City the week before the convention to cover contentious platform hearings and to write setup pieces. I had a room in a motel along the Boardwalk that smelled of anything but sea air, but was convenient to Convention Hall and the *Bulletin's* workspace in a hotel where there were better rooms for the older reporters.

Johnson, who liked secrecy, surprise, and keeping his options open, was expected to come to Atlantic City on Monday, the first day of the convention. No one was shocked, however, when he said on Sunday that he would stay in Washington until he came to Atlantic City, but he wouldn't say when he would come to Atlantic City.

More importantly, LBJ had yet to announce his choice for vice president. Earlier he ruled out Robert F. Kennedy with a flimsy explanation that he didn't want any cabinet member as his running mate. Kennedy despised Johnson and quickly launched a campaign against Republican incumbent Kenneth Keating for the New York Senate seat. The *Bulletin* poured a lot of money into covering the convention. It ran ads touting the presence of its reporters on top of the story. A sketch of me ran in the paper, calling me a trained political observer for the *Bulletin*. Now the possibility existed that not a single *Bulletin* trained observer would be in Washington to cover Johnson's announcement of his vice presidential pick—in reality the only real story of the week.

Sam Boyle, the *Bulletin* editor running the convention bureau, ordered me on Sunday afternoon back to Washington to cover Johnson. I was disappointed that I would not have more days in Atlantic City. I kept my room by the Boardwalk. At the White House on Monday morning, press secretary George Reedy said it was wise to stay loose and close. Fortunately the *Bulletin* office was only a ten-minute walk from the White House northwest gate on Pennsylvania Avenue, the access point for reporters. I made the office my home. I napped on the blue leather couch and ate at the press club. I saw little advantage to being at Fort Totten Drive, especially since I had emptied the refrigerator and cupboards in anticipation of a week in Atlantic City.

I was in the White House on Wednesday morning when Reedy invited a handful of reporters, including me, to join LBJ on the South Lawn. It was a warm day as Johnson led us round and round the cement oval talking about "this vice presidential thing." Spectators looking through the iron grill fence with the Washington Monument behind them must have marveled at the sight of the long-legged president striding rapidly while reporters jockeyed to hear whatever might pass from Johnson's lips. He artfully played with us, insisting that he had not yet made up his mind on the vice presidency. He finally said he would invite Hubert down for a conversation in the Oval Office in late afternoon.

So how do you write that story on deadline? I wrote carefully, especially as the White House continued to leak tidbits of information. What might have seemed obvious could be another devious move by Johnson. Was it an announcement that Humphrey would be the vice presidential nominee? Not for me. I wasn't going to be caught on a limb only to have Johnson saw it off. My story in the late afternoon edition read:

> "Sen. Hubert H. Humphrey (D-Minn.) flew here from Atlantic City late this afternoon at President Johnson's invitation to discuss the Democratic vice presidential nomination. Humphrey, accompanied by Sen. Thomas J. Dodd (D-Connecticut) arrived here at 4.40 p.m."

Dodd's appearance was a new twist. Reedy told me that I could write without attribution that Johnson had not made a final decision, that Dodd was still a possibility because as a Northeastern Catholic he could win votes from Catholics, New Englanders and Northern moderates who distrusted Humphrey as too far left. Reedy told me that Johnson liked Dodd more than he liked Humphrey.

I walked past the Oval Office and whom did I see there sitting on a hallway bench but Humphrey looking quite miserable; Dodd looking quite placid; and James "Scotty' Reston of *The New York Times*, perhaps the most important journalist in Washington, looking quite like Scotty Reston, quite bemused. I knew that Reston, born in Scotland, wasn't eligible for the vice presidency. My thought then, as now, is that it was Johnson's final taunt to Humphrey, unnecessary and mean-spirited, that LBJ was boss and Hubert would do his humble bidding.

Minutes later, I boarded a bus on the White House South Lawn for a ride to Andrews Air Force Base. I flew to Atlantic City and on the tarmac was told by Jack Valenti that Humphrey was the choice. I went to the floor of Atlantic City's cavernous Convention Hall. I saw Johnson announce his pick of Humphrey.

In the flight back to Andrews, Reedy and other Johnson aides provided what we called "tick-tock," a step-by-step account of this curious day in U.S. history.

After a sleepless night and trip to the Fort Totten Drive apartment for a change of clothes, I flew with Johnson back to Atlantic City for the final night of the convention—with acceptance speeches by Humphrey and LBJ. There was an amusing moment. Managers arranged a fireworks display to celebrate LBJ's nomination and birthday. Johnson went to a balcony overlooking the Boardwalk, the beach and ocean. Secret Service agents stopped me at the balcony entrance. I protested that I was with the *Bulletin* and needed to be on the balcony. I heard a voice in Texas twang behind me. I was grabbed by the arm and projected forward. "Let him out there," said Liz Carpenter, the savvy, aggressive and politically astute press aide to Lady Bird Johnson. The wall of agents opened to admit me to the balcony, where I stood a few feet from Johnson as the fireworks exploded and the band played, among other things, "Stars and Stripes Forever" and "Happy Birthday."

The night was far from over. I had a story to write. I had a couple of hours sleep in my motel off the Boardwalk before I reported back to Convention Hall, got on a bus to the Pomona air field, boarded a plane and flew to Texas. That still wasn't the end of the day. Exhausted, I was ready to crash in my room in the Driskill Hotel in Austin when I got a call from Philadelphia. Riots had broken out in North Philadelphia. The *Bulletin* wanted a comment from Johnson. It took me more than an hour to find someone from LBJ's office who was still awake. I got a comment that satisfied my editors. Finally after no more than a combined six hours sleep over four days, I called it a night.

*   *   *

Roth, Day, and McCullough were given primary responsibility for covering the presidential campaign while I set to work on chasing Humphrey and Miller. I was put into the rotation for a few days with Goldwater and a few days with Johnson. The days with Johnson were more newsworthy than anticipated.

I spent a day in Brooklyn and the New York suburbs as LBJ campaigned for Bobby Kennedy's election to the Senate. I felt sorry for Kennedy's opponent, Ken Keating. Keating had been a good source during the battle over the Civil Rights Act. But I knew from the crowds that I saw on the Johnson-Kennedy tour that the brother of the slain president would join another brother, Teddy, in the Senate.

*   *   *

I was there when real news broke in New York in mid-October. Reedy told reporters in a New York hotel room that Walter Jenkins, one of Johnson's oldest friends and closest advisers, had been arrested in Washington on a morals charge arising out of an incident in the YMCA near the White House. Homosexuality was a taboo subject in the *Bulletin,* and it was before the word "gay" was ever applied to a lifestyle or the Supreme Court struck down laws prohibiting sexual contact between consenting adults of the same gender. I led the paper with the story. Jenkins entered a hospital. The Johnsons supported his family. Miller tried to raise the issue against LBJ, but it never took off. My attitude at the time to homosexuality was consistent with my upbringing in a conservative family where sex of any description was never mentioned. I advanced over time to view gay and lesbian relationships as private choices.

*   *   *

LAWRENCE M. O'ROURKE

In the fall of 1964, the *Bulletin* gave me another assignment—the campaign for the Pennsylvania U.S. Senate seat between Republican incumbent Hugh Scott and Democratic challenger Genevieve Blatt.

I traveled with Scott and Blatt in the state for several weeks, usually as the only reporter. Scott had the upper hand from the beginning. He was by far the better campaigner, the better-known statewide politician. He had a great money advantage. He cut deals with labor leaders and black leaders who would ordinarily have backed a Democrat. Scott had another advantage: he was running against a woman in a state that was chauvinistic toward women politicians, having never elected one to major office.

I drove the point home in a controversial story I wrote for the *Bulletin*. "Dear Miss Blatt," my story began. "Where do you get your hats?" The question was put to her at a Democratic Party rally. I wrote that she "smiled under the red turban, not showing her annoyance at the question." To the question, Blatt replied, "Wherever I see one I can afford that looks good." But privately, she fumed at the sexism.

Bulletin editors split about where to put my story. This was different from a disagreement over issues that would have landed my story on page one. In 1964 Blatt's gender was a sensitive private matter, albeit one that involved half the population. Women politicians were still novelties. The issue of women's equality reached into the *Bulletin*'s newsroom where women were kept in lower-level jobs and paid less than men. Finally the *Bulletin* ran my story about Blatt and her hats and the gender issue on the back page. The story drew wide reaction. Some readers complained that I had raised the topic. Some said I should have gone much further in discussing the disadvantage faced by women in the political arena. They were right. I should have explored the issue in much greater depth. But I was the product of my own environment.

Blatt winced when she read the story because she knew the bias in Pennsylvania against women running for office. Many men regarded politics as no place for women. Many women, especially conservative ethnic women with little experience outside the home and their community, regarded Blatt as uppity.

Scott had a heavy political weight on his shoulders—Goldwater atop the GOP ticket. I wrote many stories on Scott ducking questions as to whether he supported Goldwater and would vote for him. Blatt failed to exploit the GOP fissure. Whether out of politeness or ineptitude, Blatt stuck to well-trod Democratic themes. When Johnson campaigned in Pennsylvania, he endorsed Blatt, but with muted enthusiasm. Scott worked with Johnson on tax and civil rights battles earlier in the year, and neither man had an instinct to attack each other. When the votes were counted, Scott narrowly beat Blatt as hundreds of thousands of Pennsylvanians split their tickets. On election night, I wrote the story on the Scott-Blatt election. Scott told me he went to bed not knowing if he won another term and was pleasantly surprised in the morning to get a gracious concession call from Blatt. Blatt was always gracious, always a class act, but miscast in hardball politics.

Blatt continued in public service as a member of Pennsylvania's highest appellate court. She and I talked and exchanged letters through the years and remained friends. She came to acknowledge that in 1964 she ran a terrible campaign that she should have won.

*   *   *

As 1964 ended, I looked back, as I do half a century later, with astonishment that so much opportunity and responsibility was given to me at age 25. The boy from the row house of Philadelphia found the White House, the halls of Congress, and the campaign trail not a bad place to be, not at all.

LAWRENCE M. O'ROURKE

CHAPTER 8

LBJ's Colliding Wars

IN JANUARY 1965, after a glorious year in Washington as correspondent for the *Bulletin,* the paper called me back to Philadelphia. It felt like a demotion, but Dickinson, the managing editor, told me I was being promoted as he sent me to Boyle, the city editor, for my new assignment. "Your Washington ticket has been punched," Dickinson said, adding that I needed more experience in Philadelphia before I stepped onto the ladder toward a top leadership rung at the *Bulletin.*

Boyle, who succeeded the fired Selby, was the second most powerful figure in the *Bulletin* newsroom. He was thin and sharp-featured. He wore his sandy hair close-cropped, perhaps to remind us that he was a Marine during World War II. He expected his instructions to the dozens of reporters and editors who reported to him to be carried out immediately. He delegated authority only when he had to, which wasn't often. He always appeared to worry. A graduate of Notre Dame University, a stickler for honest and unbiased journalism, Boyle was quick-to-the-point and always on edge. I attributed his nervousness on the three cups of coffee he drank every hour.

"I know you don't want to come back," Boyle told me. "I'm glad you did and I think I have a beat you'll like. You'll cover Johnson's war on poverty as a local story and as a national story based out of Philadelphia. You can travel as you think you have to. I want you to put as much interpretation in your stories as you need to. The copy desk will understand." Boyle stunned me. The *Bulletin* did not spend money easily. Dickinson checked with the publisher before major decisions on staffing or travel. But Boyle's invitation to put interpretation into my pieces was a shocker. The *Bulletin* traditionally did not permit reporters to interpret in news stories. Suddenly I was exempt.

Boyle had another surprise. "I'm giving you a $35 a week raise," he said, effectively upping my pay by more than 30 percent. My head reeling with the thought of so much money, I walked to the area for beat reporters at the rear of the newsroom. I had a desk there two years previously when I covered education. I took a desk near Frank Hanlon, the obituary writer; Harry Toland, the labor writer; and Dan O'Leary, the real estate writer. It was a quiet zone. Hanlon and O'Leary were workhorses and rarely raised their voices. Toland was more likely to be found in union halls and executive offices than in the *Bulletin* newsroom. George Staab, a loud, contrarian all-purpose reporter, was in front of me. In the months ahead, he regularly goaded me as the paper's liberal ambassador to the city's black community.

I did not have to be back in Philadelphia for the *Bulletin.* Many contacts I acquired in 1964 while in Washington were surprised when I told them I was called back—and even more surprised when I agreed to go back. I could have gotten a job that would have kept me in Washington. Newspapers were glad to add experienced young reporters to their staffs, particularly those like me who were single and would work cheaply. I was invited to go after jobs in government and the private industry that feeds on the government. I could have found a job in a congressional office. But I felt attached to the newspaper business. For me, being a reporter with the level of independence the *Bulletin* gave me was a lot more fun than answering to a boss who in the end was more concerned about his own advancement than mine. I had minimal interest in a big salary.

In Philadelphia, I moved back in with my parents and brother. My mother was pleased. She had another person in the house to listen to her stories. My father helped me tote my books upstairs. He was particularly proud of the stairs from the living room to the second floor. For months he had worked most evenings and weekends sandpapering the stairs by hand to their base wood, then staining and shellacking them. The stairs were magnificent. My father worked in silence, not listening to the radio or speaking for hours. He always seemed worried about money and so he and I talked about the additional expenses of another mouth to feed, but he graciously said he did not intend to charge me rent. My brother, ten years younger, reacted as one might expect a 16-year-old high school kid to react—he largely ignored me and I did the same to him. I came in later years to regret that there was little to connect us during his growing-up years.

*   *   *

LAWRENCE M. O'ROURKE

What I realized after I took up my LBJ war on poverty beat was that *Bulletin* managers had much more in mind than simply covering another government program. The city's demographic profile had undergone dramatic change, with whites moving out and blacks increasing. No longer were African-Americans—I and other journalists were still calling them Negroes in print—a minority that could be ignored. Newspapers were catching up with reality. Black people had become a force in politics, so politicians had to respond to them, just as with every ethnic group. The Northern press had to accept that the civil rights revolution was more than a Southern phenomenon. If only for survival, the *Bulletin* was challenged to address racial issues in its circulation area. There was virtually no overt racism in the *Bulletin's pages,* but rather paternalism and apathy. *Bulletin* editors and reporters lived in white upper-or middle-class neighborhoods. Their view of inner-city Philadelphia was through a car or train window.

In sales offices of merchants and in newspaper advertising departments, there was newfound recognition that blacks were shoppers who had to be enticed, the same as white people, to lay down their hard-earned cash for products ranging from groceries to sofas to cars. Blacks didn't have as much money as whites, but food chains, department stores and other dealers in consumer products wanted black customers. When in January 1965, I walked through Wanamaker's and Strawbridge & Clothier and other major department stores, I rarely saw a black sales clerk or customer. The department stores were major buyers of display ads in the *Bulletin.* Without the dozens of pages that they bought every week, the *Bulletin* would not be able to publish. Merchandisers knew how to market products in the newspapers to white people. That was OK with them and the *Bulletin* until black people became a potential economic force.

Black professors at the University of Pennsylvania and Temple University did read the paper as did black lawyers, government officials and schoolteachers. They were the blacks that white reporters were most likely to encounter. But most black people in row houses in Philadelphia did not get a daily newspaper. The *Bulletin* slogan "In Philadelphia, nearly everybody reads the Bulletin" was flawed. More accurately, it should have read, "In Philadelphia, nearly every white person reads the *Bulletin*."

There were multiple reasons why the *Bulletin* did not sell newspapers to black people in the same manner and at the same numbers as it did to whites The *Bulletin's* circulation, as at most other newspapers, depended on home delivery and street sales. The bulk of the *Bulletin's* circulation was home delivery, as I was aware from my days as a *Bulletin* carrier. The *Bulletin* did not push the carrier system in inner-city black neighborhoods. Because so few families in the city's poorest areas signed up to take the *Bulletin*, it was tough to get a kid to deliver the paper after school for a few dollars a week. It was easier and more cost-efficient for the *Bulletin* to try to expand circulation in subdivisions growing around Philadelphia—largely white enclaves. But sales campaigns there were now also tough. It was difficult to attract suburban white kids to deliver newspapers for pocket change. It took more time, trucks and gasoline to get the papers from 30th and Market Streets to the suburbs.

The *Bulletin* didn't make many street sales to blacks. There were far fewer blacks in business suits than whites pouring out of downtown offices at dusk to buy the fabled 4-star edition. There were fewer mom and pop stores in black neighborhoods selling the *Bulletin* at a few pennies a copy profit.

At *Bulletin* strategy meetings on how to increase sales to black readers, experts said the paper had to put in more news of interest to black readers. This notion constantly generated controversy in the *Bulletin* newsroom. Some contended that more news devoted to blacks would "drive away white readers." The phrase was virtually a mantra whenever the subject of declining circulations or increasing black readership arose.

By taking the LBJ poverty beat, I became a player in the *Bulletin's* effort to win black readers. Dickinson and Boyle made it clear that my job was to write stories that compelled a black audience. I was not to pander—a word often thrown at me by critics—but to generate copy that convinced black Philadelphians that it was important for them to read the *Bulletin*. The city desk kept a roster of beats and reporters—beats such as education, labor, politics, mayor's office, City Hall, 619 (the major police beat), and transportation. Boyle said my beat should be listed as "poverty." There were poor white people in Philadelphia, but we knew that poverty was a euphemism for black.

The previous summer, a black North Philadelphia neighborhood was badly damaged by burning and looting. Many saw it as a self-inflicted wound, only a problem if it escalated to white neighborhoods. The *Bulletin* covered the event as a police story. It was low on reporters who could go into the neighborhood and talk to the people who lived there, including the rioters, about what caused the disturbance and what

LAWRENCE M. O'ROURKE

might trigger it again or prevent it. The *Bulletin* hired a prominent black reporter named Orrin C. Evans who had exposed racism in the military as a reporter for the city's black newspaper. Evans, a cultured man in his late 50s, had no intention of serving as the *Bulletin's* missionary to the black community. He lived in an affluent black enclave surrounded by white neighborhoods in the Delaware County suburb of Yeadon. Neither by personality nor instinct was he an automatic expert on blacks in urban ghettos. Evans wanted to be a general assignment reporter. Moreover, he didn't want to be labeled "Uncle Tom." On several occasions, *Bulletin* editors asked Evans to explain events in the black community, but he did not like the role and often referred questioners to me. Orrin and I talked often and it was clear that I was in greater daily contact with younger inner-city black community leaders.

During my coverage of the school desegregation battle in 1963, I built a professional relationship with many leaders of the black community, and, in a few instances, personal ties. I had been a guest in the homes of some black leaders and had met them in their offices. Settling into my new assignment on the poverty beat, I reinvigorated many of these connections. On the education beat, I had links to black ministers who served as the closest thing to an intelligence network and street leadership for the black community. I went to the ministers again. Some planned a boycott against the *Bulletin* for what they viewed—correctly in my judgment—as inadequate reporting of areas of concern to black communities in Philadelphia. It was not my job to argue against a boycott, and I steadfastly refrained from becoming the *Bulletin's* apologist. It was my job to report and explain. I didn't see myself in public relations or advocacy for *Bulletin* management.

Reporters who wanted quotes from black leaders frequently sought out the same people, starting with Judge Raymond Pace Alexander and his wife, Sadie, distinguished members of the black community. For more firebrand quotes, reporters called Cecil B. Moore, president of the Philadelphia branch of the National Association for the Advancement of Colored People. He was always glad to respond with a fiery quote. (Cecil Moore frequently called me at home. He and my mother, though they never met, had many conversations about growing up in Philadelphia.) I expanded my contacts, writing stories about new black leaders, including some trying to wrest political control of the black community from black members of the Democratic City Committee. Black ward leaders on the city committee had their fiefdoms and reasons for maintaining power.

Outside public view, they cut deals with the Democratic organization and City Hall.

With a growing younger group of black leaders in Philadelphia, political tensions emerged over the development of a system to administer the war on poverty in the city and the appointment of leaders to run it. From the outset of the federal war on poverty program, there was conflict over who would control it. A new group of black leaders of Philadelphia wanted control of the city's anti-poverty program. These leaders wanted Mayor James H. J. Tate and power brokers in City Hall and the Democratic Party to keep their hands off the anti-poverty program. Predictably, Tate and the political establishment thought otherwise. They saw the war on poverty as an opportunity for business as usual in urban politics—rewarding friends with jobs and programs and getting the credit for it.

My new assignment plunged me into this battle because the mayor in the early days of the war on poverty, before I was on the beat, controlled the flow of information about the program by occasional self-serving statements. I got into the thick of the political entanglement because I not only talked more with black leaders than with white politicians, I often traveled to Washington to speak with R. Sargent Shriver, Jr., whom LBJ had named director of the Office of Economic Opportunity (OEO), the federal anti-poverty program. Shriver had a staff of like-minded people, such as former Trappist monk Colman McCarthy, who thought that the growing notion of black power should be tested by giving local black leaders the federal dollars allocated to the anti-poverty program and the authority to direct it. I wrote many stories about the power struggle between the feds and local black leaders on one side and the powerful politicians in City Hall and congressional and local Democratic operatives on the other.

I was not the only reporter in America who jumped onto this story. Robert Semple of *The New York Times* and Morton Kondracke of *The Chicago Sun-Times* quickly grasped the implications. But because Philadelphia was ahead of other cities in the debate—and I was a full-time reporter on that debate—Philadelphia became a national laboratory for developing a system to give power to black people and deny that power to City Hall.

Critics in the Philadelphia newsroom thought I overwrote the story as I kept plugging away at the conflict. But there was a slow building of awareness that I was on to something unique. Dickinson played my stories prominently, mainly on page one. The battle over power pitted the new wave of black figures, such as those at the Congress of Racial Equality, against long-standing black organizations like the Urban League. Another strong presence in the black community and the governance of Philadelphia was the Roman Catholic Archdiocese of Philadelphia. One key aspect of the dispute between the Church and local community leaders was the politically explosive issue of public funds to support birth control.

Birth control was a matter rarely addressed in *The Philadelphia Bulletin.* Some local black leaders told me that they intended to put federal antipoverty money into sex education and birth control. When I ran the idea past Shriver and his aides in Washington, they saw no problem with that. One evening I covered a meeting of black community leaders and agencies that served the black community, and among those present was Monsignor Edward Hughes, social affairs director for the archdiocese. I asked him point-blank if he objected to war on poverty funds going into birth control. "No comment," he snapped. The *Bulletin* rarely used "no comment," but I put the monsignor's words into my story. A desk editor wanted to cut the quote, but I argued for it. Boyle backed me, and the Hughes quote was printed and picked up by other news organizations. The Philadelphia archdiocese position stirred up interest in how to fight poverty in America.

*　　*　　*

As I wrote stories about the poor participating in the program to lift themselves out of poverty, the idea developed of a special election in Philadelphia that spring to pick anti-poverty committees of local people. The theory was that local people knew more about what their community needed than officials in City Hall and in Washington. Through my stories, I put weight behind the idea that poor people should be entrusted with significant responsibility for the allocation of federal antipoverty dollars in their neighborhoods. Mayor Tate resisted the idea on every front. He and his aides told me so in several blunt interviews. I had an inside look at the mayor's thinking and maneuvering through a source who often served as a middle man between City Hall and the OEO—Michael J. Stack, a young Washington lawyer with ambitions for a legal and political career in Philadelphia. He eventually achieved both. Mike was a great storyteller. He and I began a friendship that continued even after he became a prominent ward leader in Philadelphia and supported for mayor Frank L. Rizzo, the hard-charging former police commissioner. I didn't like Rizzo and made that clear to Mike. I had several clashes with Rizzo. Later, Mike and I, with the Rev. William J. Bryon, SJ, a wise and caring priest and an accomplished ecclesiastical strategist who later became president of Catholic University after a major controversy, set out to collaborate on a book on poverty and politics. But, alas, we talked more than we wrote and never published.

The idea of a special election in black neighborhoods (and a few white neighborhoods with a high percentage of poor residents) caught on. Opposed by City Hall, the idea might have been quietly suppressed had I not kept it alive through the *Bulletin*. Again I became aware of the power of the press. Reporters don't have to slant copy—and should not—but they have the means to move discussion in certain directions, simply by calling attention and giving credence to ideas and the people who promote them. While working the poverty beat, as with education two years before, I helped to bring new ideas and faces into the public arena. One new face belonged to Isaiah Crippens, a little-known black lawyer in Philadelphia. I believed he had talent to bridge the gap between City Hall and the black community. I advanced his reputation by giving him lots of ink in the *Bulletin*. Crippens was hired as the first executive director of the Philadelphia anti-poverty agency. The press can also squash ideas and prevent the emergence of new voices as evidenced in the claim of Southern segregationists that the Civil Rights Movement would have failed if the press ignored it.

Elections to Philadelphia anti-poverty committees were held in the spring of 1965. The turnout wasn't large. It had flaws as an exercise at grass-roots democracy, but it enabled new younger black leaders to come forward.

In the meantime, reporting for the *Bulletin*, I traveled to national projects of the anti-poverty program. On the theory that jobs and job training, much more than welfare, are indispensable to progress in the black community, I visited a key component of the federal anti-poverty program—Job Corps centers that trained young people in marketable skills. One such trip took me to Florida—with stops in St. Petersburg and Miami—not by accident during baseball's spring training season.

It wasn't hard as a reporter to gain a reputation as an expert on the federal anti-poverty program—so few of us were covering it. It was easy to write an exclusive story when no other reporter was trying for it. I often had far more poverty stories in my notebooks than even the *Bulletin*—committed to the subject—could find room for. The opposition papers, the *Inquirer* and the *Daily News*, largely ignored the subject. But my stories got me attention, if only because "rip and read" radio and TV news outlets shamelessly stole my stories from the *Bulletin*. I was interviewed on television and radio and contacted by reporters on other publications who needed a "quick fill" on the poverty program. My work in Philadelphia later served as source material for the book, "The Problem of Jobs," by University of Virginia assistant professor Guian A. McKee, in the series *Historical Studies of Urban America*, published by the University of Chicago Press.

Therefore it was not a surprise in the early summer of 1965 when the news editor of the local NBC outlet invited me to lunch at an expensive restaurant in center-city Philadelphia. I figured I'd be pumped for information on the poverty program. The local TV news manager introduced me to another lunch guest, a producer at the Huntley-Brinkley television news program in New York.

We talked about the Philadelphia version of the war on poverty. I filled them in on information that was new and fascinating to them. The NBC people said they wanted to run an idea past me—would I be interested in leaving the *Bulletin* to host a talk show on Philadelphia radio. They said they learned that I had an "obstreperous" style that would attract listeners. I wasn't sure at the time what obstreperous meant, perhaps obnoxious and undoubtedly liberal. The idea was intriguing. They hoped to air me during afternoon drive time. They said they had another idea—would I be interested in training to be a television reporter? They had seen me on TV and making speeches around town and thought I might be able to cut it before the camera. I was taken aback by the offers. I asked a lot of questions, but gave no immediate answer. They urged me to think about it and get back to them. Lunch ended on a pleasant, if uncertain, note.

Without saying a word to anyone, I went to the *Bulletin* newsroom to work on a story. No sooner was I at my desk than Boyle said Dickinson wanted to see me. Wondering if I had screwed up some story and was about to be rebuked by the managing editor, I went to Dickinson's office. He complimented me on my work on the poverty beat and said he saw a bright future for me in Philadelphia. In fact, he said that in recent weeks he and Boyle had talked about changes in the city desk setup so that beat reporters could function as a unit working under a supervising assistant city editor who would work with them closely on assignments. I had been mentioned for that editor slot, Dickinson said. He went on: The *Bulletin* has decided to expand its Washington Bureau—and while it would continue to rotate reporters from Philadelphia in and out of Washington for a year, would I be interested in becoming a permanent member of the Washington Bureau? I accepted immediately. I called the NBC people and rejected their offer. It was a more critical juncture for me than I realized. I turned down a golden chance to try my hand in the new world of talk radio and television, but I preferred to be a newspaper reporter.

I never knew if there was a connection between the job offer from NBC and the *Bulletin's* offer on the same afternoon. No matter, I was becoming what I hoped to be—a Washington correspondent for an evening broadsheet newspaper with the largest circulation in the country.

* * *

In the months I spent on the poverty beat in 1965, the country experienced the start of turmoil that was to mark the rest of Lyndon Johnson's presidency. He violated his campaign promise to avoid sending "American boys" to fight a war in Asia. LBJ expanded the U.S. commitment to Vietnam, pouring U.S. blood and treasure into a foolish and unnecessary cause. Back in Washington, I wrote a column that was effectively the obituary of the war on poverty and the notion of community involvement that I as a reporter chronicled from birth to death. Johnson trimmed the federal social budget and rearranged War on Poverty programs so there was no longer any point to poor people serving on neighborhood committees. Somewhat bitterly, I wrote in the column, "The bosses have begun to hit back" and complained that a "white backlash" triumphed. In initially declaring the war on poverty, Johnson promised to end poverty in America by the time the nation celebrated its bicentennial in 1976. There would be poverty in the third century. Mourning the end of the dream and my own naiveté, I wrote that it was "perhaps foolish to expect anything else."

* * *

While living on Fort Totten Drive in 1964 and commuting to the office, I changed buses at the corner of 14th Street and Park Road. Just a half-year later, as I looked for a new place to live in Washington, a friend advised me not to go anywhere near upper 14th Street. Buses still stopped there, but transformation of that busy corner where I often browsed for a magazine or paperback while waiting for the cross-town had been sudden and dramatic, the decline in safety as meteoric as the plunge of the war on poverty. The 14th Street corridor was in the core of a growing racial tension in Washington that fed not only on the collapse of social programs but the anti-war movement. I opted for personal safety and moved into a two-bedroom apartment on a hilltop off Lee Highway in Roslyn, Virginia. From my bedroom window I could see the Washington Monument. The bus between home and work sauntered through upscale Georgetown.

My life and my work became synonymous. Except for the monthly trips to visit my parents in Philadelphia and occasional dates, I did little other than work. When Congress was in session, usually from Monday night or Tuesday morning until late Thursday, I was on Capitol Hill. But I also had responsibility for covering stories at the Supreme Court, the Pentagon and the Justice Department. I didn't complain about the hours or demands of the job. On the contrary, I loved to work. I welcomed the challenge of jumping from one story to another, from one venue to the next. During the day, while the *Bulletin* was on deadline, I was often required to dictate stories for which I had little preparation and no time to build background. Nights were not my own any more than days. Congress often worked until late hours. I tried to cover political meetings at night. I was genetically lucky that I could get by with a few hours sleep.

I spent many weekends on the road, often in Texas in Austin and later San Antonio covering LBJ. It suited bureau chief Roth, and Tony Day, my colleague and the father of two children, that they had in the bureau someone who would drop personal plans to cover a story, in town or not. A week without several front-page bylines would have me second-guess my worth. It was not healthy, but it was reality. I had become a workaholic.

Increasingly my stories and most stories coming out of Washington had a common thread—the growing war in Vietnam and its consequences for social programs and U.S. politics. Johnson became a prisoner of the war, a pariah among the young, the poor and minorities. As he told me in the Oval Office or on his ranch on more than one occasion, his motto was, "Come, let us reason together." But he and the North Vietnamese and their allies did not reason together. Johnson called for reason while he sent the world's most powerful military force to kill. As war deepened, draft calls increased and dollars for social spending dried up, Johnson avoided venues where he faced booing, heckling or worse. Even his base constituency—organization Democrats—did not welcome him.

*　*　*

Looking to regroup his allies before the 1966 congressional campaign and his own run for re-election in 1968, Johnson called for a White House Conference on Civil Rights in June 1966. He invited more than 2,400 people, including the nation's black civil rights leaders and other prominent black and white activists, business and labor officials, and performing arts stars. The conference was scheduled for two hotels near Connecticut Avenue on the edge of Rock Creek Park. But what Johnson launched as a forum to emphasize his achievements quickly turned into a potential political disaster. Word filtered out that some invited guests would use the White House conference to protest the Vietnam War, saying that no progress could be made on social justice issues while so much money was going to the war. Rumors flew of a planned sit-in at the White House during a dinner Johnson arranged to launch the conference.

I decided to cover the conference. Security was tight. I had a White House pass that got me into conference rooms without problems, but most invitees were required to stand in long lines and undergo scrutiny by the Secret Service and White House security force. On the afternoon of June 1, I arrived at the Shoreham Hotel for a session and slipped into a seat next to a young woman. While waiting for the meeting to begin, we chatted about the conference. I identified myself and she said she was Mrs. Marcus (Rosemary) Kilch, president of the National Council of Catholic Women (NCCW). I doubted that. She didn't look like someone who would be named Mrs. Marcus Kilch. She seemed too young and lovely to be Mrs. Marcus Kilch, whatever she looked like. The woman next to me didn't have a wedding band, as I assumed a Mrs. Marcus Kilch would wear. She kept a sheaf of papers across her jacket, obscuring her badge. When she lowered the papers, I could see the name Mrs. Marcus Kilch, but my skepticism was absolute.

We sat side by side during the presentation, as I took notes. When the session was over, the woman who identified herself as Mrs. Marcus Kilch asked to borrow a dime to make a phone call. That was confirmation. Mrs. Marcus Kilch would never have to borrow a dime.

The young woman thought it was time to admit the truth. In case you are wondering, she said, I am not Mrs. Marcus Kilch. I am Patricia Coe and I am a staff associate for legislative affairs at NCCW. She said that Mrs. Kilch couldn't attend because of a last-minute family emergency, and she was sent instead.

Now that's the kind of person I admire—someone clever enough to slide past vigilant Secret Service agents and White House police on another person's credential. I gave her the dime and found out more about her. She was from Chicago and had only recently moved to Washington. I got her phone number and said I'd be in touch. I called a few days later, not to arrange a meeting under real names, but to say I was heading west on a cross-country camping trip with *Bulletin* colleague Mike Sisak. I said we'd be back in a few weeks and I'd call her then. Mike and I set off. We had a great time, sleeping in parks and sometimes alongside the road. We visited San Francisco and went to Los Angeles where, through connections via the *Bulletin's* sports department, Mike got tickets to a Phillies-Dodgers game in Chavez Ravine. We spent a few hours in Tijuana, Mexico, before we went to the Grand Canyon. Before sunset one morning we hiked down the Bright Angel Trail into the canyon. We didn't make it to the river. But we were deep enough so that it was a tough and long climb back. Mike and I drove to Salt Lake City and attended a service in the Mormon Tabernacle.

On the journey, I didn't forget Patricia, alias Mrs. Marcus Kilch. I sent her a postcard and when I got back to Washington, I called her. We had our first date at a New Orleans style restaurant in Roslyn. And to move things along, on February 26, 1967, in her apartment on 19th Street near Dupont Circle, in Washington, I asked her to marry me. Luckily, she accepted. We married six months to the day later, on August 26, in Holy Trinity Church in Georgetown. Father Tom Gavigan presided at a liturgy we substantially designed. After spending the first three days of our married life in Harrisburg, we boarded a Pan Am 707 National Press Club charter for Europe for our real honeymoon. We got off in London.

While a college undergraduate, Pat spent a semester in Vienna, Austria, and traveled widely in Europe. Since I figured it would be the only trip I ever took to Europe, I put together an ambitious itinerary: From London we went to the Shakespeare Theater in Stratford to see "Macbeth" before a trip to Huddersfield in Yorkshire to see cousins. Then there was a Saturday flight to Dublin, a drive the next morning through Athlone across the country to Dunmore in County Galway to see more cousins, then a wild drive through Macroom and southern Ireland to get back to the airport in Dublin to fly to Paris. From Paris we went to Monaco, then on to Nice, then rushed on to Florence, then sped on to Rome where we caught the Press Club charter and flew home, via a stop in Shannon where I bought an Irish tweed jacket. We did all this in a month, a real "If It's Tuesday, It Must be Belgium" kind of trip.

But let's not skip so quickly over Paris. There, as at other stops, we had $5 a day reservations through travel agent Natalie Meeks in the National Press Building. The $5 for each of us paid for the room, breakfast, and a sightseeing tour of each city. Our room in Paris was down the street from the Arc de Triomphe. We could see the Arc from our balcony on three mornings in the city of lights while we ate our petit dejeuner. We toasted our love for each other in the Restaurant des Beaux Arts on the Rue de Napoleon. We were sad to discover on our most recent visit to Paris that the restaurant is gone.

The return flight from Europe to Washington in October 1967 brought us not only to married life and back to jobs. It brought me to the absurdity of law school after missing the first month of class. I had decided in the spring of 1966, more than a year before I bumped into the person known as Mrs. Marcus Kilch, that I would attend Georgetown University Law Center. I began law school in the fall of 1966, informing the *Bulletin* that I would attend classes four evenings a week and on Saturday mornings while performing my job to their and my customary standards. Roth and editors in Philadelphia wished me well and said they didn't doubt for a minute that I could do it.

*   *   *

In enrolling in law school, I gave no thought to whether I wanted to be a lawyer. It just seemed like a neat thing to do. I had gone two years to graduate school at Villanova, the first year in theater, and the second year in political science. But my two transfers to Washington interrupted my graduate study at Villanova. Since I was now in Washington, there was scant chance of completing work on a Villanova master's degree.

In a speech in September 1966 welcoming us to Georgetown, Chester Antieau, the assistant dean, declared ominously, "Turn to your left and shake the hand of the person on your left. Now turn to your right and shake the hand of the person on your right. This time next year one of the three of you won't be here." But I made it through the first year comfortably. I often toted my casebooks to the Capitol and while waiting for some event briefed the cases for my next class. There was a lot of briefing to do as Dr Walter Yeager, the Contracts professor, insisted on ten cases for each of the three classes every week. We went from 5.45 in the evening until 7.30. We night students faced four years of this schedule. Day students had a three-year curriculum. Day and night students had the same professors and courses and took the same exams together so that no one could gain an advantage. We wrote student numbers, not names, on the cover of the exam booklets.

The ease with which I got through my first year at Georgetown contributed to my arrogance in skipping the first month of classes during my second year so that Pat and I could take the press club flight to Europe. When I finally got to class on the first Monday in October I was hopelessly behind in all classes, but especially Real Property. It was known at Georgetown as the "washout course" because it was a four-credit course that many students flunked. I was so hopelessly behind after missing the first month that I barely caught up with such concepts as future interests and contingent remainders, much less learned the arcane exceptions to those principles. Professor Don Wallace was known as a teacher with no sympathy for slow learners. After the final exam, I was convinced that I had failed. But I passed—barely, and I think I owe it to the kindness of Wallace. (In one of life's ironies, years later, I taught sixth grade Hebrew Scripture to Wallace's daughter in Sunday school at Holy Trinity. There was no test and no grade. She was a wonderful pupil. Don Wallace and I never discussed our Real Property connection.)

*   *   *

A new marriage, law school and the job as the *Bulletin's* White House correspondent were not always a happy combination. On the Saturday morning of Washington's Birthday weekend in February 1968, Pat and I shopped for furniture and made plans for dinner and a movie that evening. As we returned home from shopping, the phone was ringing. It was the White House summoning me to Andrews Air Force to take a trip with LBJ. The White House would not say where we would go or how long we would be gone. Yelling, "where's my toothbrush," I packed my suitcase and rushed out to a cab. Recalling this event, Pat said it was her "first introduction to life as the wife of a national political correspondent." It was my turn in the pool system to ride on Air Force One. It was not until we were in the air that an LBJ aide said we were headed for Fort Bragg, North Carolina, for Johnson to hail the 82nd Airborne Division embarking for Vietnam.

It was a pivotal moment in the war. Just a few weeks earlier the North Vietnamese launched the Tet Offensive that showed that they had plenty of fight left and may have the momentum in the war. In the United States, Johnson was on the ropes as public opinion swung against U.S. involvement in the war. He faced primary elections and Sen. Eugene McCarthy of Minnesota was running strong enough in the polls to suggest that LBJ could be dealt a primary defeat and certainly had a hard uphill climb to victory for another White House term in November. Effectively Johnson could not campaign since everywhere he went he heard, "LBJ, LBJ, how many kids did you kill today?" and worse. Little did reporters know at the time, but among LBJ's advisers, former Secretary of Defense Robert S. McNamara and his replacement at the Pentagon, Clark Clifford, were urging Johnson to scale back the war and open negotiations with Ho Chi Minh.

On this February morning when I was supposed to be studying law and heading for dinner and a movie with Pat that evening, I flew into Fort Bragg and watched Johnson, who appeared haggard, address the troops. I called Pat and said you'd never guess where I am. We did not change our dinner and movie plans. But from Fort Bragg we did not fly to Washington. When I looked out the window of the plane I saw the Appalachian Mountains. An LBJ aide said we would next land at El Toro, the Marine Corps station south of Los Angeles. Johnson delivered a message of hope and patriotism to the Marines. I stood near Johnson as the Marines boarded airplanes for flights to war.

That wasn't the end of a surprising day. I boarded a helicopter at El Toro and landed on the deck of an aircraft carrier off the southern California coast. For much of the night I sat up with LBJ, Walt Rostow and other LBJ aides who pushed one central thought:—that the Tet Offensive launched by the Viet Cong and North Vietnamese was a failure, that it amounted to a last gasp by the enemy, and that the United States was close to victory in South Vietnam. I didn't believe it. I was convinced that the war in Vietnam was a mistake, a trap into which the United States had fallen. LBJ's attempt to convert the debacle of the Tet Offensive into a U.S. victory was doomed.

I flew with Johnson for a quick visit the next day to former President Dwight D. Eisenhower at his home on a golf course in Palm Springs. We flew back to Washington, two days too late for Pat and me to fulfill our weekend plan for dinner and movie. I was at my *Bulletin* office the next day and in my law school class that night. A month later, on the final Sunday night of March, LBJ went on national television to announce that he would not seek, nor would he accept, the nomination of the Democratic Party for another term in the White House. Lyndon Johnson was a casualty of Vietnam.

His withdrawal from the political campaign created turmoil at the *Bulletin* and other news outlets. Plans for what had looked like a contest between LBJ and Richard M. Nixon were discarded. "Clean Gene" McCarthy was the only Democrat of any consequence in the race against Johnson, but he was not alone for long. Vice President Hubert Humphrey and Sen. Robert F. Kennedy of New York announced their candidacies. I began to travel with Humphrey and got ready to cover Kennedy's first major effort as a White House aspirant in the Indiana Democratic primary in April.

*   *   *

As Humphrey and Kennedy hastily put together campaign staffs and I made plans to travel to Indiana, tragedy struck. The great civil rights leader, the Rev. Martin Luther King, Jr., was shot to death on April 4 on the balcony of a Memphis motel. Within minutes, violence erupted on the streets of many of the nation's cities. Pat and I climbed to the roof of our apartment building at 3808 Davis Place in Northwest Washington. We looked east and saw smoke from the fires on 14th Street. We heard sirens as police converged on the riot zone. I headed downtown to the White House. The Secret Service brought in buses from the D.C. transit system and formed a wall that encircled the White House, Treasury Department and Executive Office Building. From the fenced-in White House lawn, I saw soldiers in combat gear take positions in and behind the buses. The White House West Wing had the feel of crisis, though Johnson's aides told me the president was safe and the situation was under control. There was no point for me to hang out at the White House.

From the *Bulletin* office in the National Press Building at 14th and F Streets I walked a half mile north to barricades erected by the District of Columbia police and National Guard. Cutting through an alley beyond the barricades, I walked a few blocks more until I smelled smoke and saw rioters. I wrote a story about my close look at a riot.

A few days later, I flew to Indianapolis. Richard Drayne, Robert Kennedy's press secretary, was a neighbor and friend from Holy Trinity Church. He issued me credentials to ride in Kennedy's plane and motorcades. I was with Kennedy in Hammond, Indiana, where he rode in an open car that slowly made its way through crowds of aggressive admirers to a high school football field. Kennedy removed his jacket and wristwatch and stood in a car while reaching for hands to touch. Bill Barry, his chief security man, grabbed the back of Kennedy's belt and kept yanking the senator back into the car as well-wishers pulled Kennedy in the other direction. I walked just behind Kennedy into the football field.

On another day, I flew with Kennedy into Indianapolis Airport at the end of a long day of campaigning in Eastern Indiana. There was a mix-up in scheduling. Cars and buses for Kennedy, his staff and reporters were missing. As I talked with Kennedy on the tarmac under bright lights, he called for a football from the plane. There for several minutes that warm April night we tossed the football, with Kennedy waving me down the runway so he could launch a forward pass. I wasn't very good at catching a football on the run, but I remember how delighted I was to grab a short pass from Bobby Kennedy.

I was at home on June 5 with Pat, watching on television as Kennedy spoke in the ballroom of the Ambassador Hotel in Los Angeles following his victory in the California Democratic primary. Roth was there for the *Bulletin*. Kennedy headed through the hotel kitchen. Pat laid aside the green curtain she was hemming and we talked about whether Kennedy could beat Humphrey in the final run-up to the nomination. Then came the news from the kitchen—Kennedy was shot.

The next morning, a Philadelphia editor called me at home: go to New York for the funeral. After Kennedy's body was brought into St. Patrick's Cathedral, I sat in a pew for hours, watching as a reporter, but also wondering what was to become of this country as another young dynamic leader was taken from us. I was a few pews back during the funeral Mass, choking back grief, as Edward M. Kennedy spoke of his brother as a good and decent man. I struggled to maintain professional detachment. Drayne gave me a ticket for the funeral train from New York to Washington, where Kennedy's body would be carried across the capital and laid to rest beside his brother in Arlington National Cemetery. The *Bulletin's* plan was that I cover the New York end of the

LAWRENCE M. O'ROURKE

story and Day cover events in Washington. Walking out of St. Patrick's after the mass, I decided that this was a story I wanted to give full justice to. I wanted to write it and read it before I sent it to the paper, not dictate it on the run. But I had to get in a bus to ride to Penn Station to board the funeral train.

Standing on the cathedral steps as Ethel Kennedy and other family members boarded cars, I spotted an old friend, Father Geno Baroni, an assistant pastor at a predominantly black parish in Washington—SS. Paul and Augustine. Some years previously, Pat was a volunteer teacher in Baroni's parish. I knew Geno celebrated Mass for the Kennedy family at their Hickory Hill home in Virginia and swapped ideas with Shriver and other promoters of the war on poverty. On the spur of the moment, I asked Geno if he had a ticket for the train. "No, but I'd sure like to be there," he said. I gave Geno my ticket.

As the Kennedy funeral train rolled slowly to Washington, I wrote and filed my story from New York and flew from LaGuardia Airport to Washington National Airport. On television that night, Pat and I watched the funeral procession to Arlington. As the camera fixed on Ethel Kennedy and Edward Kennedy walking up the slope to the gravesite, there was Baroni a few steps behind.

Pat and I needed to escape the sorrow that filled our lives and our city. We took a short holiday in Montreal and Quebec. In the midst of our sadness, we needed to celebrate the new joy in our lives. Pat was pregnant with our first child.

*   *   *

Roth assigned me to full-time coverage of Johnson, except for a trip to Chicago for the Democratic National Convention. I spent much of that summer in Austin where LBJ suffered while the party nominated Humphrey as his successor. I took my first foreign trip for the *Bulletin*, traveling with Johnson to Costa Rica, Nicaragua, El Salvador, Guatemala and Honduras. At virtually every stop I was forced into the protection of young men in uniform cradling machine guns. I was nervous when they swung them in my direction. I feasted on a crayfish dinner in Managua, an event that I often recalled as I wrote about the vicious war to erupt later in Nicaragua.

Pat, starting to feel and show her pregnancy, quit her job as program associate at the National Association for Housing and Redevelopment

Officials. She and I spent a month in the Crest Hotel in Austin where it hit 100 degrees every day. Among the few cool places was the air-conditioned car as I drove to the LBJ ranch and farmhouse. I came away from the conversations with LBJ—most of them not for attribution—convinced that he felt cheated by events beyond his control. He could not abide the idea that Nixon or Humphrey would take his place as the most powerful man in the world. Johnson didn't have much respect for either man, but he thought Humphrey was not up to the job. He was about to put Humphrey to the test in a manner that may have cost Humphrey the White House. Speaking on deep background, a journalistic device that prevents the reporter from even hinting at the source, Johnson told me that he expected Humphrey to remain loyal throughout the campaign and to avoid criticism of Johnson's conduct of the war. Nixon skirted direct criticism of Johnson and reassured voters that he had a "secret plan" to end the war. I never discovered it.

*　*　*

As the Democratic Convention neared, Pat and I flew to Chicago. Pat went to Grand Beach in southwestern Michigan—a summer hangout for Democrats from the South Side of Chicago—to spend time with her mother. I had a hotel room on Michigan Avenue near the Conrad Hilton Hotel. I was glad I wasn't in the Conrad Hilton. It was Humphrey's headquarters hotel and it was a fortress. When I had appointments in the hotel, I invariably found long slow lines at the elevators. My main assignment was downtown—to cover thousands of war protesters in Grant Park and delegation meetings and candidate appearances in the Loop.

Once or twice a day I visited the protesters. During daylight, many slept. They usually came out in force in late afternoon or at night to jeer delegates heading south on Michigan Avenue toward the convention site. Mayor Richard J. Daley, highly skilled at co-opting political opposition in Chicago by throwing benefits to adversaries, failed to grasp either the size or intensity of the anti-war group. Nor had he provided them with sufficient bathrooms, water and stages for their rallies. It is probable that in no case was Daley going to buy off the demonstrators, but it was the height of folly for his police to attack the demonstrators on the Wednesday night of the convention. I was on Michigan Avenue when the cops moved in, some on horses; most carrying nightsticks that they swung with passion, some firing tear gas. As a veteran of war protests in Washington, I knew better than to get caught between police and protesters. Wearing my credentials prominently around my neck, I stayed behind the police line. After an initial surge into the protest camp, the police backed up, and the protesters came forward onto Michigan Avenue in the direction of the Conrad Hilton Hotel. I stood at the northeast corner of the hotel as police clashed with protestors in the next block north. I saw police hit by flying objects, and I saw police pick up protesters and throw them to the ground and club them with their thick batons. I watched in horror as the Chicago cops tossed one protestor at a plate-glass window. As the battle edged in my direction, and I smelled tear gas, I ran to the entrance of the hotel, only to find it blocked by police. I ran around the corner and into the hotel. Through a window I could see the ugly action on the street.

After a while, the police withdrew and protestors milled about on Michigan Avenue. I returned to the street, where I made a tactical mistake. I found myself where I knew better than to be—in the no man's land between the protestors and the police. As the soldiers got closer I could see their rifles tipped with unshielded bayonets. I looked for a way around the soldiers, but was stopped by one who raised his bayonet to my chest. Waving my credentials and shouting, "press," the soldier and I had a standoff that probably only lasted a few seconds, but seemed like an eternity. He lowered the bayonet from my chest and I edged past him to the side entrance to the hotel. I dictated my story to a reporter at our convention office and headed to Humphrey's press office on an upper floor. It was jam-packed with reporters. Humphrey's staff was absent. They had reason to hide. Norman Sherman, Humphrey's campaign press secretary, eventually arrived and said a statement on the riots was being prepared—very carefully. Sherman invited me to Humphrey's suite in the penthouse.

We walked up several floors. The security team scrutinized each of us. When I stepped into Humphrey's suite, I found him on a sofa next to his wife Muriel. From the television set before him came evidence that the Democratic National Convention had nominated Hubert Horatio Humphrey to be president of the United States. The Humphreys and their friends smiled and clasped hands.

It would have been a joyous occasion except that in the room with Humphrey, I smelled the tear gas rising from Michigan Avenue. In my gut, I knew that despite Humphrey's joy, the riots had destroyed his chance for the White House.

I traveled with Humphrey to his home in Waverly, Minnesota, and spent several days there before I switched to covering Nixon. Through the fall my life was on rotation: a stretch with Humphrey, a stretch with Nixon and a stretch at the White House. I was with Humphrey the final week before the election when he came to Texas to campaign. Johnson refused to endorse Humphrey beyond a perfunctory statement. I wrote of Humphrey's agonizing effort to disassociate himself from Johnson and the Vietnam War without either alienating Johnson or coming across as an unprincipled political opportunist. Instead Humphrey looked weak, hardly competent to heal the nation.

Despite this, Humphrey's poll numbers slowly improved—because people didn't like Nixon. Johnson grudgingly decided to do his political duty for Humphrey and his party. Humphrey and Johnson made a joint appearance at a rally in the Houston Astrodome. I watched from them the press area in center field.

*   *   *

I was disappointed, but not surprised, when the country picked Nixon over Humphrey. Though I voted for Humphrey, I did so nervously, fearful that he wasn't strong enough to end the war and draw the country together. I couldn't abide Nixon personally, though I recognized his political genius. I was almost finished with covering Johnson. A man who earned my admiration by moving so brilliantly in advancing the civil rights agenda and promoting the cause of equal justice, LBJ succumbed to his worst instincts.

*   *   *

In 1971, I went to Austin to cover the opening of the LBJ Library on the University of Texas campus. While in that splendid capital city of Texas, I thought about the dozens of visits I made there, about the evening I wandered up the Drag and first heard in person the singer Willie Nelson, about the skillet breakfasts I enjoyed in the $8-a night city's finest hotel—the historic Driskill, about the Tex-Mex and steak dinners I consumed while quaffing long-neck Pearl beers on the *Bulletin's* expense account, about the time I stepped onto a scale on the Drag and discovered that I weighed more than 200 pounds and realized I was short of breath and resolved to begin running again in earnest.

I remembered the calls to get quickly to the ranch to hear LBJ talk on the condition he would not be quoted. I remembered parties with Texas politicians, boating on the lake and sightseeing down the road at the Alamo. I had the opportunity to report on one of the sorriest episodes in U.S. history. But now my story moves on—to other presidents, other deadlines, and other wars.

CHAPTER 9

Nixon:
With Admiration and Scorn

I HAD MANY a good day covering Richard M. Nixon. He was a gift to reporters. Rare was the week between his election in 1968 and his resignation in 1974 when I did not have three or four front-page stories out of the Nixon campaign team and the Nixon White House. In the dismal final months of Richard Nixon's presidency, it was day-by-day, sometimes hour-by-hour, breaking news about the president and his men.

When the Nixon presidency began, I was in the "give the guy a chance school," unlike many of my fellow White House correspondents who were older and knew Nixon closer up than I did. Shivering in the cold, I was on Capitol Hill on the January morning in 1969 when Nixon pledged to the nation that he would "bring us together." I had spent much of 1968 reporting on how divided we were as a people, primarily along racial lines. We needed to be brought together. I was determined to give Nixon my respect and what I could provide—fair and honest coverage in the nation's largest evening broadsheet newspaper. He said he had a "secret plan" to end the war in Vietnam—the issue at the top of my private political agenda. I hoped so, though I was skeptical. I was in the "lesser of two evils" crowd on Election Day. I reluctantly cast my ballot for Hubert Humphrey, despite his cowardice on Vietnam, because I thought he might, once liberated from Lyndon Johnson, move aggressively to end the war and would, in any case, govern under more enlightened and progressive civil rights and domestic policies than Nixon.

For me as a reporter, Nixon's swearing-in opened an era that I never contemplated in my wildest fantasy. I would be with Nixon in Beijing and Shanghai and in Moscow and Yalta, in Cairo and Alexandria, in Jerusalem, in Damascus, in Rome, Zagreb and Dublin. I would walk with him, each of us in white tie and tails, in the Philadelphia Academy of Music. I would sit with him on the patio of his seaside home in San Clemente, California, and in the woods of Yellowstone National Park. I would be a few feet away from him in Orlando, Florida, when he said, unconvincingly, "The president is not a crook."

And I would be on the White House South Lawn on that August 9, 1974 morning when Nixon walked from the White House to the Marine Corps helicopter that carried him to Andrews Force Base for his final journey as president. I watched as he turned and flashed his V for victory sign with his customary forced grin. I saw him do that often. He did it during two presidential campaigns and on the road when he heard taunts of war protesters. I would be with him in Limerick, Ireland and in San Jose, California, where he shaped his V sign as he dodged rocks and eggs.

When Nixon left the White House, his chosen successor, Gerald R. Ford, spoke for the nation when he declared, "Our long national nightmare is over." I shared Ford's view, even as I praised Nixon for the good he did and sorrowed in the evil he committed and the downfall he brought so unnecessarily upon himself. He had the political ability to be a good, if not great, president. I wrote in the *Bulletin* that Nixon wasn't forced out of office because he attempted great achievements and fell short. He was sent away in disgrace because he was so petty, so manipulative, so Nixonian, so "Tricky Dick."

He brought the worst of his secretiveness and paranoia to the White House. He worsened the situation in Vietnam by expanding the war. At home, instead of bringing us together, he deliberately made us a nation divided. He exploited political, racial, and economic tension in our country for his political gain. To benefit himself, he mocked the Constitution and twisted the power we granted him. I never thought that Nixon's downfall came because he tried to line his own pockets for personal enrichment. His goal was power, not money. He observed no bounds in seeking control. He acknowledged the checks and balances that make our system work only because he had to, not because he believed in them. In the self-aggrandizing interest of establishing an "Imperial Presidency," Richard Nixon abused the faith and trust of his fellow citizens.

Yet there were reasons to praise him. Even at the end, I was not a Nixon-hater. As glad and relieved as I was to see him relinquish power, I felt more sorrow for the nation at what he had dragged us through and failed to do than vindictiveness at his departure. I was there every step of the way.

*   *   *

I was there when Nixon, playing the "China card," cracked open the barrier separating the world's most powerful nation and the world's largest nation through his trip to China.

While I was with Nixon in Moscow, Leningrad and Kiev, I wrote in support of his major steps toward ending the Cold War by cutting nuclear arms deals with the Soviet Union. Writing from Jerusalem, Damascus, Jeddah, Amman and Cairo, I praised his effort to reduce tension in the Middle East to reduce the risk of war. I liked what he did to expand international trade, including steps he announced in the Azores. I admired Nixon's leadership, however reluctant and late it may have been, in expanding the federal government's protection of the environment. I have always thought that if the Democratic majority in Congress in 1969 had worked responsibly with Nixon on his welfare and health care proposals, the country would have taken real steps forward on both rather than wait decades, and Nixon would have deserved much of the credit.

*   *   *

From a personal perspective, one fond memory of Nixon came during his 1968 campaign against Humphrey. It was in reconstructed Colonial Williamsburg, Va., where Nixon paused to rest and prepare for a campaign debate with Humphrey in Richmond.

Nixon and his entourage, me at the back of the bus, had been in and out of airplanes and hotel ballrooms for several weeks. I was weary and remembered that I still had an overnight story to write and file when I headed for my room in the Williamsburg Inn. My plan was to write and have dinner with my preferred drink at that time, bourbon and water, or maybe two. I opened the door to my room and was shocked. There was Pat, resting quietly, as befitting a woman in her seventh month of pregnancy. The story of her apparition in Williamsburg unfolded. Helen Powell, the wife of Roland "Buzz" Powell of *The Buffalo News*, called Pat with a plan: they could surprise their husbands by driving from Washington to Williamsburg. Pat's presence altered my schedule. I still had to write that infernal overnight. But Pat and I managed to have dinner together in one of Colonial Williamsburg's choice restaurants. I had my bourbon and water. Pat prudently let me drink alone. The baby came first. We left each other the following day with our spirits rekindled and our dream renewed to be together again and to welcome our first child as soon as this campaign ended.

*　　*　　*

It may be hard for people who have never been on a presidential campaign to know what the experience was like for a newspaper reporter in 1968. It was nirvana for a political junkie like myself. It was customarily up in the morning at 5.30, bags in the hallway or lobby by 6, a quick call to the office while grabbing coffee and a donut, then toting a typewriter and files to the bus for the first boarding of the plane and the first flight of the day, with rushed breakfast on board while writing a new lead from a handout from the campaign staff, and then on and off the next bus, a speech, back on the bus, back on the plane, and on and on, sometimes four or five flights a day and as many speeches, and as many meals as one could grab on the run, never skipping a bathroom stop because you never know where the next one will be. For a writer for an afternoon paper such as myself, it was several new leads a day, sometimes entirely new stories if the speech seemed important enough. The workday didn't end when we reached the overnight hotel. Writers for afternoon papers—called PMs—had to write and send overnights, always staying awake until we could call the desk and assure ourselves that our copy had arrived safely. We were a small but select group, Peter Lisagor of *The Chicago Daily News*, Jerry terHorst of *The Detroit News*, Jack Horner of *The Washington Star*, John Farmer of *The Newark News*, and wire service reporters Doug Cornell and Frank Cormier of the Associated Press and Merriman Smith (a Pulitzer Prize winner who tragically took his own life in 1970) and Helen Thomas of United Press International. On occasions that our copy got mislaid before it reached our home offices, we had to track down the Western Union or AT&T agent to find out where our story was. That usually meant summoning them from the bar or bed. To get down from the high of the campaign day and the coffee that inspired the overnight, we PMers, after successfully filing, routinely gathered at the bar for a nightcap. There we might find a campaign aide who, of course, knew the regimen and was glad to give us inside information that served his candidate's interest. Sometimes we had to get that information into our stories—which meant new leads in the dark of the night. It was rare on the campaign trail that I got more than five hours sleep.

*   *   *

We kept ourselves going by telling ourselves that we were covering the most important story in the world—the election of a U.S. president. Our goal was to make it until the day after the election when we could write wrap-up stories and launch the holidays we always dreamed of taking. We talked of returning to "real life" and "real people." Even as we massaged our egos as the self-assumed leaders of our craft, we spoke about getting out of "the bubble"—the airplane, security and milieu of a White House campaign. We knew we were exhausted captives, but we would not be anywhere else. Being here is terrible, we said to one another, but not being here would be far worse.

*   *   *

We often said we felt the burdens of a campaign more than the candidate. Measured against the candidate, we got up earlier, got to bed later, wrote our own stories, passed through tighter security, stood in lines for food and telephones, and rode in narrow seats with little leg room to stretch or nap on chartered buses and in the press section of the airplane. But even Nixon, a perennial campaigner, gave in to exhaustion.

That brings me to my second personal story. Nixon ended a rough week of campaigning that included several flights through bad weather. We landed late at night in balmy Miami and went by motorcade to Key Biscayne. As the Nixons continued to their villa, we stumbled out of buses at a beachfront motel. I was so tired I barely noticed the palm trees.

I appreciated all this the next morning when after a long sleep I drew open the shades and saw the swimming pool outside my window and the sun dancing on the gentle rolling bay just beyond. I didn't have a bathing suit, since I did not expect the Nixon campaign to take a break in a resort. We didn't know when we'd stop, so suitcases were filled with more essential articles of clothing as well as extra notebooks and batteries. In the briefing room, I asked Gloria Steinem, writing for the feminist magazine *Ms.*, what Nixon had said to her during her exclusive interview aboard the plane the day before. Of course she wouldn't say. I didn't expect her to. I would have kept it for myself until it appeared in print, just as Steinem did. But I was fascinated that Nixon would grant an interview to a publication that he might reasonably have suspected would not be friendly. I had one-on-one sessions, more chitchat than interviews, with Nixon during the campaign, but never got a great story from him.

We did not stay long at Key Biscayne, just a weekend for Nixon to plot strategy with campaign manager John Mitchell, make calls for campaign contributions, cut TV ads, and share a moment with his confidant and Key Biscayne neighbor Charles "Bebe" Rebozo. Campaign clocks tick fast until the polls close. Nixon wasn't about to give away valuable campaign time. He painfully remembered going to Alaska in 1960 to keep a promise to campaign in every state. Nixon had Alaska in the bag, but he spent valuable hours off-camera on the journey. Kennedy used those hours to visit swing states that helped him eke out his narrow victory. I was grateful for Nixon's brief respite in Key Biscayne. In later years, whenever I was in Miami I drove over the Rickenbacker Causeway to Key Biscayne, passed the beachfront hotel and recalled the magic detour from the 1968 campaign trail.

*　*　*

The main thing on my mind on Election Day 1968 was not the result at the polls—I was near certain that Nixon would win—but the birth of our firstborn child. After the election, when Tony Day covered Nixon's start on putting together a government, I spent my days at the White House, where LBJ counted down to the end of his tragic presidency. Since LBJ was a lame duck, my work hours were more regular. Pat and I had time to bring our life together after my year on the road, to pick out a bassinet and to seek a name for our child, whom we called "the cub." We didn't know if we would be parents of a boy or girl. Technology for a safe in-utero determination of gender didn't exist, and, besides, we were not anxious to know. When people asked what I wanted, I said, "A healthy baby."

On November 26, the Tuesday before Thanksgiving, three weeks after the doctor said our "cub" would arrive, Pat woke me and said it was time to go to Georgetown University Hospital, a five-minute drive from our Glover Park home. Our hospital bag was packed. I drove quickly. We spent a long day together as Pat went through labor. Dads, I realized, can't do much during contractions except to count, touch and offer encouragement. It was night, after more than 14 hours of labor, when Dr. James Brew, the obstetrician, said it was time to head to the delivery room. Gowned and masked, my shoes covered with green gauze, I went along, having taken several of the classes given for fathers who wanted to be present at the delivery. And thus I was there when our son entered the world. We immediately decided on his name—Christopher.

Chris was a big healthy baby weighing 10 pounds and 3 ounces. Despite hospital regulations, I brought a bottle of champagne to the new mother's room on Thanksgiving. We toasted our son and ourselves. I handed out cigars at the White House.

*   *   *

The *Bulletin's* editors said congratulations, take a couple of days off, and quickly come back to work. That was an improvement on the old days at the *Bulletin* when they gave new fathers a shiny silver dollar, but no time off. The work editors had in mind for me was not in Washington. It was in New York, in the Pierre Hotel on 5th Avenue opposite Central Park, where Nixon was picking his cabinet and his staff and laying down policies on matters he had largely avoided during the campaign.

A few days after Chris's birth and his trip home wrapped in a blanket in his beaming mother's arms as she climbed the steps to our third floor Davis Place apartment, I took the train to New York and moved into the St. Moritz Hotel on Central Park South. From there it was a leisurely walk to the Pierre and Nixon command center. I spent my days in the Pierre, attending briefings and interviewing people who would serve as the next White House staff and Cabinet. From the campaign I knew H.R. (Bob) Haldeman, the brusque monosyllabic fellow who would become Nixon's chief of staff and gatekeeper. I had better relations with John Ehrlichman and Daniel Patrick Moynihan who would advise on the domestic agenda. In the Pierre I had my first conversation of any length with Henry A. Kissinger, incoming national security adviser, and William P. Rodgers, incoming Secretary of State. As we discovered, Kissinger and Rodgers were antagonists. Kissinger won. But all was teamwork and idealism at the Pierre.

During December 1968, when Pat was a new mother, I a new father, Chris our new baby, and Nixon about to become a new president, I lived in New York. I quickly learned that it wasn't prudent to call home at night and announce the fancy restaurant where I ate dinner or the museum I slipped into my schedule. With a hungry infant to nurse, Pat got little sleep and had little patience to hear about my adventures in the big city. I left New York for Washington on the last train on Saturday night, so that I didn't miss any story for the *Bulletin's* Sunday paper, and left Washington for New York on Sunday night with enough time to report and write a story for the *Bulletin's* Monday edition. Once I asked a *Bulletin* editor for permission to leave New York on an early train on Saturday, but was reminded that I had to wait around to see if other papers had stories I had to match for the *Bulletin*. The *Bulletin* wanted my byline on Nixon stories and they reminded me they paid the freight. I served the *Bulletin's* interests, but I didn't have much time to become acquainted with my new son in his early months. Considering it all, Pat was marvelously patient with me, not to mention exhausted. Looking back, I don't know how she tolerated it.

*　　*　　*

It was during those weeks that the *Bulletin's* top editors in Philadelphia announced that Bob Roth retired as Washington bureau chief to become a fulltime columnist, that Tony Day succeeded him as bureau chief, and I was White House correspondent and columnist. By the way, they said to me, take a couple of days at home for Christmas and then fly to California where Nixon would make additional cabinet appointments. It was a joyful, but rushed, Christmas celebration.

I flew aboard the Nixon plane to Los Angeles and traveled with the president-elect and his senior staff and wire service reporters to the luxurious Century Plaza Hotel. The rest of the press was taken to other hotels. I was the print pool reporter and housed in the Century Plaza for the entire visit. I pushed Herb Klein and Ron Ziegler, the press office contacts, for an interview with Nixon. They said I could talk with him, but he was busy putting together his cabinet. I prepared questions so that when Nixon and I sat together I could ask him about his "secret plan" to end the Vietnam War, about allegations that he intervened in foreign policy near the end of the presidential campaign by contacting the North Vietnamese to block the initiation of negotiations, and his civil rights views.

When I entered his hotel room, I barely had my greeting out of the way and my hand separated from his when Nixon began to talk about football, specifically about the Rose Bowl and running back O.J. Simpson of the University of Southern California being drafted by the Philadelphia Eagles. Nixon said he knew that I rooted for the Eagles, but in truth I knew virtually nothing about the team or Simpson.

There wasn't a pause in his monologue. Every time I tried to break in, Nixon looked irritated. Before I could get to my questions, a Nixon aide popped into the room and said time's up. So in theory I had my interview, but hadn't learned much worth telling my readers unless I was a football writer, which I was assuredly not. I wrote a few paragraphs in the *Bulletin* about Nixon, Simpson and the Eagles. They were printed in the sports pages. The Buffalo Bills as the first choice in that year's professional football draft drafted Simpson.

On New Year's Day, 1969, Nixon, the staff and I flew by helicopter from the back lot of the Century Plaza to the parking lot of the Rose Bowl. I had a great seat at the game a few feet from Nixon as Simpson ran the ball for 171 yards, including an 80-yard sprint for a touchdown. USC beat Ohio State 27-16. Nixon visited both sidelines. The president-elect told me on the record and for attribution that it was a great game. I figured, who was I to dispute him? After that event was locked into history, we spent a few more days in California before heading east and the inauguration of Richard M. Nixon as 37th president of the United States.

*   *   *

If Nixon ever put into effect his secret plan to end the Vietnam War, I missed the story. White House reporters, members of Congress in the opposition party, and most citizens historically give new presidents a honeymoon, usually the first 100 days. Nixon got more than that. For the White House press, it was virtually collective amnesia captured by the *Washington Post* cartoon by Herblock—Nixon getting a clean shave.

Life for me in 1969 could not have been better—Pat and I happy in our married life and rejoicing in the development of Chris, success in my law school classes, new friends through our religious community, Holy Trinity Church in Georgetown. I even got a few Saturdays and Sundays off work. I traveled with Nixon domestically and internationally.

The Nixon house in Key Biscayne, Florida was too exposed for presidential security. Local police barricaded the roads. The Coast Guard patrolled the bay on the edge of the Nixon property. The Secret Service occupied the house next store and installed 24-hour guard posts. Yet it was in a community and accessible through other houses and shortcuts. Besides, neighbors complained about the hassle caused by Nixon's presence.

LAWRENCE M. O'ROURKE

The Nixons learned of a house on the Pacific coast in San Clemente, California that was comfortable, secure and private. When they flew out in March to check it out, I accompanied them. I was invited to lunch with the Nixons in San Juan Capistrano, the town that welcomes back the swallows on what has in song been hailed as the first day of spring.

The restaurant chosen by Nixon for lunch looked charming. Ziegler said there was a seat for me at the table with the Nixons, and that the conversation could not be reported. Nixon did most of the talking. It was mainly about his early life in California.

Lapsing into what for Nixon was the romantic, he said that one of the first dates he had with Thelma Ryan (later Pat Nixon) was dinner in this very restaurant. He said that our lunch that day brought back many memories. He picked this restaurant, he said, because of those memories. He said that as president he had his pick of restaurants, that he could have chosen the fanciest in California. But this one, he waxed euphoric, was so gracious with its exposed wood, its fine food, and its excellent service. He called attention to what he described as "fresh flowers" on the table.

That seemed to be the breaking point for Mrs. Nixon.

I can still see her clearly across the table from me looking at Nixon, gesturing to the flowers, and saying, "They're plastic, Dick."

From then on, the conversation seemed strained. We had coffee and the meal ended.

*   *   *

The Nixons bought the house in California. The president decided to spend August at what instantly became known as the San Clemente White House. I had to cover him. It turned out to be a happy family vacation. Pat and Chris flew west with me in the press charter. I paid the White House the cost of their flight. The White House picked the Surf and Sand Hotel in Laguna Beach for the press. It was a few miles from San Clemente. Pat, Chris and I had a room on the ocean side on the fourth floor. From our balcony we watched waves roll onto the beach. In the distance we saw Catalina Island. We joyfully watched the sun set over the ocean. At night we left the door to the balcony open so that from our bed we could hear the surf.

The Nixon press office held one briefing a day, in the morning, and later in the day posted notices about public events involving the president. Since Philadelphia was three hours ahead of California, the schedule worked out just fine for the O'Rourke family. While Pat and Chris enjoyed the pool and the beach, I attended the briefing and wrote my story. By the time we had lunch, it was after the *Bulletin's* final deadline. We took advantage of this by trips to the San Diego Zoo, Laguna Beach galleries, Los Angeles, and Joshua Tree National Park. White House press secretary Ziegler often reminded me that before his involvement with Nixon, he was an announcer on the Jungle Cruise ride at Disneyland. At Ziegler's invitation, Pat, Chris and I accompanied him to the theme park where he did his spiel. Chris was nine months old. We wheeled him in a stroller and he laughed when Donald Duck and Mickey Mouse tickled his chin.

The young woman who cleaned our hotel room was a mother, and gentle and playful with Chris. Pat and I asked her to baby-sit. So Pat and I got a couple of nights out. We attended a party at the Nixon house. The Nixons graciously invited us to look around. Of course we did. Pat was appalled that reporters went into the Nixon bedroom and wrote down the names of the books at their bedsides. I told her it was pretty standard operating procedure. Reporters seize every opportunity and grab every detail that might reveal an insight into the president. And I guessed, perhaps cynically, that the Nixons or their staff for the occasion picked bedside books they wanted the Nixons to be reported reading.

*   *   *

While I was in California, there were important developments in the *Bulletin's* Washington Bureau. Bureau chief Tony Day left to become chief editorial writer at *The Los Angeles Times*. He was recruited by Otis Chandler, the publisher, and Robert Donovan, the editor. The *LA Times*, long a conservative organ and not a very good newspaper, was moving toward the center. It became an outstanding paper under Chandler, Donovan and Day. I knew that Tony would be a gifted editorial writer and editor. He was careful, precise and analytical in his thinking and writing. As Tony left the *Bulletin*, many journalists across the country applied to succeed him. The job was considered one of the best in the business. Although the *Bulletin* was not the finest paper in the land, it was the major afternoon paper. I wondered who my new boss would be.

The job was still vacant a couple of months later when I was at the United Nations covering the General Assembly. George R. Packard, who succeeded Dickinson as the *Bulletin's* executive editor, called me. Packard, a Japan scholar, said he was reluctant to name me bureau chief because I was only 31 and headed toward a law degree that likely would take me away from journalism. However, said Packard, after thinking it over, talking with others in the business, and evaluating applicants, he wanted me for the job. I accepted with pleasure, especially since it meant a big salary increase to help care for our child and another on the way.

*　　*　　*

Reporters and editors at the *Bulletin* that I worked with since my copy boy days were overwhelmingly enthusiastic about my promotion. I benefited from my record at the paper. I favor promotion within organizations unless there is a need to shake things up and go outside. As an insider with access to the *Bulletin's* decision-making hierarchy, I long advocated change, including switching the *Bulletin* from an afternoon newspaper to a morning paper. I argued for more aggressive reporting, certainly in Washington, but especially on local issues, where the *Bulletin* could use its clout to uncover sloppy and inept government leadership. The *Bulletin* had a superb local staff that was underused. I also knew that at 31, I was pushing the boundaries of my editors' tolerance when I suggested new ways to run their newspaper.

But now I had the job of making the *Bulletin's* coverage of Washington and national politics relevant and interesting to an audience that was steadily being drawn from newspapers to television. I was aware that journalism as I knew it and loved it was ending. Newspapers had to be much more competitive in news gathering and packaging. I shook up the bureau, adding Linda Heffner, Rem Rieder, and Rob Taylor, young, aggressive reporters in tune with modern culture and alert to emerging issues, an experienced political reporter in John Farmer, and an accomplished foreign policy journalist Ray Moseley. As bureau chief, I outlined coverage responsibility and gave reporters freedom and encouragement to develop their own sources and techniques.

*　　*　　*

On a few occasions, I stepped away from reporting the Nixon White House and managing the bureau on a day-to-day basis. One such time was June 1970 when I received a Juris Doctor degree from Georgetown

University Law Center. At the graduation ceremony on the Georgetown campus, I sat with a child on each knee. Chris on one and on the other Katie, our second child, born just two weeks before, on May 21, imperfect timing since I was in the middle of exams. The rules at our Davis Place apartment building stated that we could not have children of different genders sharing the same bedroom. As nonsensical as we viewed that rule, it prompted us to move into our first house at 5616 Nevada Avenue in the Washington neighborhood called Chevy Chase DC. We had a lot of unpacking to do. I suspect that Katie's exposure to the law at such an early age had little effect on her, but she grew up to be a distinguished lawyer, first as a prosecutor, then as a trial lawyer. Beyond Pat, Chris and Katie, I was blessed to have my father and mother at my law school graduation.

Graduation from law school is just a first step. Telling the *Bulletin* it would have to do without me for a while, I plunged into preparation for the bar admissions exam. I began my days before sunrise. I bundled Chris and Katie, wrapped in blankets, onto my lap in an overstuffed rocking chair and read aloud from my bar prep notes. During the day, Pat did a heroic job keeping the children quiet while I focused on the fine points of law that may test the candidate's ability to absorb vast quantities of minutiae, but which most lawyers bury in deep recesses of their mind as soon as possible, if only to regain mental stability.

In any event, I took the three-day bar exam, fretting after each session with fellow Georgetown law graduates, including Kathy Davies, John Rick, Marlene Martin, Henry Gallagher, and Dan Sullivan, that we had really screwed up that section of the test. We feared we had flunked. The test over, Pat and I and the two kids left for a splendid holiday in Green Mountain Falls, Colorado, in the villa of old friend Ann Schattman and her family. We rode horses, explored mountain towns, and enjoyed fresh trout. The children finally had their parents all to themselves. I squeezed in an interview with a law firm in Denver. Pat and I together decided we would rather remain in the east and I withdrew my name from consideration.

When we flew back to Washington, the first piece of mail I opened was the one I wanted: I passed the bar. A month later, when I was back at the *Bulletin* covering Nixon, I took the oath as a lawyer, framed my certificates and took my first cases, defending juveniles accused of delinquent acts.

Sen. Hugh Scott, the Pennsylvania Republican minority leader of the Senate, called me and said he had an important announcement to

LAWRENCE M. O'ROURKE

make that afternoon and could I be at his office to hear it. Mystified, I showed up. Before a roomful of reporters and Senate aides, Scott made a little news about some pending legislation. Then he said that the main purpose of his meeting was to announce that I had passed the bar. He presented me a lovely leather briefcase and gracious note. I was flustered, but honored and pleased. A week later, Scott called and said he scheduled an interview appointment for me with the U.S. attorney. Scott said he backed me for appointment to a federal prosecutor's job. He said I should be in politics and that one of the best routes to elected office was through the prosecutor's office. I knew that was accurate. I met the U.S. attorney and we had a fine discussion. We explored the death penalty, rules of evidence, factors in sentencing, individual rights and reports of abuses in the FBI. At one point, he said that I lacked "a prosecutor's mentality," but he would schedule additional interviews that could lead to a job as an assistant U.S. attorney if I wished. However, I knew that I would be happier as a reporter than as a prosecutor, and that was the end of it. Scott said he was disappointed because he wanted me in politics.

*　　*　　*

Working at the White House covering Nixon was too much fun to give up, especially with the foreign travel that I loved. For a guy who figured during our honeymoon trip in 1967 that I would never get to Europe again, I became a regular commuter. I came to expect as routine three or four trips a year to Europe. Who can forget that first visit to Moscow, the State Department warnings that our hotel rooms would be bugged, walking through Red Square, standing in the Kremlin in the gilded St. Catherine's Hall? Who can forget my first time at the Wailing Wall (later called the Western Wall) in Jerusalem? Or my first time at the Pyramids?

I could go on, but will mention just a few more. Thrilled to return to Ireland, I flew with Nixon at dusk into Shannon Airport and rode in a car behind him to Limerick, where hundreds of people lined the sidewalks, some were quite unfriendly, as evidenced by chants and placards that Nixon go home and end the Vietnam War. When the president left his car to speak from a platform and accept a walking stick and key to the city, he was the target of stones and eggs. Some of them hit me, but we all survived, even after Nixon displayed his V sign, and the pelting intensified. The next day, Nixon visited a town where he claimed Irish Quaker roots and went on to Dublin where it was my only look at the aged and ill Irish President Eamon de Valera.

*   *   *

While exciting, the foreign travel was but a footnote to the story that will overwhelm all else in the history of Richard Nixon—Watergate. I, like other White House correspondents, had no part in uncovering the role of Nixon and his men in the June 1972 break-in at the Democratic National Committee headquarters in the Watergate. Credit for uncovering the Watergate scandal is primarily due reporters Bob Woodward and Carl Bernstein and their colleagues, especially publisher Katherine Graham and executive editor Ben Bradlee, at *The Washington Post*.

Information about Watergate began to flow and then to flood after Nixon's victory in the 1972 election over hapless Democrat George McGovern. I covered that campaign but there was little point to it. McGovern had the right message, but you didn't have to be an experienced reporter to realize that McGovern didn't have a chance to defeat Nixon, riding high from his China trip, a decent economy and a country that wanted Nixon's stern hand, not McGovern's anti-war and liberal messages. I voted for McGovern.

I covered Watergate as it unfolded at the White House from Ziegler's dismissal of the break-in as a "third-rate burglary" to final revelations that Nixon abused powers of his office in a blatant attempt to use the Central Intelligence Agency and FBI to block the probe into Oval Office involvement. More than a year before Nixon resigned, I wrote in a *Bulletin* news analysis that he could not survive. On April 23, 1973, I wrote that Nixon was now "forced to move forward alone" in a White House where "things were out of control." I covered the resignation of the disgraced Spiro T. Agnew as vice president and his replacement by House Republican Leader Gerald R. Ford. While I talked a few times with Agnew, he preferred to keep prying reporters at a distance. I often spoke on Capitol Hill with Jerry Ford. He struck me as a politician with good survival instincts, but limited capacity for genuine leadership on tough issues.

*   *   *

LAWRENCE M. O'ROURKE

Many writers have told the Watergate story, and there's no need for me to go into it. I recall two events in which I was involved as a reporter with Nixon in his final days.

Nixon knew that the end of his presidency was in sight for many months before it actually happened. In May 1974, I went with him to Moscow for the signing of a significant nuclear arms deal—a significant Nixon achievement. Nixon went flawlessly through the protocol, but this time I was unable to speak with him as I had on previous occasions abroad. Nixon returned for a couple of weeks to the United States and then we headed across the ocean again. We flew to Cairo where President Anwar Sadat put on a rousing welcome for Nixon.

In Cairo, Sadat and Nixon boarded a train for Alexandria, the ancient city on the Mediterranean coast. I was in the car just ahead them. We were a few minutes from the Cairo station when I was taken to Nixon and Sadat. I said, "Hello, Mr. President," to each of them. We went to the next car and an open platform exposed on the left hand side as we rolled rapidly along the tracks. Nixon and Sadat sat in red upholstered chairs facing out. I stood to the side. We passed hundreds of thousands, maybe millions of Egyptians who lined the tracks, sometimes so close they could touch the Sadat-Nixon car as it rolled by. (I was later told that at least four people were struck and killed by the rolling train, but got no confirmation from either the Egyptians or Americans.)

On arrival in Alexandria, Sadat took off in a motorcade for his seaside villa. Nixon stepped into an open touring car. I, along with a dozen photographers, climbed aboard a flatbed truck. We were immediately ahead of Nixon in his open car as the motorcade pulled away from the railroad station and entered a broad boulevard lined with high-rise buildings and throngs of people on both sides. Hundreds waved small U.S. flags and cheered Nixon. Large U.S. flags hung on buildings. Many people stood on balconies and roofs. It was an awesome sight. At the same time, I found it chilling and frightening.

In my years covering the White House, I never saw a U.S. president as exposed to the public as Nixon was that day in Alexandria. Thoughts of John F. Kennedy shot in an open car in Dallas filled my head. I figured that Egyptian security could not have checked out everybody on the balconies and roofs with full view of Nixon. Nor could they be certain about who was in the crowds at street level. To me, it was no wonder that Sadat was elsewhere, not in this open car with Nixon. The route of Nixon's journey was no secret, the presence of crowds and flags made evident. There were no Secret Service agents running alongside the Nixon car, as there would be normally. I kept looking up and into the crowd, more than at Nixon, wondering if I would spot an assailant.

But the half-hour ride was all cheer and no violence. Nixon made it safely to his meeting with Sadat. After I saw the two men enter Sadat's villa, I returned to the press center and wrote a pool report. The story was straightforward—that Nixon, embattled at home, had received a warm welcome on the train ride from Cairo to Alexandria and on the streets of Alexandria.

While riding on the open railroad car and the flatbed truck on that lovely day in Egypt, I thought that Nixon had no fear because he knew that his days as president were fast running out. And I wondered, though never expressed in print because it seemed so speculative, and theoretically so preposterous that it should remain unsaid until much later, that Nixon might not have minded if he had been shot in Alexandria. It might be better for Nixon to die a martyr, I thought to myself, than disgraced as the first U.S. president to resign.

On the return flight from Egypt to Washington, I wrote that after a hero's welcome, Richard Nixon was coming home to the inescapable death of his presidency.

*　　*　　*

Revelation after revelation showing Nixon's deep involvement in the cover-up tumbled out in the next weeks. On constant deadline and with no margin for error, I wrote a chain of stories. The Supreme Court ordered Nixon to reveal incriminating tapes. Nixon reluctantly bowed to the court and late one afternoon, just minutes before deadline, I got the thick blue-covered book containing transcripts of secretly taped Nixon Oval Office conversations. Quickly, I read through it and found documentation that he had misused the power of his office in an attempt to cover-up the White House role in the Watergate break-in. The *Bulletin* delayed its final edition until I dictated my story paragraph by paragraph from the White House to Philadelphia.

I led the *Bulletin's* Washington staff in putting together a package of stories that detailed, usually through Nixon's own words, the horror that had taken place in the White House after the botched break-in. With the manuscripts stripping away Nixon's dignity and providing convincing evidence, the House of Representatives moved methodically

　　LAWRENCE M. O'ROURKE

toward impeachment. White House and Republican sources, including Hugh Scott, told me that Nixon was finished. Nixon's legal team and the leading Nixon staff apologist, Jesuit Father John McLaughlin, offered to give me secret information if I would write pro-Nixon pieces, but I insisted that everything would have to be on the record and attributed.

*   *   *

On a bright and clear August 8 morning in Washington, I encountered Pat Buchanan, one of Nixon's longest-serving aides. "It's almost over," he said somberly. He and speechwriter Ray Price and others were drafting a speech in which Nixon would announce his intention to resign as president.

I called Jerry Ford's office to see what was on his schedule for the day, but could not reach any aide who knew anything or, at least, would tell me. I knew Ford's aides reasonably well and they usually took or returned my call, but this time it was different. It was later that I learned that Ford met that morning with Nixon in the White House just a few yards from where I sat. I called Scott and he said the Senate flowed with rumors, but he better not say any more. Ditto with the other senator from Pennsylvania, Republican Richard S. Schweiker, usually an excellent source. I tried Alexander Haig, a former Army general acting as White House chief of staff, and very often an excellent source. In Washington and Key Biscayne, Haig and I frequently talked about Nixon's situation. Haig was honest and blunt, telling me what the Nixon people were doing, and never arguing that Nixon could remain in office. Haig and I had a long-established link. He was born in Bala Cynwyd, a Philadelphia suburb. He attended St. Joseph's Prep in Philadelphia and had a brother, Frank, a Jesuit. We swapped stories about growing up only a few miles apart. But on this day Haig did not call me back, adding support to my belief that Nixon was about to end his presidency.

Gerry Warren, the calm, steady, affable and competent deputy White House spokesman, would tell me nothing. He wasn't about to mislead me. He never did during the long ordeal. He and Haig were the two figures in the White House for whom I retained respect. I called the *Bulletin* in Philadelphia and said I thought this was the final day of the Nixon presidency. When wire editor Bill Townshend asked how strong were my sources, I said I was dealing with little pieces of information that added up to a resignation, but that I had no single high-placed source I could confidently rely on. Write the story as strong as you can with what you got, Townshend said. We aimed for the midday home delivery edition, the *Bulletin's* big run. From my desk at the White House, I dictated the story to a reporter in Philadelphia. Within seconds, I got a call back from the national editor. It's too strong, he said. We negotiated softer words that suggested that the resignation was imminent, but stopped short of saying it was at hand. I was ahead of the wire services in reporting the rapid flow of events that day. However, *Bulletin* editors didn't want to risk a headline that Nixon was resigning, only to have him stick it out. They had a good point. Memories of the 1948 *Chicago Tribune* headline declaring Tom Dewey's victory over President Harry Truman haunt newspaper editors. But, on the whole, the *Bulletin* did well with my story that August afternoon. Shortly before the final edition, the White House announced that Nixon asked the television networks for time that evening to speak to the nation. I asked Warren if Nixon would announce his resignation. His doleful silence and tears in the eyes of the White House staff provided the answer.

Past the 4-star deadline, with the presses holding, and editors moving my copy to the composing room paragraph by paragraph, I dictated on August 8, 1974: "Richard Nixon will address the nation at 8 o'clock tonight, apparently to announce his intention to resign as 37th president of the United States." It was with reluctance that I put the word "apparently" into my lead. What's more, the jittery typesetter failed to include the word "as" in my sentence. The editors did not catch the omission, so the *Bulletin's* fabled 4-star hit the streets with a typo. Nevertheless, that front page became a keeper in my file.

*   *   *

The next morning, August 9, 1974, Warren told me that he could get me into the East Room to hear Nixon's final speech as president to his staff and his family, certain to be emotionally devastating, or he could get me on the South Lawn for the final departure, equally to be a riveting performance. Gerry said he couldn't get me to both places because it would be a quick move and the Secret Service, Nixon family and White House staff did not want to risk any sort of a hitch, like encountering a reporter in the hallway. I chose the South Lawn and saw

LAWRENCE M. O'ROURKE

the Nixons and Fords walk across the grass, Nixon's V-sign and smile, and liftoff of the Marine helicopter. It was over.

While I admired some of Nixon's work and built a career covering his rise and fall, I was relieved to see him board the green helicopter. Standing on the South Lawn, I smiled at "good old Jerry Ford" as he and Betty, after waving goodbye to the Nixons, walked hand-in-hand into the White House. I felt relief, hope and joy when in the White House East Room, I watched Ford take the oath of office.

CHAPTER 10

Ten Days That Shaped a Career

President Richard M. Nixon startled the world on July 15, 1971 with his announcement that he accepted an invitation to visit the People's Republic of China—Communist China—in early 1972. The announcement set off a journalistic scramble as hundreds of U.S. news organizations applied to cover the visit. National security adviser Henry A. Kissinger and Chinese Premier Chou En-lai cut a deal for news coverage that resulted in credentials for 17 U.S. newspaper reporters. I was one of the 17, by far the youngest. This is my story of Nixon's trip to China, drawn from my notebooks, journals and memory.

July 16, 1971, Friday—My story on the Nixon trip the morning after the announcement emphasizes its political impact—a few months before the 1972 presidential election in which Nixon seems vulnerable. The American people are weary of the Vietnam War. Democrats are certain to point out that during the 1968 campaign Nixon declared he had a "secret plan" to end the war, but he expanded the war.

July 20, 1971, Tuesday—Senate Republican Leader Hugh Scott invites me to lunch at his Capitol Hill office. He offers to use his influence with the White House to get me a credential to cover the trip. I politely tell Scott that I would prefer that he not do so because I would rather rely on the importance of the *Bulletin* and my own position as its Washington bureau chief and White House correspondent. Scott shows me his collection of Chinese memorabilia. He suggests that Nixon should invite him on the trip. I write a column on Scott's ambition.

July 23, 1971, Friday—I send a note to White House press secretary Ronald Ziegler that I want to cover the trip. Ziegler phones and says he cannot promise anything since the Chinese are holding down the number of correspondents they will admit. Since the onset of the Cultural Revolution, no mainstream U.S. journalist has been let in. Ziegler knows that I regularly travel with Nixon and that the *Bulletin* is the nation's largest broadsheet evening newspaper. Over the years I tangled a few times with Ziegler. I was known as a reporter who was critical, but fair, to Nixon. Of course, I wanted to go, but I knew that covering it would be enormous responsibility. If I did a poor job, readers and editors would notice and remember.

August 2, 1971, Monday—I hear from the *Bulletin* grapevine that various editors and reporters in Philadelphia have proposed that if the *Bulletin* gets a credential for China, they rather than I get the assignment because they are more experienced. One rumor is that *Bulletin* managing editor George Packard, an expert on Asia as former aide to U.S. Ambassador to Japan Edwin O. Reischauer, may want to make the trip. If I am to go, I want to be prepared, so I start reading everything about China I can put my hands on. With Packard's support, I attend several programs on China, at Harvard, in New York and in Washington. I proceed on the basis that if the *Bulletin* gets to send a reporter, it will be me.

Mid-November 1971—Henry Kissinger tells me off the record that the Chinese are starting to loosen up a bit on credentials, but he doesn't have a number yet. He says he is pushing for a large press contingent but that may be counter-productive.

Mid-December 1971—Ziegler tells me that the Chinese have put a final number on U.S. news people to be credentialed, that he doesn't know the number, and that Nixon will pick.

December 23, 1971, Thursday—Ziegler calls me in Chicago where we are on Christmas holiday and asks me who will go for the *Bulletin* if it gets a seat on the plane. I say I will go. In that case, he says, you're on the plane. Don't tell anybody until we announce the list. I tell Packard and he says grand, do what you have to do to be ready.

Early January 1972—The White House releases the list of 87 U.S. news people who will be credentialed to fly into China with Nixon. The list includes television and radio technicians and reporters, magazine writers, and 17 daily U.S. newspaper reporters. I am on the list. *Bulletin* colleagues and other reporters call to congratulate. *The Boston Globe* and *Newsday* contend they were excluded because they are critical of Nixon. Ziegler declines to explain why some are on and others are off.

February 17, 1972, Thursday—I fly on the Pan American press charter 10 hours from Andrews Air Force Base to Honolulu. It feels hot after Washington. A lei is hung around my neck. I see Richard and Pat Nixon arrive on Air Force One and get the same traditional welcome.

Nixon is said to confer with advisers. I am told the president will give the Chinese a pair of musk oxen.

February 18, 1972, Friday—Ziegler warns that filing stories from China may be a hassle. The Chinese are in charge. I take a break from cramming to visit Pearl Harbor.

February 19, 1972, Saturday—I leave Honolulu in the dark at 6.30 a.m. and pass the International Dateline at 9.22 a.m. Sunday. Tom Ross of *The Chicago Sun-Times* suggests we find a folk Mass. Deputy Press Secretary Gerald Warren says we'll have lunch in Shanghai, but there will be no facility for filing. We're a day ahead of Nixon. Dr. Walter Lukash is aboard our plane and chats about health risks in China. I've gotten several shots, as recommended by the State Department. Tim Elbourne, the White House press advanceman, will get on in Shanghai with credentials. Our pilot is Ralph Hunt of Kinnelon, New Jersey

After a seven-hour and 40 minute flight, we land in Guam for re-fueling. Guam is a blur. At the PX, I buy a camera for $43.50 and a radio for $12.95. After an hour, we're off on a four-hour flight to Hung Chiao Airport in Shanghai. The Nixons will spend the night on Guam at the home of Admiral Paul E. Pugh, commander of Naval Forces in the Marianas, and come to China tomorrow.

On the press plane, we indulge in grim humor, joking about what stories will say if we're shot down by the Chinese or arrested in China. Among journalists on board are Bill Ringle of *Gannett*, Peter Lisagor of *The Chicago Daily News,* Jerry ter Horst of *The Detroit News*, Phil Potter of *The Baltimore Sun*, Chuck Bailey of *The Minneapolis Tribune*, Bob Boyd of *Knight,* Max Frankel of *The New York Times*, Dick Dudman of *The St. Louis Post-Dispatch*, Robert Keatley of *The Wall Street Journal*, and Stan Karnow of *The Washington Post*. Among columnists are William Buckley and Joseph Kraft. The TV contingent includes Walter Cronkite, Dan Rather, Eric Sevareid, John Chancellor, Barbara Walters, Harry Reasoner, Bernard Kalb, Herb Kaplow and Ted Koppel. Theodore White represents Public Broadcasting. James Michener is here for *Readers Digest,* Hugh Sidey for *Life* and Mel Elfin for *Newsweek*.

Frank Cormier, Henry Hartzenbush, and Hugh Mulligan will report for the Associated Press. Norman Kempster, Helen Thomas and Stuart Hensley will cover for United Press International.

At age 33, and a relative novice in presidential reporting, I feel privileged to travel with such distinguished journalists. As we fly west, I read, doze, and look at the Pacific. Packard advised me to write everything because readers have tremendous interest.

February 20, 1972, Sunday—It is Sunday morning off the coast of China. We're bright and sunny at 35,000 feet, with a cloud cover that breaks now and then to let me see the Pacific. Cherries Jubilee is served as I await a diet of Chinese food. Ringle suggests we feast on sea slugs. We are told we are 40 miles from Shanghai and it is very cold there. The movie, the *French Connection*, is shut off. A White House staffer on the intercom talks of a problem with toilet seats and poison sumac in China. I wonder if the Chinese have put their air force planes near us yet.

We are 30 miles from Shanghai. It is four degrees Centigrade, 39 degrees Fahrenheit, which doesn't sound too bad. I'm prepared with a warm coat with a fur collar, bought for China after we were advised to dress for cold weather. Seat belt signs come on. We're told that in Shanghai they will put Chinese navigators and engineers aboard. They don't want us flying over sensitive military facilities along the coast. Clouds make big shadows on the ocean surface. Here we are—the "running dogs of U.S. imperialism." I mix disbelief that I'm here with excitement that I am participating in a major moment in history.

As we descend, reporters talk about who gets off first. We decide it should be TV crews to film the rest of us.

There it is—China. I see brown fields. There is a small river with boats, roads but no cars. Most buildings are along the water. I see big storage bins, a few people walking. A long boat passes under a bridge. There are red-roofed houses that remind me of chicken coops in New Jersey. We fly over sampans and piles of coal. I see trucks as we descend sharply. As the plane rolls down the runway, I see soldiers with rifles, prop planes with red flags, and a blue and white fuel truck. We taxi toward a guy on the ground wearing a Mao jacket. He waves his arms in signals just as they would back home. The plane stops several hundred yards from what appears to be the terminal. It is very quiet aboard the plane, as if wonder and anticipation have frozen us. Two-dozen people in blue jackets emerge from the terminal. They are accompanied by a contingent in green uniforms with side arms. The delegation in blue includes women. They walk to our plane. The airplane steps go down. Two Chinese come aboard. It remains quiet on the plane. I see billboards with red characters. Girls emerge from the terminal and lay a long red carpet. They wear Mao buttons on their blue jackets.

A White House official says TV crews are authorized to leave. There's an announcement. Mr. Lu is the press officer for the Shanghai Municipal Revolutionary Committee. Other Chinese come aboard. They say they have our credentials in the terminal. They announce that we will have a quick lunch. "I hope you are good with chopsticks," one says, displaying a bit of humor. There's a surprise. Five long distance phones are available, and we can file from here. I can't think of anything *Philadelphia Bulletin* readers need to read over Sunday breakfast about my arrival in China. There are three Telex circuits.

I step into China at 12.25 in the afternoon. Mr. Lu stands by the red carpet. I shake his hand and say, "I'm pleased to be in your country." He smiles, says nothing, and moves me along. There are more Chinese hands for the visiting U.S. journalists to shake. We walk on the red carpet into the terminal where we are immediately served hot tea. A girl in braids does not smile as she pours my tea. She wears a blue cap, much like the one my grandfather Higgins wore. Pictures of Mao, Marx and Lenin hang on the wall.

We are ushered to a room where we are told that the U.S. journalists are members of the official U.S. delegation. Mr. Lu and his colleagues agree to answer questions.

Q. Who will meet Nixon in Peking? A. A high number of committee members.

Q. Will there be private citizens? A. Arrangements were made by the leaders. I don't know the details.

Q. Are there flights from this airport to other countries? A. Air France leaves from here.

"Attention please. Attention please. Take your seats. Ladies and gentlemen, on behalf of the information department, I would like to extend welcome to our journalistic friends of the American press corps. We will now issue press and cable cards and your press badges. Pin the badges on your coats. There are items of interest in Peking. Each of you will be issued a hotel card. Carry it with you as you go along. I wish you a pleasant stay in China and the best of health and every success."

I ask for names. A Chinese official writes in my notebook: "Mr. Lu was joined by Li Fu-Shien, official of Foreign Affairs Department of Shanghai Municipal Revolutionary Committee, and Yuan Pin, China International Travel Service, Shanghai Branch."

Lu says he will give journalists the information they need for their careers. Joe Kraft asks: Where's Lin Biao? (Marshal Lin Biao, former minister of defense and number two official in China as vice chairman of the Chinese Communist Party, had mysteriously disappeared. The Chinese government later said Lin Biao attempted to assassinate Mao. Lin Biao opposed China striking up ties with the United States or the Soviet Union.)

Kraft's question, where's Lin Biao, was clear enough. Lu avoids an answer. "Why don't we eat our lunch?" That was the end of the question and answer session.

I get plastic tags with my picture and identification as correspondent of the *Bulletin*. My hair is long in the style of the 1970s and dark. I am smiling. The identity card is for Chinese security forces. The other is authorization to use the telephone and telegraph. They are in Chinese and English. For recognition by security agents, I get a blue lapel button from the White House and a green lapel button with the word Press in Chinese and English from the Chinese.

We arrive at tables for lunch and begin toasting. A Chinese official at our table stands, raises his glass and offers his toast to peace and friendship. He does not smile. I raise my glass to him and say "to peace and friendship." It was a little like saying grace. An American stands and offers the same toast. We stand, clink glasses, and offer toasts to peace and friendship. The pattern repeats four times during lunch.

Conversations with Chinese lunch partners start with the flight and weather, but get personal. Fay Wells asks a Chinese man how old he is. He doesn't answer. I say we have been traveling 37 hours. A Chinese man said he doesn't get to travel much. I ask one of the Chinese if his country would participate in the Olympic Games. He says not as long as Taiwan is said to represent China. Conversation is stiff and awkward. It sounds forced.

Lunch is elaborate. It consists of nine courses, starting with crispy duck, followed by crispy fish, nuts, a chicken roll and a rice roll, ham, beef, mushrooms and greens, chopped fish, soup with mushrooms, watermelon, shrimp, rice and custard. I especially enjoy the duck and fish. I use large red chopsticks to lift food off the serving plate and white wood chopsticks to eat. The meal closes with another soup. Lu the leader keeps his hat on through the meal.

After lunch, I notice more signs through the window, and have them translated by a Chinese official: "Workingmen of all countries unite. Long live the great unity of the people of all nationalities of China. Workers and oppressed of the world, unite."

It is time to go to Peking. (I will use Chinese names as they were used at the time of the Nixon visit: Peking rather than Beijing, Mao Tse-tung rather than Mao Zedong, and Chou En-lai rather than Chou Enlai.) The Chinese tell us not to take pictures from the airplane as we go from Shanghai to Peking. The plan is a one hour and 40 minute flight into Capital Airport, Peking. We are told we toasted with port wine, not the potent mao-tai liquor.

Ringle says he asked a Chinese official if young boys from communes could enter another line of work than farming. He was told: "The state makes the determination on what is the best way to serve the people." "Serve the people" will be the all-purpose phrase that I hear repeatedly from Chinese for the next week.

We arrive in Peking and the airport is empty except for security guards and Chinese officials who direct us to buses. I don't see airplanes. I am told that C-141 U.S. Air Force Starlifters are there to bring equipment for the visit, but I do not spot them. Elbourne says Pung Wa, head of the information ministry, has directed we go directly from the airport to the Minzu Hotel where we will stay. We are to travel the route Nixon will take into Peking tomorrow.

Entering Peking, I write in my notebook: Brown fields, frozen creeks, cows, bicycles, few houses, some big clusters, outdoor basketball courts near military barracks, big Mao billboards, a sign in English, "Unite to win greater victory." More notes: fruit trees, walls. I see what look like open factories, but a Chinese official on the bus says they are closed on Sunday. To me, they look open.

The road into town is a divided highway with tall trees in the center strip. I'm told the trees were planted on order of Chairman Mao after trees were burned down for firewood in the days before the Chinese Communists entering the city a quarter century ago. It is a chilly, but not bitter cold, day, with heavy overcast and few people on the street. I'm struck by the unpleasant and pervasive smell of fumes from burning coal. We pass many apartment buildings, said to be for workers. They are 10-12 stories high. I see few lights in the apartments. It must have been dark inside. There are a few groups of people talking, but no significant gathering. I didn't see banners or flags, customary trappings for a visiting head of state. Workers with brooms brush away snow.

We pass Tiananmen Square and I write: three soldiers in Tiananmen, many kids, red boxes perhaps for directing traffic, a big sign: "Long live the great victories of the Indochina people in the war of liberation against U.S. imperialism," a clear reference to the Vietnam War.

On the bus, a Chinese greeter says we have free movement throughout the city, but he suggests we travel with our assigned interpreters. Buses for the airport will leave at 9 in the morning. The Nixons are to arrive at 11.40 a.m. They are to go directly to a guesthouse. Press buses will follow. The journey will take 40 minutes. There is a "possibility of a meeting in the afternoon." There will be an evening banquet.

The Minzu Hotel is simple and clean with a small lobby. I am to share a room with Don Bacon of *Newhouse Newspapers*. A Chinese greeter says to rest for a half hour, and then meet in the lobby for a 50-yard walk to the Cultural Palace of Nationalities. At the Palace filing center, I am offered a choice in coming days of five tours: the Peking #26 secondary school, the Hopingla neighborhood center, the People's Liberation Army, the China-Albania Commune, and the Wenshing Street primary school.

A Chinese official notes there was discussion in Shanghai of crime caused by racketeers and landlords. The official here in Peking says there is "no drug problem" in China. Asked about the Communist Party, he says the "theoretical basis guiding our leadership is Marxism-Leninism."

I join in asking a Chinese official for a news conference with Mao and Chou. He says, "If Americans want a press conference, they'll have to submit a request to the China information ministry, which will consider it." The room has stacks of booklets on China's achievements. I take a handful. I am told there are recreational activities in the basement. Ping-pong, I discover.

From a U.S. official I learn that today's edition of *People's Daily* attacked U.S. policy toward Vietnam. Nixon was not named. The newspaper yesterday had a brief article about Nixon's visit. Foreign diplomats in Peking will not attend the arrival because the United States does not have diplomatic relations with China. I have dinner at the Minzu. It includes skewered mutton and duck, altogether a dozen courses with wine, mao-tai, tea and orange juice. I go early into the sack.

February 21, 1972, Monday—It is hazy. I have three eggs with toast, fruit cup and coffee. I take an early morning stroll and run into David Kraslow. Bike riders come in waves. People look at me as a curiosity. I say hello, but get little response, just an occasional nod or smile. I ask if I can take pictures. Some oblige, many wave me off. When I ask a policeman if I can take his picture, he shakes his head no and points to his weapon.

Was he suggesting he did not want it photographed or would shoot me if I took the picture? Bus #140 rolls by, crowded. Most buses are red and white. Some passersby wear masks; some have fur collars on their overcoats. It is cold, but not cutting. There isn't much wind. Our hotel is across the street from a walled housing area. From the room, I look down onto the street and over the wall to see smoke curling from houses. I see a cart of furniture pulled by a horse move along the street. There's a notice in the lobby that buses leave for the Great Hall of the People today at 3.45 p.m. and no later than 5.45 p.m. for a banquet at 7 p.m.

It is now 8.22 on the morning of Nixon's arrival as I head for the bus to the airport. A father shows his child the Occidentals. A woman carrying a toddler on her back pedals by. Bus horns sound. As we pass Tiananmen Square, I see a couple of TV crews, no crowds and only a few police. We pass a marching People's Liberation Army (PLA) unit. Children with locked arms and book bags over their shoulders seem to be headed to school. People walk with arms over one another's shoulders, showing more public touching that I anticipated. There's wash hung out to dry. We go through what our bus guide says is an embassy area, large houses with guards. On the outskirts of town we pass mounds of wood and coal. The earth is brown, barren in the winter's cold. I notice few smokers, in contrast to reports of heavy tobacco use here. We pass a large area of scrub pine, dotted occasionally by small fields with horses, a few trucks, chicken coops, three mules pulling a tanker truck, people trimming trees, more schoolchildren, railroad tracks, barbed wire around fruit trees by a bus stop, a dairy with at least 100 cows. Cars with drawn curtains pass our bus in the same direction. A sign: "We resolutely support world people in their revolutionary struggle," looked freshly painted. Our guide said it has been there a long time.

Jerry ter Horst and I are to share an interpreter named Ko Chin-liang. He writes his name in my notebook in English and Chinese. He is thin, short with glasses, mild mannered and very nervous. He says repeatedly that we stay with him or tell him where we are going. Why? Does he have to report on us as well as interpret for us? In appearance and manner, he reminds me of Jimmy Smart, the *Bulletin* columnist.

Entering the airport, we see police on motorcycles. Officials arrive in cars. Ko translated the signs:

"Proletariat people of oppressed nations the world over, unite." "Make trouble, fail, make trouble again, fail again. That is the logic of the imperialists and all reactionaries the world over in dealing with the people's cause and they will never go against the logic." "Long live the great Communist Party of China. Long live great leader Chairman Mao."

Ko talks: Children go to school at 8, come home for lunch at 11.30, are back in school at 2, then head for home at 5.30. People exercise for two hours at night.

At the airport, I see the White House control room with Nixon advanceman Ron Walker and Secret Service agents. I head outside. A Chinese guard of honor with red flags on yellow and red poles marches onto the field. They are said to represent the Army, Navy and Air Force, 120 from each service. It looks like a standard drill for a visiting head of state. I notice there are no children waving U.S. and Chinese flags, nor are there flags around the airport. Military personnel with weapons on their shoulders accompany flag bearers with Chinese and U.S. flags. Guards are mainly dressed in olive drab uniforms with collars and hats bearing red Mao buttons. They wear well-polished boots. They look tall. They burst into song. Ko translates as: "Stand Up. Those who do not want to be slaves." We are told they sing "The Three Rules of Discipline" and "Eight Points of Attention."

A limo with red flags arrives at 10.15 a.m. A slight breeze catches the flags. Army Lt. Col. Vernon Coffey is the only U.S. official in uniform. Chinese troops stand at parade rest, quite still, for several minutes before snapping to attention. The musicians are more casual as they shift instruments and move their heads. They begin playing at 10.24 a.m. as Chinese officials arrive. Ko identifies them as Ye-Chen-Yeng and Li Shen-Nien, vice chairmen. He also names Chou Lin, Yeh-Chien, chair of the military committee of the Chinese Communist Party and vice chair of the national defense council, Li Hsien-Nien, vice premier of the state council, Kuo Mo-Jo, vice chair of the standing committee of the People's National Congress, Ching Peng-Fei, of the Foreign Affairs Ministry, and Madame Li Hsien, Wie-Te, acting chief of the Peking Revolutionary Committee, Pai Hsien-Kuo, minister of foreign trade, Chien Mo-Fa, vice minister of foreign relations, and Li Chen, vice minister of public security.

At 11.30 a.m., I see Air Force One circle and turn to land. Chou En-lai arrives as the plane nears the ground. The American press is on edge. Air Force One lands. There is a small ripple of applause when Nixon appears in the doorway. Nixon smiles as he walks down the steps. Chou extends his hand to Nixon and we are later told the initial conversation was about the journey. A Chinese woman interprets. The U.S. delegation includes Charles W. Freeman, Jr., of the State Department, as U.S. interpreter. Nixon tells Chou he crossed the Pacific in stages to make the time adjustment, and notes that Chou is an experienced traveler. Chou wears a gray suit. Nixon is in a blue overcoat, and hatless. Mrs. Nixon in a bright red coat follows her husband. The meet and greet goes on for a couple of minutes, then the U.S. party walks the receiving line. Bill Rogers and Henry Kissinger follow Nixon. Other members of the U.S. party include Marshall Green, John Scali, John Holdridge and Winston Lord. Ko says Chinese TV and radio are broadcasting the ceremony. National anthems, the Star Spangled Banner and March of the Volunteers, are played, followed by Hail, the Motherland. Chou and Nixon check the troops. There are no speeches. The arrival, after the hoopla back home, is matter of fact, quite anticlimactic. Nixon will later say that he did not know what to expect on arrival. Others contend that Kissinger and Chou scripted the entire visit.

Nixon and Chou head for a black Red Flag limousine with other officials scrambling behind. I race for the bus to get into the motorcade. As it turns out we're a few minutes behind the Nixon motorcade, which consists of motorcycle outriders and 18 cars. They drive fast into the city. To me it is significant there are no crowds along the way, no flags, no bunting. Not even knots of curious people, drawn by the procession of cars and motorcycles. They don't have police at cross streets holding up traffic, perhaps because there is no traffic. It's as if China yawned. So what did I expect? Nixon as conquering hero or Nixon, go home signs?

The Nixons go to a reception at the Great Hall of the People, then to their guesthouse.

I go to the filing center and start on a story of the arrival. Not sure how long it will take to get my story via Telex punched by Chinese from Peking to Philadelphia, I write fast on my Olivetti portable. We learn nothing for the next few hours, and then Ziegler says that Nixon met Mao Tse-tung inside the Forbidden City for an hour, with each man speaking in his language and with translation. We press Ziegler for details. What did Mao say? Did they shake hands? Who else was there? But he adds nothing to a short announcement of the meeting. The Chinese government releases a photograph showing Nixon and Mao shaking hands. Chinese press officials say they know nothing about the meeting.

Various stories about Nixon's visit with Mao emerge later. Kissinger says he was as surprised as anyone because the Chinese refused in advance to work out a schedule for meetings. Nixon said he was just stepping into the shower in his guesthouse when an aide stuck his head through the door and said that Mao wanted to see him immediately. Gerald Warren, the deputy press secretary, said he was waiting as ordered in a car at the front of Nixon's guesthouse with a pool of reporters and photographers. Warren said he didn't know it at the time, but he was a "decoy" to divert the press. Meanwhile, Nixon went out the back door by a roundabout route to Mao's house. It wasn't the first time, nor would it be the last, that Ziegler and the inner circle used Warren as a decoy. Nor did the Nixon staff give important information to Warren. "They didn't trust me any further than they could see me," Warren later told me.

*　　*　　*

After I wrote a story on the Nixon-Mao meeting, I head to dinner at the Great Hall of the People. I and other American reporters climb many steps and are directed to risers. Chou arrives and stands with us for a picture. We are in front of a large mural of a mountain. There are U.S. and Chinese flags at the edge. We stand with our hands at our sides, very stiff. We troop into a large banquet hall. In proletarian style, Chinese and U.S. leaders and members of the press, and other Chinese people eat and toast while the world watches on TV. A military band plays "Turkey in the Straw," "America," and other favorites. Nixon offers a toast. Chou offers a toast. In fact, pretty much everyone there offers a toast, usually to peace and understanding. I clink glasses, sit, and eat my dinner, which is delicious.

The menu is printed on a white card topped by the red seal of the People's Republic of China. It lists Hors d'Oeuvre, Spongy Bamboo Shoots and Egg-White Consommé, Shark's Fin in Three Shreds, Fried and Stewed Prawns, mushrooms and Mustard Greens, Steamed Chicken with Coconut, Almond Junket, Pastries and Fruits.

The food, I write in my notebook, includes "something in a pastry shell with orange and green decorations" and honeydew melon and tangerines. I also scribble: "It is strange to see the premier of China peel a tangerine and to see the president of the United States pick up his dinner with a chopstick."

With no security intervention, I go to the head table and clink with Chou, but not with Nixon because he is at another table. Nixon and I pass one another on that toasting round. From where I sit, not far from Nixon and Chou, neither man seems to drink anything from the glasses

Mrs. Nixon talks about meeting with Madame Chou and how exciting it is to be here. Madame Chou does not speak English. Mrs. Nixon talks about chopsticks. She notes that you don't want to sleep on a trip like this. Maybe she'll shop this afternoon.

Q. Have you tried to cook Peking duck in the White House? Mrs. Nixon: I'm trying to learn today. I'm invited to dinner by Madame Liu Chiang Mei.

Q. Are you tired? Mrs. Nixon: The trip has not been tiring at all.

Liu of the hotel tells Mrs. Nixon there are 375 cooks and the kitchen is able to prepare four different styles of Chinese cooking.

Mrs. Nixon: Do you also prepare foreign dishes? Liu. One of our two kitchens prepares Western food.

Mrs. Nixon: What kind of food do you prepare? Liu. We do our best to see that the different demands are met. Have some more tea.

Mrs. Nixon: What is your favorite tea? Liu: I like green tea and I like Northern Lake Jasmine. Green tea is so good. It has a sweet flavor. It doesn't need sugar.

Mrs. Nixon comments that the "ornamental work is so beautiful. I love the doors." She waves to the cloakroom girls. Mrs. Nixon shakes Liu's hand, waves and says, "How's everybody over there." Escorted into a gilded parlor, she says, "Oh, beautiful." In the vegetable carving room, Mrs. Nixon examines flowery vegetables while the cutter waves his knife. "Beautiful," she says. "Aren't those beautiful flowers? What was that, a little beetle? Oh, a cricket. Hello, there." She sees spring rolls being made. "Isn't that something? Does he ever get burned?"

Mrs. Nixon picks up a plate of hot peppers and offers the dish to reporters. I take one pepper from her, eat it, and do not seek a second. In the pastry room, she says, "You're all making just gorgeous food. I already saw the goldfish. You do beautiful work. So pleased we could come. Your explanation was clear as a bell." We pass through a room where fish and duck hang on hooks. "Everything looks good," says Mrs. Nixon. In the hot kitchen, she says, "everything smells good."

Mrs. Nixon is invited to lunch in another room, but she declines. "Well, thank you, I just had breakfast before I left. If I eat more, I'll need all new clothes. I'll come back to your hotel another day." She talks about menus at the White House, eating the next time she comes, taking a few plates home. "They're all so sweet. I learned a lot. Thank you very much. We hope you come to visit us someday and I'll take you through my kitchen. How about that?" Liu responds, "We would like to do that."

Mrs. Nixon says to me, "When we have the reunion at the White House, I'll do the cooking and we'll have Chinese food. I'll have to take a few pots home." She adds, "When the president gets home, he's going to have to go on a diet. He's been eating Chinese food for lunch instead of his cottage cheese." Mrs. Nixon sees tables for preparation of cakes and pastries, meat, poultry and vegetables, and a table for preparation of cold dishes, as well as the cooking area. I see bamboo shoots, sweet and sour pickles, and carved pandas. Mrs. Nixon shakes hands with a guy kneading dough. She sees cubed chicken, a tub of live eels, vegetable jade flowers that she describes as "just beautiful, all different shades." She also sees rose incense, red porcelains, and things used when the emperor worshipped gods and sacrificed.

Michener and I have a grand talk coming and going about Pennsylvania politics and his career. He says that when he is in Bucks County he reads my columns and enjoys them. I tell him I especially enjoyed his "Fires of Spring."

*   *   *

On a tip from Warren about a good story and the fact that the Nixon-Chou talks are not producing news, I go with Mrs. Nixon this afternoon to the Peking Zoo. I walk behind the First Lady and her Chinese hosts until they get to the enclosure for pandas. I hear a Chinese zoo official say to Mrs. Nixon that China will send pandas to the National Zoo in Washington in commemoration of the trip. The story gets big play back home.

*   *   *

Ziegler briefs at the press center. Mrs. Nixon goes tomorrow to the Evergreen People's Commune where 40,000 people live. She'll also go to the Peking glass factory where there are 530 workers. Nixon and Chou meet at 2 in the afternoon. The Nixons go to a gymnastics show tomorrow. The president met today for four hours with Chou, Kissinger, Holdridge and Lord. The secretary of state and foreign minister met for three hours. The Nixons host dinner at the guesthouse for Chou. Away from the room, the Nixon staff and reporters have whispered exchanges. They give us little details that they want to see in print, but don't want to say publicly. It is not exactly world-shattering news, barely enough on an ordinary day for a headline. But I write what I have and the *Bulletin* leads the paper with it. The *Bulletin* runs my story on Mrs. Nixon in the kitchen and the panda story, fulfilling its promise to use anything and everything.

February 23, 1972, Wednesday—For me, this is arguably the most important day in Peking. For it is the day of the great picture that certainly helped shape my professional identity for years to come.

I am a pool reporter, along with Osborne, Wells, and Beckman to cover Premier Chou's arrival at the Nixon guesthouse for an afternoon meeting. I am in the front room of the house when the Secret Service indicates that Chou is on his way and Nixon is coming to greet him. A door opened and there is Nixon in a suit just as Chou arrives in an overcoat. While the photographers shoot away, Chou removes his overcoat and Nixon takes it from him and passes it to me. I give it to one of Nixon's aides. Then I go with Nixon and Chou to the meeting room. After a few minutes I'm escorted out. Little did I know at that moment that the photograph of Chou taking off his overcoat with Nixon's help and me right behind them would appear in hundreds of newspapers around the United States and the world. The *Philadelphia Bulletin*, of course, gives it top billing, with this cut line: "President Nixon helps China's premier Chou En-Lai take off his coat before their third meeting in the Great Hall of the People in Beijing. *Bulletin* reporter Lawrence M. O'Rourke is at the left rear." Aside from the fact that the *Bulletin* gets the place of the meeting wrong, I enjoy the picture and the cut line, and so do my mother and every other family member and friend. TV anchorman John Facenda, an old friend, shows the picture on his WCAU news program and reports on my presence. The *Bulletin* will run the picture on the cover of its employee magazine. It will have a blown-up version mounted on cardboard displayed at places where I speak about the trip. It remains on display in our home. Nixon, Chou and O'Rourke.

I do not use restraint in my story. Here is how it appeared under my byline:

> Peking—President Nixon and Premier Chou En-lai held their third business meeting this afternoon as a gentle snow fell on Peking and the lid remained on what they're talking about. The only report on the meeting came from five US newsmen, including this correspondent, who were invited to the President's guesthouse to see Chou's arrival and the start of the meeting and then tour the rest of the house.

Chou walked up a path made slippery by the wet snow and was met by Mr. Nixon, standing coatless under a small overhang by the front door.

President Jokes

"Ni-hao," said the President, smiling and extending his hand.

Chou said, "Ni-hao,"—Chinese for hello—in return, and then slipped off his black overcoat to be photographed in his grey tunic suit.

Chou asked the newsmen through an interpreter "How are you all?"

The President cracked, "They're better than they deserve."

As photographers clicked away, Chou said, "You should take more pictures of your president."

"If they had them," Mr. Nixon replied with a grin, "They would burn them."

Meeting Room

The two men, trailed by aides, photographers and the newsmen, then walked through the house to a long room arranged for the meeting. It was the first of the three sessions between Mr. Nixon and Chou to be held outside the Great Hall of the People, the Government House.

The first impression of the meeting room was that it looked like the good setting for a poker game. The table is covered with green felt. There are liquor and glasses nearby. There's a large overhead light pouring down light on the principals.

Mr. Nixon and Chou sat across the table from each other, flanked by aides. It appeared that neither had personally brought working papers to the session. But national security advisor Henry A. Kissinger rested his hand on two black notebooks and Chinese officials carried briefcases.

A Tipoff

Ranging on the wall at the end of the room is a life-sized portrait of a young Mao Tse-tung at work at his desk in Yenan after the long march of 1934.

On the table were several plates of damp pink, green, white and blue washcloths. During the usual banter for benefit of photographers, Chou told the newsmen "if the press wants to see any more places, they can apply to our Department of Information."

Was this a tip-off that newsmen might be permitted to stay in China after the president leaves? When the question was put to the premier's information chief, he said only that it was being considered.

Visit to Wall

The President said to Chou, in what sounded like a mixture of statement and question, that he "probably would go to the (Great) Wall tomorrow."

Chou, speaking in Chinese, which was immediately interpreted for the President, said that the prediction was for the weather to "turn fine."

Mr. Nixon said, "I'll go even if it snows."

Chou then wondered whether Mr. Nixon likes snow. "I don't mind it," he said.

Nixon Quarters

Then the newsmen were ushered out so the meeting could begin.

White House Press Secretary Ronald Ziegler took us upstairs to the President's private quarters. Mr. Nixon has a queen-sized bed, a long dining room with an ample supply of wine and mao-tai, a strong liquor, an office with desk, and a workroom with rust and white silk sofa and chairs, and several radio consoles, including one that looks like a miniature ship.

The dining room table was set for two. By each plate were three glasses, a tumbler for beer or juice, a wine glass, and a small glass for mao-tai.

There is a beautiful painting in the President's workroom called, "Spring Comes to Tibet." It shows five women in bright peasant dresses working in the fields under snow-covered mountains.

There is a television set in a small room off Mr. Nixon's bedroom. Ziegler said that the President has been too busy to watch any programs. Living in the villa, which looks like a garden type of apartment, are Kissinger and his aides from the National Security Council.

Secretary of State William P. Rogers has his own villa about a three-minute walk away.

I call my parents in Philadelphia. They are thrilled about my picture on the *Bulletin's* front page, how my presence in China is a big deal on local TV, and how relatives and friends are calling.

February 24, 1972, Thursday—We walk on the Great Wall of China today and this is how I began my report to *Bulletin* readers:

Great Wall of China—President Nixon walked today on this high mountain barrier built to protect the Chinese from their enemies.

Then he descended 85 feet into the earth to visit Chang Ling, the tomb of Chu Li, the third emperor of the Ming Dynasty.

Then, having made an extraordinary entry in the history of any presidency, Mr. Nixon began his fourth business meeting with Premier Chou En-lai.

At the Chinese Wall, Mr. Nixon said he hoped for "an open world," without any walls separating peoples.

It was a mind-boggling day in which events, which only seven months ago would have sounded preposterous, seemed very routine.

* * *

Kissinger told me in the States that it would be cold in China and especially at the wall, where we might be outside for a few hours. I shopped for suitable China-wear. I purchased a heavy three-quarter length tan coat with an attached hat. I stuck a sailor's knit cap into my pocket. I also purchased a pair of ankle high fur-lined boots, just the thing for walking in the cold and possibly the snow. I put the bills for the jacket and boots on my expense account, listing them as clothing for China. The *Bulletin* paid.

What immediately caught my eye in China was the heavy blue cloth overcoat that many Chinese officials wore. I wanted one. The chance came when my guide suggested a side trip to a "dollar store." A "dollar store," he said, is where foreigners buy Chinese merchandise in foreign currency, in my case, in dollars. It is also a place where China sells rare pricy goods from abroad. Chinese with clout are permitted to use the dollar store. My interpreter Ko makes it clear he wants to go there.

At the dollar store, I purchase the blue overcoat. For about $20, I get a coat that will see me through many winters in Chevy Chase. It has buttons up the front, a fur collar and quilted inside, with Chinese markings. It is very heavy, but attention grabbing. I also buy a thin dark blue Mao jacket, worn by most of the Chinese I encounter inside buildings. I buy a bag of buttons with Mao's likeness against a red background, and half dozen copies of Mao's little red book in Chinese. I will give one to Packard.

In Washington, Bob Roth gave me $50 to buy jade for his wife, Edith. I also want to buy a piece for Pat. At the jade counter in the dollar store, I spot two oval pieces, one dark and one light. The clerk says they are genuine jade from China. I bring them home. Pat is delighted, as are Bob and Edith. I buy two bolts of silk. Pat will make an evening dress with one bolt and a jacket and long skirt with the other. I buy silk robes and pajamas for Chris and Katie, and a silk bathrobe for myself.

I buy several wall hangings, including one of a duck that reminds me of the "Story of Ping" that I read to our children. We will hang it in our living room.

February 25, 1972, Friday—Taking up Chou's invitation to ask for any appointments I wish, I tell the Chinese press office that I want to visit an ordinary criminal court to attend the trial of someone accused of a crime. The Chinese give me a variety of excuses on why that would not be possible. One is that there is no such crime in Peking. Another is that there are no courts in session. Another is that they do not have an interpreter to accompany me. Another is that trials are private closed affairs. When it becomes clear I am not to see a trial, I accept the Chinese government's invitation to visit Peking University and see how it changed under the Cultural Revolution, the cleaning and purification launched by Mao.

With a Chinese guide, I go to the campus, known as Beida, in the Haidan District of Peking. Founded in 1898, the university was one of Asia's premier centers of learning and research when it was caught up in the throes of the Great Proletarian Revolution. Some of the 30,000 students at the university formed a pivotal cadre of the Red Guard as they protested university policies. They overthrew school authorities and forced many to do manual labor. They objected to grades and "imperialistic elitism" in the selection of students and instruction. They voiced opposition in wall posters. One theme was "Smash the Four Olds and Set up the Four News."

The chaos on campus was so great that by 1966 Peking University was shut down. Gradually the Cultural Revolution ebbed. Chou En-lai led the restoration of stability by the Ninth Party Congress in April 1969. The next year, Peking University reopened with 3,000 students and 2,132 faculty members. I want to see how it is doing.

I enter the campus through a freshly whitewashed Russian Studies building and am welcomed by members of the Revolutionary Committee of Peking University. A man identifying himself as a professor of history says that while the Cultural Revolution is officially over, many effects remain. One is the need to humiliate professors.

I listen as theoretical physicist Chou Pei-Yuan confesses his offenses. Educated in Germany, Switzerland, and in the United States at the University of Chicago and Cal Tech, as well as in China, he says he was guilty in the 1950s of revisionism when he worked as a Peking University professor under a system that admitted students on the basis of intelligence and aptitude tests and stressed academic achievement. He says he wishes that his academic training had included more practical work. On this day, Chou has his students building transistor radios.

Chou speaks excellent English as he discusses his academic experience and explains his course. Chou switches to Chinese, translated into English by a member of the Revolutionary Committee, when he says he learned the error of his ways when he studied the teachings of Chairman Mao in the late 1960s. "Mao taught us self criticism. Using it, I began to understand the masses," he says. I have trouble believing him.

He explains that with his new understanding of the masses, he linked with Chang Chun-yu, a member of the Revolutionary Committee, to overhaul the university. Chang, 36, entered higher education after six years of schooling and a job as a bookbinder. Chang speaks proudly of his success in overhauling the university's philosophy department. Students now study exclusively the works of Marx, Lenin, Engels and Mao. With tests no longer required, students are selected from the ranks of workers, peasants and soldiers, those with five years of practical experience getting preference. The government provides full scholarships for all, adding pocket money.

In the past, Chang says, undergraduate studies took five years because they were "divorced from practice" and loaded with "many redundant courses. Our policy is to educate and train people, morally, intellectually and physically so that all have a socialist consciousness and students are equipped with an ability to analyze and solve problems." The school is determined to maintain closes ties between students and the masses, he says. On this day, many students are "applying theory to practice in the countryside, villages and shops," according to Chang.

I ask to look at the Peking University library. Kuo Sung-lien, who describes himself as "comrade in charge," leads me to the American literature section. I find works by Poe, Whitman, Longfellow and Thoreau. The library card at the back of Thoreau's "Walden" says it was last been checked out in 1957. A U.S. history book by Charles A. Beard was last removed in 1962. Except for a few workers, the library building is empty during my mid-morning visit.

I write a front-page story under the headline: "None Flunk Out at Peking University." It begins:

> No student ever flunks out of Peking University. There is no risk of professors isolated in ivory towers obsessed with publishing and promotion rather than classroom performance. Nor is there much chance of a town and gown squabble. And students are not going to graduate with a head full of theories, but little common sense or practical knowledge. The Great Cultural Revolution ripped apart China's universities in 1966 and 1967 and only now are they being put together again.

February 25, 1972, Friday—I meet off-the-record with Nixon at his guesthouse. When I come into the room, Nixon stands to greet me. I ask him how the visit is going. He sounds pessimistic as he describes his talks with Chou. The Chinese, says the president, are tough bargainers, not about to give anything away easily. Nixon says he and Chou have spent many hours on bilateral and regional issues. Nixon tells me that his aides and the Chinese are having problems putting together a communiqué that deals with U.S. ties to Taiwan, recognition of the government of China, the Vietnam War, trade, military issues, mutual relations with the Soviet Union and Japan, and potential trade.

Nixon seems annoyed when he tells me that the talks go on so long because Chou will speak only in Chinese, even though Chou has a working grasp of English. The effect, says Nixon, is that Chou hears Nixon in English, and has a chance to think about Nixon's words while they are interpreted into Chinese. Chou replies in Chinese, which is then interpreted for Nixon into English. As a result, Nixon tells me, everything takes twice as long. I mention to Nixon, and I'm sure he knows this fully, that his visit to China is dominating the news at home. He says he hopes expectations have not risen too high.

I ask him about how he is bearing up. He says he is tired, partly because he is getting so little sleep and has so many public duties. I tell the president he looks great and appears to be enjoying himself. A White House photographer takes our picture.

February 26, 1972, Saturday—There is an amusing incident on our last morning in Peking. Aware it would be cold in China, Don Bacon packed a set of long johns. On our final morning in Peking, Bacon tosses the long johns into a wastebasket in the room he and I shared. We check out of the Minzu and board buses for the airport. A hotel attendant arrives holding up Bacon's underwear and shouting our room number in English. Bacon has no choice but to take the long johns back with the embarrassed explanation that he wanted to throw them away. He later often told the story on himself.

In Hangchow, I go with Nixon and Chou to a lake and watch the two men feed carp. I capture the feeding on my home movie camera. I have never seen any other footage of that event and believe my home movie is unique.

I am by a bridge when Nixon and Chou, trailed by Rogers, Kissinger and their entourage and Chinese Foreign Ministry officials, arrive. There are many large goldfish—carp, the Chinese said—in the lake swimming just below the bridge. A Chinese official hands Nixon and Chou each a small bag of fish food and the two men elaborately feed the fish. The official offers Nixon a second bag of fish food. The U.S. president shakes his head and says no. The Chinese official insists and Nixon takes the bag. This time he is even more ceremonial, tossing the food with his arm extended with a follow through. When the second bag is empty, Nixon turns to give it to somebody, anybody. But no one takes it. Nixon looks at the bag, seems to study it and consider what to do with it. He crumbles it and puts it in his pocket. He and Chou walk on. It is a great piece of cinema if only because it captures the two world leaders feeding fish together. But it is especially glorious because of the look on Nixon's face as he goes through the ritual.

February 28, 1972, Monday—On our last day of the trip, in Shanghai, while waiting for the communiqué, a briefing by Kissinger, and a final banquet in a Soviet-built hall, I take a long walk down Zhongshan Road by the Huangpu River through the area called the Bund, once the center of life for the British, French, German and other Europeans who dominated Chinese business for decades. I had read that a sign saying, "No Chinese or dogs admitted" once stood at the entrance to Huangpu Park. When I asked a Chinese official about this, he was only too glad to tell me where the sign had been. When I get to the park, there is no sign. Thousands of Chinese walk along the road and waves of bicycles roll by. There are only a few cars. There is vibrancy about Shanghai that I did not feel in Peking. People seemed to talk and laugh more in public.

After the banquet, it is time to pack, and that isn't easy. I have silk, jade, Mao jackets, buttons, the Ping wall hanging, bathrobes for Chris and Katie, Mao's little red books, booklets from the Chinese government, menu cards, invitations, and my notebooks and pool reports. I manage to shut my suitcase, hoping it will hold until home. I intend to carry the big blue Chinese overcoat and to wear a Russian fur hat I bought in Peking.

I am asleep when there is a loud knock, the door is flung open, and lights flash on. I instantly have the thought that security agents are about to arrest me. It was a Chinese official with two large boxes, one covered with green fabric, the other with pink fabric. He announces a gift from Premier Chou En-lai, and leaves. The boxes. I discover, are full of tea. What was I to do with my gift from Chou? There is no room in the suitcase. I don't see how I can carry another ounce. I don't want to leave it behind. That might have been ungracious, and besides, remembering poor Bacon's long johns, I don't want a hotel employee chasing me with two boxes of abandoned tea. I put the boxes in a shopping bag I rescue from the trash. The next morning, I join my fellow journalists trudging onto the bus with their two boxes.

As we travel to the airport, I try to absorb every sight and sound. I realize I have been privileged to participate in a great moment of U.S. history, one that will stay with me throughout my life.

The departure ceremony is quick. Nixon and Chou shake hands. Nixon goes up the steps, turns, waves and enters Air Force One. Two minutes later he is heading home.

We have a few minutes to file. I send my story and by instinct head to a small airport souvenir shop, looking for that last item from China to carry across the Pacific. I hear a noise in the hallway and there is

Premier Chou walking with two security agents. I put out my hand, saying, "Thank you, Mr. Premier, for a wonderful visit to your country." It is the best I can muster at the moment.

He slows, smiles and says, in English, "I am pleased that the American journalists were here. I hope you will be able to return." And with that, the man who had refused to speak English to Nixon, continues down the hallway. There will be no questions.

Nixon called it "the week that changed the world." Maybe. What I know is that I was a bit player, a spear-carrier, at a major moment in history, lucky beyond belief to be there, and filled with memories for a lifetime.

February 29, 1972, Tuesday—Nixon returned to Washington last night. I am aboard the press plane full of exhausted but exhilarated reporters arriving a few hours later at Andrews Air Force Base. The *Bulletin* again points out that it had the city's only reporter in China. Under the headline: "President Nixon's journey: 'an apparent success,'" the *Bulletin* says in its lead editorial.

President Nixon, on his return to Washington last night from his epochal journey to China, said a start has been made in building a bridge to span the gulf of hostility and suspicion that has for so long separated two great but estranged nations.

This seems a fair assessment of the journey and of the many hours of discussion Mr. Nixon had with Chairman Mao Tse-tung and Premier Chou En-lai of the Peoples Republic of China.

This is not little accomplishment. It is clear from the sights and sounds of Mr. Nixon's mission to China that there were major immediate accomplishments, although perhaps of a short-term nature. But it will be years, as Mr., Nixon took care to point out last night, before the result of the trip can be fully assayed.

The *Bulletin* went on:

Lawrence M. O'Rourke, chief of The *Bulletin's* Washington bureau who accompanied Mr. Nixon on his mission to the Peoples Republic, wrote yesterday from

Shanghai that the president's trip should, at this point, be judged "an apparent success."

Mr. O'Rourke also made the observation that the thin areas of agreement listed in the joint communiqué were actually less important than the fact that the trip itself had been made.—and that the two sides in the historic venture were able, despite their very recent, very great, differences, to come together in issuing the document.

The bridge Mr. Nixon speaks of will have to be long. It will have to be strong. The war in Vietnam goes on. China still holds several Americans as prisoners. The communiqué seemed purposefully vague on some important issues.

But as Mr. O'Rourke found, a start has indeed been made to break down the wall between the two nations. So the trip was well worthwhile, Mr. Nixon found, as he said, no "magic formula." But for what he did find, for what he is attempting to achieve, he is entitled to the gratitude of his countrymen.

March 1, 1972, Wednesday—Kissinger met a group of us today to assess the trip. He insists we talk under deep background. We may write what he says without quotation marks but may not identify him as source. I follow the rules, as do others at the meeting, but reporters who were shut out let readers know Kissinger was the briefer. My story was headlined "Nixon and Mao Share Aversion for Details." Next to my story is a two-paragraph story headlined "Kissinger Identified as Chou Story Source." Datelined Boston and reported by Associated Press, the story says *The Boston Globe* identified Kissinger as the Nixon Administration source who talked with newsmen yesterday about Nixon's discussions with Chou En-lai. The *Globe* reported accurately that Kissinger and reporters arranged the briefing while returning from China. The Globe said it "learned of the briefing through other government sources. The *Globe* was not invited and therefore is free to identify the source of the material." The *Globe* was furious because it did not have a reporter with Nixon in China.

Observing the rules, I do not name Kissinger as source in my story, although I use his name several times. A retrospective reading of the story shows the importance that Kissinger placed on Kissinger. He pictures himself as hard at work, doing the gritty, while Nixon rested in the suburbs. It was classic Kissinger, though hardly new. He used background rules constantly for self-promotion. For reporters, it was a you-scratch-my-back and I'll scratch-yours approach. Kissinger fed us good stories, on the understanding we would write good stories about him. Get nasty, ask tough questions, challenge him, and you'll not be invited the next time and your competitors will get a good story and your editors will ask why you were beaten.

Here's what I wrote for the front page of the *Philadelphia Bulletin* of Thursday, March 2, 1972:

> Chinese Communist Party Chairman Mao Tse-tung is vigorous, alert, very quick and endowed with an earthy sense of humor.
>
> That assessment of the 78-year-old Mao is made by Nixon Administration officials reviewing last week's summit conference in Peking during which the president and Mao met for an hour.
>
> Premier Chou En-lai, 74, is also seen as vigorous and energetic with a command of facts and details that makes him a formidable negotiator.
>
> It appears to the U.S. officials that Mr. Nixon and Mao share in common an aversion to the minute details of negotiations and communiqués.
>
> The official said that Mao regards himself as the father philosopher of the People's Republic of China who prefers general principles and objectives to the smaller items.
>
> Likewise, Mr. Nixon prefers to lay out the grand strategy while others do the tactical details.
>
> Thus when the communiqué was being rewritten into final form in Peking last Friday night, the president was resting in his guesthouse in suburban Peking.
>
> National Security Adviser Henry A. Kissinger worked in a nearby villa with Chinese deputy foreign minister Chiao Kuen-Hua. Kissinger and Chiao worked out compromise language and submitted it to Mr. Nixon and Chou.

March 16, 1972, Thursday—The White House bills me for the trip. My share of travel costs, including Federal transportation tax where applicable, and lodging and transportation costs within the People's Republic of China was $2,345.12. It asked that a check be sent to Ray M. Zook, charter agent, at the White House. The *Bulletin* paid promptly.

* * *

I got many invitations to speak to groups about Nixon's trip and accepted several in the *Bulletin's* circulation area. I told high school students in Moorestown, N.J.: "China is committed to decent housing, adequate food and competent medical care. It's in those areas that great progress has been made. Much of their effort goes into rural electrification, for instance, since many of China's 800 million people are still living in medieval conditions."

The *Catholic Star-Herald* had a story about my speech by Tom Goldschmidt, a classmate at Villanova, a teacher at Moorestown. He began:

> When Larry O'Rourke told several of his fellow Villanova University freshmen that some day he would be Washington bureau chief of the *Philadelphia Bulletin*, they laughed at his self-assurance. It was March of 1955. O'Rourke and the others (including this writer) were reporters on the *Villanovan,* the campus newspaper. In 1970, after six years as a member of the White House press corps, O'Rourke replaced the veteran Robert Roth as head of the *Bulletin's* Washington bureau. By then, 'By Lawrence M. O'Rourke,' had become a familiar credit over stories about Presidents Johnson and Nixon from all over the globe, wherever our chief executives traveled.

April 1972—By invitation, I write the cover story in the *Villanova Alumnus* magazine. It has the Nixon-Chou-O'Rourke picture under the presumptuous line, "Our Man in China."

The O'Rourke family circa 1945 in Philadelphia.

At work as editor of *The Villanovan* at the printer with associate
editor Joseph Kinney.

Sergeant O'Rourke at top oversees English language trainees in
Puerto Rico in 1961.

O'Rourke walks with other White House reporters with President
Johnson and Lady Bird Johnson on White House lawn, 1964.

Meeting with *The Philadelphia Bulletin* executive editor William B. Dickinson and publisher Robert Taylor, circa 1971.

Front page story on Nixon-Chou meeting in Peking in February 1972 (O'Rourke in picture at far left).

With President Nixon in China.

Gathering with the *Bulletin's* staff at the Capitol during the Nixon
impeachment proceedings in 1974.

President Ford and White House Correspondents Association
President O'Rourke in 1976. From left: O'Rourke, my father
Lawrence, Pat, brother John, Ford, my mother Margaret.

Note from President Ford to President O'Rourke in 1976.

At White House Correspondents dinner in 1976 with First Lady Betty Ford and Edgar Allen Poe of *New Orleans Times-Picayune*.

A diversion from reporting: O'Rourke on a camel near the Sphinx, circa 1978.

Greeting President Reagan at White House Christmas party for press, December 17, 1987. (White House photo)

With President George H.W. Bush at Kennebunkport, Maine, August 31, 1990. (White House photo)

Finishing the Maryland Marathon (December 2, 1979).

O'Rourke family gathers on evening I preside as Gridiron Club
president. (Tom Brazaitis photo)

O'Rourke heads to the field as Persian Gulf War combat
correspondent in 1991.

With Bill and Hillary Clinton at White House
Press Christmas party, December 15, 1997. (White House photo)

Larry O'Rourke with his grandchildren at family cottage in Grand
Beach, Michigan in August 2011. (Katie O'Rourke photo)

CHAPTER 11

Jerry Ford: Watching His Ups and Downs

B Y ACCURATELY REPORTING what President Gerald R. Ford did and said, both domestically and internationally, I unwittingly contributed to ending his presidency, despite my personal admiration.

Unlike my view of LBJ and Richard M. Nixon as too devious and self-centered for the country's good, I regarded Ford as a simple, reasonable and admirable professional politician whose strength and charm paradoxically lay in his ordinariness and decency. I did not share his view of what the United States government can and should do in pursuit of the common good, but I thought he did the best he could in a job to which he was not elected. I always felt he acted with integrity.

He was ordinary enough to look like a klutz in meeting Emperor Hirohito of Japan in a Tokyo palace. He was ordinary enough—even though he was the most athletic of all U.S. presidents—to stumble down the steps from an airplane in Salzburg, Austria, an event I watched with horror, instantly realizing it would rerun Johnson's cutting evaluation of Ford as a man "who can't walk and chew gum at the same time."

I stood twenty feet from Ford on a sidewalk outside the St. Francis Hotel in San Francisco on September 22, 1975 when a woman fired at him with a 38-caliber handgun, the bullet missing his head by inches. A few minutes later, at the airport, I saw his dazed and stark face as Secret Service agents rushed him to the relative safety of Air Force One. Then, given a microphone and platform by the White House, I told the details of what I had seen to the world.

I was there when Ford's mind stumbled in San Francisco as he brushed off the Soviet Union's domination of Poland. I saw his stubbornness cloud his judgment and kill his last chance for a full term in the White House. Standing near him on a cold November night in Grand Rapids, I saw tears roll down his face just after his pollster told him the brutal and devastating news that he would lose the 1976 presidential election.

Members of audiences often asked me to name my favorite president during the days I covered the White House, and that was easy: it was Jerry Ford. I meant it. He wasn't the smartest president I covered during decades of reporting on national politicians. I never voted for him and I often disagreed with him. But if I were given an opportunity to pick a president as a friend, it would be Jerry Ford.

I often recalled the evening Pat and I spent at the White House attending a state dinner for Prime Minister Lee of Singapore. It was the usual glittering event, ladies in long dresses, men in tuxes, the East Room receiving line where we chatted with the Fords and their guests while our pictures were snapped, the summons to the family dining room where hand-written cards marked our places at table, dinner with filet of beef and vanilla ice cream with strawberries flambé, strolling violinists and white-gloved service, speeches with the small jokes and flourishing compliments, champagne toasts, cautious looking around to see who was invited to this shindig, knowledge that our names would be in the newspaper the next day. It was glorious decadence and an invitation to arrogance and smugness. But who would turn down an invitation?

Dinner was followed by entertainment in the East Room. Performing that evening were the brilliant New York City ballet principal dancers Edward Villella and Violette Verdy. Then Pat and I could dance until the Fords called it a night. By tradition, they were first to leave.

On this night, Pat and I left our tables in the State Dining Room to walk across the first floor of the White House to the East Room. We came upon Betty Ford by the fireplace in the Green Room. I had enjoyed several previous talks with Mrs. Ford and always found her approachable and friendly. She was again and soon Pat, Mrs. Ford and I chatted away about the evening and our children. I sensed, as one does at Washington parties, the presence of another figure joining our group, but I was so intent on listening to Mrs. Ford and Pat that I didn't pay any attention to this intruder until he had stood there silently for a minute or so. Then I turned; saw who it was, and said, "And good evening, again, to you, Mr. President." It was good old Jerry Ford, listening in, not interrupting, his wife.

Beyond my admiration for his post-Nixon modesty and lack of pretense, there were several of his policy decisions that I found praiseworthy: his decision to end U.S. involvement in Vietnam:

his plan, albeit flawed, for granting amnesty to thousands of young American men who left the country, mostly for Canada, to avoid the Vietnam War draft: his insistence that the federal government had a legitimate role in protecting the country from corporate abuse and a role in providing benefits to the poor, the ill and the elderly. His view of the role, responsibility and authority of the federal government in domestic matters was narrower than mine, but it was rooted in the Republican conservative philosophy.

I view Jerry Ford as the right man in the right place at the right time. He was fundamentally an able and effective caretaker when the country needed it; more could hardly be expected. Ford took major steps toward returning civility to relations between the White House and the press, an event I duly noted as president of the White House Correspondents Association. Though I didn't see it at the time, his defeat in the 1976 election marked for at least two generations the collapse of mainstream Republicanism. Ford's loss triggered the blossoming of the ideological split in the Grand Old Party, contributing to the political alienation that dominated our politics well into next century. Jerry Ford would not be happy with the politics of confrontation and the rise of the Tea Party.

*　　*　　*

In the weeks following the resignation of Nixon and the end of what Ford called "our long national nightmare," I dutifully reported, almost always on page one of the *Bulletin*, every morsel of information about Ford—he made breakfast, he wore blue pajamas—that White House correspondents saw and were told. Months later, Betty Ford told me privately that the image of her husband's domesticity that appeared in print and on television was a shocker to her. She said that Ford's idea of making breakfast was occasionally to pop bread or English muffins into the toaster.

I knew Ford from covering him as an amiable but uninspiring House Republican backbencher and then as nominal leader of the revolt that led to his selection as House Republican leader, replacing Charlie Halleck of Indiana. The revolt, largely directed by Donald Rumsfeld and Richard B. Cheney, gave Ford a seat at the regular GOP news conference held at the Capitol. On one chair sat the lugubrious Everett McKinley Dirksen of Illinois, the Senate Republican leader. What was known as the Ev and Charlie Show now became the Ev and Jerry Show.

LAWRENCE M. O'ROURKE

Nobody could compete with the corny and quotable Dirksen. Ford had the wisdom not to try. He plodded through his prepared material and wisely grinned and grimaced as appropriate. Dirksen was funny. Ford was ponderously serious. Though Ford was officially the main player in the GOP leadership, he conveyed little alternative strategy. It seemed his role was to make the closing floor speech against whatever the Democratic majority proposed. But behind the scenes Ford cut deals with the Democrats, and the wheels of the legislative process kept grinding. Ford's political philosophy was a combination of small town banker, real estate broker and car dealer. He was the guy who never skipped a Kiwanis Club lunch and never failed to give his vision of common sense that satisfied the small business crowd. Few in Congress or politics said anything bad about Jerry Ford.

When in 1973 Nixon picked Ford to succeed the shamed Spiro T. Agnew as vice president, Republicans and Democrats on Capitol Hill mostly cheered because they regarded Ford as fundamentally right of center, but someone who would steer the ship of state on an even course if he became president. Though Ford was mentioned after Agnew's ouster as a possible Veep, Ford did not actively seek the job. When Nixon picked Ford, I wrote that it was a wise move in several aspects. I was proved right. Watergate was unfolding. I wondered then what promises Ford made to Nixon.

A couple of weeks after Ford's inauguration as president in August of 1974, I sat in the office of Jerald terHorst, the new White House press secretary. Jerry and I were old friends. Like me, he labored long and late in newsrooms around the world and nation writing overnight stories since his *Detroit News* and my *Bulletin* were both afternoon newspapers. On many nights, Jerry and I would wrap up the day with a drink or two at the bar. Jerry and I strengthened our friendship when we were paired for more than a week with the same Chinese interpreter, Mr. Ko, during our coverage of Nixon's 1972 trip to China. Jerry championed my election to the Gridiron Club.

Now it was a late Friday and terHorst, appointed by Ford to replace Nixon spokesman Ron Ziegler, was just settling into the office of White House press secretary. His bookshelves were bare except for a few photos; there were cardboard boxes scattered about. With a characteristic chuckle, he puffed on his pipe as he showed me the stack of paper he had to go through every day, but he added that he was enjoying it despite the longer hours. He gave me on background—attribution to an unnamed White

House official, but not to him—a good story that Ford was working up a plan to extend amnesty to young men who had fled the country rather than submit to the draft during the Vietnam War. Jerry explained Ford's thinking and conceded that it would not sit well with hardliners in the Republican Party, and it would not go as far as anti-war activists would welcome. Ter Horst told not for publication but for my own planning, of domestic and foreign trips in the works. That was tremendously helpful in planning a family life. Nixon's people had rarely been helpful that way, and LBJ virtually never. LBJ and Nixon kept travel plans secret because otherwise they would yield time to Vietnam War opponents to mobilize. Jerry said that Ford would not face such antagonism because he had not been an architect of the war, had an amnesty plan and would be more active in finding a way to end U.S. involvement in the war.

Jerry signaled an end to our conversation by saying that he hoped that he and I could get together often and he would get me to see Ford in the Oval Office before long. I had a final question for terHorst: would Ford offer a pardon to Nixon. There had been rumors of a pardon. After a puff on his pipe, terHorst replied that Ford had no plan to pardon Nixon, there had been no deal between the two men, there was no talk in the White House about a pardon, that the pardon was a press story, and Ford would not pardon Nixon.

That certainly was clear, I said to myself. I boarded a helicopter on the South Lawn, as did Ford. We flew to Andrews and then to Philadelphia on Air Force One. Ford invited me to join him in his airborne office. On the short flight, Ford enjoyed a double martini on the rocks. I had bourbon and water. Also on the flight was Walter Annenberg, former publisher of *The Philadelphia Inquirer* who served as Nixon's ambassador to England. Ford told me that Annenberg wanted to leave the post and that he was looking for a replacement. At the Philadelphia airport, Ford worked a rope line, and then spoke in a tent near Independence Hall. He sang the praises of the First Continental Congress. Heading back to Washington aboard Air Force One, Ford came back to the press section where I sat and ordered Scotch. I did the same. I teased him about his promise to return to Philadelphia on July 4, 1976, the bicentennial of the Declaration of Independence. "A little political," Ford said. "But they can't say it is political because I'd be answering an invitation. I might not get another one from Philadelphia." I said it sounded as if he had just announced his candidacy for a full term. He grinned. I regarded our exchange as playful and off the record. I asked him if he ever tired of the rubber chicken political circuit. "Never," he said. Much to my regret later, I did not ask Ford about a pardon for Nixon.

It was the following Sunday morning a little before 8 a.m. Pat and I were getting the kids and ourselves together to attend Mass at Holy Trinity Church. The phone rang. A White House press office secretary said that terHorst had told her to call me and to recommend that I head immediately to the White House. That's what I did as Pat and the kids went to church. On arrival in the White House, I found two dozen regular White House correspondents gathering. We were jolted when we were given statements from terHorst's office that Ford had granted a full, complete and unconditional pardon to Nixon for any crimes he may have committed during Watergate. Stunned, my first act was to call my *Bulletin* editors and bureau members to mobilize for a story that needed to be reported in full detail to our readers.

A few minutes later, several Ford assistants entered the briefing room to meet with reporters and answer questions. I, and I believe most of my reporting colleagues, were reeling from the announcement. Some television and radio reporters were still on the air. With just a few of us in the briefing room, Ford's aides provided their version of the facts and law behind the pardon decision. I asked questions about how Ford had reached his decision. I have no doubt but that my questions were preliminary and imprecise. If I had anticipated the decision I would have done a much better job in researching the legal and political implications of a pardon. I was irritated to learn later in the day, when reporters pressed appropriately with more and better questions than mine, that some reporters were told that O'Rourke had already asked those questions. It was noted by members of the White House press office staff that I was a lawyer and that the questions and answers were available in a transcript. In other words, my name and reputation were providing cover for people who didn't want to answer legitimate and timely questions from reporters. I didn't learn about this misuse of my name and reputation until later. If I had known, I would have immediately called the White House press office and demanded an end to it. And I don't know who authorized it. TerHorst was in the process of resigning to protest the pardon and it was unclear who was running the press office. The White House evasive tactic didn't work. Before the day ended, the White House provided additional briefings and interviews with Ford's aides. My questions got better as the day went on.

TerHorst resigned that day because he viewed the pardon as a "double standard of justice," one for Nixon, the other, harsher, for Nixon aides and draft evaders. Jerry also realized that, in view of the fact that less than 48 hours before he had assured me and other reporters privately and individually that there would be no pardon, his credibility had been severely tarnished. When Jerry told his wife Louise that he was going to resign, she told him that he was "on the right track." Jerry returned to the *Detroit News* as a national affairs columnist and in 1981 became Washington representative for the Ford Motor Co. Jerry and I were friends for the rest of his life. He died in 2010 in Asheville, North Carolina, at age 87.

*   *   *

In the weeks after the pardon, I traveled extensively with Ford across the nation as he tried to sell the notion that the pardon of Nixon was consistent with his amnesty for draft dodgers—as actions to heal the nation. Ford tried unsuccessfully to switch the subject from the Nixon pardon, but doubts about his honesty and integrity flared. I kept trying to establish if Ford and Nixon had cut a deal. When Ford on October 17 made an extraordinary appearance on Capitol Hill in defense of the pardon and to insist that there was no deal, I was in the committee room. I don't think that Ford ever dispelled the idea that he told Nixon in some manner, direct or indirect, through commission or omission, that he would grant a pardon. But proving it was another matter.

My view is that Ford should not have granted the pardon when he did, but that in his mind, he and Nixon never had a deal. I think that the criminal justice process should have continued until the truth came out and history was served, even if that meant further investigation by prosecutors and putting Nixon under oath. I never wanted Nixon in jail. I would have been satisfied if the justice system had functioned to reflect the belief that no one is above the law. Ford defended Nixon's acceptance of the pardon as admission of guilt. I think that was stretching Nixon's statement much further than warranted. Nixon never owned up that he conspired to cover-up. I think he did so conspire.

*   *   *

As the firestorm over the pardon raged, Ford announced a major trip to Asia that I immediately made plans to cover for the *Bulletin*.

In the predawn hours of November 17, I took off in the press charter from Andrews Air Force Base for a trip to Japan, Korea and the Soviet Union. We made a refueling stop at Elmendorf Air Force Base outside Anchorage, Alaska. Ford delayed departure for Japan so he could watch the televised football game between the Washington Redskins and Dallas Cowboys. Ford, who four decades before had been an outstanding center for the University of Michigan Wolverines, was an avid football fan. When Washington went ahead 28-0 in the second half, Ford said we should continue to Japan.

The descent into the Tokyo Airport was the worst flight of my thousands of hours on airplanes over the years. Typewriters and briefcases of reporters were tossed from open overhead bins and crashed about the plane. Ashen-faced cabin attendants screamed at us to strap ourselves in even as they did the same. Cutlery and glasses flew around the cabin. Looking out the left window I saw the aircraft wings flapping as I had never seen before. I had been through many bad landings, but I figured this was the last one, and my colleagues expressed the same sentiment. On landing, we gratefully staggered from the plane. The pilot told us that he might have found a route around the storm or a way to avoid the worst of it had we not been behind schedule for arrival—a fact we blamed on the delayed start from Anchorage.

The next morning I was the print pool reporter at the palace guesthouse in Tokyo where Emperor Hirohito welcomed Ford as the first U.S. president to set foot on Japanese soil since the end of World War II. I watched Ford tug at the striped trousers he wore, traditional garb for meeting the emperor. When Ford dressed that morning, he discovered that the waist was far too big and the suspenders were too short. The combination was a sartorial disaster. Either he could hold up the trousers with his suspenders and thus show several inches of leg or he could cover his leg while worrying that his trousers might slip down toward his spit-shined shoes. Ford had no one to blame except himself. Before the trip, the tailor asked him to try on the outfit in the private quarters of the White House for any needed adjustments, but the president declined the opportunity. The ill-at-ease White House staff absolved Ford of blame for this, and went to great pains to have me report that when Ford, at dinner with Japanese Prime Minister Kakuei Tanaka, used chopsticks, he used them better than Nixon had during his visit to China.

Bragging about Ford's decency and honesty was part of a deliberate U.S. plan to make it clear to the world that a new man was in charge of U.S. foreign policy, Kissinger told me in not-for-attribution conversation. While I found the use of chopsticks to make that point somewhat amusing, I wrote it straight that White House officials asserted that Ford would be better than Nixon in dealing with foreign leaders, especially Soviet boss Leonid Brezhnev. Kissinger said that Nixon had a reputation for playing games with words and proposals whereas the more plainspoken Ford would come across as more direct and honest, and thus more trustworthy. The story line was typical Kissinger in his using the press to advance the president's interest, and also his own by showing Ford how he could manipulate the situation to Ford's advantage. To quote Kissinger directly: "Ford is more direct than Nixon. In terms of personality, Ford and Brezhnev are better matched than Nixon and Brezhnev. Ford is well prepared, steady and unflappable. Brezhnev is more gregarious. Ford is more interested than Nixon in the tactical side."

One official purpose of Ford's visit was to finalize agreement on a military base deal and to emphasize assurances by Ford on the safety of nuclear weapons on U.S. ships and planes operating out of U.S. bases in Japan.

After visiting Tokyo, I decided to skip a flight on the press plane to Kyoto. Instead, Bill Ringle of Gannett Newspapers and I went from Tokyo to Kyoto by the Shin Kansan bullet train. As we moved along at astonishing speed, said to be over 200 miles an hour, Bill and I had lunch, marveling that the wine in our glasses remained steady. I recall gliding past Mount Fuji in the distance.

From Japan, Ford, his staff and reporters flew to Korea, about which I will write at length later in this chapter because the stop was so important to me. After Korea we flew to Vladivostok in the eastern Soviet Union. I was print pool reporter on the train ride with Ford and Brezhnev through the snow-covered fields and thick fir forests 31 miles from Vladivostok to Usseresk. A collection of dachas served as the venue for the summit. The pool included three U.S. photographers and a six-member Soviet crew of still and film photographers. I was kept outside while Ford and Brezhnev entered a dacha, then after a few minutes I was admitted. There, under a large chandelier, in a fancy room, Ford, Brezhnev, and about two dozen others held long-stemmed glasses with yellow liquid. From 20 feet, I could hear Ford and Brezhnev talking, but could not make out a word of it. Ford and Brezhnev donned overcoats and went outside and I followed. Ford, addressing Brezhnev, pointed to White

House photographer David Kennerly, and said, "There's my personal photographer. He's in charge of me day and night. At night I'm not so sure." When Brezhnev had the words translated, he laughed. Ford turned to Brezhnev, "Thank you very much. I look forward to seeing you this evening." "Six o'clock," said Brezhnev. "Six o'clock,' said Ford.

Ford departed in a limousine to his dacha. I was driven a few minutes to a sanitarium built many years before for Russian soldiers and sailors. I filled in other reporters, wrote my story and called Philadelphia over lines that the Americans and Russians installed for our visit. Later that night, reporters were told that Ford and Brezhnev took a walk in the woods and made progress toward a new nuclear arms agreement.

During breakfast of hard-boiled eggs and cold cuts the following morning, I was invited to take a cruise through Vladivostok harbor. Since it was a Sunday with no *Bulletin* deadlines, I accepted. It was quite a remarkable show, cruising past large warships and submarines of the Soviet fleet. I was encouraged to take all the photographs I wished and as I did, I thought of the millions of dollars the Pentagon and Central Intelligence Agency had spent tracking those war vessels during the Cold War. After the cruise, I hired a cab and was driven through the streets of Vladivostok. I jotted notes about shoppers rushing with parcels and children on sleds and ice skates. One of my notes said, "An old man with a clean white beard limped across the snow." Back at the press center that evening, I told a National Security Council official what I had seen in the harbor and in the streets of Vladivostok. He said he was astonished. It was a "closed city" to visitors because of its military importance.

*   *   *

Now for the important story about Korea. It was for me the most life-changing event of Ford's visit to Asia. From Seoul, where we landed, I hired a car across the South Korean peninsula to Inchon, a harbor city best known to Americans as the focal point for the U.S. invasion of Korea that resulted in the truce that ended the war. Under the truce, thousands of American military personnel were stationed in Korea, many along the 38th parallel. It was there in 1960 that I was headed as a member of the 2nd Infantry Division before the Army decided instead to make me an English language instructor in Puerto Rico.

My trip to Inchon was motivated by a request from my sister-in-law Ann who with her husband adopted a boy from the Star of the Sea

Orphanage in Inchon. They named their son Daniel. They were anxious to learn more about the orphanage.

Here I was in Korea on a history project on a nephew. I rode across the bleak landscape and through several villages to Inchon. At the orphanage, Sister Mary Bernadette, a nun of a Canadian Roman Catholic order, greeted me. She was responsible for several hundred children, from infancy to late teens. The South Korean government provided the buildings and gave her six cents a day to feed each child. The U.S. government chipped in generously. Many of the children, she said, were offspring of Korean women and U.S. GIs who may not have known that they left sons and daughters behind when they finished their tours of duty in South Korea.

I saw that the infants were often four to a crib, keeping several young Korean women busy with normal care, but giving them no time to play with the infants. Dozens of toddlers and older children played on mats with a few toys given by volunteers from various embassies. The children appeared to be warmly dressed and nourished. Sister Mary Bernadette said they got barley at every meal, meat three times a week and one egg a week. I asked her how often they had milk. "Never," she said.

A few children were in bed, obviously ill. Sister Bernadette said sadly that they would not live much longer. There was no health service available for very sick orphans. She said that older children got enough education to join the military or take menial jobs. "Orphans have little future in Korean society," she said. Her big goal, she said, was to make sure the girls did not grow up to be prostitutes.

The nun encouraged me to talk to the children and take photographs. Some children knew a few words in English. As I took pictures, some were adroit in getting into the scene. They tugged at my coat, saying, "Pick me" or "take me." Sister Bernadette said it was their way to appeal to adoption agency representatives to consider them for adoption. Sister Mary Bernadette said she couldn't provide specific information on Danny, but she was grateful he had a new home with loving parents.

Back in Washington, Pat and I discussed adopting a child from Korea—a decision not easily taken since we were fully aware of the responsibilities of parenting and were in agreement that raising a family was a lot harder than we had anticipated, especially since my job didn't allow much time for family life. We were determined to give our children love and time. Could we be stretched further by the addition of another child and do justice to the three children we already had? Pat and I were blessed with three wonderful children: Chris, just turning six; Katie, four; and Jenny, one. Jenny was born March 23, 1973. She was a wonderful 20-month old at the time I visited the Korean orphanage.

In considering adoption, our first step was a visit in early 1975 to Welcome House, an adoption agency in Bucks County, Pennsylvania, known for arranging adoption of Korean children. We attended a weekend conference where the difficulties and risks of adoption were frankly discussed. After soul-searching, Pat and I decided to go ahead. We told Welcome House we wanted a boy to make our family two boys and two girls, and we wanted him 18 months younger than Jenny.

The adoption process began. Our children said they were delighted that they would have a new brother. We told our parents, and they were supportive. We filed a mountain of forms with the Immigration and Naturalization Service. INS told us a few months later it lost our file, and we had to start the process all over again.

Fast forward to October of 1976: I was hopping from city to city with presidential candidates when we got a call from Welcome House. Within days our son would be on a plane from Seoul to John F. Kennedy Airport in New York. Pat and I and Chris, Katie and Jenny drove to New York and were together when a two-year-old boy wrapped in a blanket was carried off the plane and handed to us, with the words, "Meet your new son." We drove to Yeadon, a Philadelphia suburb where our fourth child sat in a high chair at my parents' home. Although unable to speak English, his big smile and good humor quickly won his way into our hearts. We named him Timothy, but he quickly became known and loved as Tim.

*   *   *

In 1975, Sam Boyle, *The Bulletin's* city editor, asked me if I would be willing to leave Washington for a few weeks for Boston to cover the trial of Dr. Kenneth Edelin, a physician charged with manslaughter in an abortion case. I had the reputation among *Bulletin* editors as a guy who could write about abortion without rousing either advocates or opponents of legalized abortion to attack the paper. I had written a several-part series on abortion after the U.S. Supreme Court *Roe v. Wade* decision legalizing abortion. I covered the Court's *Roe* decision and its aftermath. It was not a subject that *Bulletin* editors easily addressed.

Bitter cold it was in Boston in the winter of 1975 when I spent my days in the Dorchester County Courthouse and my nights in the Copley Plaza Hotel writing a story where even the slightest slip would invite criticism. I kept my view of abortion out of my story. I disliked abortion. I saw it as a danger to the respect we must grant to human life. I feared that abortion would encourage promiscuous sex among teenagers and would become the ultimate contraceptive. I was clear on contraception—I believed there were instances in married life when birth control was imperative, morally obligated. But I worried that abortion would cheapen life. I saw abortion as a failure to prevent unwanted pregnancies.

But my abortion view had another side. While I personally oppose abortion, I believe that the Supreme Court's decision was right as a matter of law. As a law student in the 1960s, I had carefully studied the *Griswold v. Connecticut* decision striking state bans on artificial contraceptives. I regarded it as appropriate and consistent with personal liberty that the Supreme Court extend privacy rights and keep the government out of the nation's bedrooms. I wrote in support of federal programs that provided funding for contraceptives through clinics and school systems. My view was that the abortion decision flowed consistently and logically from *Griswold.* I did not advocate abortion. Rather I tried to deflect questions about my view on abortion to advocacy of birth control. But very often I had to give my views on the *Roe* decision to family and friends. Several family members and friends were shocked when I opposed the Catholic Church's teaching on contraception and defended the abortion decision. My conscience would not let me do otherwise.

The decision by the Boston jury that Edelin was guilty of manslaughter was no surprise. I wrote a column wondering if Roman Catholics on such a jury could set aside their religious beliefs and follow the law. The column drew considerable hostile mail from Catholics who said they detected my support for abortion. As I expected, the Massachusetts Supreme Court, following *Roe,* struck down Edelin's conviction.

* * *

A few weeks after the Edelin trial, Boyle asked me to undertake another controversial story—the decision of the Catholic Archdiocese of Philadelphia to shut down St. Thomas More High School, my alma mater. I wrote in a column that closing the school imposed a special hardship on black boys who were now forced to travel long distances to overwhelmingly white schools in the suburbs. A spokesman for the Archdiocese complained to the *Bulletin* about my column. On another occasion I spoke at a high school Communion breakfast. In a homily at the Mass, a bishop took a swing at liberals who oppose government aid to religious schools. Since I had recently written a column holding that position. I knew where the bishop was aiming.

*   *   *

While I ranged freely in my columns, my main responsibility at the *Bulletin* was to cover Ford. As a congressman, Ford rarely traveled beyond the U.S. rubber chicken circuit. Now with Air Force One, he decided to hit the road with enthusiasm. As a consequence, I spent much of 1975 using my passport. My overseas datelines that year reflected visits to Belgium, Spain, Austria (two times), Italy, West Germany, England (three times), Finland, East Germany, Poland, Romania, Yugoslavia, and France.

After a trip to Europe in June, Pat and I met in West Berlin. We had a marvelous time strolling the Kurfurstendamm, visiting the Tiergarten, and walking to the Brandenburg Gate. We climbed a viewing platform and looked over the Wall to security fences and concrete towers on the East Berlin side. Thanks to an order by Ford, I was picked up in a U.S. limousine at the Hotel Kempinski and driven through Checkpoint Charlie for a tour of East Berlin and lunch with Ambassador John Sherman Cooper, whom I knew from his days as a Republican senator from Kentucky. From various intelligence officials in East Berlin, I had extensive briefings on the economic, security and political situation on the Communist side of the Wall. I also heard U.S. officials express skepticism about German reunification. My quite highly placed U.S. government sources insisted there could never be any attribution for their highly controversial statements.

One of my favorite stops of 1975 was in Helsinki, site of a European summit. I was among a group of reporters who enjoyed a sauna where an elderly Finnish woman demonstrated how we were to pummel ourselves with reeds and move from a hot tub to an icy bath. I followed that with a splendid lunch on the waterfront where I ordered a dessert of berries that are said to grow only above the Arctic Circle. I got six very small berries at a charge of $30. That was an expensive item in 1975, and I carefully never mentioned the delicacy to my friends at the *Bulletin*. Peter Lisagor of *The Chicago Daily News* picked the place and arranged that Henry Kissinger join us. Thus my expense account was accurately able to state: "Lunch with Kissinger."

Arriving in Madrid with Ford, I get a close look at Spanish dictator Francesco Franco. His hands twitched. I skipped an afternoon in the pressroom and toured the Prado. We flew from Madrid to Salzburg, Austria. I was near the foot of the steps leading from the plane when Ford slipped and took a nasty fall. He picked himself up. White House aides passed the word that the president slipped because he wore a new pair of shoes. Presidential physician Bill Lukash said Ford was not hurt. Kissinger quipped that Ford wasn't hurt because "he was a football player." Ford had the best line before his later meeting with Egyptian President Anwar Sadat. "Sorry to stumble in on you this way."

In Rome, Phil Jones of CBS, John Mashek of *U.S. News and World Report*, and I were on the press pool to cover Ford's visit with Pope John Paul VI at the Vatican. We were with a Secret Service agent and a White House press aide a few steps behind the president just outside the pope's reception room inside the papal apartments when papal security agents surrounded us and aggressively pushed us through a door into a stairway. All of us, including the Secret Service agent and White House aide, were furious, but helpless. Our words to the burly Vatican guards were probably not often heard in the pope's antechamber. After 15 minutes, the matter was straightened out and we got into the room to see the president and pontiff talking.

After Ford returned to Washington, Pat and I met in Europe for a brief holiday. It included visits to Vienna where we saw "Patience" in the state theater and a few days in London, a sort of busman's holiday for me when we stood an hour near Big Ben before gaining admittance to an almost empty House of Commons gallery to hear a conservative backbencher speak on the advisability of military preparedness.

Pat and I were invited to the Regents Park residence of Elliott Richardson, the U.S. ambassador to the United Kingdom. After showing us the house and garden and pouring us a drink, Richardson said he feared that Reagan would deny the 1976 GOP presidential nomination to Ford. Richardson said he would be glad to return to the United States to campaign for Ford and to accept the vice presidential nomination if that would help Ford win a full term. Speaking abut the type of people who run for the White House, Richardson said that in the pursuit of power they make compromises that drive them away from the real problems affecting the American people. Furthermore, once you decide to run for president, Richardson said, you must measure every step and constantly look over your shoulder, as a consequence losing a lot of fun in life. As an example of a man obsessed with public office, Richardson cited Nixon, whom he clearly despised.

*   *   *

Back home, Ford spent many weekends on the road, usually in the early primary states where he anticipated coming under fire from Reagan in the 1976 GOP primary. Ford hoped to hold off a Reagan candidacy until 1980. Sensitive to charges that he was too liberal for conservative Republicans, Ford rejected federal assistance to relieve New York City's financial plight. Though the nation's biggest city was on the edge of bankruptcy, Ford declared that New York politicians "have run the city in a very fiscally irresponsible way." He said that New York's default on its bonds "would not be catastrophic." The headline in *The New York Daily News* proclaimed: "Ford to NYC: Drop Dead." It may have killed Ford's chances of carrying New York and other Northern industrial states, but Ford felt he had no choice. If he bailed out New York, he would give Reagan another weapon to attack him in other parts of the nation. I didn't agree with Ford's decision to deny aid to New York, but shared his fear that Reagan was a threat.

*   *   *

On a trip to California, Ford played golf at Pebble Beach while I decided on an early arrival in San Francisco. I strolled on the hills of what many consider the country's most beautiful city. After my walk, Bill Greener, an assistant press secretary, advised me to stay close to the hotel because the Secret Service expected trouble from protest groups. Greener said the Secret Service had arrested a man in Union Square Park. From my St. Francis Hotel window, I looked onto thousands of protesters in the square.

On the following afternoon after Ford spoke in the hotel ballroom, I broke away from writing my overnight story to watch Ford leave the hotel to begin his return trip to Washington. It was about 3.30 when

Ford came down an elevator with White House Chief of Staff Donald Rumsfeld and Secret Service agents.

I was on the side of Post Street by the hotel when Ford left the building to walk a few steps to his limousine. I heard a shot and saw Ford scooped up by Secret Service agents and tossed into his car. I saw agents and police dash across the street to the spot where the shot was fired. I didn't wait around to see an arrest but hopped on a bus and rode in the motorcade to the airport. I saw Ford rushed onto Air Force One. A few minutes later, I saw the arrival of a separate motorcade with Betty Ford. I had the sense that she did not yet know that her husband had been an assassin's target. As she walked toward reporters and photographers under the plane's wing where I stood, agents surrounded her and hustled her into the plane.

Because Greener knew I was an eyewitness to the shooting, he asked me to return to the hotel to brief reporters who had been at their typewriters when the shot was fired. In the ballroom, the White House led me to the press secretary's microphone. I gave an account of what I saw and took questions, being careful knowing that what I said would be reported from San Francisco to the rest of the world. In return for this service, the White House granted me access to one of the agents who responded to the shot. He identified the shooter as Sara Jane Moore and told me where she lived in Berkeley. The agent told me she was being questioned and would be charged within hours.

I called the desk in Philadelphia and said I would not return to Washington with Ford, but would stay in San Francisco to follow legal developments there. In the next few hours I wrote my story and headed to Berkeley to interview Moore's neighbors. I went back the following morning to see her arraigned. (She eventually pleaded guilty and served prison time until she was released in 2008 at the age of 77.)

The close call confirmed for my *Bulletin* editors and me the value of having a *Bulletin* reporter follow the president constantly.

*   *   *

I was rarely at home in 1976. While running around the country chronicling Ford's battle for a four-year term in the White House, the burden of maintaining our family fell on Pat. My records tell that I spent close to ten months of 1976 on *Bulletin* travel.

It is not my goal here to tell of the struggle between Ford and Reagan that Ford finally won at the Republican National Convention in Kansas City in August. The story for me was made more complicated by Reagan's decision to announce in advance that if he got the nomination, he would pick Sen. Richard S. Schweiker of Pennsylvania as his running mate on the Republican ticket. As *Bulletin* Washington bureau chief, I knew Dick Schweiker well. As a young reporter, I covered him in the U.S. House as he represented a district north of Philadelphia. He was a moderate Republican who served his constituents, but certainly was not an innovative thinker. I also covered the campaign in which he defeated Democratic incumbent Joe Clark for a Senate seat from Pennsylvania.

Moreover, Schweiker's top aide, the man recognized by many as the brains behind Schweiker, was David Newhall, my friend since our days as reporters on the *Bulletin* nightside. Newhall, a Princeton graduate, was an excellent reporter, and once he spotted Schweiker as an up and comer, Newhall became an adroit political manager.

During the Kansas City convention, the news often broke at night, leaving reporters including myself, in a constant state of exhaustion. I tried to focus on Ford, which meant spending many hours with Jim Baker, a Texas lawyer hired by Ford to secure the convention votes Ford needed to win the nomination. Baker was superb at the task. (He later became the core of the brain team that got Reagan elected in 1980, served as White House chief of staff and Secretary of State, and represented the second George Bush in his successful battle in 2000 to halt the counting of votes in Florida that gave Bush the White House rather than Democrat Al Gore. But all that lay in the future as Baker counted votes for Ford in 1976.)

The Reagan gamble on Schweiker didn't work. As hundreds of delegates chanted, "We want Reagan," Hugh Scott cast Pennsylvania's convention votes for Ford, rebuffing Schweiker (who four years later got a Reagan cabinet job and later a lobbyist's job, but was barely heard from again.) I had a story from Baker predicting that Ford would win with 1175 votes. It was after midnight when Ford won with a dozen more. Ford rushed to the Alameda Hotel to meet Reagan. Ford offered the vice presidential nomination to Reagan. Reagan turned it down. Ford begged for an endorsement. But all Ford could report was that Reagan "indicated he would be there fighting just as hard as I am." Hardly the endorsement Ford wanted. It was after three o'clock in the morning in Kansas City that I was able to sit down and write my version of these zany events.

Later that day, Ford picked Senate Republican leader Bob Dole of Kansas as his vice presidential running mate, dumping Vice President Nelson A. Rockefeller, the former New York governor and a leading party liberal. It was Ford's attempt to soothe the right wing of his party.

*　*　*

The campaign got underway. It was typical of presidential campaigns—exhausting and not particularly illuminating, focusing more on flubs than on uplifting moments—and especially reflected Ford's style of plugging away with mediocrity. I went along, only occasionally switching to Democrat Jimmy Carter's campaign plane.

There were unexpected events that made the story intriguing. U.S. Roman Catholic bishops decided to make abortion a major issue in the 1976 campaign. A delegation of bishops met with Carter in the Mayflower Hotel in Washington. Carter rejected their request that he support an amendment to the Constitution that would overturn *Roe v. Wade.* The bishops said they continued, "to be disappointed with the governor's position." I wrote the story. Two weeks later, the delegation met with Ford in the White House. I was there when the delegation spokesman, Archbishop Joseph Bernardin, said, "We are encouraged that the president agrees on the need for a Constitutional amendment." In the question and answer session, Bernardin made it clear that the bishops wanted Ford rather than Carter in the White House addressing abortion. He called the Democratic position on abortion "irresponsible."

I and just about every other reporter who watched both meetings interpreted the bishops' words as a veiled endorsement of Ford. That's the way I wrote it. That's not the way the bishops wanted it written. I got calls from associates of the bishops who tried to get me to backtrack on my story and even to denounce the stories of other reporters that were similar to mine. They played on the point that I was a Catholic who benefited from their help in developing stories of special interest to Catholic readers. One good source said that many *Bulletin* readers were Catholic and I had put the bishops' confidence in *The Bulletin* at risk. The bishops were really playing hardball, but they were striking out everywhere. I refused to budge. A few days later, Bernardin attempted a broad scale assault on the White House press corps. He said we all had misinterpreted the bishops. It was clear to me that Bernardin's tactic was to attack the messenger and avoid the bishops' poorly chosen words.

LAWRENCE M. O'ROURKE

"We reject any interpretation of the meetings with the candidates as indicating a preference for either candidate or party . . . we are not supporting religious block voting nor are we instructing people for whom to vote. Rather we urge that citizens make this decision for themselves in an informed and conscientious manner in light of candidates' positions on issues as well as their personal qualifications."

I do not know if it was ineptitude, arrogance or naiveté by the bishops. I believe that their failed effort to influence the presidential election of 1976 established abortion on the political agenda and resulted in defeat for them and their position. I think that the bishops' attempt to put abortion paramount on the political agenda undermined their authority among many Roman Catholics who may have shared their abhorrence to abortion, but felt that on this highly personal matter the bishops should preach from the pulpit, but not seek to use political influence. Abortion eventually faded as a pivotal political issue in general election campaigns. Few votes change from one election cycle to another because of a candidate's position on abortion.

*   *   *

The biggest glitch of Ford's campaign was about to occur. I was in the Palace of Fine Arts in San Francisco for the second presidential debate on October 6 when Ford declared: "There is no Soviet domination of Eastern Europe, and there never will be under a Ford Administration." Max Frankel of *The New York Times*, a panelist, gave Ford a chance to recover, but Ford stumbled on, "I don't believe that the Poles consider themselves dominated by the Soviet Union."

I couldn't believe what I heard. I knew that Ford was as sensitive to the Soviet domination of Eastern Europe as any U.S. politician. As the debate ended there was still opportunity for Ford to recover. The practice at presidential debates is for surrogates for the candidates to flood the pressroom immediately after the debate. Armed with talking points, they expound respectively on why their candidate won. It was always my practice to listen to the competing voices, to assess their perspectives, and then to write my story the way I thought it should be written. If Ford surrogates had told us at that point that Ford made a misstep in his remarks about Central Europe, the story would have been a one day wonder, at worst an embarrassment for Ford that would have been forgotten as the campaign rolled on.

As soon as Ford blundered, his campaign team in Washington telephoned the war room at the Palace of Fine Arts with advice on how to clear up the misperception left by Ford. But Ford's agents at the debate did not take the advice from Washington. Ford vetoed a plan to say that he had flubbed the answer by failing to express himself as clearly as he might have. The Ford team's failure to put the issue to rest gave Carter operatives an open door to push their contention that Ford was clearly out of touch with the Cold War and could not be trusted to run U.S. foreign policy. That's the way the story went out across the country.

As the panicked Ford political managers in Washington saw the stories emerge in the next hour, they pleaded with Ford and the traveling staff to stop the bloodletting by conceding Ford's poor choice of words. Ford continued to resist.

Reporters such as myself known to cover Ford were invited to the Holiday Inn for a session with national security adviser Brent Scowcroft, who had great credibility with reporters, and Ford chief of staff Richard B. Cheney. Said Scowcroft: "I think what the president was trying to say is that we do not recognize the Soviet domination of Europe." Said Cheney: "The President was focusing on the fact that we want separate independent relationships with each of those nations." Neither man would concede that Ford had blundered by simply misspeaking. Ford had forbidden anybody on that staff to make that concession. Asked if Ford misspoke, Scowcroft said, "I think you have to look at the transcript." One look told it all, as far as I was concerned.

It took two days for the Ford campaign to right itself. We were in Glendale, California, on Friday, October 8, when Cheney told us that Ford "obviously knows Eastern Europe is dominated by the Soviet Union. The president could have been more precise than he was." That may have put an end to the hemorrhaging, but the momentum of the Ford campaign was ended. I heard later from Kissinger that he talked to Ford five minutes after the debate ended, "but I did not have the heart frankly to beat on him." Kissinger said he called Scowcroft 20 minutes after the debate and advised him to tell Ford to authorize his aides to concede a misstatement.

*   *   *

On the weekend before the election, Ford fought tirelessly in New York, Pennsylvania and Ohio for the electoral votes that could win him four more years in the White House. All involved in the campaign—the

LAWRENCE M. O'ROURKE

president through the youngest reporter on the beat—were exhausted when we arrived at Kent County Airport in Grand Rapids on Monday, November 1, the day before the election.

Ford rode in a parade winding 16 blocks through the city that Ford called his hometown. The parade had 16 high school bands and 30 antique cars. It was dark and chilly when Ford arrived in front of the Hotel Pantlind, a brick building on Monroe Street that was the backdrop for Ford's final public rally. A "Welcome Home, Jerry" sign hung above the platform. People in the crowd held signs such as "He's making us proud again" and "We're feeling good about America." But there was another sign that I suspected caught the country's mood, "We love you Jerry, but . . ." Ford wore a black topcoat as he stepped to the platform. I could see tears roll down his face. He looked grief stricken. "Would you please be very quiet for a minute," he said. "I would hope that we might even hear a pin drop." He talked about his affection for the people of Western Michigan who helped his political career. "Western Michigan can turn the tide," he said, virtually an acknowledgement that the tide was against him.

And indeed it was, as his pollster Robert Teeter had just told him on the flight into Grand Rapids. Teeter said Ford campaign polls showed that in the critical big-vote states Ford was close, had made a good campaign of it, but was losing to Carter.

*   *   *

I was at the polling station in a school the next morning when Ford voted. I went with him to his traditional election-day breakfast of blueberry pancakes in Granny's Restaurant. Mrs. Ford had scrambled eggs and bacon. Their bills totaled $4.37 and Ford paid in cash. I sat with Peter Secchia, Ford friend and business executive, who insisted that it was a great day because it would be either the day Ford was elected to the White House or the day he learned he would be coming home to Grand Rapids.

Flying back to Washington, Greener, the deputy press secretary, told me that on the final non-stop push from October 22 to our arrival back in Washington on Nov. 2, Ford and the rest of us logged 15,705 miles in a flying time of 34 hours and three minutes.

It wasn't until 4 the next morning that the outcome was clear. Carter had 50.1 percent of the popular vote and won 23 states. Ford had 48 percent of the popular vote and won 27 states. Carter won 287 Electoral College votes; Ford won 240.

*　　*　　*

Since I had gone on virtually every Ford mile for more than two years, *Time* Magazine interviewed me about campaign travel. I was quoted in the magazine saying, "We're trapped in a steel cocoon. We're fed what they want us to know." The headline over the story said, "Trapped in a Steel Cocoon."

I got a call from Rockefeller's office; drop by and talk about the campaign with the vice president. Rocky, former governor of New York, said I could not print anything he said, but he gloated as he vented his case that if Ford had kept him on the ticket, and had not dropped him in favor of Dole, Ford would have carried New York Pennsylvania and Ohio, and perhaps other northern States where the Rocky brand of liberal Republicanism was still solid. "If he had kept me on the ticket," Rockefeller said, "he would have had another four years." Rockefeller had an arguable point. In New York State, Carter won with 3,389,558 votes, or 51.85 percent, over Ford, who received 3,100,791.791 votes, or 47.52 percent. When I asked Ford later if he regretted dumping Rockefeller, he said, "The election is over." I got the impression he realized he made a big mistake.

*　　*　　*

After the election, as president of the White House Correspondents Association, I dropped a note to Ford, praising him for making major contributions to the restoration of civility between the White House and the press corps. At a White House party in December, he thanked me for the note and said I had always treated him fairly. I saw Ford briefly on Inauguration Day, but never again did we speak. Ford did not move back to Grand Rapids. He visited it to set up his museum, but made his home in California where he lived in the dignity and grace he had always shown. Ford died in 2006. He and Betty Ford, who died in 2011, were buried in Grand Rapids, Michigan.

CHAPTER 12

With Carter: A Deal, a Departure, and Death

JIMMY CARTER'S PRESIDENCY will always be remembered by the deal he carved out between Israel and Egypt that effectively ended the risk of all-out ground war in the Middle East.

I covered the story from Camp David to Beirut and from Jerusalem to Cairo for the *Bulletin*. During Carter's first three years in the White House, I made three extended working visits to the Middle East that included high-speed dashes at night across the Beirut Green Line where militiamen vowed to shoot anything that moved. I conducted interviews in hostile Palestinian refugee camps where edgy fourteen-year-olds with machine guns monitored my every step. I traversed narrow winding paths through fields of live cluster bombs to see the raw roots of violence.

I sat in the bomb shelters of kibbutzim under the shadow of the Golan Heights where rocket fire brought terror to Jewish settlers. I trod the route in southern Lebanon where Israel smuggled weapons to allied Christian Phalangists led by a man introduced to me as Sa'ad Haddad. I heard gunfire and observed mounted weapons in the Gaza Strip. I sat in the living rooms of Jewish settlers in Yamit and of Arabs in Hebron, and I heard them bitterly condemn each other for grabbing land, though, of course, they had never met or talked to each other about their grievances. But they talked to me as a reporter and I told their conflicting stories to *Bulletin* readers.

In Cairo, I went into the City of the Dead, a vast cemetery on the edge of the city where thousands of quite-alive people resided, many in ransacked mausoleums. It was creepy. It set the scene for my story on Egypt's array of social problems.

*   *   *

But it wasn't all work.

My Middle East coverage got me on a crawl that stretched my limits of claustrophobia to deep inside the Cheops pyramid in Giza and the burial chamber of a pharaoh. An overnight ride in an Egyptian train took me to Luxor and the Valley of the Kings, where I carefully climbed a ladder down a narrow shaft to an archeological dig. In the Sinai desert, I rode a camel and from a mountaintop looked onto a mountain pass that some claim Moses surely must have taken on the great Exodus to the Promised Land.

I watched pious Jews davening at the Wailing Wall and walked reverently with them to see foundations of the First Temple built by King David and precious Torah scrolls kept for prayer. I climbed to the Temple Mount past Jordanian police to the third holiest site in Islam, the al-Aqsa mosque where pious Muslims knelt in worship. I stood silently at the Dome of the Rock where Muslims believe Mohammed was taken up to heaven.

By the Sea of Galilee, I ate what the menu in a Jewish restaurant listed as "St. Peter's fish." In Bethlehem, I crawled into the candle-lit crypt where Christians proclaim the baby Jesus was born of Mary. In Jerusalem I stood on the rock that Christians say was the site of the Crucifixion and walked to a crypt where Christians profess that the body of Jesus lay for three days until he rose from the dead on the first Easter.

I floated in the smelly Dead Sea and visited the cave in Qumran where the Dead Sea Scrolls were found.

These adventures, creating memories of a lifetime, came because Carter, though warned that his effort to bring peace to the Holy Land would fail and destroy him politically, poured himself like an Old Testament prophet to usher Israeli Prime Minister Menachem Begin and Egyptian President Anwar Sadat to the negotiating table. The *Bulletin* wanted me to cover the story in detail and depth.

I had the rare privilege as a reporter of being at the presidential retreat at Camp David where the first Begin-Sadat deal was struck. Then when it began to fall apart, I traveled with Carter on his extraordinary shuttle diplomacy between Cairo and Jerusalem that rescued the deal from the dustbin of Middle East history.

A lengthy conversation I had with Carter resulted in my unprecedented access to his Middle East team. National security adviser Zbigniew Brzezinski and top White House Middle East expert Bill Quandt made it possible for me to travel safely across the West Bank.

LAWRENCE M. O'ROURKE

There, I spent hours in Nablus with Palestinian leaders planning a street demonstration against Israel despite warnings from Israeli troops. The Israeli troops, camped two miles away, were well equipped and prepared to handle any demonstration.

*   *   *

Through my stories, I became known as someone who could be trusted to get it right and as a reporter who, when required, shielded the identity of my sources. While I never liked depending on sources who did not want to be named, it was the only way I felt I could get reliable information about Middle East peace negotiations. Knowing the range of vested interests and the use of newspaper stories as propaganda, I had to constantly gauge who could be trusted to give unbiased information.

*   *   *

In 1979, I got a call in Washington from a U.S. State Department official who said he had a good source for me on Iran. I agreed to meet the source. We first met in a nondescript office without a name on the door. The short man who spoke accented English was elegant and genial. He introduced himself to me as Ali Akbar Tabatabaei and said I should call him Ali. He said he was a former Washington representative for the Shah of Iran and current president of the Iran Freedom Foundation. U.S. intelligence sources confirmed that he told me the truth about his role in Washington. Ali warned me that the Shah was in deep trouble. Ali tipped me off that anti-Shah forces in Teheran planned some form of action against the U.S. Embassy. Ali acknowledged that he didn't know what they were up to, but that whatever it was, it would not be good for either Iran or the United States.

With guidance from Ali and information from a State Department source, I wrote about the worsening situation in Iran months before November 4, 1979, when a group of Islamist students and militants seized the U.S. embassy in Teheran. For the 52 American hostages, it began a 444-day ordeal. The awful situation dominated the news until the day Carter left the presidency and Reagan announced freeing of the hostages. The Iran embassy seizure was a significant factor in Carter's defeat. And it was an early step in the war of nerves between the United States and a nuclear Iran.

Ali called me frequently and arranged that we meet at a French restaurant on M Street just across a bridge in Georgetown. We set up our meetings on the phone. In those calls he did not say his name; I knew his voice. On the phone he gave a day and said we would meet at the usual place at the usual time. He never said the name of the place or the time. When we met, he was always there first, sitting in a corner at the rear on the second floor. I had the sense there was a bodyguard in the room. We never rushed lunch or conversation. I was always first to leave. While I thought him paranoiac and overdramatic, I was shocked and saddened when on the morning of July 22, 1980, expecting a package deliveryman, he opened the door of his Bethesda home, and a American Muslim convert, Dawud Salahuddin, shot and killed him. I lost not only a source, but also a man who had become a friend.

*   *   *

The Middle East may be the hardest place in the world for a reporter. Passions run deep. Nuances are tricky. You can't write a story without somebody claiming you are biased. I had a great time in Israel in May 1977 covering the Knesset election that changed the political landscape. Traveling around Israel, much as I would do during a U.S. campaign, I went to rallies and listened to campaign speeches by the two main candidates, Shimon Peres for the Alignment, Menachem Begin for the Likud.

The *Bulletin* counted on me to become an instant expert on Israeli politics. The Alignment had been in power since creation of the Jewish state of Israel nearly 30 years before. Led through the years by skilled and popular figures such as David Ben-Gurion and Golda Meir, it was left-of-center and secular. Israelis viewed Peres as close to the United States, Israel's main military and financial ally. The Alignment was associated with the Western European roots of the leading strain of the Jewish population.

The Likud was right-of-center, less European and Western, with more immigrants from the Middle East and Africa. Where the Alignment was a secular party, the Likud included the religious parties.

I wrote that in terms of relations with the neighboring nations of Egypt, Jordan, Syria and Lebanon, the Alignment was more open to potential negotiations over borders, water rights, and travel. In journalistic shorthand, I described the Likud as "hard line" in dealing with Arab nations and the Palestinians. I raised questions about whether the foreign policy differences between the two parties were real or cosmetic.

Based on background briefings from officials such as Israeli Embassy spokesman Avi Pazner, Quant and others on Carter's National Security Council staff, and U.S. Embassy officials, I expected that the Alignment would win the election and that Peres would remain as prime minister. The U.S. prediction was that foreign policy would not be a major issue in the campaign and that the future of the Israeli-occupied West Bank would not be debated. The Carter Administration hoped for a Peres victory; he was considered much easier to work with than Begin. Likud contended that the Alignment was corrupt, that it allowed strikes that crippled the Israeli economy, and that Peres and his co-leaders were "fat and lazy"—as one senior U.S. Embassy official put it. The Alignment countered that Likud could not be trusted and Israelis never had it so good.

In Israel, I consulted independent pollsters and talked with Israeli reporters and experts in Israeli think tanks of various political persuasions. The thinking was pretty consistent: Begin was running a good campaign on grievances, but Peres would win. That's what I cautiously suggested in my stories for the *Bulletin*.

*   *   *

But it wasn't so. Begin's stunning victory in 1977 made the story more compelling. It was a shocker and set off a mad scramble that raised questions about how Israel would change as it moved to a right-of-center government with a coalition heavily influenced by religious parties. I wrote that for the United States, the big question was whether Begin and Carter could do business together. In a sense, Begin's victory was a boon to reporters such as myself. There were new characters and plots as grist for our reports.

The story had an unusual angle as I knew from conversations with Carter and his top aides. Carter was a deeply religious man, virtually a scholar of both the Israel of the Bible and the Middle East of today. Carter held deeply the conviction that it would take strong—his—U.S. leadership to make progress before the Middle East exploded in another war. Carter believed that the next war would risk the use of nuclear weapons and bring pressure on the United States to get involved militarily. Carter made that clear to me. He feared that he and Begin would not get along. But Carter told me repeatedly that he would not be deterred.

* * *

Carter did not give up. After Begin's election, I continued to report that Carter was determined to make peace in the Middle East the centerpiece of his presidency, even though it was costing him politically. Carter said he wanted a Palestinian state. Begin said that a Palestinian state would be a danger to Israel. Their battle got bitterly personal. In a background interview on March 4, 1978 at the Israeli Embassy, Pazner, speaking for Begin, told me that Carter "has set out on a deliberate attempt to destroy Israel's image and position in this country." After interviews that included Robert Strauss, the Democratic National Committee chairman, a Carter confidant on the Middle East, and others, I wrote in a column that Carter and Begin "suspect each other's motives." A few weeks later, I wrote that the "30-year special relationship between the United States and Israel appears now to be more of a Mideast artifact than a political reality." When I tested this thesis against Brzezinski, he ominously said to me, "Appearances are not misleading."

I heard and wrote authoritatively that Carter's aides were telling the president to back down, that he had placed his party in jeopardy in the 1978 Congressional mid-term elections.

Before I flew to Israel on May 7, 1978, I asked the Israeli Embassy to arrange a series of interviews. I got them except for one—Begin. But an aide to Begin, insisting he spoke for the prime minister, told me that Begin was ready to do all he could to end the Carter presidency, if only because Begin thought Carter was doing all he could to drive Begin out of office. When I reviewed my stories, I was aware that I was serving as a medium for the two men to fire against each other. I'm not saying that I was the only U.S. journalist in that role, but that's where I was.

Then suddenly I was invited to meet with the same Begin top aide who had been bad-mouthing Carter. He told me that Carter had developed the outline of a deal between Begin and Sadat that would end the threat that Egypt's Army would cross the Sinai and attack Israel in the event of an Israeli-Arab war. I rushed to the U.S. embassy where I got confirmation of a breakthrough. But other reliable U.S. and Israeli sources contradicted the report. So what to do? Should I gamble on a

LAWRENCE M. O'ROURKE

sensational story that would be a world exclusive, knowing it could be flat-out wrong? Reporting from the Middle East was often like that with different sources giving contradictory information. This wasn't a story to go overboard on without much more information and more identifiable sources. I chose to write cautiously, thereby minimizing the play given my story by my editors.

Positive developments appeared on the horizon in September 1978 when Carter talked Begin and Sadat into convening at Camp David to discuss a deal. I was allowed onto the highly secured grounds of Camp David to see the three men together. Carter said they had prayed, but were still wide apart on peace terms. Whatever their inspiration, they announced September 17 that they had reached a framework agreement to see the withdrawal of Israeli troops from the Sinai and a pullback by the Egyptians. Watching them shake hands at the White House was one of the most extraordinary events I witnessed during four decades of White House reporting. At a breakfast Carter hosted for reporters at the White House a few days later, I listened with astonishment as Carter said that Begin had agreed not to start any new settlements in Israel. I was astonished because the president's words flew in the face of what the Israelis told me. Soon the excitement generated by the handshake at the White House faded. The deal brokered by Carter was in trouble because Begin and Sadat, and Carter, had different views on their agreement.

*   *   *

With the deal falling apart, on March 7, 1979, I flew in the press plane with Carter to Cairo on a rescue mission. The singular achievement of Carter's administration was on the verge of collapse.

After Carter conferred in Cairo with Sadat, we flew to Jerusalem where Carter opened talks with Begin. The hours that followed constitute one of the most confusing periods of the Carter administration. My reporting illustrated the confusion.

*   *   *

While Carter and Begin kept their schedules secret on Sunday morning, I walked through the Old City of Jerusalem, pausing at the Western Wall, climbing to the Temple Mount, and wandering through the Arab souk. There was effectively a news blackout by Carter and

Begin, creating a vacuum that spawned conjecture, always a risk for a journalist in the Middle East. An aide to White House press secretary Jody Powell phoned me to say I should be in room 1914 in the King David Hotel a little before midnight on Sunday. Keep it hush-hush, the aide said. It's an invitation-only deal.

When I got to Powell's suite, I found several U.S. reporters but no Israelis. Powell spent several minutes on the ground rules. There could be no recording or identification of him or any reference to any White House official as the source of what we were about to hear. There would be no government transcript, though we could take notes. If you cannot agree to those rules, please leave now, Powell said. Everyone stayed.

In somber words, Powell said the talks between Carter and Begin were headed for disaster because the parties were so far apart. Only a miracle engineered by Carter could keep another round of Middle East negotiations from being a disaster, Powell said. Carter's brilliant mediation and splendid intervention led to the framework agreement between Begin and Sadat last September but it was not working anymore, Powell insisted.

Reporters could write without any attribution, Powell said, that obviously it would be very unfortunate if tomorrow morning Carter found out that the Israeli cabinet at a late night session then underway had taken positions on issues that had no chance of being accepted by Sadat. That would bring the negotiations to a halt. Secretary of State Cyrus Vance and Israeli Foreign Minister Moshe Dayan were making a desperate salvage effort to save the deal, according to Powell. To say that the deal was hanging by a thread is too optimistic. Carter faces going home a failure, said Powell.

Powell's stunningly bleak report sent me to my portable Olivetti for an equally downbeat story for the *Bulletin* to publish on Monday morning.

It was after 3 in the morning in Jerusalem when I finished my story and telegraphed it to the *Bulletin*. After a fitful four hours of sleep, I went to the White House press office for the latest word on what was going on. It wasn't good. Go back to your room, pack your bag and hand it in to the White House charter agent, I was told. We're going home if there is no deal and at this moment there is no deal. The Carter trip seemed to have failed. I packed and deposited my suitcase. I wrote a new morning lead—It looks even more certain that Carter is going home a failure.

LAWRENCE M. O'ROURKE

I headed to the Knesset to hear Carter speak. Against the backdrop of the White House gloom and doom, I was stunned as Carter told Israel's parliamentarians that he had prepared remarks of despair, but tossed them aside to express "concern and caution and hope." Carter looked exhausted, and why not, so were we all. But the new upbeat words alerted me. Caution and hope—they were words that got me back to the typewriter to write a slightly more optimistic lead.

I chased down a reliable Israeli source. He agreed to talk, but only on condition of anonymity. He said that Begin was furious with Carter for making it appear that the Israelis were blocking a deal. According to the Israeli, Begin told Carter in no uncertain terms that he would not agree to a deal. The source said that Begin blistered Carter. Also, the Israelis had learned of Powell's midnight briefing to a select group of American reporters, but no Israeli reporters. I wrote another new lead that tried to capture the whirl of confusion. Of course, if Powell could brief without attribution, so could the Israelis.

I was invited to a room in the King David Hotel where I got an earful from an Israeli source. The high official in the Israeli foreign office told me that Dayan has proposed to Carter and Vance that they bring Begin and Sadat together in a three-way summit. Before I wrote that, I rushed to check it out with Powell. He said flatly there would be no three-way summit. It's a downer, but Powell added that the "door may still be open" to a deal. The situation had become chaotic. I was on deadline, trying to make sense of it.

In the afternoon in Jerusalem, the latest report from both sides was that Carter and Begin were locked in stalemate. The Americans set a departure time to go home. They delayed it. I speculated to myself that something positive was going on, but had nothing besides experience and hunch to go on. So I couldn't write it.

It was now 7.30 p.m. in Jerusalem. It was dark. I had trouble keeping my eyes open. An aide to Begin arrived in the U.S. briefing room. "We made great progress. Several problems are still outstanding. There is still no agreement." While exhausted, I wrote another new lead, changing the mood entirely from gloom to one of possibility.

Powell appeared. Carter is not heading out tonight, he said. He'll meet with Begin over breakfast in the morning in one last try to forge a deal. I wrote another new lead. Bags were returned to our rooms. "Get some sleep," Powell advised. I hit the sack.

It was now Tuesday morning, breakfast time for Carter and Begin. I once again packed and handed in my luggage. Carter and Begin emerged from breakfast to say they don't have a deal, but Carter has a new proposal. The White House took us in a bus to Ben-Gurion Airport. I was there to hear Carter say that he and Begin made "substantial additional progress." Facing my next deadline in Philadelphia, I hastily wrote and filed a new lead from the airport.

We flew to Cairo, landing late at night, but more importantly for me at the moment, barely an hour until the *Bulletin* deadline. That's what I focused on. I was close to an empty tank of energy as I wrote a lead at the Cairo airport and pleaded with the Western Union agent to get it out as soon as possible. Sadat was at the airport. I interpreted that as positive. I was almost too tired to stand. Some reporters collapsed in the bus and fell sleep. Sadat greeted Carter and they rode together into Cairo. I had no choice but to remain at the airport. I waited for two hours, but there was no news. Finally the White House distributed a photograph. In it, Carter and Sadat were laughing. How does one write that? I wrote a slightly more upbeat story that suggested more strongly than ever that they are very close to a deal, but I fidgeted as I sent it because there was no one around to confirm it. I didn't want to get too far out on a limb. The White House staff told us to get on the airplane. We took off. During the long flight home I had nothing new to write. I slept off and on.

On our arrival at Andrews Air Force Base at 6.26 in the morning, White House aides steered us to a pilots' briefing room. We were told we were the first people outside the official parties to know that there had been a breakthrough, and that Carter had worked out the deal. While we were flying to Washington, we were told, Sadat declared that he would accept the package Carter worked out with Begin. At Andrews, I wrote another story, dictated it to Philadelphia, grabbed a cab and got home, and fell into bed exhausted, wiped out after covering one of the most twisting, grueling episodes in recent U.S. history.

Later that day, John McCullough, the *Bulletin's* gracious editorial page editor, called me. In good humor, John said he had several front pages from the various editions of the *Bulletin* over the last few days. He said that my stories were across the top of the front page in each edition, but that each story was different. He teased me about not making up my mind. He said the staff was amazed at my effort. He congratulated me for a job well done. He said my collection of stories would have an honored place in *Bulletin* history. He said no other newspaper in

LAWRENCE M. O'ROURKE

the United States had a comparable string of stories that chronicled the amazing twists and turns of events in Jerusalem and Cairo.

Some reporters later complained that Powell deceived us and that the White House and Israelis toyed with us to make Carter look good. They believed that the deal was in the works before we ever left Washington. I don't think so. I think it was an incredible piece of work by Carter. He gave his all to wring concessions from Begin and Sadat. Two weeks later, Begin and Sadat, with Carter between them, signed the deal at the White House. I was there. I know that with great pride I will never forget those stories.

*   *   *

A few months after his inauguration in 1977, Carter asked me to meet with him in the Roosevelt Room of the White House. I was president of the White House Correspondents Association and he said he wanted to discuss with me ground rules for coverage. We sat across a long oval table. I opened our meeting by telling him that the press was independent and I had no authority as association president to make any commitments for any reporter or publication. Carter insisted that he needed more privacy, noting that reporters and photographers always seemed to trail him. I'll never forget what he said to me—that if he and Rosalyn wanted to take a walk in the woods and look for arrowheads, they should be left alone. I countered that if he wanted to be left alone, he never should have run for president. "Press coverage, Mr. President," I said, "goes with the territory." Our session was rather testy, and when I insisted on describing it immediately afterwards to the White House press corps in the briefing room, the president was not happy. But I did the briefing. I was not about to be a party to a secret negotiation with the president.

Carter and I struck a much better note later that spring when we spent more than two hours in conversation at a dinner. Out of that event, he opened doors for me to his aides, including Brzezinski and Quant of the National Security Council.

*   *   *

My good-natured conversation with McCullough after the Carter Middle East mission was just one of several he and I had in 1979. Our other conversations were more ominous as we witnessed the slow death of the newspaper we both loved, the *Bulletin*.

For several years prior to 1979, the *Bulletin's* top editors peppered me with requests that I leave Washington and return to Philadelphia in a leadership capacity. The proposals varied. One early offer was to manage beat reporters who covered City Hall, local politics, education, labor, and city government. Another offer was to become a regional editor with responsibility for more intensive coverage of the counties in Pennsylvania and New Jersey around Philadelphia using the current city staff in a different manner. I was also asked to return to Philadelphia as the news editor, responsible for story selection and placement in the paper.

I declined every offer, chiefly because I was having a wonderful time doing what I was doing—covering the White House, writing a column, managing the Washington Bureau, and running about the country and the world on important stories. But the editors in Philadelphia had a different concern—resuscitation of the dying newspaper.

They were no longer satisfied with high-class exclusive national and international stories from me and my Washington colleagues. They looked at the bottom line and saw impending disaster: declining circulation, advertising revenue that failed to keep up with rising costs, friction between the *Bulletin's* publisher and pressmen and truck drivers, and more ads going to opposition papers invigorated by the deep-pocketed Knight-Ridder newspaper chain, which had bought *The Philadelphia Inquirer* and *The Daily News*. The *Bulletin* was suffering the fate of other U.S. afternoon newspapers. Afternoon papers no longer had tens of thousands of people like my father who bought the paper to read on the train or trolley car during their ride home from work. The trend toward people driving cars back and forth to work with their hands on a steering wheel rather than on a newspaper cut drastically into circulation. Availability of evening television newscasts contributed to the declining circulation of evening newspapers. In the *Bulletin's* case, the moment for successively converting from an evening paper to a morning paper had passed.

The numbers I got from Philadelphia every month told the story. The *Bulletin's* daily circulation, once higher than 725,000, had fallen to 516,872 in 1978. The bleeding continued in 1979 as circulation fell to 446,371. As circulation fell, advertising revenue slipped when rates dropped and department stores and other major advertisers moved their dollars into television and direct mail and into the *Inquirer*. Also, big department stores were closing and consolidating. Their marketing experts saw reduced need to buy multiple pages of advertising in the *Bulletin*.

LAWRENCE M. O'ROURKE

When I declined to move from Washington to Philadelphia to reorganize the city staff to put more emphasis on suburban coverage, the reorganization took place without me. It caused bitterness and hostility among editors and reporters who were bumped from their sinecures into new assignments. The *Bulletin* had never had a newsroom union. Now unhappy reporters launched a drive to unionize the newsroom under the Newspaper Guild. The Guild held out the promise of better wages and benefits and an end to job transfers and losses. I saw little value to bringing in the Guild. I trusted that the *Bulletin* did the best it could with salary and benefits. I had to concede that the new system of assignments that put reporters into the suburbs was necessary as readers moved further from their city neighborhoods.

*   *   *

But I didn't have a voice on these matters. Since the National Labor Relations Board classified me as an executive employee, I was not permitted to discuss these union developments with members of my bureau. *Bulletin* lawyers told me that if I had even a casual conversation about the Guild, the *Bulletin* and I could be fined. So as hard as it was for me, I kept my mouth shut. On one occasion, executive editor B. Dale Davis came to Washington for an authorized discussion with bureau members in advance of an election on recognizing the Guild. I was required to absent myself from the bureau during their meeting and forbidden to discuss it thereafter. It was awkward at best. At worst, the close relationships in the bureau that I had worked so hard to cultivate were damaged.

*   *   *

As *Bulletin* editors looked to cut expenses, they studied the costs of the Washington Bureau, and took out their scissors. I lost a foreign affairs reporter and was told that when other reporters left, they would not be replaced. Looking at the money I was spending on travel, the editors decided it was too much—that the *Bulletin* could no longer afford to send me frequently to the Middle East, Europe and Asia, as it had been doing.

The demand to trim spending on travel coincided with a theory that swept through the *Bulletin* and other newsrooms, afternoon papers especially: go local. Consultants told us that most readers got all the foreign news they wanted on television. The consultants said that our survival depended on providing news that people could use, that they could not get anywhere other than in their local newspaper. So the *Bulletin* cut space for foreign and national news—the stuff the Washington Bureau specialized in—and made more columns available for local news. I moved my Washington reporters into new assignments to concentrate on the Philadelphia area members of Congress and issues in Washington that related to the Philadelphia area.

John Farmer, the national editor, laid out *The Bulletin's* new strategy in a memo: "We want less concentration on the White House. We want more reportage on what's happening in the capital that affects the lives of our readers or tells us something entertaining or significant about where our government and its main men are leading us. This kind of change would free Larry to do trend and insight pieces useful especially in the weekend papers."

Farmer continued: "One other aspect of the bureau's operation is a problem. It's morale. I sense a feeling there of isolation from Philadelphia. I think the bureau feels there is an indifference here to national news." As a solution, Farmer suggested that editors in Philadelphia make occasional trips to Washington and take us to lunch. I didn't think that the solution to our dilemma could be found through friendly banter over lunch. I encouraged bureau reporters to look for more local stories, and they did. But this occasionally caused them to miss a national story that the paper ran prominently. I would then hear a complaint from Philadelphia that we fell short on a story we should have covered. I shielded my reporters from this contradiction as much as possible. But it became very dispiriting as I watched the *Bulletin* I loved disintegrate.

With access to circulation and advertising revenue figures, I had a close-up perspective of the *Bulletin's* steady deterioration. I realized that the paper could not survive much longer. Against that backdrop, I sadly and reluctantly understood that it was time for me to move on before I was dragged down without a life jacket.

*   *   *

Taking the train to Philadelphia in the spring of 1980 and submitting my resignation to the publisher William McLean was one of my saddest journeys. I liked Bill and respected him as someone who did the best he could. But he held a losing hand.

Another terrible moment for me came on January 29, 1982 when I went to the fourth floor newsroom of the *Bulletin* to witness publication of the final edition of that proud and once-very fine newspaper. Standing in the newsroom that afternoon, I was flooded with memories of being a copy boy at $26.50 a week, of covering fires and murders on the nightside, of writing obits and investigating political corruption, of spurring on racial desegregation of public schools and promoting greater power to the poor.

I wrote the story about the *Bulletin* for my new employer, another newspaper. "*The Bulletin* died on Friday," I wrote with a Philadelphia dateline. "It was 134 and it had given this city just about the finest newspaper coverage of any big city in America. Philadelphia will be a poorer place to live because the *Bulletin* is dead . . . Until a few years ago, the *Bulletin* was a member of nearly every Philadelphia family. It reported the fires and the broken water mains, the ward politics and the obituaries. It gave prizes for spelling bees. It sponsored the Fourth of July fireworks in Fairmount Park. A wagon with its logo on the side was the best toy a boy could see on Christmas morning . . .

"I don't want to end with anything dramatic," I wrote. "I think mostly about 25 years ago, as a young nightside reporter, leaving the office at 2 or 3 in the morning, with my friends and colleagues. Night after night, we would go to the South China restaurant in Chinatown. Often until daylight we would eat fried rice and drink tea. And we would talk.

"God, how we would talk. About the stories we had covered. About our leads. About our fights with editors and our low pay and our plans for tomorrow.

"And the next morning we would rush out to see what the desk had done to our stories, to see the play in the paper, to see our byline and those golden words: '*Of The Bulletin Staff.*'

"They tried not to cry in this newsroom on Friday."

CHAPTER 13

Learning Never Ends

HOWEVER RELUCTANT I was to leave the *Bulletin*, once I made the decision, I set out in a hurry to find another job. During the fall of 1979 and into the early months of 1980, I talked with bureau chiefs of other newspapers, interviewed with a couple of law firms, explored government jobs as a lawyer, and had job interviews with two private sector monoliths. One corporation offered me a quite challenging job working with its outgoing chief executive who would spend his final year touting the benefits of an enlightened free enterprise system. I liked the executive; in the context of big business, he was progressive, almost liberal. I liked the job since it would be entirely concerned with politics and public policy rather than with profit. But it would have meant moving out of Washington where by this time our roots were deep, not to mention that our kids were in school and we were reluctant to disrupt their lives.

In early 1980, with ice on the ground and I was preparing to go to New Hampshire for the primary, I talked about my job situation during my morning run. Later that day, I got a call from running partner David Tatel, then back from government work at his law firm. His former spokesperson at the U.S. Office of Civil Rights, Colleen O'Connor, had a new job in what was in a few months to become the U.S. Department of Education. Colleen worked in the office of public affairs with the designated assistant secretary, Elizabeth "Liz" Carpenter, a legendary Texan. Liz had rich experience, including as a former aide to President Lyndon B. Johnson and Lady Bird Johnson. A battler for equal rights for women long before that issue blossomed into a national movement, Carpenter had strong opinions on many subjects, and she did not hesitate to express them. Over my years as a reporter, I had many conversations with the strong-willed Liz. Some of those conversations tuned into arguments as Liz fought for the interests of the Johnsons and I fought for public information to put in the newspaper, positions frequently incompatible.

I got a call O'Connor who asked if I was serious about leaving journalism and coming into government. She was dubious. During a long conversation over lunch at the National Gallery of Art, she told me how entering government could be a tough transition for a veteran journalist who enjoyed independence and a finely tuned skepticism to government officials and policy.

I told Colleen I was ready to take the next step—to talk with Carpenter. And so we met in Carpenter's office and had a blunt discussion during which Liz said she took the job with Carter because she wanted him to win another term in the White House and for the Democrats to continue to control both houses of Congress. I said clearly that, since I was voluntarily taking off my reporter's hat, I could express my opinion. I shared Liz's view of the need to keep Carter in the White House and Democrats in the majority. I could work for those causes, though I was on record predicting that Carter would lose in the fall to Reagan and that Carter made more than his share of mistakes as president, including ineffectual leadership on the economy. I would have no trouble working to make Carter's Department of Education a success. Carpenter pointed out the things I wouldn't be hired to do—run a bureaucracy (that would be left to people who liked that kind of thing), speak for the department (that would be Colleen's job), keep separate from the political battle (I would be in the thick of it,) and have a 9 to 5 job (never had it, never craved it).

Carpenter said I would need to stop thinking and acting like a reporter and would have to function as an advocate for somebody else. Could I make that transition? Somewhat grandiosely, I said that as the lawyer for a few dozen juveniles over the years charged with rape, arson, assault, car theft and even skipping school, I was used to fighting for people with whom I had no shared experiences.

If I got the job, Carpenter said, I would carry the long title, Deputy Assistant Secretary of Education for Policy and Planning. Carpenter said the final decider on whether I got the job was down the hall—Secretary of Education Shirley Mount Hufstedler.

As a journalist who wrote, sometimes skeptically, about Carter's decision to create the Department of Education, I knew who Hufstedler was—a progressive U.S. Court of Appeals judge from California. She stepped down from that coveted lifetime seat to come to Washington. Though a superb jurist, Hufstedler lacked what some regarded as prerequisites for a secretary of education—a distinguished record as an educator, tested political skills, and strong experience as manager of a large bureaucracy. Some members of Congress, educators and leaders of teachers' organizations said she was not qualified to be the federal government's policymaker or voice on education. But she was Carter's nominee and with Democrats in control of the U.S. Senate, she was confirmed.

I met Hufstedler in her office on the northwest corner on the fourth floor of the Department of Education Building. She was behind her desk reading when I was ushered in. My first impression of her was her intensity. She looked into my eyes with power and purpose that I found intimidating. She looked like a judge with her black hair with a few strands of gray tied severely on top of her head.

She had a husky voice and she spoke at a level that forced me to lean forward and totally concentrate on her words. She came across as the kind of person who expected to say things only once. If she meant to impress me with her seriousness, she succeeded. She probed my experience, ambition, and attitudes toward the federal government's involvement in education. She never asked about my politics, and I never volunteered information, but she made clear she would campaign for Carter's re-election and was concerned about a Reagan presidency.

Finally, she asked if I had questions. My first question concerned process. I asked if I worked for her in putting forward the ideas of the Carter Administration in U.S. public education, how much access would I have to her. She said that if we worked together, she would keep her door open to me. I put on my reporter's hat. Madam Secretary, there is talk you are first in line if a Supreme Court vacancy occurs on Carter's watch, and there are rumors that such a vacancy might occur after the court ends its session in June. You gave up a lifetime seat on the federal appeals bench in an apparent gamble to gain attention in Washington and stand at the head of Carter Supreme Court line. How will your style and substance as secretary of education be affected by the possibility that you'll be nominated to the Supreme Court in the next few months? Hufstedler was ready for the question. Like a judge scolding an errant lawyer, she said that such a possibility was speculative, premature and beyond the scope of our present conversation. She said she did not expect such a vacancy to occur, did not come to Washington on the expectation of such a vacancy, and she would not talk about it further, to me or anyone else. But, like a reporter, I persisted. Your refusal to say more won't stop reporters from asking you that question every chance they get, I said. They'll get the same answer I just gave you, Hufstedler replied. (As it turned out, the rumored resignation of a justice never happened, Carter never got the opportunity to nominate, and Hufstedler never again sat as a federal judge.)

At our first conversation, I had another thought about this woman whom I might join in the political trenches. Never a candidate, she lacked the political ease and adroit evasiveness that are the style of high-level politics in Washington. Perhaps that was a plus, but she needed help if she intended to engage in hardball politics and to deal with the press. That's where I came in. I told her that tough questions about her experience would not go away.

The pivotal question came. "In view of what I want from your position," Hufstedler said, empathizing the word I, "do you want this job and would you accept it if offered?" Yes, I said, "I would accept it." Hufstedler looked directly at me and said: "In that case, you work out the details and begin as soon as possible." We shook hands. I was now a fed.

There would be a pile of papers to fill out and an FBI security check. The White House could veto my appointment, but Carpenter said she was confident it would not object. Carpenter mentioned Stuart Eizenstat, Carter's chief domestic policy adviser, and Jody Powell, Carter's press secretary, in a way that suggested to me they had already been asked and had no objection.

I returned to the *Bulletin* office to finish a story. I called Pat and told her I accepted Hufstedler's offer. My parents were stunned that I would leave the *Bulletin*, the bureau chief's job, my column and my standing among readers after many years of a byline and my picture and thoughts in the paper. My father asked why. I said the *Bulletin* is in deep financial trouble and is close to folding.

"I can't believe that," my father said, and I know he didn't. "The *Bulletin* has been around my entire life," he said. "Everybody reads it and everybody thinks of it as the best paper in Philadelphia. The city would be different without the *Bulletin*. They'll find a way to keep it going and you may be sorry you gave up your great job."

"You are right about the risk," I told my father, especially since I believed that Carter couldn't win another term. "But it's a great opportunity that may never come again."

*   *   *

I began a transition from journalist to government official. I've never found transitions easy. This was brutal though I willed it and looked forward to the next episode.

I called *Bulletin* publisher William McLean. We agreed to meet in his office. During the train ride up to Philadelphia, I thought of the many wonderful experiences I had while working for the *Bulletin*. It was bittersweet when I entered the *Bulletin* building. I ran into old friends going home for the day. We exchanged greetings, but I kept my news until I reached McLean's office. Bill was gracious, saying little more than he understood why I was leaving and good luck. He did not concede that the *Bulletin* was on the block. He didn't have to. We both knew it. I went to the editorial board's office to tell McCullough. He said while my decision saddened him, I made the right decision and should leave proud of my work. I went to the newsroom where long ago I spent many hours learning the newspaper business. I told Nick Nagurney, the managing editor, that I was leaving the paper. I was getting emotional, as if I were burying a family member. I looked at the newsroom where I worked—as copy boy, reporter, city desk assistant, sportswriter, rewriteman, assignment editor, and makeup editor. I quickly left to avoid seeing other colleagues who might trigger memories too powerful to hide.

Ironically, *The Philadelphia Inquirer* carried the first story on my departure from the *Bulletin* to work for Carter. The *Inquirer* reporter asked if I would work, as rumor had it, for the Defense Department or the CIA. Undoubtedly deepening the mystery, I responded truthfully that I was not able to say until the Carter Administration announced my appointment. The FBI began to investigate me. Agents came to the *Bulletin*, asked about me, and read my clippings. Finally the *Bulletin* printed a story on my resignation.

Quickly I prepared to vacate my office in Suite 1296 of the National Press Building. I packed clips, books and notes, took down photographs and placards and carted the stuff home to the attic. In respect for the *Bulletin*'s integrity as an independent newspaper and my own sense of propriety, I did not want to write additional stories about Carter or politics. But I had already accepted an invitation to breakfast with Sen. Edward M. Kennedy and other reporters at Kennedy's home in Virginia. I attended the breakfast, and made no mention that this was my final day at the *Bulletin*. I felt out of step at Kennedy's home. Not only was I no longer a reporter, I was with Carter in his fight against Kennedy over the Democratic presidential nomination.

LAWRENCE M. O'ROURKE

*   *   *

On St. Patrick's Day morning, March 17, 1980, I entered for the first time the Department of Education building near the Smithsonian Air and Space museum in Southwest Washington. I took the required oath to become a government official. I moved into an office close to Hufstedler. She said that we had a lot of work to do, let's begin.

As an Education Department official, I was surprised to learn, more than 70 people reported to me. They were scattered in several office buildings. Given an organizational chart and curiosity to see my turf, I made the rounds, popping into several offices without warning. Later I learned that word spread quickly through the ranks that the new boss was coming around and they should be on guard. I learned that I instantly became publisher and executive editor of *American Education,* a glossy Department of Education magazine. It had a circulation of 12,000 and was designed to promote the department while breaking even fiscally. Editor Richard Elwell's role was to put it together in galley form and send it to my desk before printing. I was responsible for the contents. In our first conversation, Elwell complained that the magazine was too safe and therefore dull. He hoped I would allow him to print controversial articles that didn't necessarily parrot the administration's line. Perhaps naively, I told Elwell, "Go do it." I liked and trusted Elwell and never in the months ahead did I contradict his editorial decisions. He pushed the envelope, and we didn't get into trouble. Elwell was especially concerned about two pending articles, one dealing with Egypt's educational system and the other on higher education entrance exams in the People's Republic of China. He warned me that the articles might upset U.S. policymakers, at the White House and State Department, but that he had excellent, accurate writers on the projects and intended to make sure the pieces were reliable and readable. "Sounds good to me," I said. They were printed and I heard only a few complaints.

I also discovered that I was publisher of dozens of other department publications, many largely collections of education statistics. Several editors said they would like more freedom to analyze the statistics, but they warned me. The more you interpret, however honestly, the more you risk offending vested interests. As a result, they told me, government bureaucrats always play it safe. Fresh from the newspaper business where my job was often to interpret data, I naturally told these editors to do their jobs the way they thought they should be done. I got a few complaints about the analysis, but never found fault with an editor.

I quickly learned the ropes of the bureaucracy, though I found them chafing. Since we were setting up a department, we had a relatively blank slate to sketch our table-of-organization. Hufstedler delegated considerable responsibility to Steve Minter, the undersecretary, an engaging man from Cleveland. I was frequently asked to "sign off" on various locations for boxes on the organization chart and did so without a great deal of attention. I was not about to be caught up in minutiae of the bureaucracy. I came to discover that this maneuvering gave me direct responsibility for a budget in excess of $14 million. The budget was not that much by government standards, but it got my attention.

Two weeks after my arrival at the department, my secretary dropped a stack of pay vouchers on my desk, one for each employee reporting to me. The vouchers listed individual breakdowns of hours worked during the pay period. I was to attest that such hours had indeed been spent on the people's business. Since there were vouchers for people I never heard of, much less met, I had no idea how to go about checking the documents. I got a lesson from Jack Billings, a veteran federal bureaucrat: just sign them so the employees can be paid, and don't challenge government red tape in these matters because it will eat up time and you'll always lose. I signed. It was bureaucratic nonsense, repeated every two weeks.

My direct work for Carter began when Eizenstat at the White House told me to draft a statement for Carter to deliver on May 7, the day set for the Department of Education to open. I banged out the statement one evening and shipped it to Eizenstat. With minor editing, Carter approved it. It was fun to hear the president use my words.

Since the Carter Administration wanted a big splash on the department's day of birth, designated as Ed Day, Hufstedler directed me to make planning my priority. I would be at the secretary's side on Ed Day right from her early morning departure from her apartment in northwest Washington. I guided her throughout two days of celebration, including a ceremony in front of the building where Carter was the main speaker. I accompanied Hufstedler to a White House reception and a gala at the National Portrait Gallery. These events brought together glittering figures in education and politics, and got us positive press notices.

At the White House, I sat near the president and secretary and looked at my former colleagues in the White House press corps on the other side of the rope. That evening I attended a salute-to-education White

House party that included entertainment by opera star Robert Merrill, pianist Byron Janis, poet Richard Wilbur, country singer Loretta Lynn and the Dance Theatre of Harlem.

Hufstedler, reading a speech I had helped put together, told the audience a story:

> "The best teacher I ever had was Mrs. Phillips who taught me in eighth grade in Albuquerque, New Mexico. The girls of my generation learned long before we came to school that our futures were supposed to be exclusively in marriage and motherhood. A few of the more daring ones thought perhaps they would go to business school and work in an office for a while before marriage. But Mrs. Phillips would have none of that. She never let any of us be one whit less than we could be. And I'll never forget her words to me as I left class for the last time. She said, 'Shirley, you have a good mind. Use it. If you study, if you work hard, you can run your own show. You don't have to be a secretary.'"

That brought down the house. As Hufstedler spoke, I thought of my two daughters, their dreams and futures.

Since we were starting a cabinet-level department, we needed a seal and a motto. I certainly didn't have experience at creating either. Hufstedler cautioned that I should take the matters seriously because we would enter a mark in U.S. history. I helped shape the "Learning Never Ends" motto for the department and the "tree of knowledge" design on our seal. I directed that the seal be on the cover of our next *American Education* magazine. I liked the notion that "Learning Never Ends" and incorporated it in my speeches while in government service and as a theme for life.

*   *   *

I produced and directed a Department of Education show-and-tell tour the next day. I chartered a bus for the secretary and press and assigned Hufstedler to the seat behind the driver. The road show went from the department to Dunbar High School in Baltimore and to The College of William & Mary in Williamsburg, Virginia. The entourage spent ten hours on the road. It was a risk because I asked Hufstedler to take questions from reporters who had much longer familiarity than she with politically sensitive education issues. Among the reporters to whom I allotted time were Chris Connell of the Associated Press and Ted Fiske of *The New York Times*. I scheduled a brief interview for C. Emily Feistrizer, publisher of a newsletter, *Department of Education Weekly*. I need not have worried that Hufstedler would be trapped by a tough questioning reporter. For one thing, she did her homework well. "Confirmation hearings focus the mind," she told me. She had a photographic memory. She knew the numbers and the players.

At the end of the two-day celebration for the start of the new department, largely built on events I organized, we were exhausted, but it was great fun, and I had the satisfaction that I helped get the department off to a rousing start.

*   *   *

In my capacity as deputy assistant secretary for policy and planning, I was drawn into shaping the department's mission, as well as its public image. I was charged with setting out what we as a federal department hoped to accomplish. Toward that goal, I joined Hufstedler and other top officials in the department at a weekend retreat in Reston, Virginia. My eyes glazed over and my mind wandered as Mike Smith and John Danner, two bright and articulate young men on Hufstedler's staff, instructed us in the technique of "managing by objective." From now on, they said, writing on a big sheet of paper in bold strokes, "It's MBO." They also told us we would engage in "cross-cutting." Such bureaucratic jargon caused me to shudder. We spent considerable time deploring how little we could do for public education with the tight budget Carter had secured from Congress. We were long on dreams, short on cash to accomplish them.

It was at that closed-door retreat that I encountered a very serious internal challenge to my mission of conveying to the public how the Carter Administration could do a lot for public schools. I was caught in crossfire. One official lectured me about our neglect of religiously based schools. As the product of a Catholic education, I strongly believe in the right of parents to send their children to religious schools. Another official strenuously argued that non-public schools were outside our mandate, and that new ones were being created primarily for parents who refused to let their children attend racially integrated public schools.

LAWRENCE M. O'ROURKE

I believed that some of the so-called Christian schools or academies then emerging were little more than a cover for racial segregation and a threat to both racial integration and public education. The behind-the-scenes maneuvering at the retreat between two very opposed camps introduced me to a big internal and political battle that was to have me knock heads with leaders of the Catholic Church. A church official responsible for promoting Catholic schools sent me a letter sharply criticizing my refusal to endorse direct aid to Catholic schools. He came close to accusing me of being a traitor to my faith. I rejected that and stood by my beliefs.

*   *   *

On the weekend after our policy retreat, we did not use such jargon as MBO and crosscutting. We got down to the vocabulary of politics. In the Virginia woods in a private home of Tomi Jones, a Carpenter staff member, I began to help Hufstedler become a campaigner for Carter. Since this was an unofficial event that we paid for and excluded career bureaucrats, the agenda was all politics. Talk and bourbon flowed.

*   *   *

Facing critical decisions, the schedule provided opportunities to walk in the woods and think. There was almost a Trappist notion about it. Away from the cabin, on those walks, we encountered one another, but kept a sort of spiritual silence. Back in the meeting room, and off the record, with no notes taken, we talked honestly about what made us tick, our reasons for serving in government, our politics, and our values. What I vividly remember is that as we prepared for our final meal and departure, Hufstedler said privately to me that she wanted to speak to me outside. Beyond the earshot of others, she said, "Larry, we're going to be spending a lot of time together and we need to be comfortable with one another. From now on, when you talk to me privately, you call me Shirley and tell me what you think, no matter how much you disagree with me. We'll reserve our titles for official public occasions."

It was on that weekend that we formulated plans for the Secretary to campaign for Carter, with me at her side. It was not as simple as it sounds.

*   *   *

The Secretary's office made my position as political guru official by an order. It was a wonder of bureaucratic terminology, addressed to me (with copies to all concerned):

> "You are directed to supervise and work with the senior speechwriter on a.) Researching material for the speech; b.) Meeting with the Secretary and other senior staff members in obtaining ideas and review of the speech drafts; c.) Providing necessary support to the senior speechwriter: d.) Making certain that the schedule is followed so that the Secretary may have the draft by the deadline set."

Other directives made it clear that I was to travel with the Secretary to all events that could be deemed political. As a result, I had little time to work with my department staff. I mastered the technique of delegating.

I had a team of speechwriters led by Fred Register and a budget to contract with outside writers. I had the great pleasure in the next few months to work with several excellent writers. Of particular note was Harry Ashmore, the Pulitzer Prize-winning Arkansas journalist whose courage and integrity set high standards during the Civil Rights Movement. From Santa Barbara, Ashmore sent me a speech draft:

> "I am Shirley Hufstedler and I will be the first person to lose my job should Ronald Reagan become president of the United States. That is because I am Secretary of Education and Ronald Reagan has promised to abolish the Department of Education if he has the chance to do so. It took us 200 years to get a place at the president's cabinet table for education. Yet the Republican candidate stands on a platform which promises to encourage its elimination. He would rather look backward into the simplicity of the past than forward to the complexities of the future. He views education as he views many important issues—in a sort of hazy reel that runs backwards."

When I read Ashmore's draft, there was no question but that it was right on target. Nevertheless I would have to kill it, or as journalists say, spike it, if only because I couldn't use government money to pay for a political speech. Hufstedler wanted to work for Carter's re-election, but in her way, in her judicious style. She told me she would not use a political hatchet. When I showed the Ashmore speech to Hufstedler, she declared, "That's not my style. Perhaps you can find a graceful way to lay it to the side." In writing to Ashmore, I could only say that it was a terrific job but not quite the tone we needed for the first year of the Department of Education. Ashmore sent his draft to others, including Carpenter, who pressed me to push it on Hufstedler. I took the heat, disappointing some for my apparent lack of aggressiveness. But there was no way that Shirley would attack in a strident manner.

Hufstedler, her chief of staff and I developed a speech strategy. The chief of staff and I reviewed hundreds of invitations. We picked those we thought were promising occasions for her to talk about the president's commitment to public education. Our staffs checked out locations and audiences. We got frequent requests—which we viewed as strong suggestions—from the White House and campaign committee for Carter and Vice President Walter Mondale. Constantly sensitive to the fact that she was a high-profile participant in a tough political campaign, we factored in the size and political influence of audiences, the likely press coverage, and whether the speech might help Carter win the state against the Republican ticket of Reagan and George Bush.

There were other details to consider. For instance, it would not make sense for Hufstedler to speak on education in competition with a Carter or Mondale speech. We had to make sure that if she were at risk of making news with an announcement of a federal program, the White House had first dibs to grab the positive headline. Coping with such details was my responsibility.

I reserved several hours on the Secretary's schedule each week to sit down with her and my speechwriters and put before her rough drafts of what we thought she should say. The distinction between a government speech and a political speech was often difficult to see. On major speeches, she frequently had different ideas, sometimes the result of her back channel conversations with Carter, Mondale or their political staffs. Hufstedler was scrupulous when it came to separating government service and campaigning. She kept a separate telephone on her desk that she paid for out of her pocket. She used it for politics and personal calls. She reminded me often that I could not use people on the government payroll to conduct research, write speeches or otherwise help our political agenda. I wrote and edited her overt political speeches late at night—during my private time. I was careful; once we decided to make an event political, I cut out members of my government staff from participation. Likewise, we held our political strategy meetings after regular department hours.

Several times I got caught up in delicate negotiations over the political tone of speeches. Hufstedler was not a political firebrand and never would be. Some of her speeches were so bland they got virtually no press coverage and therefore seemingly did the Carter campaign no particular good. White House officials told me to make her speeches more cutting against Reagan. Hufstedler talked about her dilemma with an old friend, Deputy Secretary of State Warren Christopher. But he wasn't much of a model. Top State Department officials are loath to make partisan political speeches. In addition, Christopher was busy trying to win freedom for the hostages seized by the Iranian students in Teheran. Hufstedler and I talked often about inserting more political material in her speeches. She resisted. She made clear that she did not want to politicize her Department of Education cabinet position. By strengthening her reputation as an advocate for education and the nation's public school children, she thought she gained respect upon which she could more effectively criticize Reagan on education issues. I agreed with Hufstedler and did my best to fend off critics who felt she was letting Carter down politically. Hufstedler and I had to deal with comparable complaints from the White House and campaign committee. Left unsaid was that if Carter won without her help, she might no longer be the number one choice for the Supreme Court.

*　　*　　*

Hufstedler was occasionally willing to go after Reagan in press interviews. I talked her into a breakfast meeting with reporters gathered by Godfrey "Budge" Sperling, Jr., bureau chief of the *Christian Science Monitor*. As a reporter, I gladly belonged to the Sperling group, meeting with political leaders and public officials over breakfast three or four times a week. Sperling breakfasts gave me chances I might otherwise not have to directly engage the guests. I liked challenging politicians. Now I wanted Hufstedler to face those challenges.

I asked Hufstedler if she would attend the Sperling breakfast, alerting her that the questions would be primarily political. Reporters there had little interest in department matters. She said yes. To prepare, I grilled her on potential questions, not holding back on topics ranging from Carter's faults to her possible nomination to the Supreme Court.

I picked her up at her apartment that morning. At the Sheraton-Carlton Hotel, I introduced her to Sperling and greeted my newspaper friends, among them Roth of the *Bulletin*, Jim Weighart of the *New York Daily News*, Bill Ringle of *Gannett Newspapers*, Richard Dudman of the *St. Louis Post-Dispatch* and Tim Adams of *Cox Newspapers*. It was a bit strange being an outsider because that is what I now was. Newspaper reporters draw a line in the sand. Step across it and you are on the other side. Some say the dark side. I certainly behaved that way when I pushed a pencil for a living.

When Sperling opened the discussion with a political question, Hufstedler seized the moment to point out that she as a Californian saw Reagan damage the state's public schools and colleges. She took a crack at Teddy Kennedy and his attacks on Carter from the left. Picking up a White House theme, Hufstedler warned that unless Democrats "closed ranks, they would lose the White House." She did a good job dealing with the few questions involving education and taking advantage of her chance to push Carter and bash Reagan.

Unfortunately, Hufstedler fielded a Texas reporter's question on the burning issue in the department—whether the federal government would require the Lone Star state to instruct non-native speaking children in both English and their non-native language until the children had sufficient command of English to learn math, science and history in English. When Hufstedler replied, the reporter got the impression, legitimately I thought, that Hufstedler intended that Texas school districts pick up the bill for the double-dose of teaching. In effect, Hufstedler stepped on the message she wanted to deliver—that Reagan was a danger to public education.

The story the next day in the papers in Texas and other states with sizeable Latino populations was that Hufstedler would mandate bilingual education that would impose additional federal burdens costing millions of dollars on states. The White House let Hufstedler and me know that they did not welcome the stories or big negative headlines.

Hufstedler assured me she was not worried about the fallout from the bilingual education story. She made me prouder yet of working with her when she said she would not shade the truth when it came to compliance with the law. Sticking to this approach during a political campaign is good government, but shaky politics. She rarely made a splash in the big political pool. For the most part, stories about what Hufstedler said about Reagan and his record on education ran deep inside newspapers.

Her words may not have changed a single vote. But Hufstedler cited her Sperling breakfast remarks as evidence that she was ready and willing to play first string on Carter's campaign team.

*   *   *

For the remainder of the campaign, I mainly served Hufstedler as supervisor of speeches, schedule keeper, and frequently, advanceman—a job that I enjoyed.

One time I went to Michigan, several days ahead of a scheduled Hufstedler visit to the American Federation of Teachers Convention and various education facilities, all carefully chosen to encourage conservative Democrats—they were called Reagan Democrats—to vote for Carter. One of my goals was to generate television and newspaper coverage that would show with emotional and political impact what could be accomplished by the progressive educational policy pursued by Carter and Hufstedler. When school officials offered me a range of site visits, I picked one to show how an enlightened policy in the Carter-Hufstedler tradition would place—"mainstream"—handicapped youngsters in regular public schools. I worked with Hufstedler to make the point that Reagan would cast aside these children in a Darwinian notion of survival of the fittest.

Working with local school officials, I arranged for Hufstedler to visit a public school making a special effort to include handicapped youngsters in all phases of school activities, including access to the swimming pool. Briefing Hufstedler and department officials on the trip, I stressed the urgent need for the department to promote policies for "mainstreaming" children with physical and developmental problems. I said that the department had to show that the Carter Administration was committed to end discrimination against these children. I offered evidence that these children were often pushed to the side in regular schools or more frequently put out of regular schools and into inadequate special schools. Mainstreaming was Hufstedler's position, so it didn't take much to convince her. But to some, inside and outside the department, it was another case of the federal government imposing rules and financial burdens on states and local school systems. But it heartened me when Hufstedler used her visit to the school to emphasize "mainstreaming" and to declare it as department policy. She thanked me for putting the issue on the agenda.

LAWRENCE M. O'ROURKE

*   *   *

But while we may have secured a victory for children and scored a few political points with a modest handful of voters during our trip to Michigan, I had a rather shocking and dispiriting experience in the state.

I went to Flint, a solidly Democratic city where Carter needed a big vote to beat Reagan. I met with United Auto Workers Union officials in a makeshift focus group and asked them what the president needed to do to carry Michigan in November. There was a painful pause until one union official said, "If Carter were to ban every Japanese car import into the United States tomorrow, I still don't think he would carry Michigan." Frankly, that was the response I expected, but didn't welcome. I submitted my depressing report from Flint to Hufstedler and the White House.

*   *   *

One of my favorite trips as a Department of Education official was to Palm Springs, California, where Hufstedler was invited to address the Magazine Publishers Association. In the desert oasis, I got up early the day of her speech and ran in a 4.9-mile foot race put on by the publishers under the title Sharp Pencil Road Race. I figured I could outrun most publishers and I was in pretty good shape. I was in training for the New York and Marine Corps Marathons. I ran comfortably and through the first couple of legs of the course I had victory in sight. But then in the final 300 yards, George Hirsch, publisher of *The Runner* (later *Runners' World*) magazine, sprinted and beat me by a few yards. At the publishers' morning session, my minor accomplishment was announced and applauded. Various publishers kidded me that they did not think that government officials could run fast.

Hufstedler explored the idea of using the publishers' speech to go after Reagan in his back yard. But she stayed true to form—above the political fray. She talked about education and the media—legitimate topics to be sure, but not grist for the political mill in the late stages of a bitter campaign. But Hufstedler did get a non-partisan buzz when she told the editors: "Considering the torrents of jargon which the rest of us endure daily, the debasement of language at the hands of Madison Avenue slogan makers, bureaucrats, rule makers and even—Lord help this fall—political speechwriters, is one of the most depressing trends of our time." No doubt a lot of the editors who heard these remarks realized how their publications contribute to the jargon. I told her before the speech that the publishers wanted political red meat. I wrote for her a few lines that I thought she could say without overstepping her boundary on politics: "I'm glad President Carter gave me the opportunity to serve as Secretary of Education, and I'm signed on for four more years." In her delivery, she dropped the "more" and the entire political point was lost.

The next day, Hufstedler and I visited a Lutheran pre-school in Norwalk, California. I had been pushing for her to visit a non-public school as a signal to the Reagan Democrats. She held a news conference. Reporters gave her the chance to rip into Reagan for his statement that the Department of Education was not needed. "People who say that are not informed, "she said. It was wry understatement, but not headline material. It would have been a small step for Hufstedler, as I urged on her, to describe the Republican nominee's statement as another example of how Reagan was uninformed or out of touch with the nation's needs, but she wouldn't go there. But she did add to my surprise, "We're not going to have a Reagan Administration in 1981." I don't think she sounded convincing to a single listener, myself included.

From the news conference, Hufstedler and I went to *The Los Angeles Times* for lunch with old friends, publisher Tom Johnson, editorial page editor Tony Day, and editor Bill Thomas. Witty and erudite, Hufstedler took restrained cracks at Reagan, but again was more judicious than political. I knew that Hufstedler was not going to be a political cutter and slasher, so why fret over it?

*   *   *

While my service at the Department focused on helping Hufstedler speak and travel, I had a substantive role in federal government policy disputes with national impact. The most important and controversial policy issue that crossed my desk was the one dealing with bilingual education. We were called on to decide a policy with the potential to shape the lives of millions of children in U.S. public schools, with an impact on the nation for many years to come.

The issue was forced on us at a politically inopportune time by a 1974 Supreme Court decision in the *Lau v. Nichols* case. Decided under the Civil Rights Act of 1964, it launched the modern bilingual education movement. It required the government to take critical steps toward better education for children of immigrants. It came to the Supreme Court from the U.S. the Court of Appeals on which Hufstedler sat and joined in the appeals court decision. The Ford Administration ducked the issue and avoided the political hit. Carter had no wiggle room. We had a political time bomb in our laps.

The question for us in the summer of 1980 was drafting regulations to improve education of the 3.5 million children whose primary language was other than English. They were in more than 6,000 school districts across the nation, many in vote-rich California and Texas. About 70 percent of these children primarily spoke Spanish, but with children coming into the United States as refugees from the Vietnam War, we had significant numbers who spoke mostly, if not entirely, Vietnamese, Hmong, and Lao. We had children speaking only Tagalog from the Philippines and Chinese. As immigration, both legal and illegal, increased, the number of affected children grew. We had evidence that lots of kids were in classrooms all day without understanding the words of their English-speaking teachers. The kids got little help at home where parents and other family members spoke in native tongues. Dropout rates were three times higher for Hispanic children with limited English proficiency than for Hispanic youngsters with no language barrier. We had files of evidence that kids who didn't know English could quickly consume the time of their teachers and turn into troublemakers, much to the detriment of others in the class. The nation was condemning thousands of children to a dim future, with dangerous political and social consequences. Some school districts treated these youngsters as mentally retarded. It was indisputable that students unable to grasp fully what the teacher said were soon hopelessly behind their peers, at risk of diminished lives.

Our job was to figure out a remedy. School districts with high numbers of non-English speaking children told us that if we wanted to fix it, we should pay for it. But there was no prospect that Washington would bail them out. We recognized that 90 percent or more of the costs of public education would remain with states and localities.

The remedies that we considered were all expensive. Civil rights activists and most advocates for minority groups, particularly Hispanics, preferred a remedy known as "maintenance." The maintenance approach provided that the children be taught all subjects in their native language as well as in English indefinitely or at least until the children became proficient in English. There was a noble argument for this. In this great mosaic of our nation, children should be entitled to their own culture. But this maintenance method would require two teachers in a classroom, one teaching subjects like math, composition, history, geography and literature in the child's native language, and a second teacher instructing on the same material in English.

I thought the "maintenance" plan was unworkable and unwise. Beyond the cost, where would one find the hundreds, if not thousands, of qualified teachers skilled in teaching in Spanish, Hmong, Vietnamese and other languages?

Politicians in areas with large numbers of Spanish-speaking children contended that in our zeal to promote bilingual education, we would damage public education. I agreed with them and said so.

From outside the department, I was pressured by school officials to scuttle the approach advocated by civil rights groups and ethnic community leaders. From the opposite direction, governors, mayors, and members of city and county councils weighed in. I was told repeatedly that if Hufstedler insisted on two teachers in thousands of classrooms, there would be a political firestorm that would put the electoral votes of California, Texas, New York, New Jersey and Illinois into Reagan's column, sending Carter and the rest of us home. But my position was based on more than politics and elections.

I thought that bilingual education was bad for the kids. My attitude was shaped by the fact that I was the only official in the department with hands-on experience teaching English to non-English speaking students.

I drew on my Army teaching in concluding that the maintenance approach would be wrong for the tens of thousands of kids whose journey through public education was meant to be a path to a productive job and a sound life as a citizen of the United States. As much as I liked the concept of children enriched by their ethnic culture, I thought it a disservice to them if they did not have conventional English—the language of the nation where they intended to live and work. I felt that you only had to look in the real world to see more doors opening for people with ability at using standard English. Bosses were reluctant to hire people with limited English. They would be steered toward menial jobs.

Alone among Hufstedler's advisers, I favored a teaching method called "immersion." This method could concentrate on teaching children in English from their first days in school. I knew from my Army teaching that after eight or nine weeks of five and six-hours a day of English, we made considerable progress in getting our Puerto Rican students, aged 18 to 25, to learn a great deal of English. Would not younger children learn English faster?

I went to the press to promote my views. I told former colleagues there was a big struggle brewing inside the government that would make an excellent story. I told these reporters about the competing interests. I told them the same thing I was telling Hufstedler—that we would do these kids an immense and enduring disservice if we did not require them to learn standard English as young and as quickly as possible. To my disappointment, the national reporters I contacted declined to write stories about the fight over bilingual education at a time that public opinion, in my view, should have been engaged. I was disappointed that I failed as a "leaker."

To jump ahead with the story, months later, after Hufstedler announced her bilingual education decision favoring a compromise called "transition," reporters came awake to the implications that I had earlier urged them to write about. Now the reporters understood the effects on Carter's campaign, relations between the federal government and states, and the new obligations on thousands of school districts. Minutes after Hufstedler's announcement, I got calls from reporters who knew of my opposition to the decision. But I knew what I had to do. I supported the decision, telling reporters that it was sound, reasonable, and had the full backing of her advisers, including me. As long as I was on the team, I would play by the rules. As my mother told me as a child, using old Irish wisdom, "When a girl goes to a dance with a boy, you dance with the one who brung you."

*　　*　　*

My battle within the department on bilingual education earned me a reputation within the department as an opponent of civil rights. A few officials said that if my attitude had prevailed after the Supreme Court's 1954 racial desegregation decision, we would still have a racially separate public school system. That hurt, but we were playing hardball.

*　　*　　*

What really killed the Carter campaign, and ended my future in government, took place thousands of miles away, in the Iranian desert.

The phone rang at home in the early hours. "This is the White House operator," said the voice. "What is your name and position with the government?" I was told to stay on the line for a briefing from the White House. A familiar voice came on. "What I will tell you is off the record for now, but it will be publicly known and on the news very soon. In an attempt to rescue the U.S. Embassy hostages held by the radical students in Teheran, the President ordered the U.S. military to attempt a rescue mission. It was well planned and the administration thought it would succeed. However, it did not. U.S. helicopters crashed in the Iranian desert. Some U.S. military rescuers died. The United States was forced to withdraw."

I was stunned. "The President hopes that you will support his decision and speak publicly in support of it in the hours and days ahead."

Putting down the phone, I told Pat. "Carter's done. It was a desperate attempt and it failed. The election is settled. Get ready for Reagan." I did my duty, telling reporters and my staff that Americans would honor and respect the president for doing the right thing, no matter how politically perilous. But I didn't believe my own words.

*   *   *

On election eve, a few of us wrote our predictions for Electoral College votes, agreeing that the envelope would be sealed until the vote was counted. I predicted a Reagan victory. I won the poll as the closest in the Electoral College count. I wasn't happy that my prediction came true. How long have you thought that Reagan would beat Carter, they asked me. "I was convinced of it long before I joined this administration," I said. I could prove it. In the fall a year before the election, I spoke at the Union League in Philadelphia at the invitation of Joe Livingston, financial columnist for the *Bulletin*. I shocked many in the sophisticated audience of business executives by saying Reagan would be nominated and beat Carter. Some in the audience openly scoffed. Livingston thought I had lost my marbles. In fact, he said so in January 1981, when I accompanied Hufstedler to the same group in Philadelphia. In introducing Hufstedler, Livingston told the story of my accurate prediction. Later, I apologized to Hufstedler for allowing her to be surprised by the recollection of my prediction and any embarrassment it may have caused her. She said she was not surprised since she knew my political talent.

* * *

It was a few days before Christmas. Hufstedler was in California for the holidays. Minter was in Cleveland lining up a job with a foundation. If anybody called a meeting of the senior staff, we could hold it around a table in the employee cafeteria. Or around the fax machine where resumes were pouring out. I filled hours by enrolling in courses in the Horace Mann Learning Center in our building.

I got a call from the general counsel. She reminded me that during the day we were required to have one senior officer immediately available to deal with any crisis. We didn't want a call from the White House or Congress to slip into the bureaucratic cracks. The counsel said that she couldn't find any assistant secretaries and she knew that I at that time was an acting assistant secretary, so would I mind staying at the department while she went out for a holiday lunch and shopping. Of course not, I said.

My staff joked that I had become, in fact if not in title, Acting U.S. Secretary of Education. They called me Mr. Secretary. Shortly thereafter, my office began to smell. In fact, the air in the entire building began to smell.

A top career official ran into my office. "Smell it," he said. "They're putting new tar on our roof and the fumes have gotten into the ventilating system." "So, what do we do about it?" I asked. "You're in charge," he said. "You're supposed to be the Acting Secretary of Education. Order the building evacuated."

"Consider it done,' I replied, and in minutes employees were on the sidewalk, the building closed, and the U.S. Department of Education was shut down. By mid-afternoon, the smell went away, all returned, and my tenure as acting secretary was over. But I became known for a few days as the guy who shut down the department.

CHAPTER 14

Pounding the Pavement, Pounding the Street

TWO DAYS AFTER Ronald Reagan's election as president, I received notes from President Carter and Education Secretary Hufstedler. They instructed me to cooperate with emissaries of the president-elect to make it the smoothest transition in U.S. history. There would be no sour grapes, no sabotaging, and no foot-dragging. In a meeting with senior officials at the department, Hufstedler said we had our chance, we lost, and we should get on with it—"it" being our remaining duties in government, our lives and careers.

Ending my government service was easy enough. I got a call from the Reagan transition team. We made an appointment in my office. Two young men came by. They were very polite and cordial, and I responded in kind. I gave them a packet outlining the duties, budget and staff of my office. They took notes and graciously asked me my plans. I expected the question. I would submit my resignation for noon on January 20, 1981, the moment Reagan would be sworn in.

Reagan's emissaries engagingly asked me if I would like to work for the next Administration. I said no, that I had spent much of the year arguing against Reagan's election, and that I believed I did not share his philosophy of the federal government's role in education. The Reagan aides said they understood. There was no acrimony. They said that I should not rush to leave the department; it would be weeks before the new leadership team was in place and I could continue to manage my office, if I wished. I found that very generous and said so. We ended on a very amicable note.

In the days ahead, my staff urged me to stay on, suggesting that I "burrow into" the bureaucracy—in other words, switch from being a political employee to being a government employee. I didn't think long about that suggestion. As much as I respected my staff and government employees in general, I felt more comfortable in a more competitive atmosphere, and a freer one, where I could exercise a degree of independence, including political expression. Paradoxically, I had worked hard to keep my staff at the department from engaging in politics at the workplace, even to chastising one gifted man who brought union and political material to the office and passed it out. I told him that while I agreed with the politics he was promoting, I regarded the Hatch Act as prohibiting such activity and saw it as disruptive in the office. I told him so bluntly and he stopped his activities. The union sent me a letter of complaint, but took the matter no further. During the campaign, I distributed to my staff a stern memo saying I did not want political buttons worn to the office or political posters displayed in government offices. That was all history when just before Thanksgiving, I wrote my letter of resignation, effective when the Carter Administration expired.

*   *   *

While closing out my government career was a cinch, finding a new job suited to me proved daunting. It was not a good time for look for a job as the country was in recession, compounded by high inflation, factors that contributed mightily to Carter's defeat.

During the transition, many friends offered help. Several took me to lunch to cheer me up. I had a call from C. Emily Feistritzer, publisher of a newsletter titled *Department of Education Weekly*. In my government capacity, I provided information to Feistritzer, an entrepreneurial former nun from Kentucky. I got her interviews with Hufstedler and other officials. Feistritzer marketed her newsletter to state and local school officials and libraries; it was apparently doing very well. It was a valuable source of information to people interested in the people and policies of the federal agency.

Feistritzer called me with a proposal: she was thinking about expanding her newsletter empire through creation of a newsletter called *White House Weekly*. As she saw it, there would be great interest in the new Reagan team and policy. Would I be interested, Emily asked, in starting it up? Effectively I would be reporter, writer, editor and production chief. She would handle distribution and promotion starting with a massive free mailing. Beyond putting out *White House Weekly*, my tasks, Emily said, would be helping with the education newsletter and any others she might begin. She was ambitious to build a newsletter empire. I mulled it over as I explored other options.

I knew that if I asked Hufstedler's help in getting a legal job in Washington, I could have it. In fact, a couple of officials followed Hufstedler into the Los Angeles law firm managed by her husband Seth Hufstedler. As much as I respected Shirley and Seth, I had no interest in moving to California.

I got a call from the University of Chicago asking if I would like to join the staff of the president, Hannah Gray, as a spokesman and speechwriter. That seemed like an excellent opportunity, much like what I did for Hufstedler, including the travel, but neither Pat nor I was enthusiastic about moving to Chicago. We had four children in school whose lives we did not want to disrupt.

I asked my old *Bulletin* colleagues and old friends on other newspapers about openings for a Washington reporter. But part of me was reluctant to return to the business. I thought that going back as a reporter might be defiance of Thomas Wolfe's maxim that you can't go home again. I had enjoyed a wonderful career as a journalist at the highest level but I doubted I could comfortably re-enter the business.

I knew that I could take on criminal defense work in the District of Columbia Courts under the Criminal Justice Act, as I had while at the *Bulletin*, but I hesitated to step onto that road. My experience as a trial lawyer in the D.C. courts had been frustrating as clients and witnesses failed to show up for court dates or appointments, cases were delayed, pay vouchers were routinely cut without explanation, and working conditions were often abominable. I tolerated it all when I had a salary from the *Bulletin* and could find the time to take a few clients at a time. To do it full time and depend on it for a living was something else entirely.

Friends urged me to apply to the Justice Department and other government law offices before my tenure in the Carter Administration ended, but I was not naïve. I could not be hired before the inauguration and the Reagan people would have no difficulty dismissing my application. After all, they won the election and were entitled to exercise the hiring and policy authority that went with it. David Broder, an old friend and the top political writer at *The Washington Post*, called one day and mentioned that I might be interested in a job as a spokesman for the Democratic National Committee. That possibility was intriguing. I had a taste for national politics. But I feared that my well-honed skepticism for politicians might surface. I did not apply.

LAWRENCE M. O'ROURKE

Near Christmas I attended a party with Hufstedler and senior department officials. We were still shell shocked. Over a few drinks we swapped stories, promised to keep in touch with each other, mourned our departure from public service, and feared our embarkation for new unknown ports. It was an Irish wake, or what the Irish called an American Wake for emigrants on the eve of sailing away never to see family and friends again.

With bills to pay and mouths to feed, I put a combination package together. I would work for Feistritzer on her newsletters, take a few law cases, and continue to look for opportunities in law, politics and journalism. Most importantly, I would re-integrate myself into the family from which I had spent so much time away.

*   *   *

On the Monday after Reagan's inauguration, I reported to my new office in the National Press Building to begin work on Feistritzer's newsletters. One of my first duties was to join her at an auction where she bought two more newsletters, one dealing with health education and disease prevention, and the other with housing and urban development. I hired freelance writers for them. Concentrating on *White House Weekly*, I gradually realized that I no longer had access to all that wonderful inside information that constituted the copy of special interest newsletters. Not only did the Reagan White House staff see me as on the opposite side politically, I no longer had a White House pass permitting me to enter the White House for interviews. Finding items worth writing for a special interest audience became a terrible chore.

Two other factors undermined the possibility of success. Emily charged a high fee for an annual subscription to *White House Weekly*, more than one would pay for *The New York Times* or *Washington Post*, each of which had several fulltime regular White House reporters chasing down every piece of information about the new Reagan administration. I got a few tips about the Reagan team from Democrats, some of whom had been ousted, as had I. But that mixture further tilted the newsletter against Reagan. I didn't consciously become a critic of Reagan's new team or his plans, but I gradually assumed that role. That countered what Feistritzer felt she needed to promote her expensive newsletter to the corporate executives who could afford it, who tended, she pointed out, to tilt Republican. So it wasn't long before Emily and I realized that we were not destined to build a publishing empire together. Four months after starting, I was out.

In the meantime, I picked up cases in the District of Columbia criminal courts and a few small checks rolled in. I also served a handful of private clients, drafting wills, filing divorce actions, and threatening lawsuits on consumer complaints. While I by necessity learned new skills and bodies of law, I risked taking on too much with no support. One of my successful criminal defense cases brought me an invitation to join the defense team for a well-known drug dealer facing a trial and the possibility of a long prison sentence. While I am committed to the proposition that every defendant is entitled to effective assistance of counsel, I didn't want to become involved in that field of representation. I politely declined.

As I struggled to find a new direction, Edmund Ghareeb, a press officer at the United Arab Emirates, invited me to fly to Abu Dhabi and Dubai to attend the organizational session of the Gulf Cooperation Council. The deal was an all-expenses-paid trip in return for a couple of meetings with officials of the governments where I would explain how American journalism worked. In all my trips to the Middle East for *The Philadelphia Bulletin*, I had never been in the Emirates. I took Ed's offer and spent a couple of weeks in the Emirates and in London, learning a lot about the Gulf nations and teaching them a bit about our country and its free press.

*   *   *

Once I was back from the Middle East, Pat and I sat down to consider our financial situation. We did not need to panic. We had spent and saved prudently. When I got a raise in joining the Carter administration, we never changed our lifestyle, but kept the extra money in my checking account. I received offers from family and friends to give us or lend us money if we ran short before I found another fulltime job. I was grateful, but did not yet need to accept. Feistritzer provided health insurance but now that I was no longer on her payroll, I faced the prospect of a family with four kids lacking health insurance. That was not tolerable. At this point, Pat came to our rescue. She took a job as an assistant to executive director Richard J. Dowling at the National Association of Allied Health Professions. It had the benefit of health insurance and a small income.

Our prospects brightened when I accepted an offer to be a researcher and education consultant in the Washington office of the Carnegie Foundation for the Advancement of Education, headed by Ernest Boyer. Prior to creation of the Department of Education, Ernie served as U.S. Commissioner of Education. He was highly respected. The offer to join Ernie came through Robert Hochstein, who had worked for me at the Department of Education. These connections were typical Washington, former colleagues opening doors for each other and helping one another through hard times. At the Carnegie office near Dupont Circle in Northwest Washington, Boyer told me that he was interested in the finished product, not in my appearing in the office every day and putting in time. He traveled widely. I would be told when and where he had a speech to deliver and in general what he wanted to talk about. He was also working on a book about the governance of higher education. He would outline his thoughts and give them to me for polishing. I could do the work where and when I wanted, as long as words on paper flowed to him regularly. It was a workable arrangement for me. I was able to work from home, except on days I had appearances in court or when Boyer would be in Washington and we would meet.

The schedule worked so well that we were able to take a family holiday in August. While enjoying the chance to spend hours with the family, I worked on Carnegie material so that I had a fresh package of words for Ernie in September. Ernie asked me to join the Carnegie staff at its headquarters in Princeton. The job would also involve research, writing, and public relations work out of Carnegie offices in New York City, close enough by train to Princeton for regular commuting. It was a generous offer. I liked Boyer and the work he was doing, but again Pat and I were unwilling to disrupt the kids with a move from Washington to Princeton. I said no to Boyer.

* * *

The lack of a permanent job was getting to me. The constant worry about whether I'd have work and income weeks or months down the road was nerve racking. I didn't like it a bit. I didn't like the uncertainty or the strain of looking for a job. I had good interview skills, but the process was dispiriting. I didn't like pounding the pavement for work, an experience that often befalls American white-collar workers. I realized that I had never before as an adult been forced to look for a job. Good jobs always seemed to pop up, but not this time. I was learning what it was like to be unemployed. Some friends suggested I apply for government jobless benefits, but I resisted. Looking back, it was a valuable learning experience that made me familiar with the hard times felt by many Americans. But on the negative side, I was filled with anxiety, the kind that can drive people to anger, alcohol or drugs. For me, the remedy to anxiety wasn't a destructive substance. It was a much more benign activity: running.

*　　*　　*

Though I didn't like pounding the pavement for a job, I liked pounding the street with a group of like-minded achievers. Through hours of roadside conversations, many in the dark, we formed a lifestyle and friendship that was to last in and out of running shoes for more than a quarter century.

I wasn't a stranger to running. More than two decades before, I ran on my high school cross-country team, competing in Fairmount Park meets and earning a letter. At Villanova, I ran for exercise because I was not good enough to compete at the collegiate level on Wildcat teams that included Olympians Ron Delany, Charlie Jenkins, Don Bragg and others. In the Army, I enjoyed the running part of basic training, even when it meant carrying a heavy backpack, and I used running as a disciplinary tool in Puerto Rico when my English language students misbehaved or became complacent. Sadly, as I got caught up after the Army in long hours and late-night work, too many fancy meals and travel, I didn't engage in running or any form of exercise beyond an occasional pick-up basketball game or round of golf.

In the summer of 1968, I came back to running. My return to the sport was spurred by an event while I covered Johnson in Texas. Pat and I had been to a movie in Austin with Carroll Kilpatrick of *The Washington Post* and Connie Gerrard of the White House press office. Carroll and Connie returned to the White House filing center to see if there were developments that needed work. I had filed my overnight story and did not anticipate any more writing for the day. Pat, who was six months pregnant, and I walked slowly on "the Drag" a busy portion of Guadalupe Street on the western edge of the University of Texas campus.

As we walked we spotted a scale. Pat went first and was satisfied that her weight was within the tolerable range. When it was my turn,

I almost fell off the scale. I broke 200 pounds. No wonder I huffed for breath when I climbed stairs. We had our first baby on the way, Pat pointed out, and I needed to be in shape for the duties of a new dad.

Back in Washington, I took decisive action. I joined the YMCA two blocks from the White House. When the White House press office shut its doors for lunch—a process called putting on a lid—I ran on the Y's inside track, an oval suspended from the ceiling above the basketball floor. It was 22 laps to a mile. At first, it was not only a physical challenge to get around the track, but also mindless and boring, especially when I counted the laps. To escape that useless burden, I bought a clicker and pushed it each time I reached the bend near the staircase. That let my mind wander and soon I found myself drafting columns and tending mentally to other tasks as I ran. It took months, but I found myself running in excess of 200 laps, nearly ten miles during lunch hour. With my new health consciousness, I would have a small salad for lunch before heading back to the White House. For more than a year, I practiced total abstinence from alcohol and bread. My weight dropped steadily and I no longer huffed and puffed.

Though I was in better shape, campaigns and foreign travel frequently kept me away from the Y track at lunchtime. On the road, I toted gear and worked out as often as I could. On Sundays, Pat and I and the kids went frequently to the YMCA on Old Georgetown Road in Bethesda, Maryland so that the kids could swim. I ran in all weather on the outside track. One Sunday when I arrived for my run, our neighbors Edie and David Tatel were walking briskly around the track. Edie and Pat were members of the neighborhood baby-sitting cooperative. Edie went inside the building to the pool and talked to Pat while David and I continued walking. We enjoyed our walk and talk so much that David and I decided to meet again the following Sunday. That led to our decision a few weeks later to meet in early morning and join another neighbor and runner, David Lawrenz, a physician. The two Davids and I struck it off well. We gradually added to our regular running group. Restaurant executive Jay Treadwell, overseas aid administrator Larry Heilman, and journalist Peter Osnos ran many mornings. We met on the street in front of the Tatel home at 5.45 and ran for a little over an hour, about seven or eight miles. We adopted a couple of rules. We would not talk outside the group about what we said during the run, titling our compact "Runners' Rules." And the run would begin promptly at 5.45 because we all faced tight schedules. Latecomers had to catch up or run alone.

Not wanting to miss the group run, I fixed my digital clock at 5.11. That time became so much a part of me that on the days I didn't run and for years after I stopped running I'd wake up at 5.11, even when I didn't have the buzzer set to go off.

On Saturdays we did a longer run, slightly more than 16.2 miles for me, through Rock Creek Park and up the long hill by the Mormon Temple in Kensington, Maryland. We often had an expanded group on Saturdays including medical researcher Bill Friedewald, journalist Marlene Cimons, psychiatrist Steve Sonnenberg, lawyer Joe Bell, national security analyst Bob Bell, and journalist Milton Coleman.

We were at times joined on our Saturday runs by a homemaker from the neighborhood, Judy Flannery. Judy began running at the age of 38 and was a natural. She was such a strong runner that she competed in the Ironman competition in Hawaii and finished as one of the top three women athletes in her age division in the world. She was the oldest woman ever to be named Master Female Triathlete of the Year. Tragically, Judy was struck by a car and killed on April 2, 1997, during a training bicycle ride in suburban Maryland when a car driven by a 16-year-old swerved across a centerline. Judy was 57 years old and the mother of five.

Others filtered in and out of our running group over the years. One was Jack Block, Reagan's secretary of agriculture. We also had a few leaders in the worlds of education and philanthropy who were in town to meet with Tatel. We had frank and honest conversations along the route. Many would have made great newspaper stories for me. But I scrupulously honored the Runners' Rules. It was a great example of trust and bonding among Type-A men.

Being competitive types by nature, we were not content to jog slowly and talk. Tatel, Lawrenz and I began to run annually in the 10-mile Cherry Blossom Race, held in early April every year on a course that winds past the Washington Monument and Lincoln and Jefferson Memorials. In 1977, Tatel and I each clocked 81.41, not a great time as running times go, but pretty good for the two of us.

The Cherry Blossom not being enough for us, we ran in the Marine Corps Marathon, the 26.2-mile test held usually in early November. In our first effort at that distance in 1978, David and I clocked three hours, 40 minutes and 17 seconds. That wasn't very good and we finished well back in the pack. But fast times were never important to us. The goal was to finish, to avoid the DNF—did not finish—in the results book. We successfully ran the Marine Marathon several times. With Lawrenz

LAWRENCE M. O'ROURKE

and others from our Chevy Chase morning group, Tatel and I ran the New York City Marathon. I did a few solo races that included marathons in Baltimore and the 1979 Boston Marathon.

Had it not been for these friends and running, I would have had a much tougher time in 1981, my year for pounding the pavement in pursuit of a full-time job. Tatel figured it out one time that we ran enough miles together over the years to get us to the moon and back. I have said truthfully that just about every mile was a pleasure, though those on ice were a bit hazardous.

*　　*　　*

When I turned down Boyer's invitation in the fall of 1981 to move to Princeton, it was back to relying for health insurance and income on Pat's job at the allied health office, with a small contribution from my criminal law practice. On an early December morning, I answered a telephone call at home from Tom Ottenad, Washington bureau chief of *The St. Louis Post-Dispatch*. Ottenad and I had worked a few political stories together and had dinner on a few occasions. I knew Ottenad's recently retired predecessor, Richard Dudman, much better. Ottenad said the *Post-Dispatch* needed to supplement its bureau through the addition of an "old hand," a reporter who covered many different types of stories over many years and might be willing to mentor a staff of very bright young reporters. Ottenad did not want to take on a mentoring responsibility. He was a first-rate political reporter and he liked to schmooze politicians and travel. He didn't want to be confined to his office at 1701 Pennsylvania Avenue, NW. He would rather be in Iowa or New Hampshire or California on politics. While good with politicians, Ottenad conceded hat he lacked the tolerance or patience to bring along a young staff. Would I be interested in the job?

I went to Ottenad's office, walking past the desks of young reporters I recognized: Jon Sawyer, Gerald Boyd, Bob Adams, and William and Margaret Freivogel. They later told me that they recognized me too, and wondered what I was talking about behind the closed door of Ottenad's office. I told Ottenad I was sufficiently interested to take the next step—to fly to St. Louis to meet managing editor David Lipman. Ottenad confided that he and Lipman were not getting along.

I could understand the flashpoint between Lipman and Ottenad the minute I stepped into Lipman's St. Louis office. The loud, shaven-head

Lipman was gruff to the point of being overbearing. He made it clear that he did not tolerate people he felt were not measuring up to his standards. He said he had sent his best and brightest young people to Washington and they were not producing as he wished. He blamed Ottenad for laxity in putting pressure on the young reporters. Lipman said that if I got the job and failed to improve the copy from Washington, I'd feel his wrath. Was it bluster? I didn't know. He sweetened the offer to me. Beyond mentoring, I'd be expected to report and write, with an emphasis on multi-part series that explored important issues.

Lipman went on: *The Post-Dispatch*, like other U.S. afternoon newspapers, was in trouble, with falling circulation and declining advertising revenue. It might not make it. I might find myself in a few years looking for a job. Lipman told me that Joseph Pulitzer, the publisher and the heir to a great newspaper name and tradition, promised that the *Post-Dispatch* would go down fighting; that as long as the Pulitzer name was attached to it, it would strive for quality. I liked that kind of talk.

I spent two days in St. Louis, talking with Joseph and Michael Pulitzer and members of the *Post-Dispatch* staff. I said yes to Lipman. I was back in the newspaper business.

LAWRENCE M. O'ROURKE

CHAPTER 15

Reagan: Triumph of the Sound Bite

BEFORE I COULD begin mentoring *Post-Dispatch* Washington bureau reporters, I renewed my credentials as a reporter. I tried first to revive connections I used and enjoyed for many years, but I feared I damaged when I became a government employee.

I found young Republican staffers who distrusted me when I told them that during my absence from journalism I worked for the re-election of Jimmy Carter and Democratic control of Congress. I did not try to hide my experience in government, politics and the private sector. When the White House and congressional staffers who took over under Reagan asked about my background, I told them about my long newspaper career, Of course, many were also skeptical about *The St. Louis Post-Dispatch* with a long history as a progressive newspaper.

In my first week at the *Post-Dispatch,* I learned from a Justice Department lawyer that the department under Attorney General Edwin Meese was secretly working up a plan that would encourage and facilitate white parents, primarily in the Deep South, to transfer their children from racially integrated public schools to private all-white schools. This would largely be done through adjustments in interpretation of the federal tax code and a muzzle on the Justice Department's civil rights division. Because the administration plan was so closely held and politically sensitive, the lawyer who leaked it to me insisted I could print it only if I extended an ironclad promise to shield the lawyer's identity. Recognizing this as an important story, I made that promise.

The administration's plan was to reverse an Internal Revenue Service interpretation of tax law that denied tax advantages to racially discriminatory private schools. These schools would be transformed into private academies based on religious preferences. Advocates contended that these academies were designed to let parents bring up their children in the Christian faith, and were not, as opponents alleged, designed to exclude black children. Advocates called them Christian academies. Opponents called them segregation academies.

The Reagan administration's plan for primary and secondary schools was consistent with its effort to protect Bob Jones University of South Carolina from government action because the school practiced racial discrimination.

The *Post-Dispatch* published this blockbuster story on page one. Many newspapers including *The Washington Post* picked up my story, and it started a firestorm on Capitol Hill. The *Post* included a paragraph that named me as the reporter who broke the story. That effectively announced my return to journalism and hiring by *The Post-Dispatch.*

Since I enjoyed reporting more than mentoring, it turned out I did virtually none of the latter. I let the young reporters in the bureau know I would be glad to talk with them about their stories and Washington reporting. I quickly found that none of them needed much, if any, mentoring from me. While young and short of experience in Washington, they were bright, diligent and quick learners. They were there because they had performed well as reporters in St. Louis. The main problem in the bureau was a disconnect between the young reporters and bureau chief Ottenad, a superb political reporter who operated on the theory that the young reporters, if left to their own talent, would do well on their own. I shared Ottenad's approach, even as I encouraged him to pay more attention to the work of his younger colleagues. I also found that enthusiasm from the leader helped.

*   *   *

Tom made his phone calls and wrote his stories in his private office and disdained meetings with bureau members, individually or as a group. The reporters, me now among them, worked in a long room with open desks and no privacy. We could hear each other's phone calls, not a situation I found conducive to development of not-for-attribution conversations or exclusive stories. I was accustomed as a reporter to a private office and as *Bulletin* bureau chief I provided a private office to each reporter. My desk at the *Post-Dispatch* was at one end of the room. Before I used it, Joe Pulitzer, the publisher's son who spent a short time in Washington to learn the business, sat at the desk that was now mine. In the top drawer, I found a gracious note from Joe wishing me well. A few

LAWRENCE M. O'ROURKE

feet from me was Jo Mannies, who covered the St. Louis area delegation. Others in the room included Jon Sawyer, a thoughtful writer often sent on foreign projects, Bob Adams who covered the Pentagon and national security, and William and Margaret Frievogel, a husband-wife team who shared a job.

Gerald Boyd, the White House correspondent, sat about 25 feet from me. Gerald was the best African-American reporter on the White House beat, if not the best black journalist in Washington. Gerald's life story was exemplary. He grew up in St. Louis, working while a teenager as a grocery store bagger. He was a reporter of poise, confidence, and dignity. He had excellent contacts in the White House. I was impressed when I discovered that Boyd could call Jim Baker or Meese or other senior officials and get his call returned quickly. Gerald was largely non-judgmental, as most of us understood that reporters should be. He was so good that the *Post-Dispatch* could not keep him. *The New York Times* came knocking. Gerald asked my advice: should he stay with the *Post-Dispatch* and work his way to the inevitable: a top position at the St. Louis paper or should he go to the country's finest newspaper and compete with a bevy of talented men and women. I told Boyd he had what it took to succeed at *The New York Times*, a newspaper, unlike the *Post-Dispatch*, with durability and clout, but he should be careful he was not being exploited.

Gerald took the job at *The New York Times*. He was soon assigned to the paper's glamour job as White House correspondent. I was in the White House pressroom on the day he arrived as the *Times'* correspondent. "Welcome to the big time," said the reporter for *USA Today*, suggesting that *USA Today* was in the big time. (At the time I privately dismissed *USA Today* as big time only in motel breakfast rooms and on college campuses, where it was available without charge and offered the best sports statistics, weather map and front-page color pictures in the business. It got better, or perhaps, it seemed to get better because it survived when so many other papers folded.)

But, that carping aside, Gerald as representative of *The New York Times* was indeed at the top of White House correspondents in access to top officials and claims to good stories. However, his meteoric rise at the *Times* ended in a crashing fall. On the ascent, Gerald moved from Washington to the *Times* main office in New York where he continued his climb as city editor. He held that position when the paper won three Pulitzer Prizes. He quickly became managing editor, the number two newsroom position. I worried that Gerald was moving faster than his experience and talent warranted. I feared he was used by the *Times* as an affirmative action gesture, an issue Gerald grappled with before he joined the *Times*. In conversations I had with Gerald after he joined the *Times*, he never expressed regret that he took that route.

Sadly I saw the Boyd legacy tarnished in the scandal involving Jayson Blair, a young black reporter with a poor track record for accuracy. Blair's immediate editor, Jonathon Landman, argued against Blair's promotion, but was overridden. When Blair was caught fabricating and plagiarizing stories, Boyd and executive editor Howell Raines were blamed for promoting and protecting Blair. When Gerald and Raines resigned in disgrace under pressure, I thought that if Gerald had gotten more seasoning at the *Post-Dispatch*, he would have spent his career with great respect and dignity. I never believed, nor do I now, that Boyd shielded Blair solely because Blair was black. But it was inevitable that Gerald empathized with Blair because their life stories were so similar. I think that Gerald blundered because his rapid achievements made him over-confident, to the point of smugness. He was unwilling to listen to the counsel of others less gifted than himself. *New York Times* reporters said he always wanted to control things. In an unpublished memoir, Boyd said his tendency was to rely on no one other than himself. I grieved at the loss of a friend when Gerald died of complications of lung cancer at age 56 on Nov. 23, 2006. I remembered those days at the *Post-Dispatch* when we talked about our jobs and our lives.

*　*　*

Gerald's departure from the *Post-Dispatch* in 1983 meant a significant change in my work at the paper. I succeeded Gerald as *The Post-Dispatch* White House correspondent. Although I had resigned as the *Bulletin* White House correspondent and Washington columnist, I knew that my talents as reporter and analyst could be used effectively in those assignments. Broadening my mandate, Lipman said he wanted not only news stories and analysis from me, but also opinion in a column in which I commented on what I observed at the White House and anywhere in Washington. He asked me to write in my columns what I could not properly write as news.

LAWRENCE M. O'ROURKE

By this time in my career, I wrote most news stories automatically—fast and clean enough that the desk could fix my grammatical and syntactical errors. Speed was mandatory because when I took the White House beat, the *Post-Dispatch* was an afternoon paper. Often I attended daily briefings at 11 in the morning and from them developed stories that I dictated from the White House for the front page of the afternoon edition. Most days I went to the office in late afternoon and tried to advance the story for the next day's paper. The *Post-Dispatch* during my tenure there switched from afternoon to morning newspaper, a move that lightened the daily deadline pressure.

*   *   *

Covering the White House for the *Post-Dispatch* was a dream job. But it was also frustrating as I participated, unwillingly, in the gradual decline of newspapers. While covering Reagan, I experienced a destructive acceleration in the transformation of White House news coverage from print to the seven-second sound bite.

Don't get me wrong. I had a wonderful time covering Reagan sound bites. It was stirring to stand by the Brandenburg Gate in West Berlin and hear the president's challenge: "Mr. Gorbachev, tear down this wall." It was fun to hear him shout over the roar of a helicopter engine on the White House Lawn and to try to interpret the policy implications. His quip, "Well, I'm glad that's all out," as reported by his aides from his hospital bedroom after colon cancer surgery, was stirring. Whether Reagan's quotes were his creations or manufactured by his aides, they warmed the nation. Reagan's denunciation of the Soviet Union and other Communist totalitarian regimes as "the Evil Empire" encapsulated his foreign policy philosophy and seized the U.S. national imagination, even as it raised questions abroad about his willingness to deal with the U.S. adversary. And I admired his self-imposed rule for dealing with Soviet leader Mikhail Gorbachev, "Trust, but verify." It became part of the political lexicon.

Of the ten presidents I covered from Kennedy to Barack Obama, and the two others I met (Truman and Eisenhower), none could charm an audience, live or over television, more effectively than Reagan. He had the movie actor's delivery. He didn't just play Notre Dame's George Gipp. To millions of Americans, Reagan was "The Gipper." After the angst caused the nation by LBJ's war, Nixon's treachery, Ford's pardon of Nixon, and Carter's dour sermonizing, Reagan offered the country what it wanted: to be left alone by politicians. He convinced the nation it was "Morning in America," the best theme of any campaign I covered in 40 years.

But Reagan's quest for personal popularity led to long-lasting blunders. The most successful politician of our time presented himself as a warrior against the Washington establishment and federal spending. But instead of trimming the national debt, he raised it to new heights. As I wrote frequently throughout the Reagan presidency—often angering readers—Reagan never met a spending program he would cut or a tax cut he could resist—a deadly combine for economic disaster, but a sure road to popularity.

While advocating law and order, Reagan and his aides secretly contrived to sell weapons to Iran—the very government that kept U.S. diplomats hostage for 444 days—and arranged for the proceeds to reach the Nicaraguan Contras—in violation of U.S. law. I covered that story too, but despite all that I and other reporters accurately wrote, Reagan never felt the sting of joining a cover-up. He was a Teflon president—nothing stuck.

*   *   *

Of all the presidents I covered, either in office or as candidate, I found Reagan the hardest to understand. On the occasions I spoke with him, I learned little about what motivated him or what he wanted to accomplish beyond the rhetoric. His staff was effective at keeping a wide gap between Reagan and reporters.

As a consequence, the flubs of Reagan's staff took on enormous proportions—including Agriculture Secretary Earl Butz's wisecracks about blacks and the pope, Chief of Staff Don Regan's feud with Nancy Reagan, and White House media manager Michael Deaver's arrangement of the president's visit to the Bitburg cemetery with the graves of German storm troopers. I covered those stories and was in the cemetery when Reagan stood by the SS graves.

In columns I wrote for *The Post-Dispatch*, I hammered away at Reagan's policies, but admittedly sometimes soft-pedaled criticism because I didn't want to widen the gap between myself and readers with great affection for Reagan.

*   *   *

LAWRENCE M. O'ROURKE

At the end of the day, I am aware that I fell short in exposing the errors of the Reagan administration. On the economy alone, he broke his promise to overhaul the tax code and bring the federal budget deficit under control. Reagan's White House managers, especially Baker, were quicker at covering up Reagan's inadequacies than we were in revealing his shortcomings.

Coverage of the Reagan shouts over the helicopter's engine roar was but one example of how we allowed ourselves to fall into the sound-bite technique that Reagan so effectively exploited. As funny and curious as reporting a Reagan quip on policy through a sound bite may have been the first time, we were drawn into it as a regular practice. I often was by the helicopter on the White House South Lawn on Friday afternoon when Reagan headed to Camp David for the weekend. As Reagan walked to his helicopter, the blades spun and the engine roared. I joined in shouting questions at Reagan. He seemed to catch one word, and he came back with his quip. Often he said what he wanted reported and we reported it even if his words bore no resemblance to the question that had been shouted, And Reagan avoided the difficult follow-on questions when he wished, which was usually the case; by saying he could not hear. That was likely true. I couldn't hear either over the helicopter. In an age when sound bites were fairly new on the political agenda, the television networks' use of the Reagan remark was sufficient to meet their need for a presidential comment on a significant event. The networks took what they got and in the culture, that seemed to be enough. Sam Donaldson, top ABC correspondent at the White House and a serious newsman, was acutely aware of this media manipulation and complained frequently about the practice that he had helped to create. Donaldson emerged as the most penetrating questioner of Reagan at long-range, perhaps because he was the loudest shouter. Quickie quotes by Reagan served TV's purposes, but they were of little benefit to me in trying to write stories on serious policy issues.

Reagan had the upper hand because television coverage of the White House, government and politics in the Reagan years slid downward to little more than sound bites. TV didn't do well with complexity and choices, and it rarely tried. Besides, a reduced citizen attention span, and skillfully orchestrated denunciation of the mainstream press by conservative activists merged to undermine serious reporting. That served Reagan's interest. Meanwhile, he engaged in policies that would have been rejected if seriously considered.

The president's brain trust, Baker, Meese, and Deaver, knew Reagan's skills, strengths and weaknesses, and they channeled them into building the popularity and image of a president—a process that easily trumped press complaints about secrecy. They sold Reagan's evasiveness as cleverness. Moreover, Democratic opponents in Congress gave Reagan a free ride. They were afraid of taking on the popular "Dutch."

What the Reagan brain trust didn't do was to help me to understand and report what was going on in the mind of the leader of the free world. I offer that perspective on the presumption that Reagan had a philosophy and methodology and that he was not merely the attractive projection of his sponsors and handlers. As long as Baker and Deaver got Reagan on television every night to give the impression he was on top of events, they seemed satisfied. I increasingly got the impression that they didn't care what I and other White House reporters put into print.

After nearly two decades as a White House correspondent, covering LBJ, Nixon, Ford, and Carter, I was painfully aware when Reagan arrived that the importance of the print reporter was in decline. During Reagan's presidency, there were far fewer medium-sized newspapers putting resources into White House coverage. Some papers, like the *Bulletin,* would soon be history. It cost those papers a lot of money to pay for a full-time White House correspondent, especially as airplane and hotel charges grew. *The New York Times, Washington Post* and *Los Angeles Times* still did serious and sustained reporting, but they showed signs of succumbing to the growing power of television. Many reporters, myself included, found it necessary to match any story reported on television, however trivial it might be, because readers, as that point, expected to read about what they had seen. Increasingly TV, not major papers, set the news agenda. *The Washington Post* was often ahead of the rest of the print and electronic press in reporting on Reagan. Lou Cannon, the *Post's* senior White House correspondent, covered Reagan while he was governor of California. Lou attained access to the Reagan inner circle. I and other reporters were often reduced to chasing Cannon's stories. While we could confirm them, we rarely got more than Lou initially reported.

*   *   *

The Reagan team restructured the role of White House press secretary. The Reagan team did not want a press secretary inside the inner sanctum.

It did not want someone like Bill Moyers, George Reedy, or George Christian who tried to explain LBJ. It did not want someone like Jody Powell who did his best to explain Jimmy Carter. Reporters covering Reagan had to depend on a daily basis with Larry Speakes, whose job as press secretary was to say nothing that Baker did not want said. Speakes succeeded admirably, but that made daily briefings less useful. During the Reagan years, I increasingly saw my job as less reporting the news and more analyzing the scraps that the Reagan White House revealed and the abyss of what it didn't want the public to know.

Baker defended Reagan's way of communicating. He said that what the public really needed to know was that Reagan perfectly summed up his conservative anti-government approach in his Inaugural address declaration, "In the present crisis, government is not the solution to our problems. Government is the problem." In other words, White House reporters got the message they weren't to look to Reagan's government for solutions because Reagan didn't think it was his job to provide solutions.

The conversations I had with Reagan over those years were frustrating exercises. The president was always charming. He told wonderful anecdotes—usually about events that happened a long time ago in a place called Hollywood. He never let me see doubt or hesitation or frustration the way other presidents did. He spoke with great assurance. He had a wonderful smile. After talking with Reagan, I read my notes several times to find something I could write. Fortunately for me, *The Post-Dispatch* gave me space and opportunity to write analytically—labeling it as such—and at length. The best years of my professional career as a reporter were spent at the *Bulletin* during the Johnson, Nixon, Ford, and Carter years. The best years of my professional career as an analyst were at the *Post-Dispatch* covering Reagan.

*　　*　　*

The greatest challenge, and one I welcomed, at the *Post-Dispatch* wasn't a news story—it was writing a "war pager." During World War II, when the *Post-Dispatch* was one of the nation's great newspapers, Joseph Pulitzer established the cover page on the editorial section for in-depth reporting of the war. With maps and good stories, it was known in the industry for its outstanding presentations of critical war news.

After the war, the *Post-Dispatch* retained the page for in-depth reports and analysis of significant events. It was a serious page doing important work.

The war page became my ballpark, and I was a slugger, hitting home runs. Almost every reporter in the bureau or the St. Louis office of the *Post-Dispatch* wanted to be on the war page. I led the league in power hitting. At least once a week, I called Lipman or Jim Millstone, the excellent assistant managing editor, and proposed a war pager for the next day. I'd tell them the topic and what I proposed to say. I wrote war pagers longer, looser in style, and more heavily analytical than my news stories, and so war pagers were more fun to write. I acknowledge that I have a lugubrious writing style. I sometimes use too many words or making points not worth making in tight news stories. The war page and I were compatible.

*   *   *

The war page gave me the space to ruminate on what Reagan really meant or wanted—points usually left unclear by the president and his advisers. I wrote that vagueness and procrastination—two Reagan constants—were clever Reagan devices to keep opponents off-balance. The war page gave me space to write about topics that would get short shrift in the tight news columns. For example, I wrote often on the war page about one of Reagan's proposals that otherwise got little attention—establishment of a major network across Europe of Pershing II missiles aimed at the Soviet Union and Soviet military targets in Eastern Europe. The P-II missile story was largely unreported in other papers. Because *The Post-Dispatch* made the war page available to me to write about these missiles and their implication, sources at the Pentagon and military think tanks fed me significant information. I thought the P-II missiles increased our risk of mutual destruction, and said so on the war page.

Members of Congress from St. Louis wanted attention, as all politicians do. With the war page, I attracted leaks from members and even forced information they did not want disclosed. In return, I had good working relationships, directly and through their staffs, with Republican Sen. John Danforth of Missouri, Democratic Sen. Paul Simon of Illinois, and Rep. Dick Gephardt of St. Louis, working his way up to become House Democratic Leader and one-term Speaker of

LAWRENCE M. O'ROURKE

the House. When I seized on a topic that had both national and local implications, it was a winner.

In St. Louis, I acquired a reputation as a guy who could produce a war pager on short notice. I often got calls from Lipman or Millstone on Friday morning. They said the war pager they planned for Sunday wasn't ready, perhaps the piece didn't work or the writer couldn't get it together in time. I had a few minutes to come up with another idea and then had until late afternoon to write it. I went without lunch on those Fridays.

*   *   *

But the most fun I had during the Reagan years was not reporting at the White House, but on foreign assignment. My motto might have been: "Suitcase packed, typewriter ready, will travel on moment's notice." Lipman gave me carte blanche to follow the news. The paper was hurting financially, but Lipman said that I was not to worry about the money; I was to do the stories and let him fret about the bills.

Wanting to be where the action was, I made two lengthy trips to the Philippines, the first in 1984 to report on the despotic President Ferdinand Marcos; the second in 1986 to report on his removal from office in the "People Power" revolution that followed the assassination of political opponent Benigno "Ninoy" Aquino and the election of Aquino's spouse, Maria Corazon Cojuango "Cory" Aquino.

On the 1984 trip, I flew from Manila to Davao City on the southern island of Mindanao. Through a Washington contact, I had the name of a Canadian priest who worked in the poorest areas of Davao City. He agreed to show me through his parish—regarded as the main recruiting base for teams of assassins known as the "sparrows." They trained to flit in and out unnoticed to kill their enemies. The Davao City community could not be called anything other than a slum. To the priest and his parishioners, it was home. The priest laid down conditions for guiding me through Davao City. No visible note taking or notebook in hand or back pocket. No camera. "Don't even think about taking a picture," he said. I was not to show a tape recorder. I was to walk by his side or just behind him, and never to stray. I was to look like a missionary doing the Lord's work.

However, the priest equipped me with a tool not ordinarily carried by missionaries—a switchblade knife. He showed me how to open it. He said I might need it if attacked. The idea that I might have to defend myself in a knife fight in Davao City was among the strangest propositions of my long journalistic career. I knew I could not defeat a trained sparrow or even a casual stick-up artist in a knife fight. I didn't know if the priest was serious or was using the knife to emphasize the need to respect his plan for getting us through alive. I chose the latter explanation.

With a switchblade knife, notebook and tape recorder out of sight deep in my pocket, the priest and I entered his community. He wore a Roman collar and black trousers and shirt. I regarded him as my bodyguard as well as my guide. I had on khaki trousers and a blue shirt. I hoped that in Davao City clerics were more welcome than reporters or cops. For nearly two hours, the priest and I wandered, sometimes in the mud, sometimes on raised boardwalks over mud and through hovels. There wasn't any privacy. It was a lively community, with people dashing about, music, laundry on the line, dogs, and the smell of cooking. There were open sewers. The latrines were on the edge of the complex. I had the sense that the place was orderly, though the economy was hand to mouth. Of course, I couldn't identify a sparrow, and never felt fear. I kept my hand away from the notebook and switchblade. The priest was well known and well received. He introduced me to a few people as his assistant. I met parishioners who said they were trying to improve living conditions. I had the sense that some of them had an accommodation with the sparrows, but I didn't push that point. In Davao City, I asked questions carefully and gently.

*   *   *

On the island of Luzon, I made several forays to the Tondo district of Manila, the city's worst slum, one of the most densely populated areas of the world with 65,000 people per square kilometer, and site of the notorious dump called "Smokey Mountain."

Tondo was home to thousands of squatters, people who lived mainly in wood and corrugated metal sheds without utilities or facilities. To keep squatters from expanding into the city, Marcos had the Army and police conduct clearance raids, a weekly ritual. Sometimes, the squatters were alerted a few minutes ahead so that they could gather their meager belongings before the cops and wreckers arrived. With bulldozers and axes, crews crashed down the hovels. Dispossessed residents screamed, cried and taunted the cops and demolishers, but the squatters rarely resisted since the police did not hesitate to fire tear gas, strike with batons, and if necessary, shoot at the crowd. Those thrown from their residences would move elsewhere in Tondo, increasing the concentration and misery. But within days the shacks would again rise, and inevitably the wreckers and their enforcers would return, only to renew the cycle.

To keep current on the mood in Manila, I frequently visited "Smokey Mountain" in Tondo. Metro Manila bureaucrats called it a landfill for trash and garbage. Dump trucks brought their collections to the mountain where dozens of children gathered. When the trash and garbage were dumped, children dashed into the new mound to pick out food, bottles, metal and anything that might appear to have value. The children carted their loot to their parents, who sold it to dealers who ran a thriving business buying junk for a few cents and selling it for a profit. Dumping, scavenging and bargaining lasted from dawn to dusk. Scavenging ended daily when the last truck completed its delivery, tractors created giant piles of trash, and the piles were set ablaze. Some piles would burn for days, producing thick black smoke that gave the site its name. Health authorities said residents had damaged respiratory systems.

In watching the Tondo evictions, I thought about the evictions and starvation that took place in Ireland during the Famine years. Every few years I view the movie "The Year of Living Dangerously." Though set in Indonesia, it reminds me of Tondo and Smokey Mountain.

*   *   *

After the first trip in which I exposed readers to raw life in the Philippines, I kept on the story from Washington. I wrote about the escalation of tension in the Philippines and the implication for the major U.S. military bases, Subic Bay Naval Station and Clark Air Force Base. Several times I went to Bataan—where the horrific World War II death march took place—to see the giant U.S military complexes, the web of bars and bordellos outside their gates, and the miserable conditions under which the Filipino people lived. I reported on the role of these bases in the U.S. defense strategy for Southeast Asia and the problems the bases caused. I wrote about the movement in the United States to dismantle the bases. Though I suspected few readers of the *Post-Dispatch* had much interest in the Philippines, the paper gave my stories excellent play.

In the days after an election in February 1986 in which Cory Aquino appeared to beat Marcos, and he refused to yield power, I got information that the White House, Pentagon and U.S. military think tanks concluded that Marcos was finished. When Reagan, in my opinion correctly, decided to pressure Marcos to yield power to Aquino, a White House official leaked the story to me within minutes. Lipman told me to fly out when I wished. I was on the plane the next day. I found Manila in chaos, but that was nothing unusual; to me, it always seemed to be chaotic. Hours before my arrival, Marcos fled the Philippines on a U.S. helicopter. The government of the island nation was now in Aquino's hands.

I went to the former Marcos stronghold of Malacanang Palace where I discovered documents relating to the fallen dictator. I interviewed several people who participated in the struggle against Marcos, including a Maryknoll priest who ran guns for the rebels and a Catholic bishop, Xavier Claver, a Jesuit who advised Aquino and used his intelligence network to provide her with critical political and military information. I talked to former Marcos allies and found that now that Marcos had fled, they were ready to sign on to the new leader, thus saving their jobs and power.

I was in Rizal Park on the edge of Manila Bay on the Sunday afternoon in February 1986 when Aquino made her grand entry into the city. Not only did I write the story of the revolution that day of celebration, but I also wrote a story on my pocket being picked in the crowd. I didn't lose a lot of money. I was smart enough to have locked away my passport and credit cards in my room at the Manila Hotel.

*　　*　　*

Before I end my stories on the Philippines, I want to tell a story about journalism. Months after the revolution, Aquino came to Washington to request money from the U.S. government to help deal with some of her nation's social and economic problems. I talked to her at a downtown Washington Hotel and covered her speech to a joint session of Congress. Within hours, Congress approved a substantial foreign aid package for the Philippines. I wrote the story and Jim Millstone put a headline on it that said that Aquino had "charmed" Congress into the quick approval. Phone calls and letters hit the *Post-Dispatch* complaining that the paper had been sexist in using the word "charmed." Sue Ann Woods, the paper's ombudswoman, asked what did I think of the word "charmed" over my story. I had not used it in the story. I said I had no objection to it and did not see the sexism some readers claimed. But Sue Ann agreed with the readers and on the following Sunday in her *Post-Dispatch* column scolded Millstone and me for not being more sensitive to sexism. Millstone, who was as sensitive to racism and sexism and other manifestations of bias as any editor I ever worked with, suggested that we give Sue Ann's advice all due respect and move on. I said that maybe I should write a story about the next male foreign head of state to get money out of Washington and he could use "charmed" in the headline. But Jim advised against it.

*　　*　　*

Since I was sometimes bored and frustrated by the routine of covering Reagan day to day, I looked for diversions. Reading testimony from Capitol Hill, I learned that the National Institutes of Health was alarmed about the outbreak of a condition called Acquired Immune Deficiency Syndrome (AIDS). AIDS had gotten slim press attention, probably because the mainstream press ignored gay issues. In an interview with Dr. Anthony Fauci, head of the infectious disease section at NIH, I learned about the worldwide effort to combat AIDS and pathogens such as malaria, measles and the diarrheal diseases often spread by contaminated water. While the scientific press reported on NIH efforts, daily newspapers rarely got into it. When I told Fauci I would like to write about these issues in depth, he promised cooperation. Lipman and Millstone authorized me to travel as I needed. I spent several days at the Centers for Disease Control in Atlanta, donning protective gear to enter highly contagious research facilities. I went to university laboratories where researchers patiently explained to this political reporter and English major the significance of monoclonal antibodies. I talked to epidemiologists and public health specialists across the country, as well as to people who were infected with these diseases, including the still-mysterious AIDS.

I kept Millstone and Lipman informed on my research, and I was startled to get a call from Millstone urging me to travel to Africa where preventable infectious diseases annually took millions of lives, especially those of children. My editors and Washington Bureau colleagues anticipated that I'd be on the next plane since I had the reputation of welcoming travel anywhere and at any time. But I shocked them all when

I turned down the chance to visit some of the world's poorest and sickest nations. I had a family, with four teen-agers, that I had been neglecting and did not want to jeopardize. Millstone was correct that on-the-scene reporting from Africa would have meant better stories, and would have brought concerns about infectious disease to congressional and public attention at the ripe moment when the country was beginning to focus on AIDS. The *Post-Dispatch* gave my stories excellent play. The series won a prestigious Raymond Clapper Memorial Award. *The Post-Dispatch* nominated my infectious disease stories for the Pulitzer Prize.

*   *   *

Of the presidents I covered, none traveled in grander style than Reagan. His was not the one-day, 16-hour flight to Asia, or overnights to Europe and the Middle East where the president insisted on getting right to work upon hitting the ground, dragging the rest of us with him. Johnson, Nixon, Ford, and Carter seemed to pride themselves on being able to conduct the affairs of state after little or no sleep. Reagan was prudent about his need for sleep and that meant that reporters could count on a few hours downtime as we headed overseas. I, for one, was grateful.

How delightful it was for me when Reagan, heading for Bali, flew from Washington for a few days in Santa Barbara, California, then flew to Honolulu for a pleasant weekend, then on to Guam for an overnight, before arriving on the tropical island. The hotel in Bali was a dream. It was my first hotel with a lobby without walls. The lawn had manicured trees replete with tropical birds. I could get addicted to such luxury.

*   *   *

One travel event in Hawaii convinced me that there were advantages in being a print reporter rather than a television correspondent. On Easter Sunday afternoon in Honolulu, I went to services at an Episcopal Church with the Reagans. It was a splendid service with a fine homily and a grand music in a magnificent venue. Andrea Mitchell, the hard-working correspondent for NBC News, was next to me in the pew. She stationed her camera crew just outside the main door to the church so that when the service ended she could be there while the Reagans exited. Andrea would do what is known in the jargon of TV as her stand-up. She hoped for a brief interview with the First Couple. Minutes before the service was to end, Andrea left her seat and headed to the intended stand-up spot. With no interest at all on snagging a TV stand-up location, I waited until the service ended and walked down the middle aisle behind the Reagans toward the main doors. At the moment the president and Nancy Reagan reached the door, the sky opened. Within seconds, Andrea, exposed in her stand-up spot, was thoroughly soaked. The Reagans waited for the Secret Service to cover them with umbrellas for a dry passage to their limousine. I waited another couple of minutes for the rain to stop before leaving the church. Andrea was soaking wet and fretting that she would have to find dry clothing and another stand-up position. This was no laughing matter for a TV reporter on deadline.

As amusing as this incident might be retrospectively, the next day I was aboard the press plane flying to Asia. We were somewhere over the Pacific at 35,000 feet when Andrea had a seizure on the plane. Flight attendants curtained off a section of seats and laid Andrea on blankets. A Navy medic on our plane got instructions from the president's doctor on Air Force One. When we landed in Asia, an ambulance rushed Andrea to a hospital. She rejoined us a few days later, insisting she was no worse for the experience. Andrea Mitchell was and is one tough reporter.

*   *   *

As much fun and satisfaction as I had on my trips to the Philippines (each of which included side excursions to Hong Kong), and on working visits with Reagan in Indonesia, China and Japan, nothing compared to a journey I took across Europe in 1985, courtesy of *The Post-Dispatch*, with my daughter Katie and my mother.

I planned to travel in Europe that summer to cover Reagan's meeting with Western industrial leaders. The G-7 summit's agenda included rolling back farm subsidies that were driving up government budgets and distorting prices. On the other hand, farm subsidies in Europe helped to forge the European Community to reduce the threat of wars like those that struck the continent twice in the 20th century. I proposed to Lipman that since I was going to have to learn the intricacies of farm subsidies so that I could report the story with accuracy and understanding, it would be a shame to squander my knowledge. I proposed a series of articles on how subsidies affect the United States, including farmers in Missouri and Illinois, and the European nations that offer them.

"But do you have the time to travel around Europe to do these stories right?" Lipman asked. "It's the summer with less pressure in Washington. I can find the time, David," I said. "Do it then," he said.

I invited my daughter Katie, then 15 and in high school, and my mother, then 74 and living in Philadelphia, to fly to Frankfurt after the G-7 summit. Our first son Chris would also be in Europe, celebrating the summer between high school graduation and the start of college in the fall. Our two younger children, Jenny and Tim, opted to go to Disneyworld when Pat attended an optometrists' convention there. When I told Lipman of my plan to take Katie and my mother on my reporting trip through Europe, he said that was fine with him, as long as *The Post-Dispatch* didn't have to pay for high-priced restaurant meals he suspected I would arrange.

Katie, my mother and I met in Frankfurt and drove to Heidelberg, Munich, Dachau, and Bavaria in Germany, Innsbruck in Austria, Arco, Florence, Pisa, Assisi, and Rome in Italy, Zurich in Switzerland, San Marino, and Luxembourg. I did interviews and stories along the way, from agriculture to airplanes. I wrote about the Airbus, a competitor to McDonnell-Douglas of St. Louis, in Munich. In Bavaria, I visited a brewery and wrote for readers in St. Louis, hometown to Anheuser-Busch, a front page story on German beer-making. We boarded the train in Frankfurt and crossed the English Channel by ferry to London. After a few days there and in the Midlands, we moved on to Ireland where, of course, they had a formerly heavily subsidized farm sector transitioning to post-industrial technology, as parts of the States were. Just about everywhere I went, I found a story. *The Post-Dispatch* ran them on page one. My daughter and mother joined me on some of the reporting. Otherwise, as I worked, they saw the sights. We sought out restaurants where the locals eat and I paid the tab. The high points for my mother were visiting the Vatican, including the Sistine Chapel, and living for three days in a convent in Rome. For Katie, it was a summer of discovery, flirting with Italian boys, unlimited cappuccino, sculpture by Michelangelo, and wine with dinner in Trastevere. All in all, it was the high point of my eight years of covering the Reagan presidency.

CHAPTER 16

George Bush the First

I BEGAN TO understand George Herbert Walker Bush as we jogged on a high school track in suburban Atlanta.

I was there because Marlin Fitzwater, Bush's press secretary, asked if I would be available to run in the morning with the presidential candidate. It sounded like a neat way to start another day on the long campaign trail. When I accepted, Fitzwater arranged my ride in Bush's motorcade.

On that warm morning in 1988, as Bush and I moved along stride-by-stride, we talked about his campaign for the presidency. He didn't tell me anything I didn't know and I didn't expect him to reveal campaign secrets. He knew that I thought he was going to defeat Massachusetts Gov. Michael Dukakis, though at that point in the campaign I didn't know how low Bush would go to win. The disgraceful, subtly racist Willie Horton ads had not yet been pushed aggressively into the nation's living rooms. Bush knew that I intended to vote for Dukakis. Nevertheless, here we were running side-by-side on a lovely morning, chatting amiably.

Once we got the humdrum of the campaign out of the way, Bush and I turned to the important topic of running. We agreed that the campaign played havoc with our running schedules. We mutually deplored the short time the campaign allowed us for running. I told Bush that I was gaining weight—my usual and unwanted consequence of a presidential campaign in which the rule is to eat whenever you see food because you don't know when the next meal will be. As for losing my running edge, I think I was sorrier than Bush. I regarded myself as a serious runner, a marathoner, running at least 50 miles a week. He was a weekend jogger, not a competitor. He competed in politics.

Politics behind us for moment, the vice president asked me, "Larry, why do you run so much?" It was a reasonable question and I had an unrehearsed but well-established answer. "I like to run, Mr. Vice

President," I said. "I like running as an opportunity to meet my friends five mornings a week. We talk a lot and usually solve the problems of the world." I tried to make our morning conversations sound like casual bantering, which is what they were. I gave a brief version of the history of our 5.45 a.m. running group.

"You run every day with the same people?" Bush asked, as if that were a notion that never crossed his mind.

"Pretty much," I said, "and for a lot of years now." Indeed, for about two decades, with, I hoped, more to come.

"You ever run alone?" Bush asked. He wasn't panting. We were running at about an eight-minute mile pace. Behind and beside us were running Secret Service agents.

"Once in a while," I said. "I enjoy occasional long solitary runs. When I'm not talking, I can accomplish a lot by floating."

There was a pause. Bush turned his head to me on his right and said, "Floating. What do you mean floating?"

I explained. "Some people call it a runner's high. I call it floating. It's the word I use for those days when I forget I'm running, when my mind escapes to somewhere else. It's sort of dreaming. It's like a trip without drugs. Sometimes I use floating to write columns or think about things, make decisions or write letters. I get a lot done while I'm floating."

"Floating," said Bush. "That's a new one on me."

We ran a few more laps, talking about the campaign and states where he would win easily and states where he would have to campaign hard. We pretty much had the same political calculations. Fitzwater had insisted that Bush's remarks while running were not for publication, but I took mental notes to jot down later.

As we came around a bend, Bush said, "That's enough for me. Got to get to work." By now there were cameras and reporters at one end of the field. Bush pulled off to meet the press. I stopped too, and stood to the side out of camera range.

"A good run on a beautiful morning," a sweaty Bush said to the reporters. He took political questions, for after all, politics and not running was the day's agenda. A reporter asked about running. "Great exercise, good for you," Bush said. "Valuable time. I use it for floating. Great time to think about things in the campaign. Maybe think about speeches. Things I have to do. Time passes very fast that way."

After saying this, Bush looked in my direction, and winked. Shortly thereafter we went back in the motorcade, he in his limousine, me in a trailing car, to clean up and begin our day on the campaign trail. I considered inviting Bush to Grafton Street for a morning run. All would have welcomed him cordially, though he might not have gotten the majority of votes from our crowd.

Thinking about the exchange on floating, I concluded that Bush was a quick learner with a sense of humor. I certainly had no copyright on the "floating" term and as far as I was concerned he could appropriate it without attribution. I was delighted that he seemed to appreciate or be amused by my contribution to his linguistic repertoire.

But, not to take this event and exchange all too seriously, the experience added to what I thought for some time—that Bush's true gift as a politician was imitation, not initiation. He was not an original thinker or someone who struggled with conflicting ideas. He was a pragmatist and quick learner. He was skilled at picking up ideas from others and making them his own. Bush was born and reared in politics. Some commentators saw the Bush family as much a political dynasty as the Kennedys. Educated in private schools and Yale, Bush was tutored in politics by his father, Prescott, a U.S. senator. George Bush served Richard Nixon, who made Bush ambassador to the United Nations and Republican National Committee chairman during Watergate. Jerry Ford made Bush U.S. representative in China and CIA director. Bush captured and recited the words of Ronald Reagan, who chose Bush to be vice president and gave him almost nothing substantive to do for eight years, aside from attending funerals.

Bush succeeded by doing little that mattered on government or policy. He was good at being vice president—a role that prohibited independent thought or action. He was careful. He rarely stumbled. Texas Gov. Ann Richards, a Democrat, only partially captured the Bush psyche when I heard her characterize him as a "man born with a silver foot in his mouth." My mother might have said, he "had a silver spoon in his mouth."

*　　*　　*

Writing analysis for *Post-Dispatch* readers, I acknowledged that Bush had impressive experience. But whether he had leadership qualities and sound judgment was unknown during the White House campaign. I'm not condemning Bush for this. Alas, leadership and judgment are rarely revealed in presidential campaigns, even while I think they are the prime criteria on which voters should judge presidential candidates. I give weight to experience, but mostly when it suggests how a candidate would lead and act under pressure. I never bought the notion that bad experience is a good teacher, that, as my father would say, graduation from "the college of hard knocks" provides backbone. Certainly you learn from mistakes, but I put a premium on the wise leader who takes prudent risks and minimizes mistakes rather than the mistake-prone helter-skelter personality.

The idealistic goal of a presidential campaign is, or should be, to give voters a look at how the candidate, if elected, would govern, especially on occasions, fortunately rare, when there is little luxury for protracted study or delay but there is urgency to decide quickly and wisely. The Cuban missile crisis, the attack in the Gulf of Tonkin, the assassination of a civil rights leader, riots in the streets, the seizure of hostages in Teheran, 9/11, a hurricane striking New Orleans—these emergencies come to mind as requiring a quick presidential decision without time for background papers. In the summer of 1988, the question was if Bush could walk in the footsteps of Lincoln, Roosevelt and Truman, if events demanded.

Sad to say, because campaigns too often don't give many clues on how a president would react to any potentially catastrophic event, we pick our presidents on a hope and a prayer. Voting is speculation about the future.

*   *   *

Our presidential campaigns focus on image, not on substance. As a reporter, I'm afraid I contributed on too many occasions to image building. When you're on the road with a candidate and need to file a story, you are under pressure to take what you can get. You're too often trapped into writing what the campaign wants you to write. Your editors pay you to report and write a story. Campaigns for reporters are not for the pure or faint of heart. Campaign stories are the first cut at history, and in a 24/7 era there's little time to reflect.

Ideally from a campaign's perspective, very little of substance is decided during the heat of a campaign. Campaign managers, no matter their politics, never want the candidate making a key decision on the fly. The candidate is exhausted and has enough to do on 16-hour days of meeting and greeting and speechmaking.

The mantra of a campaign for candidates and staff is "stick to message." The message is shaped not so much by the candidate, but by highly skilled handlers and public opinion and media manipulators who may or may not share the candidate's ideology. They may even lack abiding interest in policy or governing. Their goal is to win the campaign, to get the person who pays them elected. Their objective is not necessarily to produce the best leader to govern the country although they always tell you that without doubt their candidate is superior to the opponent. My practice as a reporter was to be wary in talking to campaign managers. Shrewd mangers are rarely candid. Bush's top 1988 manager Lee Atwater was a wonder at building the image of his candidate and tearing down the image of the opponent on flimsy evidence. Witness the barely disguised racist attack Atwater directed at Dukakis on Bush's behalf through the person of Willie Horton, a black man convicted of murder in Massachusetts and sentenced to life in prison. When Massachusetts prison officials gave Horton a weekend furlough, he committed rape. Arguably, Dukakis had nothing to do with the prison board's action, but Atwater managed to link the Democratic candidate to the rape and all that some voters find fearful in black men. Bush himself in speeches didn't stress Horton, but his campaign ads did. It was ironic that Horton was the core of the Bush campaign. Al Gore, then running against Dukakis for the Democratic nomination, first surfaced Horton's story and his criminal conduct. Gore made a gift to Bush.

Thinking about cheap shots and irresponsible ads, I reflect on how LBJ scared voters against Goldwater by the daisy petal ad that suggested that Goldwater would be reckless in using the atomic bomb. LBJ's ad agency prepared the ad, but did not build a campaign around it. However, the press picked up the ad and gave Johnson untold millions of dollars of campaign advantage. I recall Reagan glossing over the nation's social and economic problems by his "Morning in America" theme. Who can forget Bill Clinton's campaign observing manager James Carville's dictum: "It's the economy, stupid."

My approach to campaign reporting was to share with readers what the candidate was saying and doing, but to try for more, to get beyond the facade to reach the levels of ideology and judgment. That's easier said than done. It is hard to catch a candidate or handler in an unguarded moment when a kernel of reality may emerge. Candidates in the lead in a campaign avoid the press as much as possible.

*   *   *

The importance of ads also makes it mandatory that the press report on them and in the process offer analysis on whether they are fair or unfair. Campaign mangers told me in the last campaign I covered, Barack Obama v. John McCain in 2008, that as many as 80 percent of undecided voters make their decisions primarily on the basis of TV ads.

*   *   *

My analysis of Bush as the campaign began was that he would be far easier to sell to voters than Dukakis, who had a funny name, a Mediterranean appearance, a short stature, and identification more with liberal Massachusetts and Harvard than with blue-collar voters in Rust Belt states. It didn't matter that Bush was an Ivy Leaguer with a Texas accent from a well-to-do patrician family. As a governor who had to make decisions, Dukakis had a record that would be far easier to exploit politically than Bush's empty record as surrogate. It was inevitable that as governor Dukakis made mistakes. I never found a public figure that dealt with serious issues who didn't make mistakes. Since Bush hadn't dealt as a decision-maker with serious issues, he had less vulnerability. It is not by accident that the country turns often to senators who can talk a good game without being responsible for the consequences rather than to governors or mayors who actually have to experience the consequences of their decisions.

*   *   *

As a reporter, my role was to tell voters who the candidate really was rather than restrict my coverage to the images and messages presented by the campaign. I tried to bring a healthy skepticism to my political reporting. That often put me in conflict with the candidate and managers who insisted I was trying to disrupt their campaign and generate controversy. That was a standard charge against any reporter trying to do an honest job. Since campaigns limited my face-to-face time with a candidate, there was little opportunity for probing questions. Politicians, after giving empty answers to questions, would often brush off follow-up effort with a terse, "I already answered that." Of course, they had not, but reporters don't want to argue with candidates. But after 40 years in the business, I was never satisfied with my ability to find out what made candidates tick. I could generate volumes of newspaper copy, but I constantly wondered if I had gotten to the truth and presented it adequately.

*　　*　　*

As I covered campaign after campaign, I recognized that in the imperfect worlds of U.S. politics and journalism, newspapers, or any medium, could not cover a campaign the way I would like to see it covered. I had well-defined, and probably naive, ideas on how a newspaper should provide perfect coverage. Finally my moment of truth came.

In 1988, David Lipman called from St. Louis and asked me to prepare a strategy for *Post-Dispatch* coverage of the upcoming presidential campaign. Excited by the notion that I might be able to test my model campaign ideas, I drew up a plan that involved reduced daily coverage of candidate sound bites and travel and more emphasis on candidate records. "Let's focus our coverage on issues, not personalities," I told Lipman.

He said he liked the concept, but wasn't sure it would work. To test it, he proposed that I pick an issue and explore in depth where the candidates stood. I picked education. It was an issue I understood as well as any national political reporter, having covered it as a local reporter in Philadelphia, written about it often in Washington, and served as a federal government official. Bush said repeatedly that he wanted to be "the education president" and Dukakis touted his work for schools in Massachusetts.

I worked on the project for two weeks. I collected information on decisions the candidates made that affected public and private education. I interviewed their domestic advisers. I wrote an article that ran several columns in the Sunday *Post-Dispatch*. I believed I had done as much as any journalist could do to inform readers how the candidates as president were likely to deal with American education.

Lipman furnished pictures and charts to complement my story. He ran it under a large headline on page one. The *Post-Dispatch* promoted my story through radio ads touting my effort as offering insight into how the candidates stood on the issue of education—a matter of importance in St. Louis and its suburbs.

Early on the Monday morning after the story ran, Lipman called to compliment me and said the paper had calls from school officials in St. Louis and teachers saying they were going to discuss my story in their classrooms as a way to encourage students to follow the presidential campaign. One teacher, said Lipman, intended to use my story to instruct students how the press should cover a political campaign. I was thrilled that the story had been so well received and that my idea of covering the campaign on issues rather than on personalities and sound bites had worked.

The euphoria didn't last long. Lipman called that evening. He had just gotten a report from an independent marketing survey retained by the *Post-Dispatch*. Despite the play in the paper and despite the advance promotion, he said, fewer than 20 percent of Sunday's *Post-Dispatch* readers told interviewers they were aware that the paper ran a big story on education and the candidates. Of that theoretically informed crowd, fewer than ten percent read the story. "Your story reached about four percent of our readers," Lipman said, based on whatever mathematical formula he devised. "Instead of using your long story on education, I could have put stories in the paper that attracted just about everybody who bought the paper. You worked on your story for two weeks. We promoted it. We gave it big play. But it had almost no impact. And it certainly didn't sell extra papers. You seemed to have a good idea, but it didn't work." With editors, success was always a shared achievement, failure an orphan.

Goodbye to my idea about devising a new model for covering a presidential campaign. I was back to personalities and the bubble of the campaign plane.

*   *   *

I found life as a political reporter adventurous and challenging, but it didn't always provide creature comfort. As per custom with political reporting, I spent much of the winter of 1987-88 in a place where few people go voluntarily during the icy months to work outdoors—except on the ski slopes. The place was New Hampshire, site of the first-in-the-nation presidential primary. Read those words again: first-in-the-nation presidential primary. How many thousands of times have I and other reporters typed those words over the years? As cold and icy as New Hampshire gets in the weeks before the February primary election, every political reporter in the nation want to be there. In a sense, the New Hampshire primary is an alumni gathering, bringing into the same hotels and meeting halls and restaurants and buses hundreds of political junkies who may not have seen one another for four years. The competition is intense. You wouldn't be there as a reporter unless you proved to your editors that you could produce insightful, readable stories that were a credit to the newspaper and worth the cost.

For candidates, managers, volunteers and reporters, it is politics all the time. Some reporters take rooms in Manchester, the state's largest city and home to its largest and most influential daily newspaper, the *Union-Leader*, a dreadful journal that under longtime publisher William Loeb turned its pages into a political organ for Loeb's personal Republican favorite.

I didn't usually join the crowd of reporters in taking a room in Manchester. Instead, I booked a room a year or so before the primary in the Marriott Hotel in Nashua. There was some argument for this. Some candidates made their headquarters in Nashua. The main north-south interstate highway in New Hampshire ran by the Marriott. As a rule, New Hampshire's highway department did a good job clearing the road after snow and ice storms. But I picked the Nashua Marriott for largely personal reasons. I liked Marriott points, dreaming of the day when I'd be able to spend them on an exotic vacation. I liked the hotel's small gym where I worked out on a treadmill and bike while the snow fell. When it didn't snow or ice over, I ran on roads close to the Marriott. I liked several nearby restaurants where I could get a table quickly and could linger over breakfast while reading the *Union-Leader*, *Boston Globe* and *New York Times*. A local restaurant served a magnificent baked German apple pancake that I treated myself to after a hard run. Besides, it took a half hour to prepare—an excuse for lingering over the paper and drinking strong black coffee while snowflakes fell.

Such languorous mornings were the exception more than the rule in New Hampshire. Often I'd be up in the darkness and off in my rented car over slick roads to Portsmouth or Keane or Concord or Dover for a candidate's speech. I was never fond of driving north into the mountains. Not only did those drives eat up lots of time in the car, but they also seemed to rarely produce any news. One exception to going beyond Concord was Hanover and Dartmouth College. It was always fun to visit the campus and experience the energy of the students as they turned out for rallies.

In 1988, I struck up a good working relationship with New Hampshire Gov. John Sununu, a conservative Republican who displayed the twin ambitions of trying to get out of the state and trying to climb the political ladder. He backed Bush. Bush's leading opponent, Senate Republican leader Bob Dole of Kansas, had the backing of New Hampshire Republican Sen. Warren Rudman. There was little ideological difference between Bush and Dole. As GOP leader, Dole had a fatter record. As a skilled and pragmatic legislative leader, Dole cut many deals along the way, often in Reagan's service. When Bush won in New Hampshire, Dole complained bitterly—and with cause—that Bush should "stop lying about my record." The quote went right into my lead for the morning edition. The Bush campaign did misrepresent Dole's record, but who plays by rules in love, war and politics.

Sununu, Bush's key man on the ground, and I talked numerous times during the campaign in his office in the state Capitol in Concord. Sununu usually returned my phone calls. With a great sense of accomplishment, he explained how he turned his organization of thousands of Republicans in every part of the state over to Bush managers Andy Card and Ron Kaufman. Sununu pushed a strategy to humanize Bush. Bush didn't talk issues. Rather I spent many days with him when he visited three locations for breakfast and shook hands and chatted. It was retail politics at its finest. Bush met thousands of people wearing galoshes and heavy coats to survive the New Hampshire frost, while saying little of substance.

Sununu took credit for one of the top photo opportunities of the campaign—at Cuzzin Richie's parking lot in Hampstead. However ridiculous the event was, it boosted Bush's drive to the White House.

I stood in the cold next to a beaming Sununu as Bush drove an 18-wheeler around Cuzzin Richie's lot. Out of camera sight, a Secret Service agent crouched inside the cab, ready to hit the brake if Bush lost control. Sununu artfully explained to me how the event showed that Bush was a man of the people in contrast to Dole, an inside-the-Beltway political wheeler and dealer. Sununu also adroitly suggested that Dole could not drive an 18-wheeler, a reference, deliberate or accidental, to Dole's effective loss of an arm during World War II combat.

Sununu convinced Bush to pledge in New Hampshire that he would not raise federal taxes if elected president, a position Bush knew was untenable and which Dole more honestly rejected to his political peril.

As I write elsewhere in this memoir, Bush's "read my lips, no new taxes" pledge came back to haunt him. It humiliated him when circumstances forced him to increase taxes as an element of budget and spending deals with congressional Democrats. What Sununu created in 1988 opened Bush to conservative GOP attack that cost him re-election in 1992.

I was also fortunate in New Hampshire in 1988 of good regular access to Bush operatives Kaufman and Card, brothers-in-law who slept many nights on cots in their campaign headquarters in a small office with computers and stacks of files. Bush, who entered the New Hampshire campaign trailing in the polls to Dole, was so grateful to his New Hampshire team that he made Sununu his White House chief of staff and Kaufman his White House staff manger for finding government jobs for political supporters. And after Sununu resigned in disgrace as chief of staff in 1991, Bush made Card the White House chief of staff.

In covering the White House during Bush's term as president, I believed that Sununu was way beyond his depth in trying to advise the president. As brilliant and affable as I found Sununu to be, I never had the sense he cared about or understood foreign policy, national issues or the workings of Congress. To his eventual downfall, Sununu did know how to exploit White House perks. He was accused of running up $615,000 in costs for traveling on personal trips that he classified as official. The final moment came when he enjoyed a White House limousine drive from his home in Washington to New York City so that he could buy $5,000 in rare stamps. By my philosophy Sununu also made a positive contribution to the Bush legacy. He convinced Bush to nominate David Souter as a justice on the U.S. Supreme Court.

*   *   *

I don't know what Dukakis would have done as president when Iraqi President Saddam Hussein invaded Kuwait in the summer of 1990, but I am convinced now, as I tended to think then, that Bush mishandled it, plunged the nation into an unnecessary war and expanded hostility to the United States from many parts of the Islamic world.

I spent several weeks in 1990 covering Bush at his home in Kennebunkport, Maine, and wrote as best I could to raise doubts about the wisdom of Bush's decision to draw a line in the sand and threaten an invasion of Iraq. My doubts about the soundness of aggressive rhetoric and plans for war were strengthened one night when I had a not-for-attribution dinner with Bush national security adviser Brent Scowcroft in a restaurant in Maine far enough from the hangouts of the press and staff that we were unlikely to be discovered. What struck me most about Scowcroft's words was the assertion that while Saddam had misjudged by moving into Kuwait, there was no evidence that he intended to move further into Saudi Arabia. While Saddam's move had to be reversed before it seriously threatened the world's oil supply, it was more a political miscalculation on Saddam's part than an act of naked aggression, Scowcroft suggested. As such, there could be a political solution. It might take time, but Saddam probably could be pushed out of Kuwait through a variety of means other than a U.S. military assault, Scowcroft insisted.

I listened intently as Scowcraft privately made a case that to my ears contradicted what the commander in chief was daily declaring that the United States had no option, barring a humiliating and therefore unacceptable withdrawal of Saddam from Kuwait, other than war.

Scowcroft and I talked about the story then emerging—that U.S. Ambassador to Iraq April Glaspie, in a meeting with Saddam on July 25, 1990, may have left Saddam with the impression that the United States would not become involved in a conflict between Iraq and Kuwait. The State Department later released a cable that quoted Glaspie as telling Saddam that the United States had "no opinion" on Arab-Arab conflict. The cables also revealed that the State Department, then run by Secretary of State James A. Baker, instructed her to "broaden and deepen our relations with Iraq." I've wondered why Baker or someone at the department did not read the cable from Glaspie reporting on her visit to Saddam in time to send a new set of instructions clarifying the U.S. position. But it is clear to me that Saddam at the very least thought he had a green light to enter Kuwait.

I believed then, as I do now, that the United States stumbled into the war and that Bush need not have initiated it, and that a political solution was both preferable and possible. My conversation with Scowcroft that night in a Kennebunkport area restaurant and subsequent brief exchanges with Bush at Kennebunkport, in the White House and elsewhere never changed my position that going to war was a Bush mistake.

*   *   *

LAWRENCE M. O'ROURKE

I write elsewhere in this memoir of my travels with Bush to Europe and eventually my time in the sands of Saudi Arabia during the troop buildup that resulted in the start of the air war in January and the ground invasion the following month. That chapter details my coverage of the war. Here I will only address what I regard as a matter linked to the war—Bush's greatest flaw as president—the so-called "wimp factor." Whatever negative connotations the word wimp bears, I do not consider Bush a wimp. But I can clearly understand how to some people he came across as such. Lest some dismiss this as curbstone psychology, let me hasten to add that there is no one in my knowledge who engaged more in evaluating the human characteristics of people than George Bush. He tended to rely on his own evaluations and CIA studies to assess foes and friends. Before Saddam invaded Kuwait, Bush had never been tested under fire. He certainly lacked Reagan's appearance of deep conviction and Dole's reputation for hard in-fighting—matters against which Bush was measured during the 1988 primary. I believe that it was anxiety to avoid looking weak, internationally against real and potential enemies, and domestically in negotiations with Congress and in confrontations with political adversaries, that caused Bush to blunder into the Gulf War.

It was in 1988 after the New Hampshire primary that I first wrote of Bush and the wimp factor. I was in the Florida Panhandle to see how Bush was faring in the battle for the Republican nomination for president against a fading Dole and the religious right candidate, broadcaster Pat Robertson. I brushed off Robertson as a serious contender for the Republican nomination, but I wanted to know how his supporters would feel about Bush as a nominee, considering Bush's reputation as pro-choice and willing to spend federal dollars on education and environmental protection.

In a column I wrote out of Panama City after visiting many Christian Fundamentalist political activists, I wrote that Bush might not project the strength that voters wanted in the White House. "Questions about Bush's toughness will not go away," I wrote. "If he wins the nomination and he is well on his way to doing that, he will have to face in the fall a Democratic ticket that will find new ways to raise the wimp factor." Writing a few days later in Jackson, Mississippi, I said that Dole was hindered by his reputation "as an alley fighter and of meanness." In contrast, Bush came over as a "nice guy." To Saddam and other adversaries, "nice guy" may have come across as "wimp."

It turned out that I was right about the Democrats trying to raise the wimp factor in the fall campaign, but clearly I underestimated their capacity for incompetence. In fact, when Dukakis sought to show how tough he was by wearing a helmet and riding in a tank, the move backfired on the Democrats and made Bush look more stable than his opponent.

*   *   *

The wimp factor also figured in my thinking of why Bush picked the unknown young senator from Indiana, Dan Quayle, as his vice presidential running mate in 1988. I believe that Bush, aware of his soft reputation, wanted a running mate who came across as younger and less experienced than Bush, both in public presentation and record. If anything, Quayle was seen as a golf-playing lightweight not ready for the big time.

I had been in New Orleans several weeks, setting up the *Post-Dispatch's* workspace for the Republican National Convention, covering the contentious platform hearings that pitted Republican moderates and religious conservatives, running along the Mississippi levees before morning coffee and beignets at Cafe du Monde, and enjoying many fine dinners in the Crescent City's excellent restaurants, when word came that Bush would announce his vice presidential choice.

As I watched the arrival of a paddleboat carrying Bush pull into a dock on the mighty Mississippi River, I speculated that Bush might pick Jack Kemp, a favorite of conservatives as a House member from upstate New York and a former outstanding quarterback for the San Diego Chargers and Buffalo Bills. Kemp competed against Bush in the 1988 New Hampshire primary, but dropped out. I had many conversations over the years with Kemp and while I thought his ideas on economic issues were zany, I always enjoyed his graciousness and enthusiasm. He would bring youth, vigor, and strength to the Bush campaign. Kemp was no wimp.

When Bush stepped off the paddleboat that August day and announced that Quayle would be his running mate, I joined other reporters in the instant reaction, "Did he really say Quayle?" Like many other reporters who covered the Senate, I never invested much effort on Quayle, regarding him as inconsequential and a predictable party-line voter. But in the hours that followed, as I wrote of the selection of Quayle, I found out a lot more about him—as I picked up reports from sources that he used political connections to avoid the Vietnam War, had a love for golf trips that included a holiday in Florida with lobbyist Paula Parkinson, and lacked any substantive experience. Quayle made it worse the next day by an inept performance at a news conference I attended.

*   *   *

A lot of jokes, many deserved, were made at Quayle's expense after his election as vice president. I helped by a story that in a letter to a St. Louis man, Quayle in a hand-written note, spelled the vegetable "potatoe." With sympathy for Quayle, since I'm prone under deadline pressure to misspellings, I called David Beckwith, a friend from the journalistic ranks who became Quayle's press secretary. When I told David I would write a story suggesting that the vice president was either inept or dumb, he said, "Don't worry about it, Larry. You're not the first and you won't be the last."

I had sympathy for Quayle after I talked with him in his Executive Office Building suite in January 1989, about changes in his life brought by his election as vice president. He came across as the guy next door suddenly propelled into a regimen beyond his control. "The biggest change is not being able to get in the car and go out and get pizza on Sunday night," Quayle said. "Or to get in the car and go down to get milk and eggs." Before he entered his new life, said Quayle, "We went to church on Sunday and I'd always go to the 7-11 and pick up donuts. I still cook the scrambled eggs, but no longer do we get our donuts there." He said his kids were annoyed at the movies because people would reach across them to get their father's attention or autograph. He laughed without mirth when he said how painful it was to see his school transcripts with their low grades published. "My academic record in college is certainly a very useful tool; to tell my kids what not to be," Quayle said. I had to feel sympathy for the guy.

*   *   *

While I spent most of the fall of 1988 watching Bush campaign around the country, starting with his cutting fish in the San Diego harbor on Sept. 7 to asking for votes and God's help in building a "kindler and gentler society" in Houston on the eve of the election, I had the most fun breaking away on solo enterprise stories.

One such came in the Central Valley of California where I set out to discover if the so-called Reagan Democrats—mostly blue-collar Democrats who had broken away from their party to support Reagan in 1980 and 1984—were sticking with Bush or returning to their party to support Dukakis. On that trip I interviewed Anthony Podesta, the state manager for the Dukakis campaign, who conceded to me that voters saw Dukakis as a "wimp." Podesta, the brother of John Podesta who became chief of staff for President Bill Clinton, added that voters who liked Reagan also saw Bush as a "wimp.' With Dukakis or Bush the choice, it was clearly the year for wimps.

*   *   *

I got my big break of the 1988 Bush-Dukakis campaign—and I use the words in their precise meaning—when I called Maya Lindsay, a Dukakis organizer in Modesto, and said I wanted to interview Reagan Democrats she was trying to bring back to the straight-line Democratic fold. Lindsay invited me to accompany her to a pancake breakfast in a firehouse in the foothills of the Sierras followed by a hike to the mountain in Yosemite National Park called El Capitan. The 3,000-foot vertical monolith is a favorite for rock climbers. As I approached it that morning with Lindsay and a few of her friends, I had a bag over my shoulder with tape recorder, camera, extra notebooks and pens and a bottle of water. It wasn't heavy. I was talking with the Reagan Democrats, taking notes and not paying attention to where my feet were landing when I slipped, my shoulder bag swung forward. I fell—right onto jagged rocks. But the interview had to go on. I picked myself up and kept taking notes. I was more embarrassed than hurt.

I went to sleep back at the hotel in Modesto but in the middle of the night I awoke with a terrible pain in my rib cage. Not wanting to be carted off in an ambulance, I drove to a local hospital. They took X-rays and told me I had broken several ribs. The doctors said that in the old days they would tape me and have me take it easy for six weeks while the ribs healed. The current treatment for broken ribs, they said, was taking it easy, making sure I didn't get bumped, and taking as much pain killer as I needed to get through the bad moments of the day.

LAWRENCE M. O'ROURKE

Political campaigns involve a lot of bumping and many bad moments. I was in exquisite pain as I wrote my story that Reagan Democrats would probably not come back enough to Dukakis in sufficient numbers to win him the White House. A day later, I boarded a flight out of San Francisco and sat rather still in the plane as it brought me to Washington. I didn't have the luxury of skipping the campaign, so it passed rather painfully. Climbing on and off buses while toting a bag that often included a computer was an exercise inappropriate for someone with broken ribs. The ribs got better as the campaign ended. I was able to fly four round trips across the country in the final ten days, only occasionally getting more than four hours sleep at night and constantly updating stories. I didn't complain to my editors, of course, lest they for whatever reason use my big break of 1988 as an excuse to yank me from the campaign.

*　　*　　*

As president, Bush's motto might have been, "Have airplane, will travel." My job was "wherever he goes, I go." His journeys got me inside the emperor's palace in Tokyo, and into the cabinet room in Number 10 Downing Street where British Prime Minister Margaret Thatcher encouraged my rapid departure and her officious secretary chided me for bumping into a piece of furniture as I beat a hasty retreat. That trip also got me into Buckingham Palace where I stood by silently in the Music Room as Bush and Queen Elizabeth walked by. I was lectured in no uncertain terms by the Queen's household attendants that I was there at their sufferance. They made clear that I was not to move from the designated spot or utter a sound. I did hear Bush say, "It's very quiet." I heard the queen say, "You must be awfully busy." The president and the queen turned, smiled, stood for a few seconds while cameras snapped, and walked on.

In lesser pomp, Bush's travel took me to the shipyard in Gdansk where Lech Walesa and fellow Polish workers initiated the successful "Solidarity" revolution against their Communist overseers. When I met Walesa in his home in Gdansk, he struck me instantly as a warm-hearted man who would have been a successful politician in the States. A high wall topped with concertina wire ringed Walesa's home. Guards with dogs patrolled it.

Bush's travel got me a handshake and conversation with Mikhail Gorbachev on a Soviet luxury liner in Malta (that I write about elsewhere) and also let me pepper Gorbachev with questions at the U.S. Embassy in Paris.

*   *   *

I also had a chance to mingle with Gorbachev at a diplomatic reception on another reporting trip—in June 1989. Gorbachev's visit to West Germany turned out to be pivotal for ending the Cold War that gripped the world since the conclusion of World War II. I was on the street in Bonn as Gorbachev worked the crowd as effectively as any politician I've ever observed. I was briefed by several officials of the then government of West Germany, known as the Federal Republic of Germany. Based on past stories, I trusted the German sources. But I still was skeptical when they told me that the Gorbachev visit should be written as a sign that major changes were in the works in East-West relations.

But the upbeat West German analysis wasn't shared by the dour East Germans and the perplexed American officials I interviewed. I went through the Berlin Wall to meet with contacts I had arranged with help from the Bush Administration and Soviet Embassy in Washington. The hard line leaders of East Germany, known as the German Democratic Republic, told me they had every expectation of continuing the GDR's separate existence and their close ties to the Soviet Union. A high GDR official in the office of Erich Honecker told me: "The two governments are not compatible. We are not carrying out democratization. We would welcome reunification of a socialist basis, but do not anticipate that occurring." Senior U.S. officials I interviewed in Bonn, East Berlin and West Berlin, and Washington rejected speculation that the Gorbachev visit would end the division of Germany.

But to see, as I did, the enthusiasm for Gorbachev among German people on the streets on Stuttgart and Bonn, suggested that more was at work than expressions of goodwill. West German officials said there hadn't been as much excitement since JFK visited Berlin nearly three decades before. It was incredibly thrilling just five months later, in November of 1989, to see the Berlin Wall smashed. Among my memorabilia, I have a small concrete chunk of the wall and a strand of the barbed wire that adorned it.

White House correspondents would say now and then, "It's hard work, but somebody's got to do it." And so it was on July 13, 1989, the eve of the 200th anniversary of the fall of the Bastille. I was in Paris with Bush. He had dinner with French President Francois Mitterrand and other dignitaries at the Musee D'Orsay. I had dinner at the Tour d'Argent, regarded as one of the world's finest restaurants.

Leo Rennert, Washington bureau chief of McClatchy Newspapers, arranged the dinner party. Leo had a well-earned reputation for dining at excellent restaurants wherever the White House press corps stopped. When he said he had an opening at his table at Tour d'Argent, I jumped at the invitation.

In its penthouse location on the Left Bank, with its magnificent views of the River Seine, Notre Dame Cathedral and across the city to the white Sacre Coeur Basilica on the summit of Montmarte, the highest point in the City of Lights, it was an ideal place to celebrate the triumph of the French Revolution and the advance of individual freedom.

After water was poured into silver goblets and wine ordered from a cellar said to contain 450,000 bottles ready for selection from a 400-page list with 15,000 offerings, we started with Kir Royale pastry salmon, according to the notes I jotted as inconspicuously as possible in my notebook. I didn't want to be gauche. I had the house specialty, Caneton Tour d'Argent—pressed duck. I'm afraid I didn't write down what I had for dessert, but I recall drinking some wonderful wine, though not as much as a newspaper colleague. He and I decided to walk from the restaurant to our hotel off the Champs Elysees near the Arc de Triomphe. We went through the streets of Paris with their merrymakers, firecrackers popping all around us. The walk meant crossing the streets of Paris, where more than a few drivers ignored red lights at high speed. Several times I pulled my colleague back from disaster. The next day, he thanked me for saving his life.

On the 200th anniversary of the fall of the Bastille, I watched a military parade and saw Bush meet a series of foreign leaders. In the afternoon I saw the president and other heads of state at a garden party at the Elysee Palace. Chef Jany Gleize prepared a lunch of terrine of lamb Provence, fried sea perch with mashed courgettes, and bitter chocolate shells filled with ice cream sweetened with lavender honey. I, of course, didn't get to taste it. My job was not to eat, but to report how our leaders celebrated.

CHAPTER 17

Gridiron Club President

FIVE MINUTES BEFORE seven in the evening of Saturday, April 1, 1989, George H.W. Bush and Barbara Bush arrived in the secluded entranceway to the Capitol Hilton Hotel at 16th and K Streets, up the street from the White House. Pat and I welcomed them.

In white tie and tails, the 41st president stepped from his limousine and said, "Looking forward to the evening, Larry. Looking forward."

When the First Lady left the limo, I was taken aback. Blond curls substituted for her famous silvery hair. She grinned mischievously. My first thought was that Barbara had dyed her hair. She said, "I'm pleased to be here. It will be a good evening. Not too tough, I hope." "Not at all," I said. "Remember, the Gridiron Club may singe, but it never burns." Civility was a cherished tradition of the Gridiron Club, an organization of 60 active Washington newspaper reporters, columnists and bureau chiefs, often described as movers and shakers of national politics. It was the night of our annual spring dinner. As Gridiron president, I was responsible for the evening.

Pat and I and President and Mrs. Bush chatted amiably as walked through hotel corridors, empty but for Secret Service agents, into a room where Vice President Dan Quayle and his spouse Marilyn and Democratic National Committee Chairman Ron Brown and his spouse Alma, greeted us. We heard the buzz from the ballroom 50 feet away. I picked Quayle and Brown to speak as representatives of their parties.

"Barbara, whatever did you do with your hair?" asked Marilyn Quayle. Barbara Bush laughed, "Even George didn't know about it." She said it was her April Fool's Joke. "I didn't find out until we were dressed and ready to go," the president said. "It was a surprise to me."

"Mr. Vice President, Mr. Brown, ladies. It is time to go," said Bush's military aide. The Browns and Quayles went to the ballroom. A minute later the First Lady of the United States and the First Lady of the Gridiron Club were announced. They entered the ballroom to applause.

Then the announcer intoned, "The President of the United States and the President of the Gridiron Club, Lawrence M. O'Rourke."

As the band played "Hail to the Chief," I enjoyed the momentary attention as I walked with the president in the spotlight. There was tremendous applause.

I looked at the audience, 625 people, men in mandatory white tie and tails, ladies in long dresses, standing behind their chairs along both sides of 11 tables that radiated from the head table. Across the room was the stage, dark now, but I knew that the Gridiron Chorus was behind the curtain. Bush waved to the audience. I went to the podium.

Instantly, the lights in the room went out, leaving on only a lamp on my reading material at the podium. My text was there in big bold letters. I also carried a copy, a security blanket in case the primary edition disappeared. The hotel, at my insistence, put a flashlight under the podium—in case all lights in the room went out, leaving me unable to read what I had written and rehearsed for days. The hotel electrician said I was paranoid, but I would leave nothing to chance.

And so began the 108th annual spring dinner of the Gridiron Club of Washington, D.C., I had Bush on my right, Quayle on my left, with Brown a few chairs away. Pat was between Quayle and Supreme Court Justice William Brennan. The glitterati of American government, politics, and press waited. To Bush's right stood Joseph Pulitzer, holder of the greatest name in American journalism, and publisher of *The St. Louis Post-Dispatch*.

My first role, which I now steadied myself to undertake, was to deliver the Speech in the Dark. After four Gridiron members sang our opener, Music in the Air. I began:

> Mr. President, Mrs. Bush. Joseph Pulitzer. Emily Pulitzer.
> Ladies and Gentlemen. Mr. President, you've had a few bumps
> in your first 100 days in the White House. But you're in the
> wrong place if you're expecting sympathy. The Gridiron Club
> offers none of that kinder, gentler malarkey. In the Gridiron
> Club, Mr. President, there are no wimps.

The room exploded in laugher and applause, just as I hoped and expected. But I was not sure. You never know if the Speech in the Dark will launch a rollicking evening, or will be a dud. I wanted to make my Speech in the Dark memorable—if only for five minutes, until the guests had their first glass of wine. Then my words could be forgotten.

With that first wave of approval I felt as if a ton was lifted from my back. The work of writing the speech, throwing parts away, drafting new one-liners, testing it on Pat, my children, my fellow morning runners, my officemates, my Gridiron friends Dick Ryan, Milton Jaques and David Broder, was behind me. Suddenly it looked like my speech might work. Defying advice of old hands, I wrote my entire speech, insisting, perhaps arrogantly, that my one Gridiron speech would be my product. I moved ahead:

> For one thing, Mr. President, we don't let our spouses push us around. When we say we're lifetime card-carrying members, we mean it. We stick to our guns.

This, too, brought boisterous laughter, whistles and applause—as the savvy audience knew it was a reference to Mrs. Bush leaning on her husband to ban illegal sub-machine guns widely used by street gangs. The politically powerful National Rifle Association opposed Mrs. Bush. "The Gridiron Club is not about to give up its musical weapons, especially the semi-automatic ones," I said to laughter.

The Speech in the Dark is meant to be topical, and to chop at highly vulnerable targets in both parties. When you get a two targets in one, so much the better. I twinned two issues fresh in the guests' minds. The first was the refusal of Michael Dukakis, the losing Democratic presidential nominee in 1988, to endorse a Constitutional amendment making flag burning a federal crime. Bush had also pinned Dukakis as an opponent of mandatory recitation by schoolchildren of the Pledge of Allegiance. The second reference was to John G. Tower, the senator from Texas and Bush's nominee as Secretary of Defense. The Senate rejected Tower after a bruising fight that included charges that Tower consumed too much alcohol too frequently. The Tower reference needed to be addressed delicately:

> You remember the 1988 campaign, don't you, Mr. President. The one in which you made big issues out of the flag and the pledge. Now a lot of people said, Mr. President, that the pledge was not a burning federal question. But you knew

better. First, we had a Democratic candidate for president of the United States who didn't want to take the pledge at all. Then we had a Republican candidate for secretary of defense who didn't take it soon enough.

That line got the audience's attention big time, with whoops and whistles. Quayle groaned. I had more:

You took the pledge, Mr. President. 'Read my lips. No new taxes.' Admit it here tonight, Mr. President. By next year that pledge will be worth less than a ticket to the inauguration of Michael Dukakis.

Laughter rolled across the room. Quayle groaned again when I waded into his reputation as a lightweight. Still addressing Bush, I said,

I know you were surprised, stunned after the Tower vote when Vice President Dan Quayle went out and made that speech about McCarthyism. Quayle must have heard about McCarthyism back in college. In the (pause and articulation) book he read.

I took jibes at Bush campaign manager Lee Atwater, Republican firebrand Newt Gingrich and Speaker of the House Jim Wright before wrapping it up with the traditional,

In 104 years, the Gridiron Club has had but three rules, often more observed in the breech than in the performance. Ladies are always present. Reporters are never present. And the Gridiron may singe, but it never burns. Please be seated.

A large electric Gridiron on the wall behind me was lit, there was applause, hubbub, and we sat down to dinner, My Speech in the Dark, I knew, would be discussed positively for the mandatory five minutes, probably judged good or OK and relegated to my memoir and the Gridiron file. But I got through the ordeal, and it was on with the show.

*   *   *

I handed Bush our elaborate seating chart and our show book with the schedule, my speech, and lyrics. We print a dozen of the books, with the most critical copy going to the floor manager, responsible for moving the evening along smoothly. My floor manager was Bill Ringle of *Gannett Newspapers*, one of the finest people I ever encountered, a warm and gentle man, but whose duty that night was to crack the whip on hotel staff, performers, musicians and others who needed it. I authorized a schedule and program that would end before 11 p.m. For years, I believed that the Gridiron dinner went too late. Since most people in the room were in what might be called the mature generation, keeping them beyond midnight was a burden. Furthermore, the night got longer as post-dinner parties proliferated. Earlier in the spring, Bush complained to me, albeit good naturedly, that the dinner went too late. (Under Bill's hand, the curtain came down on our evening a few minutes before 11.)

The president barely opened his copy of the show book when the orchestra played a fanfare and David Broder of *The Washington Post*, the Gridiron vice president, speaking before the closed curtain, said the Gridiron Club was about to continue a tradition started when the legendary march king, John Philip Sousa, directed the United States Marine Band and served as Gridiron musical director. The ballroom doors opened and in marched the Marine Band, resplendent in red tunics, their instruments shining in the spotlights. They played the national anthem, a medley to the armed forces, and several marches, drawing well-deserved cheers.

While Bush read the show book and seating chart, I worked the head table. I said hello to Brennan, three other Supreme Court justices, several cabinet members, congressional leaders, and a half dozen ambassadors.

Warren Weaver, of *The New York Times*, a classy guy I picked as music chairman, appeared before the closed curtain. He said that it had been 200 years since George Washington's inauguration, and it was time for Gridiron Club members to re-live that event. The curtain opened as Maureen Ribble, costumed as Betsy Ross, sang to the music of My Fair Lady's Ascot Gavotte:

> Every Washington and Lee is here.
> Every patriot who should be here.
> This rhetoric, possibly historic spectacle.

The Gridiron's annual exercise in political satire has depended heavily through the years on music, with fees paid, from Broadway musicals, folk songs, and hymns, with frequent reliance on Irving Berlin and Cole Porter, and an occasional opera. The words crafted by Gridiron members do not have to fit the music precisely, especially when our special members, people who make their living on other than journalism, but who can follow a tune, take over. Among soloists that evening were lawyers Bob Stranahan and John Duvall, government worker Ernie Sult, printer John Bigby, oil executive Tex Ritter, and Marine band singer Master Sgt. Michael Ryan. Mike patiently tried every year to get Club journalists to emphasize the right vowels and consonants. He rarely succeeded.

Journalists in the Mighty Gridiron Chorus take pride in their efforts to sing on key and stay on the beat under the baton of the Marine colonel directing us, but frequently fail to accomplish either ambition. Our music leader during my presidency was Col. John Bourgeois, who valiantly got us through rehearsals and actually made us sound OK.

The opener skit ended as the Gridiron Chorus sang to the music of Lambeth Walk.

> Any George can change with flacks
> Who can rearrange the facts
> Since Valley Forge
> Onward from George to
> Onward from George to
> Onward from George to George.

The curtain came down to thunderous applause. Spurred by Ringle, waiters cleared dishes from the first course of lentil soup, filled the second wine glasses, and served the next course of avocado with crabmeat.

I barely touched my food and ignored my wine. I had a lot more to do this evening and I did not want the experience blurred in even a modest alcoholic haze. Nor did I want alcohol to throw off my attention or timing. Bush barely tasted his wine as he nibbled at his food.

With 40 minutes until the next event, the president and I chatted. As he read names on the seating list, he made small asides, some derogatory. I was aware that his remarks, even if accurate, would create international incidents if published. I did not intend to publish them. I think Bush knew that and felt comfortable offering me his candid views.

I became aware that as the president and I talked, Pulitzer sat silently to the president's right. I spoke loudly to get Pulitzer involved. Getting him to talk wasn't easy. He was a quiet, dignified, shy man, reluctant to intrude. Pulitzer was the opposite of the image of a hotshot publisher throwing his weight around. Bush asked Pulitzer about St. Louis, *The Post-Dispatch*, and the newspaper business. The president mentioned relatives in St. Louis.

The room buzzed. Some guests worked the tables, no easy task considering narrowness of the aisles and the bustle of waiters. Others went to bathrooms, since timing is essential at Gridiron dinners, for the audience as well as performers. You don't want to leave or arrive during a skit, and you don't want to be outside when a fanfare sounds. You learn timing by experience.

The conversation among Bush, Pulitzer and myself was interrupted by a fanfare. Carl Rowan, columnist, former ambassador and my predecessor as Gridiron president, stepped onto the stage. "Ah, this a fine day for the Irish, it is. We may have the finest gathering of the O'Rourke clan this side of County Galway. All to express pride in the inauguration of the 104th president, Lawrence M. O'Rourke." He introduced the family, Pat at the head table, and at a table stretching from us to the stage, Chris, Katie, Jenny, and Timmy. Then my parents, Lawrence and Margaret, and my brother, John. There was the Ambassador of Ireland and my friend, Father Andrew Greeley, the priest, sociologist, author and Grand Beach, Michigan neighbor.

Rowan introduced the Pulitzer group, Joe and Emily at the head table, and at a floor table, *Post-Dispatch* publisher Nicholas Penniman, editor William Woo, and managing editor David Lipman. Seated with them was St. Louis Mayor Vincent Schoemehl.

I was pleased to have old friends there, including Gene Ruane of Villanova, who was instrumental in my selection as editor of the *Villanovan*, a big step into journalism.

Also present were *Post-Dispatch* co-workers, Jon Sawyer, Bob Adams, Bill Lambrecht, Charlotte Grimes, Bob Koenig, and the Freivogels, William and Margaret. Years later, I had the pleasure of sponsoring Sawyer for Gridiron membership.

With introductions out of the way, the senior active member of the Gridiron, Edgar Allen Poe of *The New Orleans Times-Picayune*, sauntered from the stage to the head table bearing the ivory gavel given to the Gridiron in 1900 by Mark Hanna. The gavel is a symbol of power of the Gridiron presidency. I took it from Poe and laid it aside, not wishing to damage it, and continued to use the unadorned gavel provided by the hotel. Poe took an umbrella from under the head table and danced back to the stage to "When the Saints Go Marching in," also a tradition. Eddie introduced our two new members, Jim Perry of *The Wall Street Journal* and Adams of *The Post-Dispatch*. Jim and I worked together at the *Bulletin* a quarter century before. I ended the initiation skit with the customary instruction to Perry and Adams to retire to the back row of the chorus, not to be seen again for 10 years.

I announced the head table, starting with Barbara Bush, who smiled and bowed in her wig of curly blond hair, Marilyn Quayle, Alma Brown, and "my own Pulitzer Prize, Patricia Coe O'Rourke." I asked Supreme Court Justices at the head table to stand. Besides Brennan, who spent most of the evening talking with Pat, there were Byron "Whizzer" White, Sandra Day O'Connor and Anthony Kennedy.

Jack Germond and Bob Novak, fellow travelers on the political journalism trail and past presidents of the Gridiron, came onstage to introduce other guests: Secretary of State Jim Baker, Defense Secretary Dick Cheney, Treasury Secretary Nicholas Brady, former Attorney General and Governor of Pennsylvania Dick Thornburg, federal drug czar and Chevy Chase neighbor Bill Bennett, Secretary of Health and Human Services Secretary Louis Sullivan, Secretary of Commerce Bob Mosbacher, Secretary of Veterans Affairs Ed Derwinski, White House Chief of Staff John Sununu, and National Security Adviser Brent Scowcroft. Through years of reporting in Washington and Pennsylvania, I met them professionally and socially. I preferred as a reporter and political columnist to maintain an arms-length distance from public figures, thinking that gave me more flexibility for objective praise and criticism. Germond and Novak continued introductions, including Federal Reserve Board Chairman Alan Greenspan, Lee Iacocca of Chrysler, and Bush budget director Richard Darman.

We had sports figures, including quarterback Doug Williams of the Washington Redskins and New York Yankees owner George Steinbrenner, and TV personalities Bryant Gumbel of NBC's Today show, Connie Chung of CBS, and Bernard Shaw of CNN. Bernie and I competed as young reporters, me for the *Philadelphia Bulletin*, and he for Westinghouse radio. We became friends. I respected him for his energy and integrity, and later for courage, when he reported live from Baghdad as the United States launched its attack to force Saddam Hussein to remove his troops from Kuwait.

Germond and Novak continued introductions: Soviet Ambassador Yuri Dubinin, Chairman of the Joint Chiefs of Staff Admiral William Crowe, movie actor Robert Duvall, brother of Gridiron singer Jack Duvall, who years later died prematurely when as a Christian Scientist he refused medical treatment. We had Christie Hefner, publisher of *Playboy* magazine. They introduced Bob Strauss, the longtime Democratic powerhouse, chairman of the Democratic National Committee, ambassador to the Soviet Union, and quintessential Washington insider. It was a joy of my professional life to spend hours with Strauss smoozing over politics and government.

When introductions ended, Bush asked me about our kids and their education. The president said he would like to meet the O'Rourke family. They got a presidential handshake. Then the kids met Mrs. Bush. Jenny recalled that the First Lady was gracious and asked questions about their schools. Brennan told Pat he would like to greet the O'Rourke family and the kids had a handshake with the great jurist.

At 8.15, the waiters served what I had dubbed Irish filet mignon. We didn't give guests much time to eat because Ringle sent Cheryl Arvidson of *The Dallas Times-Herald* and producer of the Democratic skit, to the stage. In appointing Arvidson, I broke the Club's sorry taboo against giving leadership to women.

With typical Gridiron hyperbole, Arvidson said that the Democrats had it tough in the first year of the Bush presidency, showing "signs of classic schizophrenia: bizarre, sometimes deflationary, behavior and intellectual and emotional deterioration," The curtain opened to a hospital emergency room. Sen. Robert S. Byrd of West Virginia, the Senate president pro-tem, played by Stranahan, sang to the tune of "Handle me with care" these Gridiron lyrics: "We're so tired of being losers. Damn Dukakis did us in. Won't you give us, please, another chance?" Speaker of the House Tom Foley of Washington State, played by Ritter, chimed in, "We've been Cartered. We've been Mondaled, Willie Horton and Roger Ailes. Everything we've tried has failed." Senate Democratic Leader George Mitchell of Maine, played by Don Larrabee, added: "I am just a guy from Maine learning that Jim Wright's a pain, Got this pay raise to explain."

And so it went for 20 minutes, Adon Phillips playing Sam Nunn, Hank Trewhitt in the role of T. Boone Pickens, Mike Ryan singing as the arrested Washington, D.C. Mayor Marion Barry, with cameo appearances as hospital orderlies by Jim McCartney, Sandy Grady, Helen Thomas, George Condon, and Finlay Lewis, with a rock dance ensemble of Haynes Johnson, Jerry ter Horst, George Anthan and Marianne Means.

The audience responded with applause and laughs to the satire and sight of journalists in silly costumes. The skit ended as Duvall played Brown to the music of "Sit Down, You're Rocking the Boat":

> I dreamed last night we were headed for the White House.
> The taste of cornpone lingered in my mouth.
> I'll take a stand on each side of ev'ry issue.
> But my butt keeps getting kicked from the South.

When the curtain closed, I introduced Brown. Using Gridiron humor, lines that work well in the room before a politically sophisticated crowd of insiders, many of whom have had their humor bones lubricated by several drinks, the first African-American to head a major political party committee, got to work:

> Good evening, Mr. President, Mrs. Bush, Mr. Vice President, Mr. Speaker, President O'Rourke, members of the Gridiron, Ladies and Gentlemen. They said I made history when I was elected chairman of the DNC. They told me that America was really getting better. But what's the first thing to happen after I was elected? The chairman of the Alabama Democrats says he's going to secede from the party. And then I go to Chicago, and they picket me. And so, tonight, I was looking forward to this dinner. I arrive here feeling good about myself . . . Resplendent in this white tie . . . Proud of my accomplishments. And I see Bob Novak at the door. He walks up to me with a big smile on his face, and he hands me his coat and a quarter. Frankly, I was a little offended. At least Strauss gave me a dollar.

Self-deprecating humor works better than anything else at the Gridiron, I advised Brown when I invited him as my Democratic speaker. He took it to heart.

I'm a lot more comfortable here than I was at that unity dinner in Chicago. Chicago has been rough. You may have read that my good friend, Congressman Gus Savage, called me an Oreo. But that's all right. I've forgiven him. I've been called a lot worse. Fig Newton . . . I suspect that many of you don't know much about me. Just like Dan Quayle. I've been criticized for my exceptional good looks, my well-heeled background, and my reliance on connections in high places. But that's not how I got to be a partner at the firm of Patton, Boggs & Blow. I got there the old-fashioned way—on a basketball scholarship . . . and now I'm settling in at the DNC. The first thing I did was clean out all the special interests. So I could make room for my clients.

He gently poked fun at Republicans and fellow Democrats, before concluding: "We gather tonight in that unique atmosphere which is the Gridiron. Where humor never burns. It just warms, like beverage alcohol." Turning to Bush, Brown said,

You and the First Lady lead a remarkable family that in many ways is now America's own. My wife Alma and I are especially touched by the devotion and affection you show each other and your family. We Democrats will not always see eye to eye with you on every subject, but your call for making our national family closer, kinder and gentler is a call we must all heed . . . From the inner cities to the suburbs to rural America. Our country aches for leadership that will make that dream real. As adversaries and as partners, we Democrats are, above all, committed to that endeavor.

Brown was a hit and got a justified standing ovation. I was honored to have him as a speaker and told him so, but that didn't keep me from covering him as I would any politician. I was sad and felt I lost a friend when Ron died in an airplane crash.

As waiters removed the main course dishes, refilled wine glasses, and brought dessert, Bush, Pulitzer and I got into a conversation that burned into my memory. Though I took no notes, I jotted my recollections quickly thereafter, not writing a word in print until now. Turning serious,

LAWRENCE M. O'ROURKE

Bush listed decisions he faced. The economy, he said, was worse than he anticipated, and needed a bipartisan solution.

Bush said that it was becoming increasingly clear that the country could not spend its way out of its economic hole. With that, Bush refuted Reagan's economic supply side theory formulated by economist Arthur Laffler. Reagan's record of cutting taxes and refusing to veto spending bills kept his popularity high, but resulted in record deficits. Against that backdrop, Bush and I plunged into a serious discussion of economic and fiscal policy. Pulitzer listened.

Bush said it would be difficult to cut spending. He noted his campaign promise to be the "Education President" and said the Pentagon needed more money.

"What you have to do, Mr. President," I said, looking Bush in the eye, "is generate more revenue by raising taxes."

"Won't happen on my watch," he said. "Bad policy. I'll stick to what I promised in the campaign, Read my lips. No new taxes. You got it right here in your show book."

"I don't agree with you, Mr. President," I said. "The only way out of this situation is more tax revenue and some spending cuts."

"Told you," Bush said. "No new taxes."

"Then you're stuck with explaining higher deficits every year and moving the country deeper into debt," I said. "I think you should try to cut a deal now with Congress. They go for spending cuts or controls. You agree to higher taxes. Sure, it would look like you were breaking a campaign pledge, but you could say you were forced because you found the situation worse than anticipated. It's better to do it now when you're beginning your term than later. You have time for the issue to fade before the next election and you'll have an improving economy to talk about in 1992."

"Higher taxes are off the table, Larry," he said. "Now and for my entire term."

"I think you're wrong, Mr. President," I said.

Our exchange ended when Ringle signaled it was time for the Republican skit. But the matter did not fade away. Pulitzer, who had listened but said nothing, told Woo and Lipman that he had been shocked by the conversation, that he never heard anybody disagree so bluntly with a president to his face, and had never expected a reporter in his Washington Bureau to be so tough with the president.

Bush and I returned to the issue later in his term after he ruefully accepted in December 1991 a deal with Congressional Democrats to raise taxes and cut spending. His concession on higher taxes cost him a second term in the White House as the Republican conservative wing led by Newt Gingrich with help from Pat Buchanan destroyed Bush and paved the way for the election in 1992 of Bill Clinton.

I believe, as I told Bush, that he had the political flexibility 100 days into his Administration to cut a deal that would be accepted by his party, endorsed by the country, and largely forgotten as a campaign issue four years later. Instead, it became a reminder of Bush's broken promise for years to come. "Read my lips. No new taxes." It was not only a line in our show, and the basis for our amiable debate on Gridiron night, but the standard against which his own party mocked him.

*　　*　　*

Ringle signaled me that the Republican skit was ready. I told Quayle his act was set to start. He said he was as ready as he ever would be for his first major inside-the-Beltway speech as vice president. He looked nervous. I saw him shaking. Several times during the evening, his aides brought index cards to him. He had a team of speechwriters in a corner room, tuned into the ballroom, recasting his remarks. Pat told me that Quayle barely glanced at his food, did not touch his wine, and talked little to her. So she spent the evening talking to Brennan about his family. He expressed pride in his children's public service and spoke enthusiastically about lawyers taking pro bono cases for indigent clients.

The fanfare sounded and Lars-Erik Nelson of *The New York Daily News*, the GOP skit producer, strode onstage, declaring:

> After eight years, there is a new party in town—the Grand Old Party, the party of parties, lawn parties, coming out parties, alumni parties and a Texas barbecue. These days it's a kinder, gentler nation. The sign on the door of the Cabinet Room reads, 'The Episcopal Church welcomes you.'

The curtain opened to the Gridiron Chorus dressed as cowboys and Ivy Leaguers under the leadership of Atwater, played by Lee Bandy, an outstanding reporter on Southern politics. To the music of "Look Out Here We Come," the chorus sang:

When Reagan up and left us, I felt my life was done.
The Reagan revolution seemed over and dead.
Then far off in the distance, I thought I heard some stumbling
So I raised my eyes and I lifted my head.
Look out here they come, they're coming
Watch 'em as they hit the ground running
Some are up from Texas, or maybe down from Maine
Their mouths are full of pork rinds and Copenhagen snuff.
They've got doo doo on their Guccis
Let's watch them do their stuff.

For the next 20 minutes, Gridiron members outfitted as Sununu, Scowcroft, Bob and Liddy Dole, Yasir Arafat, Jack Kemp, Bill Bennett, Tower, Cheney, Nixon, and Quayle performed. The final song went to Nixon and Quayle, with Quayle, played by Richard Cooper of *The Los Angeles Times*, singing, "Look at this face. I could use a wrinkle, a gray hair or two; perhaps a South American trip would improve me, like you." Nixon, through John Hall of *Media General Newspapers*, serenaded Quayle, "I agree with you. I agree with you."

After a rousing sardonic parody sung to the Battle Hymn of the Republic, the curtain fell. I nodded to Quayle as I said, "And now the man who has found steady work—of a sort, the Vice President of the United States," Shaking visibly, Quayle began:

President Bush, President O'Rourke, Secretary of State Baker, Secretary of Defense Nunn, ladies and gentlemen, I'm delighted to be here. I'd been hoping for months that I'd be one of the speakers here tonight, but for a while it looked like I wouldn't be invited. So I made a phone call. I said, 'Hello, Dad . . .'

It's great that President and Mrs. Bush could come. Although, if I'm here, who's watching the grandkids?" But the president has been so supportive of me. The other day he called me into the Oval Office and said, 'I know you've had some rough times, and I want to do something that will show the nation what faith I have in you, in your maturity and sense of responsibility. Would you like a puppy?

To me, sitting next to Quayle, I thought that he got off to a great start by poking fun at himself, by spotlighting his reputation as a young flyweight with little to do.

Quayle said that Bush made him feel a part of the Administration's effort to take its case to the public. "On a typical weekend, you might see John Sununu on Meet the Press, Jim Baker on Face the Nation. And me on American Bandstand."

Against the backdrop of charges that the Bush Administration lacked a vision of where it wanted to go, Quayle declared: "I've tried to stick up for the president. In recent weeks, some started saying the White House didn't have an agenda. We have an agenda. It's just that when Ronald Reagan left, he took it with him." This produced the sort of gulp of air that takes place at a Gridiron dinner when the audience realizes how close to the truth the speaker actually got.

The grandchildren humor wasn't finished. "We'd probably get more done at the White House if it weren't for all the Bush grandkids," the vice president said. "I no sooner get in my office than there's a knock on the door and I hear, 'Can Danny come out and play?'"

Touching on the military service issue that subjected his candidacy to such widespread ridicule, Quayle declared:

> Our military is well represented tonight. Secretary Marsh is here for the Army. General Welch for the Air Force. General Gray for the Marines. And, of course, I'm here representing the Indiana National Guard . . . I guess I wasn't in the world's toughest National Guard unit. I mean, when we were eating our K-rations out on maneuvers, our guys would say things like, 'Pardon me, do you have any Grey Poupon?' When I look back at my earlier years, I have to laugh at some of the things I did—the initiations, the beer-drinking contests, the pranks, and the panty raids. But enough about my career in Congress.

Turning to his wife, Quayle described the day they met. "You remember, honey, when you caught me peeking over your shoulder during the bar exam?"

The vice president ended his tour of Gridiron humor with a story about Tower, the rejected defense secretary:

John was on a fact-finding tour in the Caribbean. He decided to enjoy the sunshine up on the hotel roof. Seeing no one around, he stripped to the buff and lay down, modestly putting a towel over his behind. . . . Suddenly the hotel manger burst upon the roof, yelling, "Senator, you must come down at once. This is indecent." "What do you mean?" John replied. "I'm covered with a towel." "But, Senator, you're lying on our dining room skylight."

With that image floating across the ballroom, Quayle sat down to raucous laughter and applause. By Gridiron standards, he did well. "Good job," I said to Quayle, shaking his hand. He thanked me, and reached for his wine glass. He sat beaming as people from the head table and the floor shook his hand and congratulated him. Brown came over and the two men exchanged compliments. The waiters served coffee and champagne.

I called on Al Cromley, the Gridiron secretary, to raise the curtain for our closer, traditionally music and words without bite. The chorus sang:

We'll see you again.
When politics breaks through again
Though fate and fortune go wrong
Laughter and song
Can live forever
Each fond memory
From year to year will guarantee
Fellowship still warm and bright
Leaders searching for the light
Writers wondering what to write
Good night.

As the curtain came down, I had one ceremonial task. Raising my champagne glass, I declared the traditional words: "In its 104 years, the Gridiron Club has had but one toast. Ladies and gentlemen, to the President of the United States." The audience rose, gestured their glasses toward Bush and clinked with one another, while I touched Bush's glass with mine and did the same with Quayle, Brown, Brennan and Pat.

"The President of the United States," I said, stepping back to let Bush take the microphone.

> Thank you, Larry O'Rourke. I must say I'm impressed. I thought both Ron Brown and Vice President Quayle did good jobs. They were a couple of yuppie Bob Hopes. By the way, whom do I see about getting an earlier spot in the show?

Bush had been using his left hand to change his lines on his three-by-five cards through the evening. He had scratched out several attempts to work something on daylight savings time in his remarks. He went on:

> Barbara told me to ban assault weapons. What should have been banned were those last three acts. Believe me, I know what it's like to follow a tough act. Let's face it: If I was funnier than Ronald Reagan, I would have won in 1980. And he'd be up here tonight trying to laugh away the Bush deficit.

He poked fun at himself. "People say I'm indecisive." (Pause, then hesitatingly, his cue cards read.) Bush followed script and said, "Well, I just don't know about that," and the audience erupted again. Bush made a few presidential jokes about the McLaughlin Group talk show, his dog Millie, Boris Yeltsin campaigning in an 18-wheeler to lead the Soviet Union, his staff, Atwater, and his grandkids.

"Even my grandkids are staring to pick up bad habits from the media," the president said. "The other day, one of them asked for a candy bar and I said, "No." Then she said, "I'd like to ask a follow-up." He made a crack—that drew a few groans—about crime in the nation's capital. "Seriously, I am concerned about the crime situation in D.C. I went aboard Marine One and asked the pilot where to sit. He said, 'Back there, behind the tail gunner.'

And then Bush's cue card said in double parenthesis: ((Last Joke)). "You'd think the White House would be safe from crime," the president said. "But last night Barbara was headed out the door to walk Millie. Looked back, and said, 'cover me.'"

As the laughter died and the room quieted, the president turned to the traditional tribute to the Gridiron's diet of laughter:

We do a lot of kidding around in this town, but it's important to be able to laugh. Because even though humor isn't singled out in the First Amendment, as tonight's friendly competition shows, it's darn near a national imperative. Americans are supposed to take their responsibilities seriously—but not themselves. . . . Laughter is part of the magic of America, part of the magic of our politics and our press.

A year from now, heck, a week from now, there will be all sorts of new material. My misstatements alone should give you plenty to work with. And there's things yet unthought-of, as unlikely as tainted grapes or horseshoes at the White House, I wish you happy hunting. And I wish you laughter in your work.

The president got a standing ovation. I shook his hand, said, "wonderful," and took the microphone back. "In concluding our evening, ladies and gentlemen, the Gridiron Club's senior singer, Adon Phillips, will lead us in singing Auld Lang Syne."

I grasped Bush's hand to my right and Quayle's to my left, as all in the room grasped hands or locked arms. We swayed and sang, "Should Old Acquaintance be Forget."

Pat and I walked with the president and Mrs. Bush to their car, thanked them for gracing our evening, wished them a good night and exchanged waves as they were driven toward the White House. The 104th Gridiron dinner was history.

*   *   *

My year as Gridiron president was a wonderful experience, but it had rough moments. The first came at the meeting in January when Gridiron members pick guests from an auction list made of distinguished guests we want at our dinner. Gridiron Club officers draw up the auction list. As president, I had veto power. I was responsible for the auction list. At a preparatory meeting, one of Carl Rowan's appointees mentioned that the club should invite Ronald Reagan. I agreed, especially since during a conversation I had with Reagan, I asked if he'd like to come to our dinner after he left the White House and he said yes. Another officer said he would like to have Jerry Ford back. I said how about Jimmy

Carter. We agreed that it would be wonderful to have all of them at our dinner.

Then someone noted that the only living former president we were not inviting was Richard M. Nixon. We all laughed. Not one of us wanted to invite Nixon. But I was concerned that the Gridiron would be criticized for excluding Nixon. Would that be seen as another slight from the Washington press corps, and would that not be out of step with our insistence that the Club was pledged to good fellowship. Some officers supported my point. No one objected to putting Nixon on the list. I had appointed Richard A. Ryan of *The Detroit News*, Godfrey Sperling, Jr., of *The Christian Science Monitor*, and Helen Thomas of United Press International to the executive committee. I had confidence they would advise me if I strayed off track. Also at the meeting were Broder of *The Washington Post*, and James Free, a retired Alabama journalist, the club historian. No one objected to putting Nixon on the list. I thought that was especially significant since Broder's *Washington Post* brilliantly broke the Watergate story that forced Nixon's resignation.

For the next six weeks through another executive committee meeting, a membership meeting and a dinner for club members in December, not a word was said to me about Nixon on the auction list.

However, at my first meeting as president, it was clear that I had a problem. Mary McGrory, a superb columnist for *The Washington Post,* passionately demanded that I instantly delete Nixon from the auction list. Joan McKinney of *The Baton Rouge Morning Advocate and State Times* offered a motion to delete Nixon. I argued that such an action, if reported, and I expected it to be reported, would present the Gridiron as petty and vindictive. McGrory and Arvidson spoke on behalf of McKinney's motion. Rowan opposed it; saying that a club dinner was not a state function, that members should have the right to pick and chose guests. That gave me the argument that no one had to pick Nixon's name. But in a move designed to end the debate over Nixon, I said that if Nixon stayed on the list, I would exercise authority and would select Nixon, thus sparing members a decision on Nixon.

I called for a vote on the McKinney motion to delete Nixon. It was soundly defeated. A few members walked out. I opened the auction, and picked Nixon as my guest.

That wasn't the end of it. Reports about the Gridiron fight over Nixon spread across the city. I heard about it from Bush's aides when I returned to the White House directly after the meeting. I got calls from other reporters. I refused to discuss it, saying that it was a private matter for a private club. Radio picked it up. Television stations called me with invitations to appear on weekend shows to discuss the controversy. I did take one call—from McGrory. She said she would write a column about the Nixon flap and would quote me. I advised Cromley, the club secretary, that I had calls from the press. He asked McGrory not to write a column on inside Gridiron business, but she refused.

She explained her opposition to the Nixon invitation in the column published in the *Washington Post* and across the country. (Cromley said McGrory broke club traditions of good fellowship and pushed the Gridiron where it did not want to be—in the political spotlight—by airing in public what we had historically viewed as private, but I thought it wrong and unwise for a journalist such as myself, always trying to open up government and politics, to argue against publication. I did not ask McGrory to kill the column.)

> You wonder why presidents treat the press any way they want? I will give you a case in point," she wrote. "The Gridiron Club, an organization of print journalists that is considered so elitist that my old friend, Ed Lahey, used to call it, 'The College of Cardinals,' had a meeting the other day. President Larry O'Rourke, White House correspondent of the *St. Louis Post-Dispatch*, announced that the board had decided to invite Richard Nixon and all the other ex-presidents to its spring dinner. This is a white-tie occasion of much pomp, attended to the point of unanimity by official Washington.
>
> I felt I had standing in this issue because I was on Nixon's enemies list. I asked why Nixon was invited. O'Rourke said that the matter had been discussed seriously by the board and that Nixon's offenses against the press had been recalled, including his wiretaps of four reporters. The executive board still wanted him to come to the dinner.

In her usual way, McGrory made her case effectively. She was probably the most stylish newspaper writer of her time. To my argument that we should not single out Nixon for exclusion, McGrory quoted McKinney as saying that Nixon should be an exception because he was "an exceptional president."

Within the Washington press community, the controversy ignited a firestorm. Another excellent national columnist, Marianne Means of *Hearst Newspapers*, weighed in with a column that the *Post* put prominently at the top of its op-ed page:

> Chatting over the asparagus does not mean endorsement of everything Nixon did, nor even send a message that he's been rehabilitated. Nixon, of course, is not your ordinary ex-president. This distinction was amply and heatedly noted by McGrory and others. But O'Rourke and a club majority felt that to discriminate against him would be making a political statement improper for the club that is, despite the makeup of its membership, strictly social. "We do not invite our guests to honor them," O'Rourke said, "we invite them because they are interesting people and some member of our club would like to see and talk to them. It is not our role to single out who's a scoundrel and who's not.

Means that said a "little good-natured joking goes a long way toward preserving a civilized society. "Nixon, though he let us all down badly, is no exception to this process. An invitation from the Gridiron Club will not change his disgrace in the eyes of history. But if he wants to come, the Gridiron Club will welcome him politely, as it should."

I sent Nixon an invitation. A Nixon aide called and said he would not attend. I chose not to raise the incident in my Speech in the Dark, and told my music committee to avoid it in the show. McGrory and I spoke regularly thereafter, never mentioning the Nixon fight. She did not take an active role in the Gridiron, declining invitations to serve on committees and to appear in our annual show. She resigned from the club.

*   *   *

We had another controversy on the eve of our spring dinner. For more than 100 years, the club rented costumes from the Jones agency in Baltimore. Jones also dressed Broadway shows, Gilbert and Sullivan operettas, and local theater and high school groups. The club sent the script to Jones manager George Goebel, along with recommendations for costumes. In the final week of rehearsals, the Gridiron president and a few others went to Baltimore to examine the costumes. Once approved, the costumes were shipped to Washington.

What made the costume trip to Baltimore especially memorable was the lunch *The Baltimore Sun* threw for the Gridiron visitors. *Sun* publisher Reg Murphy renewed the invitation to lunch in a letter to me in January and reminded me that the tradition was 67 years old. The lunch would be held, as usual, in the posh Maryland Club. Great, I wrote to Murphy, thanks and we'll be there. I told Weaver, as music chairman, to plan the visit and to submit a guest list to me. The trip to Baltimore was highly coveted in the club. Only two dozen Gridironers could attend. The *Sun* publisher would make a speech expressing joy in the 67-year-old link between the *Sun* and the club. I would thank Murphy, toast the *Sun*, praise the tradition, introduce my music chairman, and sit down. Weaver would outline the show and allow a singer to give a sneak preview of a song.

Distracted as I was with show preparations, including encouraging, cajoling, and soothing personality conflicts, I put the costume trip in the back of my mind. I was jolted five days before the trip when Arvidson called and asked what I knew about the Maryland Club. Nothing, I said. "The Maryland Club doesn't admit women members, but allows women to come to lunch," Arvidson said. "You should call off the costume trip."

I called Murphy. I knew him as a reporter and editor in Atlanta. He struck me as a good guy and solid professional. "Reg, I hear that the Maryland Club is segregated against women. We can't go there for lunch," I said.

"That's outdated information," he said. "Let me check it and I'll be right back to you." A few minutes later, he called back. It was true, he said, the Maryland Club continued to segregate against women. He had understood when he made the arrangements that it would drop its ban by the time of our lunch. But that didn't happen. Murphy said *Sun* executives, including him, were pressuring the Maryland Club to drop its ban on women, but that it could not be done by next week's lunch. "So we'll have to call the lunch off, Reg," I said. "Please don't act so quickly," he said. "Let me get back to you."

He called back in a half hour. It would be a "terrible embarrassment to him and to *The Baltimore Sun*" to cancel the lunch at this last minute, he said. He repeated that he had not known the ban still existed, but was assured it would be changed very soon. Murphy and I went back and forth on this several times over the next two days. I conferred with my executive committee and various members, including the women. The consensus was that I should work it out so that the lunch and tradition could go on.

I agreed to go ahead with the lunch on several conditions—that it would never be held again at the segregated Maryland Club or anywhere else in Baltimore with any form of discrimination, and that he and I would issue public statements incorporating these points and expressing individual views that we deplored the segregation. Murphy and I drafted separate statements, read them to each other, and agreed to move ahead with the lunch.

I read the statements to Gridiron Club members at the rehearsal. There was overwhelming approval from members, but Arvidson and a few others balked. James McCartney of Knight-Ridder Newspapers, a gracious and concerned man as well as a splendid journalist, sought to take some of the sting out the controversy by encouraging Arvidson and other women to go on the costume trip, review the costumes, but then go to lunch with him at a restaurant in Baltimore. He picked Haussner's, a famous Baltimore dining spot. Arvidson, Helen Thomas and Ann McFeatters of *Scripps Howard News Service* accepted his invitation. Other women members chose the Maryland Club.

Once again, the Gridiron Club got into the news and the journalistic gossip circuit. I told *Washington Post* reporter Eleanor Randolph that Arvidson had acted "quite properly." I added: "Next year, we know for darned sure we won't go to a segregated club." Arvidson told the *Post* that she did "not want to make a big thing about this." Our comments were printed in the *Post* and in other publications, including the *Sun*.

* * *

I never regarded the Gridiron Club, as Lahey and other members did, as the College of Cardinals. That was far too pretentious for a group of reporters who were lucky to stand on the edge of history and, occasionally, help shape it. I had a lot of fun in the Gridiron and on the whole, my year as president, despite the controversies, was enjoyable. Not to make too much of it, but the Gridiron was a forum for needling the pompous that had great authority over us. They could send Americans to war, set taxes, and safeguard health. Too many politicians tend to get arrogant. The Gridiron couldn't correct that, but once a year, it could remind our

LAWRENCE M. O'ROURKE

leaders that they, as my old Army platoon sergeant said frequently, put on their pants, like the rest of us, one leg at a time.

Over my years in Gridiron, I played many roles, including clown and chef, offered a few song and skit ideas that found their way into the show, and did my best to keep on key as a member of the Gridiron Chorus.

I was admitted to membership in March 1974 when Robert Roth of the *Bulletin* was Gridiron president. I retired as an active member, switching to associate status, in November 2005.

One memorable moment came on Feb. 16, 2005, as I was gestures chairman. I was to listen to the music and instruct the chorus in on-stage movements of their hands. I began to feel warm. Since I enjoyed a glass of red wine and wore a black Irish wool sweater, I figured I'd take off the sweater and get a glass of ice water. I did both, but I felt even warmer and weak. Perhaps the onset of a cold, I thought. I'll head home to shake it off.

I asked my friend, Milton Jaques, to walk me to the Metro Station so that I could get to my home in Chevy Chase. He prudently told Jerry Seib of *The Wall Street Journal,* that O'Rourke wasn't feeling well. Jaques and Seib forced me into a cab and rushed me to George Washington Hospital. At GW, Jaques demanded that a doctor see me quickly. He had trouble convincing the young woman at the reception desk, who was on a telephone, that it was an urgent matter. He became quite loud and insistent. The door to the ER opened and a nurse stepped out to assess the commotion.

It was a heart attack. Within hours, doctors performed an angioplasty to open blocked valves, inserted stents, and ordered me back a few days later for even more stents. I called Jaques from the intensive care unit the morning after my heart attack and thanked him. He sent an email to Gridiron members that O'Rourke survived. I did not make it to the Gridiron show that year. As I rested at home on Gridiron night, my mind floated to the hotel and 30 years in the Gridiron.

I made it back to the show the following year, when I sang in the back row of the Chorus.

In my years in the Gridiron, I participated in many changes. I advocated elimination of the outrageous ban on black members. My first vote was to admit women. I announced before accepting membership that I would vote to end the bans on blacks and women. Both were gone in my first months in the club. As Gridiron president, I tried to get club members to contribute to charity as a gesture that while we cavorted, drank and ate at high cost inside the ballroom, others were hungry. But my plan lasted only during my presidency. Some members called me a liberal do-gooder trying to impose my values.

Toward the end of my active years, Broder and others proposed that we drop our rule restricting membership to full-time print journalists. Cromley led a fight against admission of TV personalities, labeling them "sparklies" and predicting they would claim the glory of Gridiron membership, but do none of the work. I agreed with Cromley and voted against the rules change, but we lost. Tim Russert of NBC News was elected into membership, the first of several sparklies, all fine people and journalists, but not print journalists. Unfortunately, Russert, an outstanding journalism and a friend, died of a heart attack not long after entering the Gridiron Club.

Perhaps fine TV journalists such as Judy Woodruff of the News Hour on PBS, Andrea Mitchell of NBC and Bob Schieffer of CBS will pump new vigor into the Gridiron Club and guarantee its continued presence in Washington. As the 104th president, I hope that a man or woman will preside as the 140th president or the 204th president, and give a nod to those who a long time ago got some laughs through a Speech in the Dark.

CHAPTER 18

At War

THE EVENING BEFORE the early January day in 1991 that I was to leave home to cover the U.S.-led war against the forces of Iraqi President Saddam Hussein in the Persian Gulf, David Lipman, The *Post-Dispatch's* irascible managing editor, called from St. Louis.

"Write me stories like Ernie Pyle," he said, referring to the famous *Scripps-Howard* correspondent who chronicled GI Joe in World War II. "Make readers cry. Make them feel like they're in the desert with you." Good advice, I thought. "And get a lot of people from St. Louis into your stories," he said. I recognized the wisdom of that point. The *Post-Dispatch*, once one of the nation's great papers, by 1991 was a regional newspaper with declining circulation and fighting for survival. Going local was the mantra of survival. Why not turn the Persian Gulf War into a local story?

Lipman wasn't finished. "You don't have to do any more columns like the one you did on your last visit to Saudi Arabia, the one about the meal in the desert with the Saudi family," Lipman said. "That one was over the top." I didn't agree. I thought that my column about sitting on the floor scooping by hand a meal of rice, chicken and dried fruit, and drinking tea, while discussing with Saudis our philosophies, hopes and dreams for our children, provided insight into Saudi society few readers understood.

"Let's see what happens," I said to Lipman, as noncommittally as I could. Beyond being irritated at his suggestion about what I should not write in my column, I knew Lipman to be a man of strong opinion, impetuously expressed, never in doubt, but occasionally wrong, and bursting with ideas soon to be forgotten, if not contradicted, often by himself. Despite his inconsistency and bombast and our sporadic shouting matches, and unlike some of my colleagues, I liked David. He wanted the *Post-Dispatch* to do significant work. He was a serious journalist. He felt deeply, and, besides, he opened the newspaper's checkbook for my assignments and constantly pushed me to do more and better stories anywhere in the world. For months he called every week to ask how I was doing on getting into North Korea. He said the *Post-Dispatch* would support whatever I needed, even if it meant spending time in South Korea, just to get me into North Korea. Trying for an entry visa through various governments and the North Korean mission to the United Nations, I got nowhere. Lipman wasn't giving up. But now the matter before us was the Persian Gulf War.

Lipman had more to say that January evening. "You tell Pat I just insured you for $1 million. She doesn't have to worry." I thought I hope she's worried about more than $1 million. But all I said was. "Thanks, David. I'll tell her." Lipman footnoted: "The insurance was expensive, so make it worthwhile."

"One more thing I want you to remember when you're at the battlefront," Lipman said. "A dead correspondent," he said, "is of no use to the *Post-Dispatch*." I didn't know quite what to make of that. I didn't intend to have my family collect the $1 million.

*   *   *

I flew the next day via Heathrow to Saudi Arabia, landing late at night in Jeddah and enduring a protracted scrutiny at immigration and customs. My papers were in order. In the fall, I got a multiple-entry visa at the Saudi embassy in Washington. In November and December, I reported from Saudi Arabia on the build-up for war. From there I went to Turkey, writing about that nation's dilemma as a neighbor to Iran and Iraq, its ambition to join the European community and its struggle for economic and social development—a hefty package of stories. I got valuable insights from Morton Abramowitz, the U.S. ambassador to Turkey. I had breakfast with him at his residence, and as we rode together to his office, we were in the center of a heavily guarded motorcade. The *Post-Dispatch* put my Turkey stories on page one. Lipman and other editors said they were not only good, readable pieces, but drew positive notices from St. Louis scholars on Turkey.

I spent Christmas with my family in Washington, always mindful that in the new year, I'd be back in Saudi Arabia to cover a war.

I flew from Jeddah to Riyadh and on to Dhahran on the Persian Gulf. Dhahran was the staging point for reporters assigned to cover the fighting. In weeks ahead, as I experienced harrowing moments in

LAWRENCE M. O'ROURKE

the desert, I pondered Lipman's counsel that a dead correspondent was of no use to the *Post-Dispatch*. But I want to be upfront with a disclaimer. I did nothing heroic. I was harassed and discomforted, but never did I feel my life or health at risk. While I would not use the word fun to describe my experience, neither would I wish it away. I avoided some high-risk ventures. I turned down an Air Force invitation to fly a re-fueling mission. The idea of being in the sky close enough to another airplane to pump aviation fuel into it did not entice me. Once at a suspected minefield with an engineering company, I stayed behind the soldiers as they searched by probing the sand with sticks for explosives buried to kill them.

I was offered the chance to ride in a tank during combat, but I said I was content to ride during a training exercise. My position was strengthened when I asked a tank commander about rules of engagement in combat. "Kill or be killed," he said matter of factly. He explained how desert combat might involve tanks of several nations of the U.S.-led coalition, including Egypt, swirling around Iraqi tanks or gun emplacements. His greatest concern, the commander said, was "friendly fire." Warriors in tanks, he explained, don't have much time in the thick dust and tension of combat to know if the weapon pointed at them is enemy or friend. There are markings on tanks, and electronic devices in the tanks to disclose their identity. But you never know for certain, the commander said, if you will be able to read the markings or pick up the electronic signals in time to evaluate. And there were always minefields planted by Iraqis to think about, he said. Considering all this, while the invitation to ride a tank in combat opened the door to potentially great stories or the thrill of a lifetime, I said no. I wasn't happy inside the tank even during the exercise. It was cramped, hot, dark and noisy as I watched an electronic display and monitored rapid-fire messages among the tankers.

To complete my disclaimer, I was in the war zone during both the build-up to war and the "air war" that preceded the "ground war." I left Saudi Arabia 48 hours before the ground war started, clearing the way for Bob Adams, a colleague in the *Post-Dispatch* Washington Bureau, to be there for the ground war. The Saudi Embassy in Washington balked at granting a visa to Adams while I held mine. When I agreed to leave, I surrendered my visa so that Bob could get his. Before leaving the States, Adams sent a message that he wanted to report from the battlefield. I forwarded that request to military authorities in Dhahran. A man with a strong sense of daring, Adams got his wish. He was on the scene during the 100-hour ground war while I reported on the war in Washington based on briefings at the Pentagon and White House. Although Adams was a short distance from the scene and I was thousands of miles away, it fell to me to write that U.S. airmen discovered that killing fleeing Iraqi Republican guards was like "shooting fish in a barrel" on the "highway of death."

I wrote approvingly in my column about President George H.W. Bush's decision not to pursue the Iraqis into Baghdad or to attempt to kill Saddam. I knew that Secretary of Defense Richard Cheney and Allied commander Gen. H. Norman Schwarzkopf wanted to keep going until the Iraqi military was wiped out and Saddam was in his grave. Bush's prudent decision had the unfortunate effect of keeping Saddam alive long enough to provoke the misguided decision a dozen years later by the second President Bush to invade Iraq. On the second try, the U.S. succeeded in capturing and executing Saddam. As despicable as Saddam was, I could never figure out how his hanging helped bring stability and peace to the Middle East.

A few months after the first Gulf War, during a conversation with the first President Bush, I told him that I admired his decision to end the bloodshed before an invasion of Baghdad. He looked into my eyes and said, "Thank you. It was the right thing to do."

*　　*　　*

As I arrived in Dhahran in January 1991, war drums were sounding with a fierce battle underway—between the U.S. press and the U.S. military. Hostility was palpable. Some Army officers who fought in Vietnam were convinced that the U.S. press cost them victory in Vietnam, in their minds humiliating and demoralizing the Army. It was hard to keep civil a conversation with a major or colonel who served in Vietnam. Journalists were enemies as far as many of them were concerned. Though I had not been in Vietnam, my opposition to the war against the North Vietnamese and Viet Cong would not help matters. In discussions with military people, I avoided comparison of the Vietnam War and the Persian Gulf War, considering both misguided.

These angry Army veterans of Vietnam commanded troops readying for the Iraqi battlefield. They were not about to cooperate with reporters asking to join them and their troops. Officers in the field are responsible for security of their operational areas and their troops. They largely can say who can be with their troops and in their zones. While I understood their hostility to the press, I thought the American people had a right to know what their government was doing. The barriers to press coverage were dangerous obstacles to the flow of information needed by a self-governing people.

Denial of access to reporters was more than pique by disgruntled officers. Schwarzkopf wanted to control every aspect of the war, including information flowing into American homes through print and television. In limiting coverage, Schwarzkopf did the bidding of Bush and Secretary of Defense Cheney.

Saudi Arabia during preparation and conduct of the war was not a good time or place for rational debate over press coverage. Reporters fought with their weapons—words—for the right to report against soldiers who had weapons and power to inhibit or ban that right. The military won easily. The question of war coverage will endure as technology increases real-time access to both sides of the battle line.

Field commanders used a variety of techniques and threats to keep reporters away, ranging from roadblocks manned by troops to threats such as shooting out tires on reporters' cars and arrests of reporters. I had conversations with field officers that were ominous. They made clear that if reporters tried to play an end-run game with the Army, consequences for reporters could be severe. I took the threats seriously.

The argument over the role of the U.S. press in Vietnam, which had raged for years, took on new life as tens of thousands of soldiers moved north in Saudi Arabia into position to cross into Iraq and Kuwait. We were there to cover the troops.

To gain access to troops in the field, editors cut a deal with the Pentagon. The deal created a system of pooling by correspondents in which a few reporters would be allowed access to the troops to gather information that would be subject to censorship before it was distributed to other reporters for general use. This system was to be implemented by a military office in Saudi Arabia known as the Joint Information Bureau, or JIB.

The JIB was up and running when I arrived in Dhahran. JIB offices were in the Dhahran International Hotel on the edge of the airport for civilian and military planes. JIB rented space for its leader, Col. William Mulvey, a West Point graduate and Vietnam War squad leader, his assistants, a workroom, and a ballroom available to reporters to sit, wait and to write stories that might come their way. A television set occasionally broadcast CNN and college basketball games from the States. The Saudis turned it off at prayer time and often refused to turn it back on for hours. (The Saudis did not allow broadcast of the Super Bowl game in Tampa where the New York Giants beat the Buffalo Bills, 20-19. But I saw the game on a color TV in a tent in the desert in the company of soldiers. The military set up satellite service for the broadcast and on that early morning in Saudi Arabia the war was put aside. I stood at attention with the soldiers during a stirring rendition of the Star Spangled Banner by Whitney Houston.)

The JIB briefing room staff had a team of Saudis who placed long-distance calls and sent copy by Fax, on condition of immediate payment. They, of course, did not work during prayer time, and they were gone extended periods for meals. They were unenthusiastic about helping reporters.

Bedrooms in the Dhahran International Hotel were filled with JIB officers and reporters. Based on my previous stay in Dhahran, I booked a room at the Royal Hotel in central Dhahran, about a ten-minute drive from the International. I chose to stay at the Royal rather than at the International or a luxury hotel on the beach for several reasons. I figured that the Iraqi military would target the airport, with the hotel as possible collateral damage. I doubted the Saddam would target central Dhahran. That would be politically counter-productive.

I preferred the Royal because I wanted time and space every day away from what amounted to my office at the JIB. I never liked the idea of living above the shop. As for a seaside hotel, I stayed in one in the fall, but found it pretentious. The staff at the Royal was friendly and cooperative. The hotel, owned by Saudis, was managed by a Palestinian and staffed by Filipinos. The stories the Filipinos told me about their treatment were shocking. The Filipinos, hired to work in Saudi Arabia under long-term contracts, were required to surrender their passports to the hotel owners. The workers, all men, could not bring their families; they could take vacation home only after two years in Saudi Arabia. To keep the foreign workers in line, the owners gave them monthly a small part of their salary for transfer to their families. The owners withheld the bulk of their pay until they completed their term of service under their contract. If they messed up in some way in the view of the Saudi owners and were sent home before the contract expired, they'd lose their accumulated back pay. The Filipinos had little money—to keep them out of trouble, the owners said. When the Filipinos learned that I had reported from the Philippines, they invited me to their parties, all non-alcoholic in compliance with Saudi law and Muslim religious practice. At these parties, the workers' stories gave me insight into Saudi and Filipino society that would have fascinated sociologists.

There was another reason why I picked the Royal Hotel. It was close to the waterfront, with a long promenade where I could run much easier than I could near the airport. My typical day in Dhahran was to sleep until 11 in the morning, run for an hour, grab breakfast at the hotel, read and listen to Armed Forces radio (Bette Midler's "From a Distance" was the war's inspirational theme song), get an ice cream cone near the beach around 4, arrive at the JIB at 5, and stay until I filed my final story of the day to the *Post-Dispatch*, around 4 in the morning Dhahran time. I got to sleep about 5 a.m.

There were occasions when I didn't get six hours sleep as sirens warned people to head to bomb shelters. We had a shelter in the hotel basement. But I went in the opposite direction. At the siren's call, I stood on the roof of the hotel and watched for lights or explosions in the sky that I believed were missiles, sometimes Patriots from the U.S. side and Scuds from the Iraqis. When I saw and heard an explosion overhead, I went inside the hotel for cover in case the shrapnel headed my way. On many daily runs, I saw shrapnel on the path along the gulf. As for running, U.S. government officials alerted me that I might be stopped for running in short pants in public, but that did not happen. Most Saudi runners wore long pants and long-sleeved shirts. I never saw a woman running.

From the JIB, I got the credential needed to get into the ballroom and use the phones and Fax. Mulvey was pleasant when I filled out my application. He immediately approved it and I sported on a neck chain a badge with my picture, name and affiliation in English and Arabic. Mulvey said that if I wanted an interview, I should fill out a form and it would be considered. He promised nothing except the right to submit an unlimited number of requests.

I submitted requests for meetings with soldiers, particularly from St. Louis, to write on such human issues as food, shelter, mail, showers, and anticipation of combat. I wanted to know about religious services, about how the troops got recreation, how they endured the hot days and cold nights. I filed a request saying I wanted to go north to the Saudi border with Kuwait and Iraq. I asked to see military medical facilities. I requested an interview with any U.S. solider who spoke Arabic. Mulvey's initial pack of handouts touted close cooperation between the Coalition and Kuwaitis who fled south when Iraq troops first crossed the border. I asked to speak to Kuwaitis. I asked for an interview with Schwarzkopf, though I knew that would be a long shot. It never happened.

JIB gave me a list of "media ground rules." Most were reasonable. If allowed forward, I could not reveal "number of troops . . . number of aircraft . . . numbers regarding other equipment (e.g. artillery, tanks, radars, trucks, water, etc.) . . . information on intelligence collection activities to include targets, methods, results . . . information on special units, unique operations methodology/tactical (air ops, angles of attack)."

I agreed to abide by those rules. I wasn't in Saudi Arabia to analyze military strategy or preparedness. Military details weren't essential to my story dream list. I wanted to write about young men and women in uniform. I acknowledge that armies are entitled to secrecy on information that could jeopardize the lives of soldiers. I agreed to a provision that became critical after the 9/11 attacks and during the second Persian Gulf War when the United States interrogated terrorism suspects and other prisoners at Guantanamo, Abu Gharaib prison in Baghdad and other facilities. That provision banned disclosure of information I might learn about "intelligence collection activities to include targets, methods, results"

I had several opportunities to observe troop numbers and equipment in the field—pieces of information that I pledged not to write, and did not disclose. I never got information on intelligence activities other than deliberate and authorized leaks to me by U.S. military and civilian intelligence sources. They spoke to me, always on condition that I not identify them by name, title or country, with an apparent purpose—to serve their interests while tricking the Iraqis. I was told, for example, that Marines planned an amphibious landing on Iraq and Kuwaiti beaches. Another U.S. official in whom I had considerable confidence told me that the leaks about a Marine beachhead were designed to deceive Iraq into deploying troops into the reported landing areas and away from the Kuwait frontlines. Wrestling with this bundle of conflicting information, I decided I was not going to allow myself to be used to distribute information that I knew was wrong from unnamed and therefore unaccountable sources. So I sat on the information, using it later only to offer evidence in a story that truth is often the first casualty of war. I was aware other reporters were getting the same information and using it, even though they were skeptical. The leaked stories illustrated the use and abuse of the deep background briefing system so routine in Washington and wherever U.S. officials worked. I also surmised that if I had used the false information I could have been handed more of it.

Several times I asked the JIB people how they were coming with my requests for interviews. They told me there was a tremendous backlog of requests, but that they were working on mine. When I discussed this with other reporters, we concluded that we would be waiting a long time, possibly forever, for the JIB to say yes to any request.

I did what any reporter should do—go out and find the story. I called contacts I made during my previous tour in Dhahran. I went to bazaars where I occasionally ran into GIs on a brief respite from their desert encampments. I went to gathering places such as ice cream parlors, shopping areas and restaurants and asked loudly "anybody here from St. Louis?" I got a number of stories, including some involving soldiers from the *Post-Dispatch* readership area. I drove as close to the border as I could before being turned around at roadblocks.

While I was frustrated by my inability to get more stories, Lipman and others at the *Post-Dispatch* told me almost every day that my story that day had been fine and on page one.

One story I didn't get haunts me still, and I still second-guess myself on whether I did the right thing.

In Dhahran I met an American from near Gettysburg, Pennsylvania. I had often been to the national historic battlefield and visited my Great-Aunt Ann, a St. Joseph's nun assigned to a parish in nearby McSherrystown. The American and I initially talked about the Civil War battle. I told him I reported for the *Bulletin* before I became a *Post-Dispatch* reporter. He said he was a mechanic brought to Saudi Arabia by the Army. He told me how he repaired trucks and tanks damaged by desert sand. He said the military had new equipment and techniques for saving vehicles from the sand. The effect, he said, was to keep current vehicles running, and cut down the need for additional tanks and personnel carriers. Innovative hardware was saving the governments hundreds of thousands of dollars, he said.

In the war zone and in Washington, government officials talked about holding down the cost of the war. The president insisted that the war's cost would be minimized and shared among allies, thus sparing the U.S. taxpayer.

I decided that before I wrote the story of Pentagon thrift, even though based on a reliable source, I wanted to see the operation through my own eyes. The mechanic gave me the precise location of the retrofitting center. It was outside Dhahran, off a highway that Saudis drove on every day. I had driven by it several times on trips to other stories.

I drove to near the repair yard and walked over to look through the fence. I could see a lot of military vehicles and garages. I wasn't at the fence more than three minutes before U.S. soldiers with weapons showed up and asked me what I wanted. I was wearing my press credentials and said I was there to write a story about the facility. I was hauled inside, berated, threatened with arrest, and eventually released with a strict command never to come back. I pointed out that I hadn't gone inside the facility, but had only looked through a fence along a public highway. But while here, I said, let me look around at the good work you are doing. Not a chance, they said. Back in the JIB, I was summoned to a room where two officers complained that I tried for a story without permission from the JIB. The officers told me that if I ever did such a thing again, I'd be stripped of my credentials and put out of Saudi Arabia.

I had to make a decision. I had enough to write a story, and it would have made the Pentagon look pretty good—saving tax dollars. I couldn't see how it might jeopardize anyone other than managers of the JIB and their ability to maintain absolute control over the story. But suppose Mulvey and his aides were serious with their threat. I would be gone from Saudi Arabia. I had several story ideas in the works. The *Post-Dispatch* made a considerable outlay in getting me there and seemed happy with my work. If I were tossed, the *Post-Dispatch* would be without a reporter in the war zone. We were then pushing for Adams and Bill McClellan, an outstanding columnist from St. Louis, to join me. They might have been denied entry. So I did not go back to the repair facility or write the story.

*   *   *

As more troops arrived in Saudi Arabia to begin the war, and as more reporters showed up at the JIB, frustration grew in the press corps. I, at least, had contacts and experience to keep me busy producing stories. Many of the newly arrived reporters lacked these resources, but they were talented people anxious and ready to do their jobs for their publications. Joseph Albright of *Cox Newspapers* had the unenviable job of negotiating with the JIB on behalf of the reporters in Dhahran. He was the press pool coordinator, and in that capacity served as whipping boy for frustrated reporters and, his desire to the contrary, as shield for the JIB. I often saw Joe verbally attacked by fellow reporters in the JIB briefing room for not getting this or that reporter into the field. I knew from conversations with Joe and others that he was aggressively pushing for more pool assignments to the field, but beating his head against the steel wall of the military.

From Washington, I knew Joe, who came from a distinguished journalism family, to be an excellent reporter and manager for his newspaper. Before the war, I had social contact with Joe and his wife Madeleine, who was a college professor teaching history and foreign policy. One evening at a party in the home of Mike Waldman, a *Newsday* reporter, with whom I had worked at the *Bulletin* 20 years earlier, I chatted with Madeleine about journalism and events in Europe. The Albrights later divorced, and Madeleine became Secretary of State during the Clinton Administration.

As the number of frustrated reporters in Dhahran grew, Joe Albright's task worsened and he enlisted other reporters to help in the negotiations with Mulvey and the angry press. Nicholas Horrock, Washington bureau chief for *The Chicago Tribune*, an outwardly gruff man, signed on to help Albright and eventually replaced Joe as the print pool coordinator. Charles J. "Chuck" Lewis of *Hearst Newspapers* brought his Pentagon managerial experience to the negotiations. John Fialka, a highly-experienced military affairs reporter for *The Wall Street Journal*, served for a time during the buildup and air war as a print pool coordinator. At the start of the ground war, he was in a tank at the front with the Army's 3rd Armored Division as it attacked Iraqi ground forces fleeing Kuwait. From several long conversations with John during the air war, it was clear he intended to be where the action was when it really counted. John fully understood the risks and never shirked. I lacked the Pentagon experience and organizational clout that Fialka and Horrock brought to the post of pool coordinator. They recruited me to perform grunt work, such as distributing pool reports and advising arriving reporters on the mechanics of credentialing. Through my ties with the coordinators, I was privy to their pitched battles with Mulvey.

Mulvey and his associates read our stories closely. In a memo to Albright forwarded to me, Mulvey said U.S. reporters were revealing information that was of "great service to the enemy." That was a serious charge. Mulvey wanted us to remind all reporters "not to use 'near the Kuwait border' or any other specific locations or specific units. They can say 'with U. S. forces near the northern Saudi border' or 'with U.S. forces near Iraqi troops or Iraqi front lines.'" While I could not see any difference between saying I was with troops near the Kuwait border—as opposed to saying I was near the northern Saudi border—since the border was the same border, I saw no point in arguing the point with Mulvey or his JIB lieutenants. Even on a few occasions when I suspected I might be in Kuwait or Iraq, though didn't know for sure, my practice was to use locations such as "in the northern Saudi desert" or "in eastern Saudi Arabia."

Some pool coordinators had sympathy for Mulvey, who at times seemed uncomfortable, almost apologetic, in censoring copy or explaining why he was not able to do what he was supposed to do under the Pentagon-press agreement—get reporters into the field and respond to their requests. While I skirmished with Mulvey on numerous occasions, our exchanges never became personal, partly because I recognized that if I truly created enmity between us, I'd never get any cooperation from the JIB.

From the hotel in Dhahran, Mulvey had no authority to order officers in the field to accept reporters. When they told him that security and logistical problems made that impossible, Mulvey could hardly argue. Without the backing of Schwarzkopf, Mulvey was almost as much a special pleader as the reporters. Editors in Washington bombarded Cheney, Gen. Colin Powell, chairman of the Joint Chiefs of Staff, and Pentagon spokesman Pete Williams with pleas to intervene, but there is no evidence they did. Their obduracy didn't hurt their careers. Cheney became vice president and Williams became legal affairs correspondent for NBC News. Mulvey retired and became a consultant with a defense firm. Powell retired with full military honors and served as Secretary of State before settling into a comfortable private life. But his reputation was tarnished after he testified in February 2003 before the United Nations that Iraq seemed intent to use weapons of mass destruction. Critics suggested that Powell was not adequately skeptical of the information that he was stating as absolute fact. Powell later called it "painful" and conceded it would "always be part of my record."

In mid-January, all of us in Dhahran knew it was only a matter of days, if not hours, before the United States began bombing and strafing Iraqi targets in Baghdad and along the border. Calling a meeting of reporters in the JIB briefing room, Albright announced that under the deal between the Pentagon and news organizations, 14 combat press pools were to be organized to work in the field with the troops.

I was to be one of the combat correspondents in the field.

For the *Post-Dispatch* and me there was both an upside and downside in my accepting assignment as a pool correspondent. The upside was obvious. I would move into the action. Potentially I would get a firsthand view of the military operation. Albright and Horrock told me that as a combat correspondent I would primarily deal with health and medical stories. This was potentially a critical pool assignment. Much of the talk in the war zone was that Saddam and his Iraqi military would use poison gas against advancing Coalition troops. I was to be in the field in uniform at facilities where soldiers would be treated for gas or other wounds of war.

While this view of the war from an aid station or field hospital would be myopic, it would be better for me as a reporter than sitting in the Dhahran press room awaiting and rewriting reports from pool correspondents with the troops. I accepted the assignment.

I did so after considering the downside. On assignment at a health care station, I would get only that perspective on the war and there would be no guarantee that anything I wrote would get to St. Louis for publication.

Mulvey authorized me to get back into military uniform—nearly 30 years since I had stepped out of uniform after my Army tour of duty.

At a military supply depot much like the one I last visited in Fort Dix,—except that I didn't have to strip naked or salute—I was outfitted from head to toe with the gear of a front line combat soldier—with the exception of weapons. There would be no rifle, side arms, bayonet or grenades for me this time around. I would be armed as a journalist—typewriter, notebooks, pens, tape recorders and camera.

Other than weapons, I got the standard gear of a foot soldier—camouflage desert fatigues, a Kevlar helmet, a flak jacket, combat boots, gas mask, and a set of chemically coated coveralls to ward off a poison gas attack. I was given a special kit with a vial filled with antidote in case I was hit with a gas attack. I got a lesson on using the antidote and putting the chemical suit on in a hurry. My favorite piece of gear was a pair of night-vision goggles. I was delighted late one night in the desert to see a passing camel caravan.

I got a new identification card issued in accord with the Geneva Convention. It identified me as a non-combatant and was primarily for use, the JIB people said, if I fell into the hands of the Iraqi Army.

I lugged this gear to my room in the Royal Hotel, where late one night I was reading a book when sirens sounded in Dhahran. In civilian clothes, I grabbed my gas mask, dashed to my car and drove to the press center. The lights of Dhahran were turned off. Saudi police stopped me and asked where I was going. I told them and showed credentials. They ordered me to turn off my car lights and they allowed me to keep going. I navigated in the moonlight, driving through additional checkpoints, At the hotel, I ran to the JIB briefing room. On the TV in the briefing room, CNN, broadcasting out of Baghdad, showed explosions in the first-ever live action of the start of a war. Bernard Shaw, Peter Arnett and John Holliman described the beginning of Operation Desert Storm from suite 901 in the Al Rashid Hotel and I watched from a ballroom in the Dhahran Airport Hotel. It was eerie.

I called St. Louis and said I'd file soon. I called home and heard from Pat that she and three of our children, Katie, Jenny and Tim, were watching reports from Baghdad, the White House and Pentagon, and Dhahran. We had a crisis at home that she wanted me to help resolve. Katie, in her junior year at the College of Wooster in Wooster, Ohio, was scheduled to fly to Italy for a semester in Florence. There was news about rising anti-Americanism in Europe from opponents of the war. Some colleges were canceling their semester-abroad programs; some not. Should Katie go to Italy or return to Wooster?

As we talked, soldiers ran into the JIB briefing room shouting, "Incoming Scud." My call was abruptly cut off and I rushed with everyone else, including JIB officers and Saudi phone and fax operators, into the basement kitchen and food storage area. As directed by soldiers with weapons, I sat on the concrete floor, in front of a giant refrigerator, looking at the dishwashers. I put on my gas mask as ordered. There I and fellow journalists and others, including cooks and waiters, sat for more than an hour, mostly in silence, wondering if there would be a boom. The soldiers dashed about in frenzy, shouting at us to brace for a hit by one of Saddam's missiles. I had no idea how to get ready to be hit by a missile, but it was unnerving.

Finally, the siren sounded the all clear and I returned to the briefing room. I called St. Louis. My editors wanted a first-person account of what it was like to be in a war zone—albeit in an underground hotel kitchen. The *Post-Dispatch* was on deadline. It was after midnight in Dhahran but evening in St. Louis. You don't have time to write, they said, telling me to dictate. I obliged. Without a note, I told the story of

LAWRENCE M. O'ROURKE

my first awareness that the war had started, and revealing what it was like to sit in a gas mask on a concrete floor in a kitchen in Saudi Arabia wondering if we would be struck by an incoming Iraqi missile. I could hear my editor snatching my story paragraph by paragraph out of the reporter's typewriter in the St. Louis newsroom. The *Post-Dispatch* ran my story in larger than normal sized type across three columns on the front page—from their reporter sitting on the floor of a hotel kitchen. A bit of overplay, I thought, not exactly heroic journalism. Oh no, said Lipman, "it brought the war as a local story to St. Louis readers."

When I ended dictation to St. Louis, I called home again. From the perspective of those on Rosemary Street, my call ended a suspenseful couple of hours. As Pat put it, when we were talking earlier, CNN reported that a missile was coming into Dhahran, and then the phone went dead. They didn't know what had happened to the missile or me. Giving a cheerful report from my end, I wished them a good night. Katie did not go to Italy, but returned to Wooster. It was daylight in Dhahran and past deadline in St. Louis when I drove back to the Royal Hotel. The war was on.

* * *

Later that day, I got my first notice from the JIB to move closer to the fighting as a combat correspondent. Come dressed in your gear tonight to the JIB and you'll be escorted to the departure site. A friendly Marine sergeant in the JIB made an off-the-record recommendation—that I wear an article of clothing showing that I was not a soldier. He said that would be useful in any confrontation with enemy or friend. I surmise that I could have passed at first blush as an old soldier since I had a short haircut from a barbershop on the Dhahran waterfront and my gray hair wasn't evident. Though I was 53, too old to be an ordinary soldier in the field, I may not have looked it instantly in a uniform. I was trim and in good shape—the result of many years of distance running.

When I showed up at the JIB that night, I wore dungarees. Otherwise, I was in military gear with a two-day supply of meals ready to eat (abbreviated as MREs). I felt the weight of the unusual accessories. Under my desert cammy, I wore a tan fisherman's vest with many pockets I had filled with notebooks and pens, tape recorder and camera. I carried a typewriter.

Driven the short distance to the airport, I joined a group of men that I immediately recognized as roughly my age. They were officers of a civil affairs unit headed for Kuwait or Iraq. Their job, once the fighting in their sector had ended, was to move into a town and become its de facto mayor, police chief, water commissioner, school superintendent—any civilian task that needed to be done until the local Iraqi or Kuwaiti authorities were permitted to take those jobs. The Americans on the tarmac that night were mostly reserve officers—weekend warriors—whose real lives were as lawyer, lobbyist, government contractor, police officer, school principal, and other civilian jobs. Many lived in Northern Virginia and we talked about how our paths might have crossed back home. My first job as a combat pool correspondent was to accompany them to a position where they could be ready to move into a town in Iraq.

As we waited to board our aircraft, planes took off, loaded with bombs to drop on the Iraqis dug in along the border. It was very noisy as plane after plane climbed into the dark sky. We saw sites ready to launch Patriot missiles against incoming Iraqi missiles.

I boarded an Air Force C-130, taking a seat on canvas that stretched along the side of the aircraft. I tucked my typewriter between my legs. By turning my head, I could see through a cut in heavy padding that revealed a window. The ramp at the back of the plane was closed. A young man came in with directions. He said we had to be prepared in the event the plane was struck by "triple A"—artillery anti-aircraft flak fired by the Iraqis. This was my first indication on where we were going, somewhere, it appeared near or across the border. If we were hit, he said, there was a possibility we might have to jump from the aircraft. So we put on parachutes and got a short course on how to use them. He had my full attention as he explained that we would line up with a hook attached to a wire than ran down the plane to the side door through which we would jump. And once pushed through we would count to three—as I recall—before we pulled straps that opened the parachutes that would get us safely to the desert floor. I was handed a parachute and put it on with the help of the crew. I strapped myself onto the canvas seat. I was apprehensive. I didn't know the next stop.

With aircraft engines roaring around us, we were off. Once the lights of the airport and Dhahran disappeared, I saw nothing through the small portion of window behind me. I looked sporadically at the parachute wire. I wondered what the others were thinking. We didn't talk. About 45 minutes later, I felt us start to descend. Twisting my head, I saw blue lights flash on and off. We landed on a makeshift runway built on metal plates across the sand, the lights flashed once more, and there was darkness. The plane halted. I ran out the back ramp into a concrete bunker dug into the sand. I took off my parachute and returned it to the crew. The C-130's ramp closed and the plane immediately took off. From the bunker I heard explosions and saw flashes of light. I guessed that we were still in Saudi Arabia, several miles south of Iraq, and that noises and flashes of light were from U.S. bombing of Iraqi lines.

At that point, I asked myself for the first time, "O'Rourke, what are you doing here?" I remembered Lipman's words that I was insured for $1 million. I thought of what they were doing on Rosemary Street.

We were picked up in trucks, driven to a large tent in a field of tents and told to pick a bunk. I didn't sleep well, so it wasn't much of a disruption when we were alerted to an incoming Scud. I put on my gas mask and chem suit, and lowered myself into a bunker cut into the sand. I saw lights cross the sky, but had no idea if they were Scuds, Patriot missiles, airplanes, shooting stars, or exercises of imagination. A half hour later, it was back to the bunk, and after tossing and turning, I fell asleep.

Breakfast the next morning was better than I expected. I could preserve my MRE for another time. I joined the troops enjoying juice and coffee, eggs, sausage and pancakes, served in a tent with tables. When I got back to the tent, the civil affairs officers were gone. To where, I don't know. But I did think of them a few weeks later when a Scud missile hit a building in Dhahran that housed civil affairs officers, killing dozens of them. It was the largest single loss of life for Americans of the war. I could not help but think of our journey aboard the C-130 into the desert of northern Saudi Arabia.

I was taken that day to an Army field hospital for my first view of how the military prepared for the wounds of war.

*   *   *

I didn't see any killing or dead or wounded people in Saudi Arabia. My flight into the northern desert was as close as I got to action during the war. I tried to get closer when Iraqi troops invaded the Saudi border town of Khafji. I had earlier been further north than Khafji, to the town of Hafar al Batin, a crossroads near the Iraqi border. I spent a few nights in a dump of a motel in Hafar al Batin, interviewing soldiers passing through either to or from U.S. positions. The hotel was little more than a cell of cinderblocks with a mat for a bed, but you couldn't beat the location if it came to war on the border. There was even a telephone at the hotel that I used to call St. Louis.

Several reporters who disdained the pool system and were determined to get stories on their own—called "unilaterals" in the jargon—settled into Hafar and stored food and water. They awaited the start of the ground war when they intended to latch onto the military force heading into Kuwait and Iraq. In the interim they had to stay below the radar because the U.S. military was determined to keep them out as both a threat to Coalition security and as a violation of the pool plan orchestrated in Dhahran. The local Army commander said that reporters in Hafar would pose a "terrorist threat" and were subject to being treated as the enemy. I gave passing thought to holding up in Hafar, but decided it would make little sense. Big newsgathering organizations might be able to spare a reporter, but as the only *Post-Dispatch* reporter in the Persian Gulf Theater, it would have been inefficient to go the unilateral route.

On a road from Hafar to Dhahran, I passed close enough to Khafji so that when the Iraqis invaded it on Jan. 30 I knew where to find it. I drove north, but was stopped by military police more than 20 miles south of Khafji. I was not the first reporter turned around, nor the last. Some reporters got through. I knew that U.S. Marines had been killed and wounded in Khafji. Although Khafji was not militarily important, it would have been a political disaster for the United States and its allies to lose the first battle of the war. Schwarzkopf ordered his forces to use whatever it took to regain Khafji and minimize the significance of Iraq's temporary control of the town inside Saudi Arabia.

When the fighting in Khafji ended, I was taken by jeep to a Navy medical facility on the Gulf in Jubail. The wounded from Khafji were there. Joan Lowy of Scripps-Howard and a JIB escort officer joined me. He was a young reserve lieutenant from Washington State with a civilian job in public relations. At the Navy facility, an admiral awarded the Purple Heart to two young men wounded in the battle for Khafji. The two were in blue hospital pajamas in beds. When the brief medal ceremony ended, our escort officer turned to leave, but Joan and I insisted we talk to the wounded men.

Our escort listened as Navy Corpsman Clarence Conner of Hemit, California, talked about how he had been wounded. As Joan and I pressed Conner for details, he had a complaint. After he was shot, he laid in pain on the ground for more than three hours before a Medevac helicopter arrived to carry him back to the fleet medical facility. As Conner talked, our escort officer grew obviously agitated and urged us to end the interview and return to the JIB to file a story on the awarding of the Purple Hearts. Conner said that in great pain he pleaded for morphine and shouted, "hurry, hurry, hurry," until he was medicated and removed. Another corpsman told a comparable story.

I told the escort that we needed to talk to someone higher in the chain of command about the experience undergone by Conner and the delay in rescue. The escort left, and returned with the Navy commander of the fleet hospital. The commander blamed the delay on the Marine Corps, which ran the evacuation system. I asked to speak to someone in authority in the Marine Corps. The story had become much more than a report on a Purple Heart ceremony. Another Navy official arrived. He said that quick evacuation of battlefield wounded was a priority for Schwarzkopf. As an officer in Vietnam, Schwarzkopf complained about delays in evacuating his wounded troops.

I had a story that the military did not plan on. Back in Dhahran, I asked our escort for a contact to put the matter before Schwarzkopf. The escort replied he didn't think he could put me in touch in any way with Schwarzkopf. Instead, he suggested that I not write the story right away, but put the question to Schwarzkopf at his next briefing. Joan and I said we would write the story the way we saw fit.

After I handed the story to Mulvey's staff for clearance for general distribution as a pool report, a Mulvey aide asked that the story be held until the Marine Corps replied. When I pointed out that the military had been on notice for more than two hours what the story was going to say about the delayed evacuation, my discussion with JIB became more pointed. I said that if the JIB would not release the story, I would appeal immediately to Pentagon spokesman Pete Williams for his ruling—the agreed-upon procedure for dispute resolution. The JIB had a counterproposal: If Lowy and I would agree to tack on a statement by a Navy spokesman, the story would be cleared immediately and available to all reporters. Wanting to get all sides into the story, I agreed. With the addition, the story was cleared by the JIB and handed out. Joan and I sent our versions to our papers.

The story got considerable play in U.S. newspapers. It also got Schwarzkopf's attention. The day after the flap I was in a corridor in the JIB when a Marine who worked at the JIB came from the other direction. He grabbed me by the arm and pulled me into a side room.

"I know the problem you had yesterday about getting that story about Khafji approved," he said. "This morning we heard some more. When Schwarzkopf heard what happened, he called the Marines and really chewed ass. He said he didn't want any more stories like that and he certainly didn't want any more troops lying wounded and begging for evacuation for three hours. You know, I'm really not a JIB guy. I'm going to be back in the field someday and I certainly wouldn't want my troops and myself to wait three hours for evacuation."

With the possibility that my story benefited the troops, I've often thought that's one battle with the JIB I'd be glad to fight again.

*　*　*

During those weeks in uniform in the Persian Gulf, I wrote many medical stories that focused on what might happen if Saddam used gas against Americans or if the Iraqis and Coalition forces waged a protracted bloody ground battle. The long bombing campaign that started in January and lasted for six weeks rendered the Iraqis virtually impotent when it came to fighting on the ground. The ground war lasted only 100 hours and produced few Coalition casualties. As it turned out, if I had been in Saudi Arabia, Iraq or Kuwait during the ground war on pool assignment to cover medical matters, I would have had little to write about.

*　*　*

The story that hit me the most unfolded during a visit I made to a hospital in Central Saudi Arabia. The Army called it Medbase America.

I interviewed Army Surgeon Glenn Tripp, a pediatrician from Tacoma, Washington, a reservist called up as triage medical officer in what was designed to be a major treatment center for wounded fighters. The facility had an air strip and planes to fly the wounded to hospitals outside Saudi Arabia if the number of injured mounted.

I toured the facility, starting with landing pads where helicopters would bring the wounded. The great fear was that gas would contaminate the entire medical system, including the surgery and makeshift wards. During several days I spent at the base, I watched mock exercises in which helicopters landed with wounded. They were unloaded, stripped

LAWRENCE M. O'ROURKE

naked, doused with liquids to counteract poison gas, and wheeled to Tripp. It was all a rehearsal, but I got a sense of what could be.

Tripp said that as triage officer he would make a "rapid assessment of the level of urgency. That doesn't leave a lot of time to get to know the patient."

He carried a grease pencil. His responsibility, after a quick assessment, was to write a letter on the patient's forehead. He might write "E." That would not be good. Standing for "Expectant," it anticipated that the patient had a low likelihood of survival, no matter what medical intervention might be employed.

Tripp might write "D" for "Delayed." If casualties were high, the Ds could be bandaged, treated for pain and stabilized for later treatment.

Or Tripp could write "I" for "Immediate." Those marked immediate would be wheeled as quickly as possible into the surgery because they were in bad shape but had a decent chance to live.

"You go for the greater good for the greater number," Tripp said.

Working with Tripp as triage officer would be Duke Kimbrough, an emergency room physician in Austin, Texas. "I have never made an 'expectant' decision and I suspect it will be one of the hardest things I ever do in my life," Kimbrough told me.

As I followed the 100-hour ground war via television from the White House and Pentagon, I remembered my visit to Medbase America and was relieved they had no casualties to mark as expected to die.

*   *   *

I was not trapped into going to war. I could have told the *Post-Dispatch* that I did not wish to go, as I did when the *Bulletin* two decades earlier sounded me out on reporting from Vietnam. With a spouse and young children at home, I declined. But in 1990 I was ready, willing and able to go to the Persian Gulf for the *Post-Dispatch*.

My regret was that I didn't get better stories, but who did get good stories? I and other reporters lost our battle with the Pentagon to tell firsthand and in depth much of what happened in the Persian Gulf. And I believe there were other losers. They included the brave men and women in the field who barely got their story told. Above all the battle between the Bush Administration's leaders in the Pentagon and the press undermined the right of the American people to learn and assess the information they need and are entitled to in the exercise of their right to govern themselves as free people.

*   *   *

I stand by what I wrote on my return to the United States:

> "I left Saudi Arabia convinced that the pool system practiced there—set up, incidentally, by a committee that included editors and bureau chiefs working with the Pentagon—did not work. It must be re-examined in more peaceful circumstances.
>
> "As I sat on the C-141 flying out, and continued my journey aboard a more comfortable commercial airliner across the Atlantic, I daydreamed about what I left behind.
>
> "My thoughts on those long hours were dominated by faces of soldiers and the feelings and ideas they shared with me.
>
> "I looked at my watch and wondered what I would be doing if I were "in country" at that moment. I confess I had already built up a certain nostalgia for the place. I was glad to be coming home. But I was also glad to have been in Saudi Arabia and to have covered the war."

LAWRENCE M. O'ROURKE

CHAPTER 19

Too Much Stuff

I F I MAY interrupt the story, I'd like to pre-empt questions that any reasonable reader might ask. Starting with: How does he remember all this? The answer is multi-layered. It begins with my mother. But before I get to her, I need to explain the source of what constitutes the core of this work—the "stuff" of my newspaper career.

As a reporter, I collected stuff. It was stuff needed in my job. Whether it had intrinsic value, I leave to the reader. Since much of the stuff was government-issued paper, judgment on value may involve political considerations that I would not presume to influence. During my working years, I kept most of my stuff in my office in the National Press Building, but I brought a significant quantity home. I stuffed the stuff in filing cabinets in my basement office and under the attic eaves, wherever space could be found without creating either a collapse of the upper floor or an imminent fire hazard.

*   *   *

When I retired from newspapering and yielded my downtown office, I brought the office stuff to our home. With help from my friend Milton Jaques, an excellent reporter retired from the *Toledo Blade*, I moved office stuff to our Rosemary Street home, initially filling the garage to the point that there was hardly any room for the car or my collection of broken lawn mowers, other gardening utensils, rocking horse, and bicycles.

On her customary gracious days, Pat would ask, "What are you going to do with all that stuff?" Sometimes she would say, "You've got to get rid of that stuff." She might occasionally say, "That moldy stuff is making me sick." I knew the time would come when unless I got rid of the stuff; somebody would do it, not as gently as I might do it.

I was reluctant to yield the stuff until I used it to write this memoir. One barrier that seemed to keep me from the memoir was time given to other activities. After retirement from journalism, I put together a family history, practiced law, and occasionally taught and consulted. Also, I read more books, quite often Irish history and politics, than I did while a journalist. Through all those endeavors, naturally, I acquired more stuff.

An additional filing cabinet bought for stuff I wanted to keep in perpetuity quickly was filled with law case files. It's amazing how often I talked with clients and how much they had to tell me. In addition, retirement, as those who have done it know, brings on Social Security, Medicare and pension funds, not to mention appointments with doctors and purchases at drugstores. Most documents generated by those entities have a line, "Retain for your records." There was the suggestion that an Internal Revenue Service agent might pounce on me for delinquent record keeping. The bottom line was that I was ever more buried in stuff.

So what to do? I talked to other retired journalists. Those who tossed out their stuff because they moved to smaller quarters or simply to clean house were unhappy about it. Very few reported themselves cleansed or liberated by dumping their stuff. Bill Ringle told me that he once wanted to remember details of a great experience several years ago, but could not because he had thrown away his stuff. Dick Ryan said he put his stuff away because to go through it would take valuable time from golf. The only logical inference was that once he shot par consistently or abandoned the game altogether would he open his boxes of accumulations. Jim McCartney said he had his stuff, but ignored it.

I knew that politicians acquire even more stuff than journalists, but often have staffs that share the sorting-out. I was my sole staff member. George Arnold, an American University librarian, suggested that journalism or modern history departments might be interested in my stuff. On little more than a wing and a prayer, I wrote a note to Villanova, my alma mater. To my surprise and delight, after negotiations that involved an appraiser and university lawyers, I had a deal with the Villanova archives. They sent 60 cardboard boxes and said to use their account with United Parcel Service for shipping my stuff to the campus.

*   *   *

Among the first loads shipped were loose-leaf binders the White House gave to reporters who traveled overseas with the president. The binders' covers bore the presidential seal and other official-looking

LAWRENCE M. O'ROURKE

information about the trip. Contents included minute-to-minute schedules for the president and traveling party, and background notes on foreign leaders and issues to be discussed. We reporters were not given the sensitive information available to the president and top aides. But the more than 30 presidential travel briefing books I accumulated over the years contained enough information to make them worthwhile. Besides they looked neat, stacked one beside the other, covering presidents from Johnson to Clinton.

I sent Villanova boxes of material on Nixon's finances and impeachment. The Library of Congress undoubtedly had it, but I figured that my collection could save researchers hundreds of hours. I sent Villanova boxes of pool reports filed during the Persian Gulf War in 1990 and 1991. I brought home with me from Saudi Arabia what I believe was as complete a set of war pool reports as any human being without a truck could tote. The Pentagon and Villanova Archives are unique in storing a vantage point on the war.

Copies of presidential and congressional speeches, Supreme Court briefs and opinions in major cases, position papers from federal agencies and lobbyists, hundreds of memos and documents that touched on the management of the *Bulletin*—these were included in the boxes for Villanova.

*   *   *

Before boxing material, I reviewed it—a process that ate hundreds of hours. Looking for stuff for this memoir, I removed material that might reflect badly on any person who worked with me at the *Bulletin*. Not that there was much of it, but in the course of evaluating employees, and now and then fighting with editors I regarded as incompetent, I wrote intemperately, even harshly, and I saw no value in exposing such material.

From the perspective of this memoir, the most important items that went to Villanova were thousands of my notebooks over 40 years. Most of the notebooks contained words and phrases in my handwriting that were not easy to read, even by me, much less of importance, in my judgment. When I showed a professional archivist my stuff, I suggested that I toss the notebooks. He let me know sternly that the notebooks had to be preserved as "raw material" of history. I thought that was fantasy, but who was I to argue.

While it was easy to go through presidential briefing books and congressional documents on such historic moments as the Nixon impeachment and the civil rights debate, vetting notebooks was a tougher task.

My stuff was not only the product of Washington reporting. I had notes from the *Bulletin* in the 1950s and 1960s before I ever came to Washington. I had stuff from Army days and school days, including first-grade notebooks. Much of the old stuff was packed in boxes that we moved in 1980 from our Nevada Avenue house to our Rosemary Street house. I hadn't time to go through it for 40 years. When I finally had time, I found the stuff well preserved. Paper lasts longer than you might expect. (For the sake of brevity, I won't catalog files of basketball and baseball statistics, newspapers and magazines I cherished as historic records, and my collection of running supplies, including worn-out shoes, shirts that no longer came near to fitting, and tubes of dried-out shoe repair glue.)

*   *   *

As a reporter for four decades, I was a pack rat, gathering and storing most documents I touched. Washington and institutions of government generate enormous quantities of paper. A wise and normal human being would ignore most of it, and trash it. But not reporters. At least not this one. I may have been fundamentally flawed, but I regarded every piece of paper I laid my hands on as a potential story, if not now, then later. If I read the document, it had to be filed to verify what I wrote. If I didn't read it, I felt guilt that perhaps I should have and might need to at some point down the road. Perhaps this Catch-22 analysis had become a mental disease or condition, I had to admit.

*   *   *

As for accumulating paper and memories used in this memoir, I give credit to my mother. She was a great storyteller in communities that put great value on stories. She planted a love of stories in me. More than that, she encouraged me to write things down. I was ten years old when she gave me a diary. I have it still. The entries are those of a ten-year-old. On review, I have yet to find anything profound or insightful.

When I became a journalist at the *Bulletin*, Al Shrier, publicity man for the Temple University sports department, gave those on his long contact list a small red-covered annual diary, with a few lines for each day. Between Christmas and New Year's every year, I'd get an envelope with the little red book and a few friendly words from Al. I looked forward to the little red book and made a point of dropping Al a couple of sentences of thanks. There was just enough space in the little red book to jot down, even with the tiniest printing, no more than 15 to 20 words. I suspect that the book's designer and publisher sold it only as a daily appointment reminder. It wasn't meant to record history. It certainly wasn't intended as a diary. But I for several years used that little red book as a primary diary, developing a shorthand-style system that noted where I was, what I did, whom I saw, with an occasional personal reference. At the end of each year I put the little red book into a bureau. Over decades, I shaped several long rows of little red books. They have been invaluable in writing this memoir.

*　　*　　*

Not only did my mother write on average three letters a day to me while I was in the Army, she kept up a steady flow to Pat and me after we married in 1967. She wrote to our children. She wrote to relatives in Ireland. In 2008, John Coleman, an Irish cousin, brought to our home in Washington stacks of letters from my mother that the Irish relatives had saved. To some, that might confirm that there is in my family a genetic predisposition to accumulate. I was pleased to get those letters, so full of chirpy details of our lives. They are a treasure of family history. They tell the good with the bad, births and deaths, lost opportunities and dreams. After turning 90, my mother wrote few letters—a fact she talked about with sadness during our long final visits. "I have trouble seeing and I don't have the energy to write letters anymore," she said.

She brought out her stuff, including letters written a century ago by her mother, her grandfather's records from the Civil War, her prized collection of old newspapers and photographs, and hundreds of pieces of paper on which over a lifetime she jotted her thoughts. I still have my mother's stuff. It is not headed to any university archive. I don't intend to trash it. Perhaps future generations will find some use for it.

CHAPTER 20

Clinton and a New Direction

B ACK FROM WAR and a trip to Disney World to re-connect with family, it was time to chart a new direction. I had been away from White House reporting and 24/7 coverage of President George H.W. Bush for more than four months, and I enjoyed it. I liked freedom from the White House schedule and agenda. While covering the Persian Gulf War, my life was more under my control than it had been in Washington. Back home, I was always either at the White House or awaiting a call from it, or on a trip with the president.

In the Persian Gulf, though I railed at the military restrictions, I re-discovered the pleasure of often being the lone or one of few reporters on the story, as opposed to the pack journalism that increasingly was the case at the White House. As a competitive reporter, I welcomed the chance to go for targets of news opportunity that looked exclusive, or, at least, would allow me to develop better stories than my peers. It had become less satisfying for a writer at the White House serving a discrete audience of newspaper readers to compete with television broadcasters delivering news in snippets to millions.

Realistically, while reluctantly, I was forced to acknowledge that the era of the U.S. newspaper was on the down slope—as a consequence of many forces, helped by CNN's you-are-there coverage of the war. I was on the inevitable path of history—much as stagecoach haulers must have felt when they first saw railroads rolling across the prairie.

Yet I wanted to remain a newspaper reporter. I enlisted as a lifer in the business, but I realized that I didn't want to serve out my time at the White House.

* * *

While I had a job that many reporters coveted, I was weary of White House travel, the early check-ins, and the endless delays and hassle created by tightening security. A fourth trip with a president to London or Brussels or even Paris or Tokyo loses some excitement. With the high level of security now necessarily wrapping every president and virtually every other official, I found it ever more difficult to gain access to policymakers that I needed to write a good story. As protective as the U.S. Secret Service could be, foreign security agents had never seen me before, and had no discernible understanding of the White House press corps, so they limited access in ways that were often rude at best. I was unwilling to be pushed around by cops who didn't care that I wore a slew of White House-issued press credentials around my neck.

Foreign travel for the White House press increasingly involved hours in hotel ballrooms waiting for press secretaries with canned reports or pool reports from colleagues who were lucky that day to get out of the hotel and into the bubble of a motorcade and presidential movement. The appearances by press secretaries might be the only opportunity of the day to crack the protective shell in which world leaders, including the U.S. president, operated.

In bygone days of presidential travel to Europe, whenever I was not on a pool or the president was cloistered, I got up early, ran, ate a quick breakfast, and took off for half a day at a museum or historic site—anywhere that reminded me that here I was in this wonderful place on my publisher's money. A half-day in the Prado, the Hermitage or the Louvre refreshed the spirit. I would return to the hotel—and it was no problem to do so—to report and write my stories or columns. It was a lot of fun for free.

Perhaps the greatest argument for leaving the White House beat was the sense that the *Post-Dispatch* was under growing pressure to cut back spending on news coverage, with foreign travel at the top of the list. There's no doubt that my White House beat was the most expensive. P-D editors never complained to me about what I spent, but I felt a measure of regret that I was cleaning out the newsroom's budget, leaving little for other reporters, including those on local beats who wanted and needed occasional out-of-town visits to develop their skills and stories.

With these ideas percolating, I began to think about leaving the White House beat, embarking on a new direction that would force me to compete against other reporters, some of them already in beats I might want to explore. There would be no shortage of reporters at the *Post-Dispatch* who wanted to succeed me at the White House.

When I mentioned to friends that I was getting tired of White House reporting, they laughed and expressed envy at the job I had. I kept asking myself: are you in a mid-life crisis? Perhaps I was, but there was something more than that.

Stories from the White House were important and got splendid play in the paper, but they were stories that too often for my sense of competitiveness were matched and sometimes beaten by other reporters with even better sources than I had. Their sources were better usually because of the reach of their publication or because they had cut deals, tacitly if not overtly, with news sources. You could as a White House correspondent, especially if you were lazy or content, become little more than a stenographer, taking down the words of the artful officials who worked there, and massaging them a bit for your readers. You could look like a world-class journalist because you were writing stories that caught the world's attention. If you had a reputation as a friendly reporter, you could get a bigger share of leaks than the reporter like me who resisted the temptation to rely on the word of sources that had to be anonymous.

And I didn't hide my head in the sand. If a source wanted maximum impact on a leaked story, that source would go to *The New York Times* or *The Washington Post* or one of the networks, not *The St. Louis Post-Dispatch*.

Lest I come across as holier than thou, I concede that I cut my share of informal deals with sources. Such agreements were never spelled out. I believe that leaks to me came about mainly because sources respected my professionalism, including my accuracy and fairness. I did not play a political card. I worked with conservative Republicans and liberal Democrats. For example, I earned access to John Ehrlichman, Nixon' s domestic adviser. He leaked me several stories and filled in the background on others. Among Democrats, I got help from such figures as Ted Kennedy and Earl Pomeroy of North Dakota, as well as Speaker Richard Gephardt of St. Louis. I had a good working relationship with several Democratic and Republican staffers on Capitol Hill who could not be named in my stories because their bosses would not approve, or sometimes because they disagreed with their bosses. But these staffers leveled with me about policy implications and strategy. I had good sources in the Justice Department. I valued them because while sometimes they leaked me information, I mainly relied on them to explain calculations and implications of official acts, and to steer me away from wrong information.

LAWRENCE M. O'ROURKE

One of my techniques was to maintain contact with lobbyists, activists and think tanks. While they hoped I would write stories that reflected their point of view, I routinely mined them for information that I would thoroughly check out before printing. I didn't write based on rumor, but I aggressively pursued rumors. While I was open to the views of all, I never expressed a point of view in my column if I didn't believe it.

As a White House correspondent, I considered it my job to provide an honest and complete presentation of the administration's position, but to do more than parrot the officials or their spokespeople. Whenever possible, I put analysis, background, and alternatives into my stories. Decisions in government, as in life, are rarely simple. They involve upsides and downsides, certainty and risk. I did my best to spell all that out.

*   *   *

Other reporters in Washington, including many covering Congress, had a tendency to envy and deride White House correspondents. One major charge against White House correspondents was that we were spoon-fed and didn't dig. While there was some truth to that, I tried as the White House correspondent for three decades for the *Bulletin* and *Post-Dispatch* to do more than stenography. I tried to interpret events, to point at flaws in official arguments, to find out more than they were willing to tell us, and to bring in opposing views. That was good and important, and wasn't easy.

It was perhaps that I was so successful as a White House reporter that I wanted to see if I could do as well reporting in other areas. When I returned to the White House from the Persian Gulf in late March of 1991, I was 53 years old. If I wanted to do something else with my career, it was the right moment. Also, if I wanted to spend time with my family before I became more an absentee father than a presence in the home, it was time.

In the nearly three decades that I covered the White House, the beat changed. The White House press corps became more aggressive and skeptical during the Watergate scandal as a pair of young *Washington Post* police reporters uncovered the malfeasance of Nixon and his top aides. Television's beaming of White House events to the world 24 hours a day raised the profile of the White House correspondent, as I realized after family members, including those in England and Ireland, told me they saw me on TV.

Television appearances brought celebrity. Whenever I asked a question at a presidential news conference or appeared on C-Span on a call-in show or panel discussion, I'd get telephone calls and letters in much greater volume than when I wrote a story. Even my editors would say, "I saw you on television this morning" more often than they'd say, "That was a good story you wrote." I was skilled enough on television that a few times I was invited to try out for a job as a broadcast correspondent. But I was never enthralled with the idea of reducing a complicated story to a sound bite. In complaining about covering the news in seven-second bursts, I had a kinship with such TV luminaries as Tom Brokaw of NBC, Dan Rather of CBS, and Sam Donaldson of ABC—fine journalists and honorable men who had the special skills needed to star in the highly-competitive world of White House journalism. Nevertheless, they concluded that people who relied solely on them for news of the president were short-changed.

*　　*　　*

The White House beat brought me opportunities and excitement that I in my wildest dreams as a nightside reporter in Philadelphia in the 1950s could not even have dreamed about. The White House beat propelled me to more than 60 countries, a virtual guarantee of front page stories several times a week, prestige inside the newspaper and out in a way that won me frequent speaking invitations and plenty of stories to tell at weekend dinner parties, but too often I wasn't at the family's dining table during the week to tell the stories to my spouse and children. As a White House correspondent for major newspapers, I had a White House hard pass that got me into the West Wing whenever I wished to enter, a desk and telephone in the White House workspace, and the likelihood that White House staffers and agency officials would return my calls.

I surmised that if I did the job reasonably adequately, and I did it much better than that, I could be the *Post-Dispatch* White House correspondent as long as I wished and as long as the *Post-Dispatch* published or wanted White House coverage. I could envision being the *Post-Dispatch* correspondent until I got my first retirement check.

But even as I assessed my own ambitions and needs, I was nagged by concern over the *Post-Dispatch*. I saw signs that it was heading in the same direction as the *Philadelphia Bulletin*—into the graveyard of journalism history. Lipman told me not to worry about how much money I spent covering the Gulf War, and I spent a lot of it.

While Lipman and editor Bill Woo authorized me to spend what I needed to cover the war or the White House, the Pulitzer brothers, who controlled the voting trust, and Penniman, the publisher, spoke of shrinking profit margins and a bleak outlook. In the first quarter of 1991, as I returned from the Gulf, the company showed a net loss of $726,000. Lipman announced a freeze on travel for all others in the bureau and told me to look for domestic White House trips that I could skip. I felt sad and a bit worried as I wondered about a paper for which I had deep respect and affection.

The decline of the *Post-Dispatch* was especially tragic because the newspaper had a reputation for never stinting in either foreign or domestic coverage. But the excellent stories from trips by me and other fine reporters such as Jon Sawyer in the Washington Bureau did not draw more readers. Facing declining circulation, Woo put me on a committee to develop ways to increase circulation among young people and to draw more advertising in the *Post-Dispatch* targeted to them. After thinking about my children and their interests, I proposed that the *Post-Dispatch* hire a rock music critic and pay more attention to the music clubs along the Mississippi River. Certainly not many in the younger generation would be impressed by my stories on the overthrow of the Marcos government in the Philippines, the farm economy in Europe, or even the Persian Gulf War, considering the absence of a military draft. To young people of a certain age, rock music trumped politics and government. *Post-Dispatch* editors eventually hired a pop music critic. (Years later, when I thought about connecting with young people, I speculated that I might have well suggested that the paper hire a consumer electronics reporter rather than a music critic.)

Increasingly drawn into what I thought were management issues, I discussed with Woo and Lipman that they bring me to St. Louis as a newsroom executive. I said that if they made Lipman the executive editor I'd be glad to become managing editor. Perhaps they scoffed at this idea in the privacy of their offices, but Woo rejected the idea in his usual courtly style. "Some people are talent, some people are management," the gentlemanly Woo said. "Larry, you are talent. We can get management people more easily than we can get people with talent like yours." As flattering as this may have sounded, it was a No.

It wasn't the first time that my joining the Pulitzer Publishing Co. as an executive was raised. In 1986, when Pulitzer bought the then-*Chicago Southtown Economist* from Bruce Sagan, Lipman asked me if I'd like to move to Chicago as editor or publisher. The idea was not without charm. Not only did Pat come from Chicago and had her mother and other family members still there, but also we enjoyed the family vacation cottage in Grand Beach, Michigan, an hour's drive from Chicago's South Side. I gave passing thought to the idea that if I worked in Chicago, we could winterize the Grand Beach cottage and make frequent weekend trips there. But Pulitzer decided, correctly I believe, to keep the paper in the hands of editors far more familiar with the neighborhoods and journalism of Chicago than I could ever be.

* * *

Woo and Lipman clearly sensed that I was anxious to do something after the Persian Gulf War other than return to White House. Lipman called and offered possibilities. The *Post-Dispatch* would re-title me chief Washington correspondent and give me a second column a week. I would be free to take up or abandon White House coverage whenever I chose. They clearly went out of their way to keep me at Pulitzer Publishing. At no time was money for me an issue in these negotiations. After weeks of agonizing, I made the decision to pursue a new target of opportunity. The bottom line was that the *Post-Dispatch* was fading while some newspapers still had a fighting chance for survival. I did not want to go through the throes of another newspaper dying.

* * *

Through the newspaper grapevine, I learned that the McClatchy chain, based in Sacramento, California, with several dailies, starting with *The Sacramento Bee*, and a national news wire, was looking for an experienced Washington reporter to cover national politics and Congress. Not only would the McClatchy reporter have a larger audience than I had in St. Louis, but McClatchy looked to be on considerably sounder financial footing than the *Post-Dispatch*. It had the prosperous Central Valley of California to draw readers and advertisers. The valley's population was growing, whereas there was little prospect of a population increase in St. Louis.

I flew to Sacramento to meet Erwin Potts, the chief executive of McClatchy Newspapers. Potts, a reporter and editor before stepping into the corporate office, advocated quality journalism. With high hopes all around, I accepted McClatchy's offer as national political and congressional correspondent.

The Washington bureau had two national reporters—Leo Rennert, who managed the bureau, and Muriel Dobbin. Leo had a well-deserved reputation for taking complex issues such as arms control and presenting them to readers in lucid prose. Dobbin, a native of Scotland, had a marvelous ability to write feature stories. But the thrust of the McClatchy bureau was regional coverage to the chain's newspapers, and nobody did that better than McClatchy.

The regional reporters included David Whitney for *The Anchorage Daily News*, Michael Doyle for *The Fresno Bee* and *Modesto Bee*, Les Blumenthal for *The Tacoma News Tribune*, and Laura Mecoy for *The Sacramento Bee*.

*   *   *

Over a weekend in the summer of 1991, I dismantled my office at the *Post-Dispatch* and moved into my new office at McClatchy. The trend in journalism was to go local, to emphasize news and information as close to the readers' homes as possible. There was nothing revolutionary about this. The *Bulletin* wanted a story on every fire, every accident, every crime, and every death in the Greater Philadelphia area. For years, the formula worked. Going local, as newspaper consultants urged, was going back to roots.

Consistent with this approach, the mechanics of Washington seemed to matter less to McClatchy editors than the wheeling and dealing of the politicians closer to home. A top *Bee* editor cautioned me that newspaper readers in Eastern and Midwestern U.S. cities—the kind of people I served as a reporter for more than three decades—were older, had more leisure time to read, and had greater interest in the inside of national politics and Congress than the readers they were trying to attract in the Central Valley of California. David Favrot, a young editor in Sacramento, told me the paper's readers were "people whose greatest thrill in life is going to the Arco Arena and watching the tractor pull." I thought Favrot's description was so powerful and colorful that I wrote it down. Favrot left the *Bee* to work for a magazine.

I also found one big obvious difference between the *Bulletin* and *St. Louis Post-Dispatch* on one hand and the *Sacramento Bee* on another—time and distance. *Bee* editors had the luxury of three hours over the East. They could wait until late afternoon in California to see how stories developed. They could read over the wire how *The New York Times* played a story. What may have looked in the morning in Sacramento to be a good story by evening in California had been overtaken by a better story. The *Bee's* editors were quite right in picking stories that were important and appealed to their readers. But for me this often meant working on a story all day, only to have it tossed aside or pushed into the back of the paper as dusk settled over Sacramento. Many a late afternoon I'd get a call from Favrot that they wanted a front page story from me on an event that had taken place ten hours before and which I had not covered.

To my surprise after I had been with the chain for only a few months, McClatchy dispatched me in October 1991 to Madrid to cover an international conference on the Middle East attended by President George H.W. Bush, Soviet President Mikhail Gorbachev and leaders of Israel and key Arab nations. Here I was again as a White House correspondent.

*   *   *

As McClatchy's national political reporter, I reported on the battle inside the Republican Party as its conservative wing champion Patrick J. Buchanan tried to deny Bush a second-term. Indeed, Bush's own rhetoric burned him. While he had intoned, "read my lips, no new taxes," he had finally, out of necessity, cut a budget deal late in 1991 that included new taxes. I spent the usual weeks in New Hampshire and other primary states covering Bush's effort to retain his occupancy of the White House.

*   *   *

My national political assignment for McClatchy also entailed chasing the Democratic governor of Arkansas, Bill Clinton, from Iowa to New Hampshire to South Carolina to Florida and Pennsylvania. On a trip to Arkansas in 1991 to check out Clinton's record as governor, I picked up—and suppressed—information about Clinton. I've been haunted by the story ever since. From a very close friend and political associate of Clinton, still alive as this is written in 2011 and whom I even now do not want to identify, I got a prediction. If Clinton were elected president, this Clinton associate told me, the country would be in "for a series of bimbo eruptions the like of which we've never seen." In blunt terms, the Clinton associate said that Clinton could be an excellent president, but he had no self-control over his sexual desires and that sooner or later he would succumb to temptation in the White House and the country would be dragged through a terrible scandal.

I returned to Washington not knowing what to do with this information. It was clearly conjectural. I was working for a responsible newspaper chain, not a supermarket tabloid. I suspected McClatchy would not publish the story even if I put aside all my scruples and wrote it. But the paramount issue for me was not whether McClatchy would publish it, but whether I should write it or even discuss it in the first place. I felt that even to bounce the idea off other Clinton associates would be spreading the kind of rumor that would tarnish my reputation and violate my own integrity. My rule was never to write malicious gossip, and this, at this moment at least, was no more than malicious gossip, perhaps even fiction. Even in those cases that I knew of that involved sexual activity by politicians outside their marriages, I never published the information until it emerged through an arrest or a court case. I don't really know if I'm an old-fashioned conservative in these matters or a modern believer in the principle that what consenting adults do sexually is no one's business but their own. It's a different matter, of course, when children are involved and in cases of hypocrisy.

Home from Arkansas, I talked over with Pat my dilemma on what to do about the Clinton story. She offered wise counsel, but the decision to sit on the story was my own.

As the Clinton sex scandal developed later, I often thought about what I had known and wondered if I had written the story, would that have altered history. Let me add that I am confident that at least two other Washington political reporters had the same information and, like me, sat on it. If I had it to do over, I'd so it the same way.

* * *

Covering presidential campaign debates as I did for McClatchy was a challenge not easily undertaken or mastered. Working reporters on deadline rarely go to the room where the debate is held. They usually do not have time to wait until the end of the debate, return to the filing center, write and send the story, and meet the deadline. Reporters covering presidential campaign debates know that the story will lead the paper and that editors in home offices are waiting for it, often on delayed deadlines.

On many occasions, I needed to start writing before the debate ended, and that meant writing from notes and listening for new material simultaneously. With the clock ticking, it was necessary but difficult to recheck the accuracy of quotes. There was risk that I misheard a candidate. Major papers such as *The New York Times, The Washington Post* and *The Los Angeles Times* and the Associated Press didn't have this problem as severely as I did as a sole reporter. They had back-up reporters and transcribers verifying quotes. While I figured out my lead and searched through pages of notes to find the right quotes, the spin began in the filing center.

As I focused on the typewriter or later the small computer in front of me, spinners—aides to the candidates—and eventually even the candidates, wandered about, ready to explain why their candidate had won the debate. It would have been useful to listen to their conflicting reasoning, but there was little luxury for that. Before the evening was over, the debate sponsor passed out a transcript of the debate and I used that for the second or third version of my story to verify the accuracy of quotes and to add any good quote I missed in my first story. On a typical presidential debate story, I wrote at least three new leads and one or two total write-throughs.

In retrospect, all this was a great challenge and great fun, and I don't regret for the minute the chance to have done it many times over the years. Now as I listen to presidential debates, but don't have to write them, I think about what my lead would have been and what quotes I would have included.

*   *   *

When the Clinton sex stories broke in his second term, I was reporting for McClatchy on Capitol Hill and thus was right in the eye of the hurricane generated by the Republican majority in the House of

Representatives. In covering the Clinton impeachment proceedings, I had the distinction, I believe, of being the only reporter in U.S. history whose career included serving as lead writer for different newspapers on two sets of impeachments. My work for the *Bulletin* on Nixon was the first; my work on Clinton for McClatchy newspapers was the second.

From day one of the Clinton scandal, I regarded the House GOP's effort to throw Clinton out of office as payback for Watergate, an abuse of power, and destructive to the nation's political tradition. In the payback category, it was a Democratic-controlled House that came to the edge of impeaching Nixon, a situation he avoided when he resigned in disgrace. In the Clinton case, it was a Republican-controlled House attempting to even the score. There was a fundamental difference. Nixon abused the power of government. Clinton committed a private wrong.

Thanks to excellent Republican sources I developed in the offices of Speaker Newt Gingrich, House Majority Leader Richard Armey, and House Judiciary Committee Chairman Henry Hyde, as well as advocates for Clinton, I was able to compete on the Clinton impeachment story with *The New York Times, Washington Post, Los Angeles Times*, and other national newspapers. Rare was the day for months that I did not have a page one story in the McClatchy newspapers on the Clinton impeachment proceedings. When the Senate trial on Clinton started, I had an assigned seat in the Senate gallery. I watched very minute of action on the floor. After the proceeding closed for the day, I spent long periods on the phone calling people for more information and refining my story. As one of the McClatchy executives said when he handed me a bonus check after the trial ended in Clinton's acquittal, there was no need for any McClatchy paper to correct any fact I put into one of my stories. In mentioning Hyde, I'm reminded that he was among many senior Republicans who told me the effort to impeach Clinton was a bad idea that would not succeed and would come back to haunt the country and the Republican Party.

*   *   *

The second set of Congress v. White House stories that I enjoyed covering for McClatchy involved the shutdown of the federal government in 1995 by the Republican majority in the House led by Gingrich. Weeks before the shutdown, as Gingrich and Clinton played chicken, I predicted that, based on conversations with Gingrich and Armey, that the government would be shut down, even though it was clear to me that a majority of voters would be critical. I adjusted our family vacation and alerted my Washington Bureau colleagues to stand by to cover a major moment in U.S. political history.

Within minutes after the shutdown began, the Clinton Administration dramatically showed the need for a government to mail Social Security checks, patrol the border, keep national parks open, and perform the myriad of services Americans take for granted. After several bruising days, Gingrich capitulated. But his exercise of power undercut Republican chances in the 1996 election and ended his tenure as Speaker. The aspiring 1996 GOP presidential nominee, Sen. Bob Dole of Kansas, said Clinton's second term was assured the minute the government shutdown started. Unlike Gingrich, Dole never underestimated Clinton's political adroitness.

*   *   *

My recollection of Clinton's presidency would be incomplete without two personal stories.

The first: Pat and I were invited to the White House for the president's annual Christmas party for the press. We stood in line to exchange a few words with the president and first lady and to have our picture taken. It was ritualized. I did it many times. You shake hands with the president and first lady, you have a drink, you eat a few of the finger sandwiches and Christmas cookies and you look around to see who of your colleagues and other guests are there. Pat and I always strolled through the first floor to admire the tree and decorations. In some years the White House threw two parties for the press and two parties for Congress. That invariably produced speculation about who was on the A list and who was on the B list. I've always thought that presidents and first ladies must have loathed the approach of the Yuletide.

The receiving line at the Christmas party was quite an ordeal at best for any first couple, but little did we know what was going on within the Clinton household as Pat and I awaited our chat and picture with the Clintons. Pat has a unique memory of the event. "I was just about to shake President Clinton's hand when the button on my pink jacket fell to the floor. I bent to find it and pick it up. I found the button and straightened up to find the president holding out his hand to me. I had the button in my hand when I shook Clinton's hand. He never let on that anything was odd, but he definitely must have felt a lump in my hand. I certainly did. Then I turned to Hillary. I moved the button to the other hand and shook hands with her. We said a few words to each other. We all posed for the traditional photo and then Larry and I moved on to the food table.

"I had the sense right away that something was odd about the event and my quick conversations with the president and Hillary. They seemed very tight, very strained, not the way they usually appear at these events. I didn't think it was my button that caused it. But I didn't know what it was. I knew that something was odd. It was just a few days later that Clinton revealed publicly that he had the sexual encounter in the White House with Monica Lewinsky. I think that on this Christmas Party night Hillary knew about it and was furious at Bill, but she trying not to show it. The picture shows us all smiling."

Christmas parties often produced the unexpected and were therefore memorable. Some presidents give Christmas gifts. Lyndon Johnson gave me a tie clasp and a very nice note, and then there was a knock on my apartment door in Northeast Washington and a White House driver presented me with a box he said was a gift from the president. I opened the box and found several pounds of sausage and a note from LBJ saying that it was deer sausage from the Hill Country of Texas. They were the days that I ate sausage and I enjoyed it, as did colleagues at the office and my family in Philadelphia. Ronald Reagan gave White House reporters red and green knit hats. Jimmy Carter made a big fuss about serving alcohol in the White House. He ended the open bar and provided only beer and wine, and not much food. But that practice was reversed when Reagan arrived and provided a complete bar and tables laden with food. I was pleased when one year Nixon opened the party to children of invited reporters. One year I ran into the president and Mrs. Ford near the tree and was amazed at how much Mrs. Ford was able to talk about the tree and decorations.

*   *   *

But the Christmas party I most remember was in the late stages of the Clinton presidency after the GOP attempt to remove Clinton from office. There had been speculation in late fall that Clinton would not throw a party that year, so angry was he at the press and Congress. But the invitation arrived. It would be an unusual party, without a receiving line, but with food and drink served in a tent on the South Lawn. Instead of the receiving line, we were told the Clintons would mix and mingle under the tent, if they could break away from their duties elsewhere. It didn't take much analysis to understand that this was the Clintons' way to avoid having their pictures taken together with their guests and to have the flexibility to move along quickly, and not necessarily together.

The White House said that the president decided to hold the party under the tent so that he could accommodate a much larger crowd than could fit into the first floor of White House. One of Clinton's aides said that Pat and I should bring our children and my mother, then in her upper 80s, as well.

My mother came down from Philadelphia and on the night of the party, I drove Pat, Tim and my mother to a garage two blocks from the White House. It was a cold night. We walked toward the entrance to the East Wing of the White House. When I turned the corner off Pennsylvania Avenue I discovered that the line leading to the East Wing was very long, and once we got into it, I realized that it moved very slowly. It was more than an hour before we reached the Secret Service checkpoint. I asked my mother if she wanted to skip the event, but she gamely insisted that she would attend.

We finally entered and left our coats in the White House Theater, converted for the evening into a cloakroom. The White House said the tent would be heated and we wouldn't need coats. Before heading to the tent we checked out the tree and decorations. We decided that we should visit bathrooms before entering the tent. We went down stairs to the bathrooms. A Secret Service agent, spotting my mother, graciously suggested that she and I take the elevator up to the first floor rather than the stairs. When we got to the first floor, my mother spotted a chair and said she would sit there until Pat and Tim made it up the stairs. I turned away to look for Pat and Tim.

Not more than a minute later, a Secret Service agent tugged on my arm and said there was an emergency involving my mother. She was in the White House medical unit. When I got to the unit, my mother was prone on her back on a table with a medical team working over her. She kept insisting, "I'm fine. Let me up." The doctors told her to lie still and within minutes she was hooked up to monitors and an IV line. Spotting me in the corner watching all this in amazement, my mother said, "Larry, get me out of here." But before I could say a sword, the agent tugged me into another room.

Fifteen minutes later an ambulance arrived and my mother on a stretcher and I were put into the ambulance. With siren blazing, we arrived at the emergency room of George Washington Hospital. Along the way, my mother insisted that nothing was wrong with her. She said she had only sat on the chair at the White House to rest for a minute and somebody had interpreted that as an emergency. She said she protested to no avail as two people lifted her from the chair and carried her to the White House medical complex. Now she wanted to go home. At GW Hospital, the ER door opened and several people stepped out, one saying, "It's the White House case." With stunning efficiency, they wheeled her into an emergency room. A nurse stopped me and advised that I come back in 45 minutes. I walked to the cafeteria and had a cup of coffee.

When I got back, a nurse took me to a small office where I found a team of what I presumed were doctors sitting at a table. The event comes back to me as if on a newsreel. "Mr. O'Rourke," said one. "We have given every available test to your mother and have found nothing wrong with her. You may take her home." The doctor said my mother appeared to be a bit dehydrated. She told them that in preparing for the White House party she had neither eaten nor drunk during the day. I could have told them that. My mother had a curious aversion to using any bathroom but her own and I'm certain that she passed up eating and drinking that day to limit her use of the White House facilities.

While all this was going on, Pat and Tim had no idea where we were. When Pat couldn't find me in either the White House or the tent, she went to the Secret Service for help. "They told me to go outside the gate and wait for you," she said. "I knew that if I went outside the gate we would probably not be able to get back in." Finally, after Pat had asked everyone in sight if they had seen us, a Secret Service agent told her that we were at George Washington Hospital. Those were the days before cell phones, so neither of us had the ready means to reach one another.

I took my mother from the hospital to our home in a taxi. She said to me that she told every one of the medical people who had treated her—at the White House and at the hospital—that if they would only give her something to drink, she'd be fine in two minutes. At home that evening she poured water, juice and tea into her and wolfed down a couple of sandwiches. She was her usual self, talking away in detail about her escapade at the White House. It was no doubt a far more memorable White House Christmas Party for our family than a visit to the South Lawn tent would have been. Pat told us later that in the tent there were several bars, but no real food. She said she never saw either of the Clintons and there were no chairs.

The Clintons invited us to the White House for the Christmas Party the following year, but we did not attend. I didn't even suggest that my mother might want a return visit.

*　　*　　*

Even as McClatchy Newspapers faced the same trends—less money, less space, and fewer readers—as other papers, I had many opportunities during my final years at the chain to do important and quality work for readers.

As national political correspondent for McClatchy Newspapers, I covered the 2000 White House campaign in which George W. Bush triumphed over Al Gore. I spent several weeks during the campaign in Florida, writing that the key to the White House would go to the victor in that state. I was proved correct, though in a way I did not expect. On the afternoon of Election Day, I was leaked exit polls commissioned by the television networks and national campaigns. Based on interviews with people who had voted earlier in the day, the exit polls gave projected state-by-state percentages and an Electoral College vote tally that awarded Florida and thus the election to Gore. I drafted a story that Gore had been elected president but kept it in my computer awaiting confirmation after the polls closed and votes were counted.

As the results came in during the night, they followed the exit polls—except for Florida. With exit polls and early returns showing Gore slightly ahead in Florida, it appeared that Gore had won Florida and the presidency. But I wrote cautiously that the outcome was too close to call. I wrote half dozen stories through the night, every time avoiding any prediction on the ultimate outcome. Late in the night, as new returns from Florida's Panhandle were reported, Bush took the lead. The networks called the election for Bush. I finally wrote a story for the final editions of the California papers that came close to calling Bush the winner and suggesting that Gore was ready to concede. I based my story not only on what the networks, with their significant resources were saying, but on reports I was getting from the national committees and campaign offices.

LAWRENCE M. O'ROURKE

I was not alone in having trouble in figuring out how to write the election night story. McClatchy deadlines were past when at 4.15 in the morning in the east the networks began calling the election for Bush. To the surprise of those who relied on exit polls, Bush captured the White House by winning Florida. But there were problems with the Florida ballots, raising questions about who had won the presidency. In the McClatchy Washington Bureau, Mike Bold, the editor processing election copy, told me to pack a suitcase and get to Florida.

With the world looking on in wonderment about the next U.S. president, I spent weeks in Tallahassee, the epicenter for the legal debate over the flawed ballots, the central argument being whether there should be a complete recount. To see what a recount would mean, I drove across the state to West Palm Beach to a hall where disputed ballots were being checked out by hand. I watched the process. To me, the hall had the feel of a church. The heads of the people counting were bowed as if in prayer. They whispered. They passed documents as if they were exchanging passages of ancient scripture. They dutifully examined the ballots for flaws such as hanging, dimpled and pregnant chads. Of course, it was a holy moment in our Constitutional system—as citizens made decisions that would establish the next president. McClatchy newspapers ran my story on page one.

I wrote of the courtroom arguments by the Gore camp to recount the ballots and the response of the Bush camp to end the counting and declare Bush the winner. As the case reached the U.S. Supreme Court, I was back in Washington for the oral argument and I teamed under deadline pressure in reporting on December 12 the late-night decision by the high court to end the counting, and thus make Bush the next president. I wrote the story of Gore's announcement that he would end the fight.

*　　*　　*

Nine months into Bush's first year as president, I wrote stories that I wished I had never had to write. Setting aside emotion, but knowing that American life had changed for the worse, I reported on Sept. 11, 2001 as terrorists hijacked airplanes and crashed them into the Twin Towers in lower Manhattan, the Pentagon and a field in Somerset County, Pennsylvania. On that horrific 9/11 morning, I was at home after a long run eating breakfast while reading the morning newspaper when my son-in-law, Simon Tiffen, called me from Chicago and alerted me to the news on TV. I quickly commandeered a taxi and spent hours looking at the damage to the Pentagon and at the security measures instituted at the Capitol, the White House, the airports and the mass transit system. In the following months, I covered the creation of the Department of Homeland Security and watched Congress and the political system adjust to the terror that had been brought to our nation. Like every other reporter on Capitol Hill, as well as staff members and even members of Congress, and eventually the re-admitted public, I began to experience the new security steps established in the aftermath of 9/11. Gone forever were the days when I, recognized by the guards, could walk in and out of the White House and Capitol without showing a credential.

My assignments for McClatchy later took me with members of Congress deep into the hole in the ground left by one of the collapsed towers. There I stood as congressional leaders vowed to never let it happen again. I made repeat trips to the Pennsylvania field, where stands a memorial to private citizens who courageously resisted the terrorists aboard their plane and prevented the crashing of the hijacked airliner into the Capitol or White House.

*   *   *

As the nation regained stability and as political and legislative business returned to the new normal, I covered Congress and politics for the McClatchy chain. I wrote scores of stories on Bush's failed attempt to transform Social Security from a government-based entitlement to a program that would premise benefits on the rise and fall of the stock market. I covered every step of Bush's initiative to provide a prescription drug benefit to Medicare beneficiaries.

I had the opportunity while at McClatchy to cover Hillary Clinton's successful campaign to become the Democratic senator from New York. I was there when she announced her candidacy in Purchase, N.Y. I walked with her through the woods during a campaign stop on a lovely crisp morning in Jamestown. I watched her outdebate her Republican opponent in Buffalo, and barnstorm through Brooklyn and Long Island.

In frequent visits to Illinois, I covered the progression of the young community organizer and backbench state legislator with the curious name of Barack Obama from the South side of Chicago into the

LAWRENCE M. O'ROURKE

Senate and into the White House as the nation's first African-American president. At the Democratic National Convention in Boston, I was in the convention hall when Obama electrified Democrats and the nation with a keynote speech. The next day I had lunch with him. He modestly brushed off suggestions that he was destined for Hail to the Chief.

From Virginia, I wrote about Oliver H. North's effort to win election to the Senate from Virginia. It was one of the first modern battles between Republican centrists and Republican far-right conservatives, a preview of the coming power of the "tea party." From Pennsylvania, I wrote about liberal Republican Sen. Arlen's Specter successful battle to fend off a challenge from a GOP right-winner Pat Toomey. On the next Senate go-around in Pennsylvania Specter switched parties and Toomey was elected. In Colorado, I covered the election of a Latino to the Senate and in Michigan I covered the victory of the old House Democratic bull, John Dingle, in a furious battle with a liberal Democrat pressing to move her party further to the left. These and others were wonderful stories—the sort I did for 40 years with joy.

Also for McClatchy, In the New Orleans suburb of Metairie, I had a long interview with David Duke, the former Grand Wizard of the Ku Klux Klan running to be governor of Louisiana against Democrat Edwin Edwards. The Republican Party repudiated Duke, who said his constituency was the "white majority." Duke told me during the interview in his office that he favored separation of the races, but insisted, "We're not racists. We believe in equal rights for everybody." When I pressed him on how he managed to hold such apparently opposite points of view, he described me as a Northern liberal reporter who didn't understand the South. He said I was one of the "Northern media attacking his Christian faith." While Duke lost with 38.8 percent of the overall vote, he said he actually won the election because he got more than 50 percent of the white vote. In an interview I had with the Democratic candidate, Edwards told me that Duke was a "merchant of hate and bigotry and a master of deceit." Edwards, a four-term governor of Louisiana who struck me during the interview as a sleazy quintessential good old boy politician, also had character flaws. He was convicted of federal racketeering charges and spent nearly nine years in prison. I had a great time in that campaign, not only because of the foibles of the candidates and the great eating in New Orleans, but for hours of door-to-door interviews in the Bayou with salt-of-the-earth people who didn't at all object to a Yankee reporter.

Being in New Orleans as a reporter, or as a tourist, I have found over the years is a great deal of fun. In 2002, I was in the Crescent City covering the Senate campaign between incumbent Democrat Mary Landrieu and Republican challenger Suzanne Terrell, when both candidates said they'd take the night off. Liberated from campaign coverage, I went to a casino in downtown New Orleans. I am not a gambler, but I bought a $25 roll of quarters and headed to the slot machine. I put my first quarter in, pulled the handle, and out came $30 in quarters. Figuring my luck had been exhausted, I pocketed the winnings and the roll of purchased quarters minus one, and left. I paid for admission to the wonderful D-Day museum in New Orleans in quarters and spent others on coffee and beignets at the picturesque Cafe du Monde in the French Quarter.

*　　*　　*

On a grimmer note, from Capitol Hill, the Pentagon and the White House, I reported on the war initiated by Bush to oust Saddam Hussein as leader of Iraq. I covered the hearings at which Bush Administration officials insisted that Saddam Hussein had weapons of mass destruction that he intended to use against the United States and its allies. I covered later appearances at which the same officials tried to explain why they had been wrong.

*　　*　　*

Though my editors and readers at McClatchy's newspapers may not have had the same level of interest in Ireland as I did, I had a number of stories published on Irish topics. In Washington, I wrote stories based on interviews with several Irish politicians including Taoiseachs (Prime Ministers) Charles Haughey and John Bruton and Foreign Minister Dick Spring. I covered a conference Clinton organized of Irish-American business executives and investors to convince them to put more U.S. green into Ireland to encourage the peace process. I reported from Ireland as citizens of both Northern Ireland and the Republic voted for the Good Friday Agreement of 1998 that put both sides of the border on record in support of a peaceful political resolution of their opposing loyalties.

One night shortly before the treaty was announced. I was in a pub in Kilmallock in County Limerick and I got into what I thought was a friendly discussion of the difficulties political leaders have in reaching a deal that may not be satisfactory to all their constituents. The week before I had been in Belfast and Dublin. British, Irish and U.S. officials briefed me on background on progress toward an agreement. I came away from those briefings with a high expectation that something could be worked out. I said so to the big fellow next to me at the bar, adding that David Trimble, the political leader of the Northern Ireland Protestant majority, was to be praised for sitting down with Sinn Fein leader Gerry Adams, and the main political spokesman for the Catholic minority. My suggestion that Trimble had political hurdles he had to overcome was a bridge too far for the Irishman on the next barstool in Kilmallock.

"Let's go outside and talk about this," he said, in a manner I did not consider friendly. Though I was half way through my first pint of Guinness, I suspected that going outside with the lad might be detrimental to my appearance and limbs.

Fortunately for me, the pub owner had been listening and recognized the precariousness of my situation. His two sons, rugby-sized lads, came from the back room and gently led my companion to another place in the pub. Thus I learned that in 1998 it was unwise for a visiting American, at least this visiting American, to venture too far into Irish politics and history in the West or Ireland.

But I have the consolation that I was right in anticipating a deal. Within a week, thanks to the brilliant and high-stakes leadership of Trimble and John Hume of the Social Democratic and Labor Party, and with concessions from Adams, a deal was cut to establish an "exclusively peaceful and democratic" framework for power sharing in Northern Ireland. The deal had significant contributions from former Senate Majority Leader George Mitchell who spearheaded negotiations, British Prime Minister Tony Blair, Clinton, and Irish Taoiseach Bertie Ahern. Trimble and Hume were awarded the Nobel Peace Prize in 1998.

But my work for McClatchy was not all politics.

I was there on the Hill in the Rayburn House Office Building when some of baseball's greatest hitters—such heroes of mine as Mark McGwire, Sammy Sosa, and Rafael Palmeiro—denied under oath before a congressional committee on March 18, 2005 that they ever used steroids—denials later refuted, modified, and withdrawn.

Though newspapers were losing circulation and advertising, and laying off Washington reporters, I was fortunate enough to avoid the worst of it, and had a wonderful time covering some of the most important events of the era.

CHAPTER 21

Transition and Reflection

I LEFT THE newspaper business in October 2005, a few years earlier than I hoped. I was 67 and planned to work until I was 70 because I loved what I did—reporting on government, the people who manage it and the wannabees. But declining energy and failing health spurred me to seek a less physically strenuous and stressful lifestyle. I meant it when I told colleagues that I felt as good as ever while reporting news until 11 at night, but found it harder to work beyond that to 1 or 2 in the morning—McClatchy West Coast deadlines for big stories. Besides, there were a lot of new things I wanted to try.

For someone as committed as I was to quality journalism, I left at the right time. Newspapers were struggling for survival. The decline in circulation and advertising in U.S. daily newspapers was underway and speeding up. Many newspapers had stopped hiring reporters and widespread buyouts and layoffs to reduce staffs were underway. There was still plenty of superb journalism, but the number of good, experienced reporters watching and writing about government and politics from Washington—my way of life—was sharply down as newspapers revamped to put more emphasis on local news and on entertainment, from sports pages to movies to features.

It was understood within the business that, on big breaking national and international stories, newspapers could not keep up in speed with the CNN, MSNBC and Fox cable networks and the commercial networks. Many newspapers were backing away from giving resources and space to breaking news on the theory that people had already seen it live on television, and weren't willing to read a print version 12 hours later. "Don't duplicate the wires," became a motto for editors. In short, if you're a writer in Washington for a regional newspaper, don't write the story if the best you can do is to copy the wire services and what the TV reported. The approach made sense. Believing they had to advance the story, newspapers moved more into analysis, a factor that widened the gap between many newspapers and some readers who didn't like the analysis offered by the newspaper. As I knew from experience, there was no way to please every reader, and displeased readers were poised to complain. Reports that newspapers were biased to the left increased, with impetus from the right. While I believe that most national political reporters believe that government must be the "safety net" for the poor, children, the ill and others unable to care for themselves—as Reagan contended—I rarely in all my years as a political reporter saw any political reporter set out to slant a story to the left. I know I never did.

With pride, I can say that no national politician I ever covered—and that includes Nixon, Ford, Reagan and Bush—ever accused me of writing a biased story.

My columns, of course, reflect my beliefs. They were marked in the newspaper as opinion. I managed to observe the line between columns with opinion and news stories that were fair and accurate.

As I left the business, my view was that the greatest damage to print journalism stemmed from the loss of young readers who began to get the news and information they wanted—and often they were too busy, distracted or preoccupied to want government and political news—from their alternative electronic sources—online, blogs and tweets and the social networks. Advertisers recognized that these young people, at an age they looked to buy houses, furniture, cars and diapers, were not reading newspapers in the same numbers as their parents had the generation before. As advertisers looked for customers, they moved their dollars to where the potential customers were—and away from run-of-the-press space in newspapers.

The loss of younger readers created a dilemma for newspaper editors. They simultaneously tried to include content of greater interest to younger people while trying to retain older readers—all at a time of a diminishing news hole. Young people were not seemingly as interested as older people in government policy and politics—the goods in trade of Washington correspondents such as myself.

Though concerned about the future of newspapers, I retired from journalism proud of my record, satisfied with the career path I chose more a half-century ago, and exultant in the memory of my experiences. As a young man, I wanted to make a contribution to my country, and I did. I wanted adventure, and I found it. I wanted challenge and excitement, and I got it.

*   *   *

In my final years in the business, my stories appeared in a growing number of newspapers as McClatchy bought publications in the Carolinas and Minneapolis.

Like other newspaper organizations, the McClatchy chain was approaching the beginning of its decline—a decline not caused by anything journalists did wrong, but rather by the rapid acceleration in the way Americans get the news. Even as skilled a journalist as Howard Weaver, an executive with McClatchy who wanted to make the chain's newspapers great, underestimated the transformation. In a meeting in Washington, Weaver said that newspapers would survive indefinitely because Americans are like primates—they want to hold something in their hands. Sadly, Weaver was wrong about young readers wanting to hold broadsheet newspapers. Not long after my departure, McClatchy reduced its editorial workforce through buyouts and refusal to fill job vacancies. It froze salaries, mandated unpaid days off, stopped contributing to retirement funds, curtailed travel and tried such unorthodox steps as hiring editors in India who through technology could work for less than homegrown editors. McClatchy found out, to the disappointment of Gary Pruitt, its top executive, that rising revenue from on-line services didn't make up lost newspaper revenue.

*   *   *

In planning to work until age 70, I intended to do what I enjoyed doing—and doing well. Seventy was an arbitrary age, but one I locked in on during my 60s. Then came a series of events starting in 2003 that left me no choice but to call it a career.

The events began with my mother's rapid decline—at 92, she was suffering physically, emotionally and mentally. She hated the nursing home where my brother and I placed her when she became unable to live alone. To offer what help I could, I began to travel every weekend to Philadelphia—a consumption of time and energy that began to sap my strength and emotions. Her condition rapidly deteriorated in the early summer of 2003 and in August she died. We celebrated her life and three weeks later a close family member called and said he had been diagnosed with prostate cancer and needed to undergo surgery quickly. His diagnosis reminded me that I had not had a prostate cancer screening for three

LAWRENCE M. O'ROURKE

years—a foolish mistake explained only because I felt wonderful and was running more than 50 miles a week. Alarmed by my relative's illness, I took the tests, and in September, just a month after my mother's death, was diagnosed with prostate cancer, had surgery to remove the diseased organ, and spent a month recovering at home—when I had time to read and play music, more so than at any previous time in my life. The time away from the office and the grind of daily journalism got me thinking that just maybe it was time to do something else.

In January 2004, three months after the cancer surgery, with the permission of my doctors and the encouragement of my editors, I went to Michigan to cover that state's primary. I ran around as if I were 30 years younger, driving hundreds of miles some days to political events, staying up late at night and rising early in the morning, writing and eating on the run as I had for 40 years. I also had a troublesome growth on my knee that a dermatologist discovered was a MRSA infection.

With Michigan behind me, I was home in mid-February 2004 getting ready to head to another primary state when I suffered the heart attack at a Gridiron rehearsal—perhaps the consequence, the cardiologist said, of inflammation of my coronary arteries linked to the inflammation on my knee. Whatever the cause, I underwent two emergency procedures to clean out my arteries and open them with stents. The cardiologist said I should take it easy for a couple of months.

I was determined to be in harness for the 2004 presidential campaign, but I knew that I could not attempt to chase candidates with the wild abandon of previous years. I attended the Democratic National Convention in Boston and the Republican National Convention in New York City, writing daily stories that included covering street demonstrations and attending early-morning breakfasts and meeting late-night deadlines. They were fun as usual, but I knew they were my final national political conventions. When I stood on the floor of the convention with my son Chris on the final night of the GOP convention that re-nominated Bush, I said to myself, it was a great run and I can't think of anyway I'd have done it differently.

*   *   *

Once I decided right after the presidential election of 2004 to leave reporting in 2005, I set out to figure what I would do next. Not given to leaving things to chance and determined not to just relax for an extended period, I enlisted as a pro bono *guardian ad litem* in the Washington office of Lawyers for Children America, a national organization committed to providing legal representation to abused and neglected children.

What I found most compelling about this practice of law was the human element—these were real children and real parents, not characters in a TV series or in the pages of novels.

I also took cases of poor adults who sought help from non-profit organizations, including the volunteer legal service office of the Roman Catholic Archdiocese of Washington.

*　　*　　*

When I called it a career in October 2005, newspapers were in significant decline—growing slimmer, with fewer reporters, and searching for different content. It mattered to me not so such that the journalism I knew was so fragile and that prosperous newspapers were but a fond memory for the old-timers, but that their loss could—and in my judgment likely would—have a profound effect on our system of self-government. I believe that newspapers have the protection of the First Amendment to the Constitution primarily so that they may fully participate without fear of reprisal in the political debates essential to self-government. As the Framers saw it in Philadelphia nearly two and a half centuries ago, newspapers were to be the lead medium by which citizens would be informed about the affairs of their government and the actions of those freely chosen as leaders of the government. There was an implicit understanding that newspapers were to be one of the watchdogs of government—free without fear of government to criticize, to question, to challenge, to investigate and to offer ideas and opinions that could well be unwelcome by government. Newspapers were to be governed by the people—through the marketplace—and protected from the government.

Through the years, newspapers as a group have performed well the myriad tasks given to them. Some have not done it well. Some protected government when government was at its worst. Some risked all to expose government and those vested with its authority.

The exercise by newspapers of their fundamental responsibilities—whether at the national, state or local levels—was understandably weakened by the loss of revenue that accompanied the decline in readership and advertising. For newspapers, the more labor intensive the better; for society, the more reporters watching government, the better as a whole will be the job done.

While I am confident that we will always have quality newspapers, I believe that never again will this nation have as many good, experienced newspaper reporters gathering, analyzing and writing information on government and politics. The loss in numbers of reporters will be significant because it means that more members of Congress and federal officials have a chance of having their deeds and misdeeds escape public attention. But there may be ways to remedy that—a more vigorous two-party system, combinations of investigative reporters, a movement of television reporting away from the visual to the factual, a focusing of bloggers on substance and away from gossip, and a commitment to accuracy.

What disturbs me most is the electronic media's emphasis on setting out to generate confrontation, to the point of making political disagreements personal and often leading to more shouts and insults than rational debate. I believe that this new journalism of the angry shout contributes to the notion that political positions are irreconcilable and that deals are traitorous to personal beliefs.

Politics is, or should be, the art of the possible. The United States was created on deals—starting with the insistence on a separation of powers theory that no one branch of government would have too much power. The creation of a bicameral legislature was built on a deal—that no state would have the power through the size of its delegation to heavy-handedly impose its will on a state with a smaller population. It was a deal that the House of Representatives, the chamber closest to the people, would initiate legislation dealing with spending and taxation, and the Senate, at that time more beholden to the states, would be the saucer that cooled the passions of the "people' s House."

What I fear most about the loss of print newspapers is the destruction of the notion of a deal at the end of vigorous debate. Newspapers, if they do their job correctly, tell us how political decisions are choices among competing interests, usually all legitimate. I do not know a single event in my 40 years in which progress was not built on a trade-off of interests. While such trade-offs, one can hope, are always for the common good and help create a more perfect union, political choices create winners and losers.

*　*　*

Not to be alarmist or sound like a Luddite, but I fear that the loss of newspapers will force significant changes in democracy, as we know it. I do not think that the loss of newspapers will end democracy. But it will make democracy different, and I think that the differences are potentially significant and need to be understood.

The loss of newspapers puts us at greater risk of extreme political rhetoric by elected government officials who are charged with making critically necessary decisions in the national interest, not in partisan interest. I welcome a good lively aggressive partisan debate, but in the end, our leaders of divided government must cut deals. And it becomes harder, if not close to impossible, when those who must sign on to these deals are locked into positions by their own inflammatory rhetoric. The risk for politicians also is that the deals they must eventually cut are ridiculed by those who do not bear the responsibility for government, with the result that cynicism abounds and public confidence in government and the political system falters.

* * *

I think that the loss of newspapers removes from the self-government process a mechanism for a slower and more reasoned consideration by the public of the choices involved in government and political decisions. Newspapers, by their nature, slow down the mind because they force readers into different thinking processes than viewers who see arguments in flashed seven-second sound bites. I readily grant that I believe that millions of Americans do not want to be drawn into the decision-making process. Millions of Americans are content, if not bored, even by seven-second sound bites. For whatever reason—cynicism, distrust, boredom, laziness, or distraction—they are not interested in affairs of state. But I continue to believe in the U.S. system of self-government and hold fast to the principle that "we the people" have the best chance ever in history of getting things right and holding our nation together.

* * *

The loss of newspapers erodes many of the small but vital local keystones on which our communities and our country have been built. We risk being less exposed to problems within our own communities.

LAWRENCE M. O'ROURKE

With the dialogue depleted of common information on which we can discuss choices, we abandon the political playing field to individuals who can plead their cases and secure special access because they are special interests with unique knowledge and the money to buy access. That exposes us to the risk of being the best government that money can buy—because without newspaper reporters asking questions, how can we be sure we are getting the information we need if we are to assess government decisions. To this I would add, that among those not mourning the demise of newspapers are well-heeled special interests that see less to fear about exposure of cozy insider trading with friendly politicians.

*   *   *

What I tried to do as a journalist for 40 years—sometimes succeeding, sometimes not—was to present the choices facing government and those charged with governing or trying to win that right, responsibility, and power. It was my hope in writing my stories that readers would slow down a bit at reading about these choices, and realize that the simple answer is not the only answer or not even the best answer. I hoped to give information so that readers might be at least respectful, even in disagreement, with those who prefer different choices. Politics, like life, is a series of choices, and it has been my goal as a journalist to shine some light on the choices. I feel a tremendous sense of accomplishment that I contributed to my country as a journalist during the golden age of American print journalism, and had a good time doing it.

INDEX

DeCurcio, Nick, 35
Department of Education, 266-67,
    272-74, 276-77, 282, 293
Department of Education Weekly, 274,
    289
Department of Homeland Security,
    406
Derwinski, Ed, 343
DeSimone, Louis, 42
de Valera, Eamon, 180
Devil's Tower, 98
Devine, Danny, 29, 35
Devine, E. J. "Barney," 50-53
Dhahran, 362
Dickinson, William "Bill" B., 16,
    100-106, 143, 151-52
Dietz, Jerry, 52, 97
Dilworth, Richardson, 68, 118
Dingle, John, 407
Dirksen, Everett McKinley, 131, 230
Dobbin, Muriel, 395
Dodd, Thomas J., 138
Dole, Bob, 246, 250, 326-27, 329, 400
Dole, Elizabeth "Liddy," 349
Donaldson, Sam, 305, 392
Donovan, Robert, 176
Dougherty Hall, 55, 59, 61
Dowling, Richard J., 292
Doyle, Michael, 395
Drayne, Richard, 160
Dubinin, Yuri, 344
Dudman, Dick, 188
Dudman, Richard, 279, 297
Dukakis, Michael, 317, 321-23, 330,
    332, 338-39
Duke, David, 407
dummy, 60, 102
Duvall, John, 341
Duvall, Robert, 344

E

East Germany, 241, 334
Ed Day, 272
Edelin, Kenneth, 239
Edwards, Edwin, 407
Edwards, Joseph M., 83
Ehrlichman, John, 172, 390
Eisenhower, Dwight David, 14, 74, 90
Eisenhower, Mamie, 34
Eizenstat, Stuart, 269
Elbourne, Tim, 188
El Capitan, 332
Elfin, Mel, 188
Elizabeth (queen), 333
El Morro, 90-91
Elwell, Richard, 271
En Transito, 94
Evans, Orrin C., 147
Evil Empire, 303

F

Facenda, John, 202
Fannon, John "Misty," 35
Farmer, John, 169, 177, 264
Fauci, Anthony, 313
Favrot, David, 395
federal antipoverty program, 148, 150
Federal Republic of Germany, 334
Feerick, Jim, 29, 43
Feistritzer, C. Emily, 274, 289,
    291-92
Fialka, John, 371
Filipinos, 311, 366-67
Finnegan, James, 33
Fiske, Ted, 274
Fitzwater, Marlin, 317
Flannery, Judy, 296

flimsies, 51

floating, 318-19

Foley, Tom, 344

Ford, Betty, 222, 229-30, 244, 250

Ford, Gerald "Jerry" R., 167, 180,
    183, 228-37, 241-50

four-star, 24, 101, 104-5

Franco, Francesco, 242

Frank, Barney, 52

Frankel, Max, 188, 247

Frayne, Tom, 109

Free, James, 354

Freeman, Charles W., Jr., 196

Freivogel, Margaret, 297

Freivogel, William, 297

Friedewald, Bill, 296

Friel, Jack, 29

"From a Distance" (Midler), 367

Fulbright, J. William, 136

G

Gale, Mary Ellen, 109

Gallagher, Henry, 178

Gates, Thomas Sovereign, Jr., 74, 79

Gephardt, Richard, 308, 390

Gerfin, John, 67

German Democratic Republic, 334

Germond, Jack, 343

Gerrard, Connie, 294

Ghareeb, Edmund, 292

Gibbons, Frank, 47-48, 50

Gilligan, Joseph, 58

Gingrich, Newt, 339, 348, 399

Giuliani, Al, 35

Glaspie, April, 328

Gleize, Jany, 335

Goebel, George, 356

Goldschmidt, Tom, 64, 214

Goldwater, Barry, 120, 126

Good Friday Agreement, 408

Gorbachev, Mikhail, 303, 334, 396

Gordy, John, 109

Gore, Al, 245, 321, 404

government shutdown, 400

Grady, Sandy, 345

Graham, Katherine, 180

Gray, Hannah, 290

Greeley, Andrew, 342

Green, Bill, 13, 130

Green, Marshall, 196

Green, William J., 130

Greener, Bill, 243

Greenfield, Elizabeth, 118

Greenspan, Alan, 343

Greenup, Gary, 84-85, 94

Gridiron Club, 336-42, 351, 355,
    358-59

Grimes, Charlotte, 342

Griswold v. Connecticut, 240

Gulf of Tonkin Resolution, 136

Gumbel, Bryant, 343

H

Haig, Alexander, 183

Haldeman, H. R. "Bob," 172

Hall, John, 349

Halleck, Charlie, 230

Hammerstein, Oscar, 111

Hanlon, Frank, 52, 144

Hanna, Mark, 342

Hardie, Tom, 35, 43

Hartzenbush, Henry, 188

Haughey, Charles, 408

Hauptfuhrer, Fred, 110

Heffner, Linda, 177

Hefner, Christie, 344

LAWRENCE M. O'ROURKE

Malacanang Palace, 312

Malcolm X, 133

Mannies, Jo, 301

Mansfield, Mike, 131

Mao Tse-tung, 192-93, 196-97, 207, 213

Marcos, Ferdinand, 309-10, 312

Marin, Luis Munoz, 89

Martin, Marlene, 178

Mary Bernadette (nun), 238

Maryland Club, 357-58

Mashek, John, 242

Maya's, 93

McAlee, Larry, 29

McCarthy, Colman, 148

McCarthy, Eugene, 158

McCarthy, Joseph, 124

McCartney, Jim, 345, 384

McCauley, Gerald "Gerry," 42

McClatchy, 394-99, 404-9, 412

McClellan, Bill, 370

McCord, Fred, 12, 52, 97

McCormack, John W., 120

McCoy, Jim, 29

McCullough, John G., 12, 134, 260

McDevitt, Gerald, 41

McFeatters, Ann, 358

McGonigle, John, 37

McGovern, George, 180

McGrory, Mary, 354-56

McGwire, Mark, 409

McKee, Guian A., 151

McKinney, Joan, 354

McLaughlin, John, 183

McLean, William L., Sr., 101

McManus, James E., 89

McNamara, Robert S., 90, 158

McNulty, Mary, 31

Means, Marianne, 345, 356

Mecoy, Laura, 395

Medbase America, 380-81

Meeks, Natalie, 156

Meese, Edwin, 299

Meir, Golda, 254

Merrill, Robert, 273

Michener, James, 94, 188

Midler, Bette
    "From a Distance," 367

Miller, William E., 120, 122, 125-27, 140

Millie (dog), 352

Millstone, Jim, 308, 312

Minter, Steve, 272

Minzu Hotel, 192-93

Mitchell, Andrea, 314-15, 360

Mitchell, George, 344, 409

Mitchell, John, 171

Mitterrand, Francois, 335

Mondale, Walter, 277

Monica (coworker), 47-49, 401

Moore, Cecil B., 116, 147

Moore, Sarah Jane, 244

Morrison, Jack, 107

Morse, Wayne, 136

Mortimer, James "Jim," 43

Mosbacher, Bob, 343

Moseley, Ray, 177

Moyers, Bill, 307

Moynihan, Daniel Patrick, 172

Mr. Lu (press officer), 190

Mrs. Marcus Kilch, 154-56

Mrs. Shalet (Jewish widow), 29

Muddy. See Waters, Robert Bruce

Mulcahy, Robert, III, 61-62

Mulligan, Hugh, 188

Mulvey, William, 365, 367-68, 370-73

Murphy, Len, 52, 97

Murphy, Leonard, 110

R

Raines, Howell, 302

Randolph, Eleanor, 358

Rather, Dan, 188, 392

Raymond Clapper Memorial Award, 314

Reagan, Nancy, 304, 315

Reagan, Ronald, 276, 319, 350, 353, 401

Reagan Democrats, 280, 282, 332-33

Reasoner, Harry, 188

Rebozo, Charles "Bebe," 171

Red Detachment of Women, 198

Reedy, George, 138-40, 307

Regan, Don, 304

Reischauer, Edwin O., 187

religion, 41, 89

Rennert, Leo, 335, 395

Reston, James, 139

Ribble, Maureen, 340

Richards, Ann, 319

Richardson, Elliott, 242

Rick, John, 178

Rieder, Rem, 177

Rife, David J., 83, 94

Ringle, Bill, 188-89, 192, 236, 340, 348, 384

Ritter, Tex, 341

Rizzo, Frank L., 150

Robertson, Pat, 329

Roche, Billy, 29

Rockefeller, Nelson A., 134, 246

Rodgers, Richard, 111

Rodgers, William P., 172

Roe v. Wade, 239, 246

Romney, George, 135

Ross, Betsy, 340

Ross, Tom, 188

Rostow, Walt, 158

Roth, Edith, 206

Roth, Robert, 12-13, 18-19, 129

Rowan, Carl, 342, 353

Ruane, Eugene, 59

Ruane, Michael, 59

Rudman, Warren, 326

Rule 9, 40

Rumsfeld, Donald, 230, 244

runner's high, 318

Runners' Rules, 296

Rusk, Dean, 136

Russell, Richard Brevard, 132

Russert, Tim, 360

Ryan, Cleveland, 198

Ryan, Jack, 58

Ryan, Michael, 341

Ryan, Richard A., 9, 338, 354, 384

Ryan, Thelma, 175

S

Sa'ad Haddad, 251

Sacramento Bee, 394-96

Sadat, Anwar, 181-82, 242, 252, 256-61

Sagan, Bruce, 394

Salahuddin, David, 254

Salinger, Pierre, 13

Sawyer, Buck, 53

Sawyer, Jon, 297, 301, 342, 393

Scali, John, 196

Schaeffer, Phil, 52

Schattman, Ann, 178

Schoemehl, Vincent, 342

Schwarzkopf, H. Norman, 364-65, 368, 372, 378-80

Schweiker, Richard S., 109, 183, 245

LAWRENCE M. O'ROURKE